A READER IN

EUROPEAN
INTEGRATION

A READER IN
EUROPEAN INTEGRATION

DAVID DE GIUSTINO

LONGMAN
London and New York

Addison Wesley Longman Limited
Edinburgh Gate
Harlow, Essex CM20 2JE, England
and Associated Companies throughout the world.

*Published in the United States of America
by Longman Publishing, New York*

First published 1996

ISBN 0 582 29200-XPPR

British Library Cataloguing-in-Publication Data

A catalogue record for this book is
available from the British Library

Library of Congress Cataloging-in-Publication Data

A catalogue record for this book is
available from the Library of Congress

Set by 3 in 9½/12pt Linotype Sabon
Produced through Longman Malaysia, LSP

CONTENTS

CHAPTER IV

GROWTH AND PARALYSIS, 1963–1983 173

DOCUMENTS

CHAPTER V

A WORLD POWER, 1984–1996 232

DOCUMENTS

ACKNOWLEDGEMENTS

Although primarily designed for the use of university students, most of this book was written when I was far removed from my teaching responsibilities at Griffith University in Brisbane. I am thankful to the University for the provision of a sabbatical during 1995 and for secretarial help provided by the Faculty of Humanities.

I am grateful for the advice and encouragement of colleagues: Dr Andrew Bonnell, Dr Barbara Misztal, Professor David Moss, Dr Martin Travers and Professor Richard Yeo in Brisbane; Professor Eric Hahn, Professor Sid Noel and Jim Langdon at the University of Western Ontario. The European Union's Legation in Canberra assisted greatly by helping to secure permission to publish a number of the documents in this collection.

Special thanks go to Robyn Smith in Brisbane for her ever-patient and always welcome advice about the format and presentation of material. Above all, I must mention the role of students in Brisbane, Ann Arbor and London, Ontario: they pointed to the need for a reader of this sort, and it is my hope that it serves them well. The errors, omissions and misconceptions are all my own; the idea of the book was theirs.

We are grateful to the following for permission to reproduce copyright material: Cassell plc for an extract from THE SINEWS OF PEACE: POSTWAR SPEECHES BY WINSTON S CHURCHILL edited by Randolph S Churchill (London: Cassell, 1948); the editor, CURRENT DIGEST OF THE POST SOVIET PRESS for the articles 'The Communist Commonwealth' & 'Soviet Reaction' translated from PRAVDA 17 June, 1962 & 26 August, 1962 in CURRENT DIGEST OF THE SOVIET PRESS, No 24, pp. 3–8 & No 34, pp. 9–16; Walter de Gruyter Co for articles 'The Nazi Organization of Europe' & 'A Wartime Manifesto' translated in DOCUMENTS ON THE HISTORY OF EUROPEAN INTEGRATION edited by Walter Lipgens, vol 1 (Berlin, Walter de Gruyter 1985) pp. 132–7 & 479–82; Office of the President of the Czech Republic for the text from a speech by Vaclav Havel addressed to the European Parliament on 8 March, 1994; Harper Collins Publishers for extracts from PERESTROIKA by Mikhail Gorbachev. Copyright © 1987 by Mikhail Gorbachev; Orion Publishing Group Ltd for extracts from Paul-Henri Spaak's THE CONTINUING BATTLE: MEMOIRS OF A EUROPEAN, 1936–1966, translated by Henry Fox (London: Weidenfeld & Nicolson, 1971); The Orion Publishing Group Ltd/ Librairie Hachette, Paris for extracts from Konrad Adenaeur's MEMOIRS, translated by Beate Ruhm von Oppen (London: Weidenfeld & Nicolson, 1965).

LIST OF ABBREVIATIONS

AASM	Association of African States and Madagascar
ACP	African, Caribbean and Pacific states
CAP	Common Agricultural Policy
CEEC	Committee for European Economic Cooperation
CMEA	Council for Mutual Economic Assistance
COMINFORM	Communist Information Bureau
CSCE	Conference on Security and Cooperation in Europe
EAEC	European Atomic Energy Community
EBRD	European Bank for Reconstruction and Development
EC	European Community
ECJ	European Court of Justice
ECSC	European Coal and Steel Community
ECU	European Currency Unit
EDC	European Defence Community
EDF	European Development Fund
EEA	European Economic Area
EEC	European Economic Community
EFTA	European Free Trade Association
EIB	European Investment Bank
EMS	European Monetary System
EMU	Economic and Monetary Union
EPC	European Political Cooperation
EPU	European Payments Union
ERDF	European Regional Development Fund
ERM	Exchange Rate Mechanism
EURATOM	European Atomic Energy Community
FRG	Federal Republic of Germany
GNP	Gross National Product
NATO	North Atlantic Treaty Organization
OEEC	Organization for European Economic Cooperation
SEA	Single European Act
TEU	Treaty on European Union
VAT	Value Added Tax
WEU	Western European Union

GEOGRAPHICAL EXPRESSIONS

In this book, the term 'east-central Europe' refers to the territories of Poland, Hungary, Czechoslovakia (the Czech Republic and Slovakia after 1992) and the post-Yugoslav republics of Slovenia and Croatia.

The term 'eastern Europe' refers to Rumania, Bulgaria, Serbia-Montenegro, Bosnia, and to the USSR (the Russian Federated Republic, Belarus, Ukraine, Moldova, Armenia, Georgia and Azerbaijan after 1991), as well as the Baltic states Latvia, Lithuania and Estonia.

INTRODUCTION

Our perception of history since the close of the Second World War is framed – and often confused – by a variety of developments. The enormous growth of the world's population, the rise and fall of Soviet power, environmental issues, nationalism in the Third World, international terrorism, global communications and 'youth culture' – these are but some of the phenomena which help us to distinguish 'contemporary history' from all preceding periods. The most crucial development, however, is one which cannot fail to influence political calculations and economic activity everywhere: the integration of Europe.

It is the purpose of this book to bring the history of European integration closer to the reading public by providing a selection of extracts from original sources. Although many of the sources have appeared in other collections, they have been so abbreviated that they resemble sound bites in a newscast. The *Reader* has tried to avoid a reliance on very brief extracts and offers instead generous versions of the original sources. Of course any collection of documents must contend with those sources which, in their original state, are truly massive. A policy of ruthless pruning is then unavoidable. Certainly the Treaty of Rome and the Euratom Treaty required repeated pruning before they could fit into a *Reader* of this size. But even those sources have retained a measure of their formidable length and more of the scope and design than has been their fate in other sourcebooks. It is, moreover, the plan of this *Reader* to provide ready access to sources which are either very dispersed in libraries or not available at all.

The forty extracts in this *Reader* come from a variety of sources. Many are 'official' because they relate directly to some of the institutions and agencies of integrated Europe, or because they are treaties involving a number of national governments. Other documents represent more personal views and recollections. Obviously there are many gaps. Some countries, events and organizations are not mentioned at all; both the documents and the commentaries seem to pass them by. But no one can write about European affairs without neglecting one or another corner of Europe or without excluding aspects of European society and politics. The apparently clever remarks 'Europe stops at the Pyrenees', 'Russia is only half European' and 'Scandinavia is European but not *in* Europe' will occur to any writer as persistent rebukes – and as excuses. The limited number of documents in this *Reader* produces yet another curious portrait of Europe.

Even so, the ingredients of a fairly balanced survey exist. This *Reader* does not give quite as much attention to Britain as do other sourcebooks and monographs published in the UK. It makes a point of assessing the essential role of Benelux and the hesitant attitudes of Scandinavia. Small countries (e.g. Luxembourg, Bosnia and the Czech Republic) are not ignored, nor are developments in the communist states, where a different model of political and economic cooperation emerged. The *Reader* also attempts to assess some aspects of European integration which have affected the lives and working conditions of ordinary Europeans.

The documents and commentaries are arranged in five chapters. The introductory chapter, concerning the interwar period, contains a brief commentary and only four documents. The remaining chapters (II to V) are more extensive and serve the same general purpose: to link the documents in a continuous narrative. The documents are not always considered in strictly chronological order. In Chapter V, for example, they are divided into two groups, the first involving the internal and structural growth of the EC (later the EU) and the second dealing with external relations.

The spread of documents is rather arbitrary: nine for each of the four postwar chapters. In preparing a book of this sort, there is no particular virtue in symmetry. On the other hand, the importance of the four longer chapters obliges us to give them fairly equal treatment. Of course, another ten or twelve documents could have been distributed across the chapters, thus insuring a greater variety of sources and issues. As a reference book combining documents and commentary, however, the *Reader* has probably already acquired its natural proportions. Students who require a much more extensive range of sources are advised to consult the collection begun by Walter Lipgens (Walter Lipgens and Wilfried Loth (eds) *Documents on the History of European Integration* (Berlin and New York: Walter de Gruyter, 1985–1991)) which now embraces four volumes for the years 1939 to 1950.

Europe's progress toward unity has long been the subject of academic research. One can easily compile an immense bibliography on virtually every phase of European integration. Among the most comprehensive and best written surveys of European integration, the general reader should become acquainted with Derek Urwin's *The Community of Europe: A History of European Integration Since 1945* (London: Longman, 1992) and his *Western Europe Since 1945* (London: Longman, 1989). Another welcome contribution is John Pinder's *European Community: The Building of a Union* (Oxford: Oxford University Press, 1991). This *Reader* is intended to complement rather than supplant the excellent books of Urwin and Pinder. It is also designed to serve students and other readers who want the period 1945 to 1995 to 'come alive' through the words of Europeans who observed or assisted in the integration of their continent.

MAPS

1965

- European Community
- Member states of EFTA
- Member states of Comecon

ALB....ALBANIA
B ....BELGIUM
DK .....DENMARK
L ....LUXEMBOURG
N ....NETHERLANDS

European Integration 1965

1975

- European Community
- Member states of EFTA
- Member states of Comecon

ALB....ALBANIA
B ....BELGIUM
DK .....DENMARK
L ....LUXEMBOURG
N ....NETHERLANDS

European Integration 1975

European Integration 1997

CHAPTER I

THEORIES AND EXPERIMENTS

1919–1943

The truce signed in the forest of Compiègne in November 1918 brought an end to the battles of Europe's major armies. The battles of the spirit raged on, as Europeans struggled to understand the causes of the Great War and its implications for their future. Huge questions now occurred to victors and defeated alike. What was to become of their disgraced institutions, their battered economies and their place in world affairs? How was Europe to be restored to life and what steps should be taken to insure a just peace? Borders, truce-lines and demilitarized zones were no barrier to such questions; they came as a plague upon the whole of Europe. The peace treaties of 1919 did not solve these questions but instead generated feelings of revenge in the defeated countries. Across a confused and divided continent, there was little disposition to trust and cooperation. There was instead a general apprehension that the Versailles Treaty, far from being the foundation of European harmony, might only be the terms of a very long truce.

Most Europeans hoped that the postwar treaties would promote the security of their continent by affirming the principle of national sovereignty. They wanted the peace conferences to establish (or in some cases to re-establish) the territorial integrity of nation states. The attempt to accommodate nationalist aspirations resulted in a very different map of Europe. Many territories were transferred (France regained Alsace-Lorraine, Italy took Trentino and Istria, Rumania annexed Moldavia and Transylvania). Elsewhere the concern for nationality led to the reconstitution of Poland and the re-emergence (after several centuries) of Lithuania. Many other states (Finland, Latvia, Estonia, Czechoslovakia, Yugoslavia and, briefly, Ukraine) appeared on the map for the first time. Germany was compressed on the east by the new Polish republic and on the west by Allied troops on the Rhine. The venerable empires of Austria, Russia and Turkey, long regarded in western Europe as autocratic or illiberal, disappeared from view, their former provinces occupied by a host of 'successor states'. With the multiplication of border crossings, customs stations and national currencies, Europe was more remarkable than ever for its fragmentation.

The realities of postwar Europe were soon apparent. Thanks to the recent war, virtually all the nations, old and new, were close to bankruptcy. The Allied states owed money and resources to one another and they were all in debt to the United States. Modern technology reminded Europeans how small and vulnerable their countries were. It would not be long before some countries would use radio broadcasting to stir up disaffected minorities in neighbouring states, and of course

1

the development of the aeroplane added immeasurably to the future perils of war, especially as far as cities were concerned. Above all, the political fragility of European states promised an uneasy, if not turbulent, peace. The precarious existence of weak governments (in Italy, Hungary and Germany), the inclusion of large and hostile minorities in many of the successor states (Ukrainians in eastern Poland, Poles in Lithuania, Hungarians in Czechoslovakia and Rumania), and the failure of representative democracy across Europe: all these conditions indicated the delicate nature of the postwar settlement.

Only one mechanism existed to mediate disputes and to encourage the peaceful cooperation of states. The League of Nations, with its headquarters in Geneva, was the symbol of the idealistic diplomacy which accompanied the end of the war. The imperfections of the League were obvious in its membership. Although it claimed to be a world organization, the League did not include the USA and the USSR. And although almost half of its members were European states, the League was never intended, nor could it ever serve, as an effective clearing house for European issues. Within only a few years of the signing of the peace treaties, secret diplomacy, exclusive alliances and the use of force undermined the idealism of the League. The French occupation of the Ruhr, Italy's gunboat diplomacy over Corfu and Poland's seizure of the Vilnius region of Lithuania were only some of the occasions when the use of military force was preferred to diplomatic conciliation. The French attempt to contain Russia and Germany by a system of alliances with the successor states clearly showed that some countries were not yet ready to give up the old-fashioned idea of hegemony in Europe.

The 1920s also witnessed the emergence of a very different solution to Europe's problems. The recognition that hypercharged nationalism had very nearly destroyed Europe in a suicidal war led some Europeans to search for an alternative to the concept of national sovereignty. They were attracted to the idea of limited state sovereignty and they wanted an association of European states which agreed to share economic resources and which accepted an entirely new framework of interstate relations. The most celebrated publicist of these ideas was the Austrian aristocrat, Count Richard Coudenhove-Kalergi. In 1923 he founded the Pan-European Union, the first popular movement for European unity. Coudenhove-Kalergi travelled extensively and constantly in Europe to promote the Pan-Europe concept and in October 1926 he organized a large meeting in Vienna. Almost 2,000 politicians, industrialists, educators, journalists and businesspeople attended this first 'Pan-European Congress'. Branch offices were then established in all major capitals; the Union attracted people from many political parties in all countries, from Portugal to Finland.

The bible of the movement first appeared in 1923, when Coudenhove-Kalergi published his book *Pan-Europe*. It was a melange of political sentiments, demographic information, economic forecasts and, above all, proposals for a number of world regional federations or groupings of nations. Coudenhove-Kalergi was inclined to grand, if not grandiose, ideas. He saw nothing improbable about huge geopolitical associations, such as the United States with the *whole* of Latin America ('Pan-America') or China with Japan and Korea ('East Asia'). On the other hand, he expressed a very durable west European notion (persisting into the 1960s) that most of Africa, independent or not, should be closely associated with Pan-Europe. Moreover, Coudenhove-Kalergi was not mistaken when he pointed to Britain's reluctance to join a European federation (DOCUMENT 1).

The Pan-Europe Movement blossomed during a special moment of the interwar years. The mid- and late-1920s constituted a brief period of optimism, at least in western Europe. The French had evacuated the Ruhr, the Americans devised a formula for the payment of war reparations and the Locarno Conference generated a remarkable degree of trust and hope. French–German relations were decidedly more cordial, thanks largely to the efforts of Gustave Stresemann, the German foreign minister, and his French counterpart, Aristide Briand. Indeed, their friendship was prophetic of the parade of French and German statesmen who, after the next war, were to build the new Europe on the indispensable rock of French–German cooperation. The 'Spirit of Locarno' and the Pan-Europe Movement were complementary and Coudenhove-Kalergi expected three great advantages to come from a European federation. The first was a new polity which submerged the sovereignty of individual member states and fostered the conciliation of old enemies, such as Germany and France or Italy and Austria. European institutions were to resolve European problems, such as the potentially explosive border dispute between Poland and Germany in the region of Silesia. The second benefit was economic: a European Union was expected to encourage the better use and distribution of resources and capital, thus insuring a higher standard of living across the continent. The third advantage of a federal union was as a counter-weight to Bolshevik-style revolution, a shield against Soviet ambitions elsewhere in Europe. If, as Coudenhove-Kalergi hoped, the Pan-Europe Movement eventually produced the United States of Europe, there would be a federal association of democratic states which valued their security and prosperity more than the outdated (and dangerous) *accoutrements* of national sovereignty.

In the same year as the Pan-Europa Congress in Vienna, the Hungarian economist Elemer Hantos published an article which focused on the economic needs of Europe (DOCUMENT 2). Like Coudenhove-Kalergi, Hantos had been a citizen of Austria-Hungary, the huge multiethnic empire of central Europe. Hantos was among those who thought that the old empire made economic sense: it brought together many different peoples of the Danubian region and created a larger market for their products. The collapse of the empire at the end of the Great War served the nationalist interests of new states (Czechoslovakia, Poland, Yugoslavia) as well as Rumania and Italy, but it also led to the appearance of many new trade barriers. Shorn of their imperial dependencies, Austria and Hungary both re-emerged as very small countries; Austria's survival was very doubtful. Hantos deplored the creation of customs duties and 'unpopular tariffs' in the successor states. He urged a very different solution, not only for the Danubian region but for Europe generally: a customs union.

Hantos assumed that the unfettering of European commerce would bring about a unified economic region. In his view, a European customs union was the logical parallel to a new European political structure. In fact, he doubted that any plan for a European federation could succeed without arrangements for an effective economic union. There were, of course, dangers in proceeding too quickly and Hantos did not want the inauguration of the Customs Union to disgrace Pan-Europa by causing large-scale unemployment. In both its political and economic manifestations, European union had to be extremely sensitive to public opinion. That is why Hantos stressed a populist economic agenda for federation: people would support European unity only if it insured high levels of employment, low prices and an expanding market economy. In short, Hantos perceived a Europe of consumers and consumerism, and he insisted on economic security as the true foundation of political stability.

The idea of a customs union gained many advocates during the first ten or twelve years after the Great War. Businesspeople and industrialists, particularly in western Europe, saw immediate financial advantages in the creation of international markets, relaxed border controls and more liberal investment conditions. The postwar transfer of populations raised the question of labour mobility, and the need to rebuild areas devastated by the war seemed to require a more rational use of energy, raw materials and capital. However attractive the arguments might have been, a pan-European customs union was never attempted. The Scandinavian states took a few tentative steps toward banking and investment cooperation. Austria, barely able to survive on its own after the war, hoped for a customs union with Germany, but the peace treaties did not allow this. The only formal customs union was that negotiated by Belgium and Luxembourg in 1922.

Apart from intergovernmental agreements, it was always possible that some degree of economic integration might take place under the auspices of the cartels. Like the International Steel Cartel, these large supranational agencies gained strength in the prosperous mid- and late-1920s. Some economists and politicians looked to the cartels as sponsors of harmonized production standards, working conditions and commodity pricing. But the cartels never fulfilled these hopes, partly because of the Depression of the 1930s and also because of the continuing force of national suspicions and restrictions.

The most comprehensive plan for European integration during the interwar years combined the political ideas of Coudenhove-Kalergi and the economic notions of Elemer Hantos. This was the proposal advanced by the French foreign minister, Aristide Briand. As one of this century's most respected and far-sighted statesmen, Briand believed that Europe's geography, political institutions and cultural affinities already afforded a large measure of unity; he was also convinced that the same factors must someday underlie a political federation of states. For Briand, the League of Nations was not enough: Europe must have its own regional organization to develop a 'collective solidarity' and a 'harmonization of interests'.

Briand's first proposal for a United States of Europe was made in 1929 with the promise of a more detailed memorandum for the next year (DOCUMENT 3). Briand's audience, both in 1929 and 1930, was the Assembly of the League of Nations, and his first concern on both occasions was to reassure his listeners that the federation of Europe would not mean the secession of Europe from the League. Briand expected European diplomats in the League (and in 'certain international bureaus') to represent a European consensus rather than the views of individual European governments; this unity of purpose and expression would, he thought, speed up the decision-making process of the League and add to its moral force.

The Memorandum was never intended as a precise blueprint for a European superstate. True to its name and to its function, the Memorandum simply presented the main features of a European federation as Briand saw it. It is not surprising, therefore, that the areas of European cooperation were so briefly expressed (part IV). Certainly there is some evidence of a modern imagination (the call for economic assistance to poor regions, for example, anticipates the Treaty of Rome in 1957) and the provision for a European regime of postal and telephone communications and broadcasting still awaits attention in the 1990s. What unsettled Briand's audience in 1930, however, was something more basic than a European system of postal services and broadcasting. They were worried by the emphasis which the Memorandum placed on a new political or constitutional organization of Europe.

Briand insisted that his plan left the sovereignty of states intact and that a European federation must first depend on the approval of parliaments in all prospective member states. But the replies of European governments to Briand's Memorandum revealed a general and profound scepticism. Was it not suspicious that economic cooperation should be subordinate to the political? Would member states be able to retain their sovereignty in the long term? Did not the commitment to common policies on the part of at least twenty different states imply the sacrifice of national interests? Europe's national governments answered these questions for themselves and decided that the priorities of national states were still far more important than Briand's theory of a federal Europe. It was their quiet indifference, combined with the economic and political catastrophes of the 1930s, which sealed the fate of Briand's plan.

It seems that Briand realized the special timing of his Memorandum. In 1929–30 he knew that the spirit of Locarno still animated the chanceries of Europe and that western Europeans had made some progress toward solving problems left over from the Great War. At the same time, Briand sensed a 'stringent necessity' to take important steps fairly soon, lest the prize of Europe's talents and resources were lost to an undeserving and selfish management. Until now, most theories of European unity had rested unequivocally on the principles of collective responsibility, the voluntary association of states, the supremacy of public opinion and the willingness to redefine state sovereignty and to raise the standard of living of all Europeans. None of these principles formed part of a very different notion of Europe among those who disdained Briand's message of conciliation and integration.

Europe's fascists and Germany's National Socialists did not always profess the same creed. Their economic and cultural policies often differed and (in the case of Bulgaria, Rumania and Hungary) their nationalist aspirations frequently collided. Even after the war began in 1939 the fascist regimes of Italy and Hungary occasionally (and politely) entertained views about Europe's 'New Order' which did not agree with those of their Nazi allies. Generally, however, the Axis states agreed about the dangers to the state of 'internationalism' and 'cosmopolitanism'. They placed the destiny of their nations far above the supposed benefits of European unity. Their first concern was the 'geopolitical security' of the state based on the return of 'lost provinces' and the annexation of territories comprising quite different ethnic and national populations. But soon after their virulent and expansive nationalism produced another war, the Nazis saw the advantages of propaganda which suggested that serious planning for the peace and prosperity of Europe was already under way.

Encouraged by their military victories of 1940, the Germans began postwar planning in earnest. Most of the schemes in the years 1940 to 1943 envisaged wholesale transfers of populations and the fantastic redrawing of Europe's boundaries, guaranteeing the Reich *lebensraum* at the expense of Poland, Belarus, the Baltic states and Ukraine, as well as the creation of small client states in Wallonia, Burgundy and the Balkans. As an Axis victory began to appear less certain during 1943, Nazi propaganda increasingly stressed the idea of a single European civilization threatened by the intervention of 'two alien forces', the USA and the Soviet Union. Of course Nazi war aims did not discard the concept of a Greater German Reich, nor did they give up the idea of a German-directed Europe. But in addressing the European public about the likely features of the postwar New Order, Nazi propaganda tried to adopt a somewhat more plausible tone.

Among these carefully crafted statements was a memorandum prepared in June 1943 for the German Ministry of Foreign Affairs. The memorandum was intended as a planning document for arguments which might later be presented in broadsheets and on radio (DOCUMENT 4). The memorandum foresaw a 'European community', a 'closer community', of countries which voluntarily embraced 'European solidarity' and 'European obligations'. There was a beguiling defence of national sovereignty and the right of European states to conduct foreign relations and to develop national institutions as they saw fit. But the memorandum saw no reason for watering down Germany's vision of a *völkisch* future. It was surprisingly frank in its prohibition of any activity which was incompatible with the military security of the continent as Germany saw it. While the memorandum apparently upheld the claims of other European states vis-à-vis their African colonies, it spoke of a European imperium in Africa and grandly referred to the continents of Europe and Africa as the *grossraum* of the New Order. In fact there was a strong suggestion that the old colonial powers (France and the UK) might lose African colonies, presumably to Germany and Italy.

Much of the memorandum proceeds as a geography lesson, dealing with regions of Europe, the Middle East and Africa as geopolitical features of the New Order. The expression of ideas in grand continental terms is certainly evident in the memorandum but so too are the Nazi fears of revealing their real plans in any detail. Were the two small states of Norway and Denmark, for instance, to become independent countries again after the war or were they to be incorporated into the Reich? Would France regain its territorial integrity and independence after the war? German propaganda avoided such issues for good reason. Similarly, there were only hints of the latitude which European states might enjoy in participating in the reconstruction of their continent. The memorandum allowed for general discussions of such fields as foreign trade, the press and education but took it for granted that postwar conferences would represent the views of 'responsible' governments. Besides, it is clear that Germany had no intention of reversing the decisions which it had already taken. The decision to settle the 'Jewish Question' by means of the Holocaust is the most obvious indication of the New Order as Germany's *diktat* to Europe.

The pathos of Nazi wartime propaganda sprang essentially from its desperation. Once they found themselves in control of western and central Europe, and particularly after they had overrun much of Russia, the Nazis felt obliged to justify their conquests. This they did by posing as the champions of a Europe united against external foes and as the saviours of European civilization from the predations of Soviet communism. But their arguments were always too self-serving (and too hastily composed) to be very convincing and in any case the Nazis' self-appointed role as the organizers of a new Europe meant very little to populations confronted by their brutal expansionism. The wonderful paradox of the Nazis' European experiment was that it kept alive the humane ideas of Aristide Briand and other theorists of the interwar period. It was to those tentative definitions of a federal, democratic union which Europeans now turned.

ADDITIONAL READINGS

R. E. Herzstein: *When Nazi Dreams Come True* (London: Abacus, 1982).

J. Jacobson: *Locarno Diplomacy* (Princeton: Princeton University Press, 1972).

P. King and A. Bosco (eds): *A Constitution for Europe* (London: Lothian Foundation, 1991).

W. Lipgens: *A History of European Integration*, vol.I (Oxford: Clarendon, 1982).

S. Marks: *The Illusion of Peace* (London: Macmillan, 1976).

A. S. Milward: *The New Order and the French Economy* (Oxford: Oxford University Press, 1970).

F. T. Murphey: 'The Briand Memorandum and the Quest for European Unity, 1929–1932', in *Contemporary French Civilization*, 4 (1980), pp.319–30.

C. H. Pegg: *Evolution of the European Idea 1914–1932* (Chapel Hill: University of North Carolina Press, 1983).

M. L. Smith and P. M. R. Stirk (eds): *Making the New Europe. European Unity and the Second World War* (London: Pinter, 1990).

P. M. R. Stirk (ed.): *European Unity in Context: the Interwar Period* (London: Pinter, 1989).

R. Vaughan: *Twentieth Century Europe* (London: Croom Helm, 1979).

1

PAN-EUROPA

The leading advocate for European unity in the interwar period was Count Richard Coudenhove-Kalergi, founder of the movement known as the Pan-European Union. The following extracts are taken from 'Three Years of Pan-Europe', published as a 'Supplement' to his book *Pan-Europe* (New York: Alfred Kopf, 1926), pp.197–8, 205.

This book appeared in 1923, the year of the Ruhr occupation, the darkest and most discouraging year that Europe had known since the World War.

The following year, 1924, passed under the sign of the French May elections, of the Dawes Plan, and of the London Conference. The road was opening to a European understanding.

The year 1925 was the year of Locarno, which led to the first practical step toward European understanding and unification. Thus Pan-Europe was a utopia in 1923, a problem in 1924, and a programme in 1925.

The world-political tendency of these first three years of the Pan-European movement was:

(1) The stabilisation and liberation of the new Europe grown out of the World War [...]
(2) Increasing weariness of Europe on the part of America, Asia, Russia and England [...]

Asia is striving more and more for emancipation from Europe. Hand in hand with the cultural Europeanisation of this continent goes its political de-Europeanisation [...]

Russia is supporting this anti-European policy and is itself becoming more and more an Asiatic Great Power [...]

The greatest differences of opinion prevail regarding the English Question: that is, whether England without risking its world position can become a federal state of Europe. England alone can answer this question of destiny. Its answer might be a compromise, as Locarno indicates. For the negotiations left no doubt regarding the fact that this security pact was the most extreme guarantee England could assume with respect to Europe without jeopardising its Empire.

Hence British policy with respect to Pan-Europe is affiliation, but not membership; understanding, but not federation.

_____ 2 _____

EUROPEAN CUSTOMS UNION

In 1926 the Hungarian economist Elemer Hantos considered some of the problems likely to accompany a European Customs Union. His article 'Der Europäische Zollverein' appeared in *Weltwirtschaftliches Archiv*, vol.23 (1926), pp.229–39.

The victory of the Pan-European idea in the intellectual world of contemporary Europe has given new life, in economically oriented minds, to the idea of a European customs union [...] Why is the Pan-European idea carried over into the economic realm, appearing above all in the form of a European customs union? Is it perhaps that customs barriers most strongly thwart the free circulation of economic forces? In the times before the war one could answer this question affirmatively. To conduct trade policy meant, at that time, to utilise customs. Custom rates were the most important mechanism in trade policy. The arsenal of postwar trade policy worked with more comprehensive armaments; new weapons appear alongside the old. Exchange rate fluctuations, transfer difficulties, obstacles to transport, import and export bans, sales taxes and railway tariffs are barriers which exceed the highest customs dues in their effectiveness. Yet a European currency union or a European transport union is scarcely discussed: a trading union, on the other hand, is pre-sented as the be all and end all of economic cooperation. The cause of this phenom-enon is perhaps to be sought in this, that despite the inflation of currency advisers and theorists of money, there are yet more people who have an insight into, and trust their own opinion on, customs matters than is the case with financial policy or the technical problems of transportation. Moreover, the logic of things leads more easily from the well-known starting point of unpopular tariffs to general conclu-sions which are intelligible to broad circles. The syllogism, persuasive to every layman, runs: the maintenance of customs dues means higher prices; higher prices bring a reduction in purchasing power; a reduction of purchasing power produces a shrinking market; a shrinking market leads to a reduction of production; a reduc-tion of production creates poverty and misery. The European customs union, on the other hand, brings, through the abolition of customs dues, cheaper prices; lower prices create higher purchasing power; higher purchasing power produces an expan-sion of the market; expansion of the market leads to higher production; higher production creates prosperity and wealth [...]

However well one may agree about borders, however convinced one may be of the correctness of the goal of a European customs union, the difficulties of managing the transition from today's divisions to a unified economic region are not thereby overcome. Even the most enthusiastic defender of the idea shrinks back from a leap out of the current situation into the desired one and wants to allow far-reaching transitional measures. The sudden abolition of customs borders would condemn part of Europe's stock of factories and produce great unemployment. The considerable number of enterprises that are kept viable only by the customs tariffs of their homeland would be the first victims. Also, those factories which today can dump exports because of the high prices within their protected domestic markets, would be condemned to go under. Hardship could scarcely be avoided in the economic transformation. It could, however, be mitigated through a planned reduction which would set the date, for each branch of industry and for each customs area, at which customs must be completely set aside [...]

International industrial interests could pave the way for the economic unification of Europe more effectively than the multilateral, staged reduction of customs tariffs. Syndicates and distribution agencies of individual branches of the economy, cartellization or the horizontal development in large-scale industries, could be a surrogate for customs tariffs. They could also be more effective than customs tariffs as equalization mechanisms, in the sense of protecting weaker groups against stronger ones and may even promote the general equalization of production costs more quickly than the dismantling of customs barriers. One can see that a harmonization of the conflicts in the creation of an inter-state economic union may occur not only from state to state. The planned cooperation of private economic interests in international production, distribution, transport and consumer organizations would vigorously promote the European division of labour without doing deep damage to individual economies, without shaking productive life [...]

For the near future, therefore, a regime of free trade in Europe is not to be expected. One needs only to recall how slowly and under what difficult circumstances the German customs union came about [...] In that case the presuppositions were incomparably more favourable. It was a question of an understanding between peoples of the same origin and the same political aspirations. It would already signify great progress if areas that were previously economically united would return to mutual free trade. For the present it is not a question of final goals but of tendencies and movements. The realization of a European customs union will have to wait for a long time, but the idea itself must underlie all political and economic measures.

3

BRIAND MEMORANDUM

The following translation of Briand's Memorandum appeared in a *Special Bulletin* (June 1930) of the journal *International Conciliation*, published by The Carnegie Endowment for International Peace (New York, 1930).

No one doubts today that the lack of cohesion in the grouping of the material and moral forces of Europe constitutes, practically, the most serious obstacle to the development and efficiency of all political or juridical institutions on which ... to base the first attempts for a universal organization of peace. This scattering of forces limits, no less seriously, the possibilities of enlargement of the economic market, the attempts to intensify and improve industrial production, and for that very reason all guarantees against labour crises which are sources of political as well as social instability. Now, the danger of such division is still more increased by the circumstance of the extent of the new frontiers (more than 20,000 kilometres of customs barriers) which the treaties of peace had to create in order to do justice, in Europe, to national aspirations.

The very action of the League of Nations, the responsibilities of which are the greater because it is universal, might be exposed in Europe to serious obstacles if such breaking up of territory were not offset, as soon as possible, by a bond of solidarity permitting European nations to at last become conscious of European geographical unity and to effect, within the framework of the League, one of those regional understandings which the Covenant formally recommended.

This means that the search for a formula of European cooperation in connection with the League of Nations, far from weakening the authority of this latter must and can tend only to strengthen it, for it is closely connected with its aims.

It is not at all a question of constituting a European group outside of the League of Nations, but on the contrary of harmonizing European interests under the control [contrôle] and in the spirit of the League of Nations by incorporating in its universal system a limited system all the more effective. The realization of a federative organization of Europe would always be attributed to the League of Nations as an element of progress to its credit from which extra European nations themselves might benefit. [...]

In fact, certain questions concern Europe particularly for which European States may feel the need of an action of their own, more immediate and more direct in the very interest of peace and for which furthermore they enjoy a special competence arising from their ethnical affinities and their community of civilization. The League of Nations itself in the general exercise of its activities, has had more than once to take account of the fact of this geographical unity which Europe presents and which may call for common solutions, the application of which could not be applied to the whole world. Preparing and facilitating the coordination of the strictly European activities of the League of Nations would be precisely one of the tasks of the association contemplated.

Far from constituting a new contentious jurisdiction for the settlement of disputes, the European Association, which could not be called on in such matters to exercise its good offices except in a purely advisory capacity, would be without authority to treat thoroughly special problems, the adjustment of which has been entrusted by the Pact or by the Treaties to a special procedure of the League of Nations or to any other procedure expressly defined. But in the very cases in which it might be a question of an essential task reserved to the League of Nations, the federal bond between European States would still play a very useful rôle in preparing a favourable atmosphere for the pacific adjustments of the League or facilitating in practice the execution of its decisions. [...]

The European organization contemplated could not oppose any ethnic group, on other continents or in Europe itself, outside of the League of Nations, any more than it could oppose the League of Nations.

The policy of European union to which the search for a first bond of solidarity between European Governments ought to tend, implies in fact, a conception absolutely contrary to that which may have determined formerly, in Europe, the formation of customs unions tending to abolish internal customs houses in order to erect on the boundaries of the community a more rigorous barrier, that is to say, to constitute in fact an instrument of struggle against States situated outside of those unions.

It is important, finally, to place the proposed inquiry under the general conception that in no case and in no degree can the institution of the federal bond sought for between European Governments affect in any manner the sovereign rights of the States, members of such a *de facto* association.

It is on the basis of absolute sovereignty and of entire political independence that the understanding between European Nations ought to be effected. Furthermore, it would be impossible to imagine the least thought of political domination in an organization deliberately placed under the control [*contrôle*] of the League of Nations, the two fundamental principles of which are precisely, the sovereignty of States and the equality of rights. And with the rights of sovereignty, is it not the very genius of every nation which can find in its individual cooperation in the collective work the means of affirming itself still more consciously under a régime of federal union fully compatible with the respect of the traditions and characteristics special to each people?

It is under the reservation of these observations and in the light of the general preoccupation recalled at the beginning of this memorandum that the Government of the [French] Republic, in accordance with the procedure decided upon at the first European meeting of September 9, 1929, has the honour to submit to the consideration of the Government concerned a summary of the different points on which they are invited to formulate their opinions.

I

In a formula as liberal as possible ... the signatory Governments would engage to make regular contacts, in periodical or extraordinary meetings, for the examination in common of all questions which might concern primarily the community of European peoples.

1. The signatory Governments appearing thus committed to the general orientation of a certain common policy, the principle of a European union would henceforth be removed from all discussion and placed above all procedure of daily application: the study of ways and means would be reserved to the European Conference or to the permanent organization which would be called upon to constitute the living bond of solidarity between European nations and thus to incarnate the moral personality of the European union.

2. This initial and symbolic pact, under which would be pursued in practice the determination, organization, and development of the constituent elements of the European association, should be drawn up in a sufficiently brief form to

limit itself to defining the essential rôle of this association. (The possible extension of this pact of principle into the conception of a more definite charter would belong to the future, if it should be favourable to the development of the European union.) [...]

4. In order better to attest the subordination of the European Association to the League of Nations, the European pact would, at first, be reserved to European States which are members of the League.

II

A. **Necessity of a representative and responsible organ, in the form of regularly establishing the 'European Conference',** composed of representatives of all the European Governments which are members of the League of Nations and which would be the essential directing organ of the European Union, in liaison with the League of Nations.

The powers of this Conference, the organization of its presidency and of its regular or extraordinary sessions, should be determined at the next meeting of European States, which shall have to deliberate on the conclusions of the report on the inquiry and which, subject to indispensable governmental approvals or parliamentary ratifications, should give assurance that the project of European organization will be perfected.

In order to avoid any predominance in favour of one European State over the others, presidents of the European Conference should be elected annually and function in rotation.

B. **Necessity of an executive organ, in the form of a Permanent Political Committee,** composed of only a certain number of Members of the European Conference and assuring, in practice, to the European Union its organization for study at the same time as its instrument of action.

The composition and powers of the European Committee, the manner of designation of its members, the organization of its presidency and of its regular or extraordinary sessions, should be determined at the next meeting of European States. As the activity of this Committee, like that of the Conference, is to be exercised within the framework of the League of Nations, its meetings should be held at Geneva itself, where its regular sessions might coincide with those of the Council of the League of Nations. [...]

III

A. **General subordination of the Economic Problem to the Political.** All possibility of progress toward economic union being strictly determined by the question of security, and this question being intimately bound up with that of the realizable progress toward political union, it is on the political plane that constructive effort looking to giving Europe its organic structure should first of all be made. It is also on this plane that the economic policy of Europe should afterwards be drawn up, in its broad outlines, as well as the special customs policy of each European State.

economic followed by political union

The contrary order would not only be useless, it would appear to the weaker nations to be likely to expose them, without guarantees or compensation, to the risks of political domination which might result from an industrial domination of the more strongly organized States.

It is therefore logical and normal that the justification of the economic sacrifices to be made to the whole should be found only in the development of a political situation warranting confidence between peoples and true pacification of minds. And even after the actual accomplishment of such a condition, assured by the establishment of a régime of constant and close peaceful association in peace between the peoples of Europe, there would still be needed, on the political plane, the intervention of a higher feeling of international necessities to impose on the Members of the European community, in favour of the collectivity, the sincere conception and effective prosecution of a truly liberal tariff policy.

B. **Conception of European political cooperation** as one which ought to tend toward this essential end: a federation built not upon the idea of unity but of union; that is to say, sufficiently flexible to respect the independence and national sovereignty of each of the States, while assuring them all the benefit of collective solidarity for the settlement of political questions involving the fate of the European community or that of one of its Members.

C. **Conception of the economic organization of Europe** as one which ought to tend to this essential end: a rapprochement of the European economic systems effected under the political responsibility of the Governments working in unison. [...]

IV

A. **Determination of the field of European cooperation**, particularly in the following spheres:

1. *General Economy*. The effective realization, in Europe, of the programme drawn up by the last economic conference of the League of Nations; the control of the policy of industrial unions and cartels among various countries; examination and preparation of all future possibilities regarding the progressive lowering of tariffs, etc.

2. *Economic Equipment*. Realization of coordination between great public works executed by European States (routes for heavy automobile traffic, canals, etc.).

3. *Communications and Transit*. By land, water, and air: Regulation and improvement of inter-European traffic; coordination of the labours of the European waterways commissions; agreements between railways; European régime of posts, telegraphs and telephones; radio-broadcasting rules, etc.

4. *Finances*. Encouragement of credit intended for the development of the

economically less developed regions of Europe; European market; monetary questions, etc.

5. *Labour.* Settlement of certain labour questions peculiar to Europe, such as labour in inland navigation and in glass trades; questions having a continental or regional character, such as the regulation of the social consequences of inter-European emigration (application by one country to another of laws respecting labour accidents, social insurance, workers' pensions, etc.).

6. *Hygiene.* General extension of certain methods of hygiene subjects essayed by the health organization of the League of Nations (in particular, reclamation of agricultural regions; application of insurance against illness; regional schools of hygiene; European epidemiology; exchange of information and officials between national health services; scientific and administrative cooperation in the struggle against great social scourges, against occupational diseases and infant mortality, etc.).

7. *Intellectual Cooperation.* Cooperation by universities and academies; literary and artistic relations; centralization of scientific research; improvement of the press system in relations between agencies and in transportation of newspapers, etc.

8. *Interparliamentary Relations.* Utilization of the organization and labours of the 'Interparliamentary Union' for the development of contacts and exchanges of views between parliamentary circles of the various European countries (in order to prepare the political ground for the accomplishments of the European Union which would necessitate parliamentary approval. [...]

9. *Administration.* Formation of European sections in certain universal international bureaus. [...]

The time has never been more propitious or more pressing for the inauguration of a constructive work in Europe. The settlement of the main problems, material and moral, incident to the late war, will soon have liberated New Europe from a burden which bore most heavily upon its psychology, as well as on its economic system. It appears henceforward to be ready for a positive effort and one which will fit in with the new order. It is a decisive hour, when watchful Europe may determine her own fate.

Unite to live and prosper: such is the stringent necessity which will henceforth confront the nations in Europe. It seems that the feeling of the peoples has already been made clear on this subject. It behoves the Governments to assume their responsibilities today, under penalty of abandoning to the risk of individual initiatives and disorderly undertakings the grouping of material and moral forces, the collective control of which it is incumbent on them to keep, to the benefit of the European community as well as of humanity.

_____ 4 _____

THE NAZI ORGANIZATION OF EUROPE

A large part of Nazi propaganda looked to the establishment of a 'New Order' in Europe after the war. The following draft of a memorandum, prepared for the German Ministry of Foreign Affairs in June 1943, expressed the Nazi 'plan' in very broad, general terms. It was published in *Documents on the History of European Integration*, edited by Walter Lipgens, vol.I (Berlin: Walter de Gruyter, 1985), pp. 132–7.

BASIC ELEMENTS OF A PLAN FOR THE NEW EUROPE

The more the war situation presses towards a conclusion, the more urgent it becomes to give shape to our plans for the reorganization of Europe and make the utmost possible use of them. Our adversaries are at a propaganda disadvantage in regard to post-war planning, as they have nothing new to offer the world and their disunion is becoming more and more obvious despite attempts to cover it up. It would be of value to our war effort to exploit the propaganda advantage that this gives us.

The plan must be realistic. Its basic principles should be intended sincerely; the propaganda element should only apply to the manner of their presentation. The plan itself must stand the test of sober examination by responsible governments.

To carry conviction and be attractive the plan must satisfy the nations' longing for peace, a just settlement of national problems and economic and social well-being.

The basic features of the plan are here outlined as briefly as possible, without arguments of a political or propaganda kind. To develop the ideas further would require a closer study of individual problems in association with competent experts.

I. THE ESSENTIAL BASIS

The plan for a new order in Europe must be based on the continent's history but reflect the new insights of National Socialism.

The firm historical basis of present-day Europe lies in the old, shared culture of its peoples and the destiny that has brought together in a small area independent nations of many tongues with a strong sense of identity, whose task is now to organize, protect and if necessary defend themselves against the typical feature of modern times, the interventionist and expansionist drive of two alien continents. *[US USSR]*

The insights of National Socialism that must be used for the reorganization of Europe are the principle of leadership in the sense of mutual loyalty (in contrast to the old ideas of hegemony and imperialism); the principle of efficiency, seen in the nations' historic achievements and their performance in the present war; the principle of organic order in contrast to the anarchy of formal equality among all

organizations, hierarchy of states

states; and the racial [*völkisch*] principle, which is decisive in regard to ethnic groups and the handling of the Jewish problem.

II. THE POLITICO-MILITARY ORGANIZATION OF EUROPE

(a) The political and military organization of Europe must be seen as an interconnected whole. The continent must have a viable, healthy structure before the rules governing its life can become effective. This is only possible by means of the individual, organic regulation of relations among states and peoples.

The backbone is formed by the German–Italian Pact of Steel and the Tripartite Pact. By the well-judged politico-military integration of other European countries these elements have been developed into a fully satisfied European community for the purpose of joint constructive effort and cooperation in repelling external dangers, and all this on a voluntary basis.

(b) Apart from the tasks which have to be fulfilled jointly, the geopolitical conditions of Europe are such as to necessitate regional subdivision. The most important region is the Greater German Reich with the Germanic and 'sub-Germanic' (Eastern or South-Eastern) peoples that look towards it. The organization of this power centre, which is responsible in the first instance for security *vis-à-vis* the border state in the East and for protecting the whole of Northern Europe, must take account of the variety of local conditions. The different forms of association with the Greater German Reich, a process in which Italy has its part to play, lie between the two extremes of (i) integration involving the loss of capacity to act as a subject in international law (e.g. the Protectorate of Bohemia and Moravia) and (ii) loose association by politico-military treaties, with the retention of separate diplomatic representation etc. The chief features which may, according to circumstances, figure in politico-military treaties are: uniformity of foreign policy, mutual political information and consultation, military aid in the event of warlike involvement with extra-European countries (possibly with periodical staff talks) and, so far as necessary for this purpose, all-European military installations such as bases and fortifications.

Next to the area centred on the Greater German Reich comes that of the Mediterranean. Italy is the leading power here and must therefore see to the political and military organization of the region with German participation. Africa's link with Europe as its natural and necessary complement is of importance here, especially as Italy has far-reaching territorial (imperial) rights and claims in that continent.

The third region is the Atlantic area. This could be organized by means of individual treaties between the Axis and the European countries of the Atlantic seaboard. The Iberian peninsula plays an important part as guardian of the access route from the Atlantic to the Mediterranean, as well as the crossing to Africa and the colonial tasks there. The functions of France in the Euro-African area will be largely determined by the peace treaty with the Axis and the resulting territorial settlement. What part England will play in the Atlantic area and in Africa cannot be discussed at present: it depends on whether, after the war, there is a new England that is prepared to give up its old claims and domineering methods in Europe and become part of its new order.

Special treaties will govern the political and military status of Africa as a dominion of the community of European nations. In particular, the territorial situation in colonial Africa must be confirmed or modified as the case may be, and basic questions affecting the natives must be regulated.

A special political settlement will be required for the Near East, with Turkey as a link with Europe and keeper of the Straits, while Egypt forms a link with Africa and acts as trustee for the Suez Canal. The organization of the Near East should be left to the countries of the area as independent national states with the right to determine the form of their own union. Europe as a whole would have to take care that no outside powers interfere in the Near East and that its economic interests (oil) are protected.

III. RELATIONS BETWEEN EUROPE AND OTHER CONTINENTS

(a) It must be a basic principle that Europe and its member states do not interfere in the affairs of other continents or embark on political or military conquests there, and that in the same way any interference or political or military conquest by other continents in Europe or Africa is excluded. Any such attack or interference would meet with united resistance on the part of Europe as a whole.

(b) Next to the principle of non-intervention is that of preferences to be accorded by European states to one another as against non-European countries, primarily in the economic field. For the rest, Europe's relations with other continents, and those of its African dominion, should be governed by the general rules of international conduct, on the basis that Europe desires to live in peace and friendship with the others and to carry on commercial and cultural exchanges to the benefit of all concerned.

(c) In so far as European powers still have territorial possessions in other continents at the end of the war, they must be regarded as the special concern of those powers, which the other European countries are not obliged to help them defend. Complications arising from the existence of such possessions are only of concern to Europe as a whole if they threaten to lead to an attack on European or African territory by non-European power.

IV. MAINTENANCE OF PEACE IN EUROPE

(a) The maintenance of peace in Europe itself will be ensured by a European peace pact which will not only provide the usual machinery for the peaceful settlement of disputes but will also embody certain material principles. Among these might be:

(1) The independence and freedom of all European countries which have freely chosen to associate in a closer community.

(2) The right of each country to organize its national life as it thinks fit, provided it respects its obligations towards the European community.

(3) European countries should be free to conduct their mutual relations as they wish, within the framework of European solidarity and European obligations.

(4) Freedom to conduct relations with non-European countries in any way compatible with European solidarity and European obligations.

(5) European countries should not interfere in the affairs of non-European states, and correspondingly the latter should not be allowed to interfere in European affairs.

(6) Any disputes between European countries should be settled peacefully; any question that presents a threat to amicable relations can be adjudicated by peaceful means.

(7) If there is a threat to friendly relations due to the fact that the areas of settlement of particular peoples do not coincide with political boundaries, they should be adjusted as far as possible by peaceful agreement and if necessary resettlement. If this is not possible the way of life of ethnic groups living within the territory of a different people should be protected by the authority of the state, if necessary by treaty.

(8) Every country is responsible for ensuring that no actions are committed on its territory that are incompatible with European solidarity and European obligations. [...]

V. THE JEWISH QUESTION

The settlement of the Jewish question is an important aspect of the pacification of Europe. A European convention should frame the necessary measures and set up an agency which should remain in existence at least until the question has been settled by complete elimination of the Jewish element from Europe.

VI. THE ECONOMIC ORGANIZATION OF EUROPE

(a) Whereas in the politico-military sphere and in that of peace-keeping, associations like the League of Nations are to be avoided, the conference system is advantageous in economic matters. The European economy must here be considered in the broadest sense, to include labour and social questions. A permanent European Economic Congress should be created with a presidium representing the leading powers and some other countries, which would summon it as occasion arose and direct its activity. It could be divided into separate Conferences for (1) trade and industry; (2) financial and currency questions; (3) labour and social questions; and (4) food, agriculture and forestry. Any state might join the Congress provided it belonged to the European peace organization.

(b) The task of the Economic Congress, its Conferences and their Committees would be to prepare and enact European economic conventions for the settlement of economic problems of the Euro-African *Grossraum* with an eye to making it secure against blockade, e.g.:

(1) Trade based on the principle of European preference *vis-à-vis* non-European countries, with the eventual objective of a European customs union.

(2) A European clearing centre and stable currency rates in Europe, with the eventual objective of a European monetary union.

(3) Harmonization of labour conditions and social welfare, in the direction of improving standards.

(4) Long-term planning of production in industry, agriculture and forestry.

Within the framework of the European economic convention and its objectives each European country would have the right to conduct its economic relations with other European countries as it wished. Its economic relations with non-European countries would also be free in so far as they were not restricted by the Convention, especially the rule of European preference.

(c) In addition to the European Economic Congress and its specialized Conferences, European specialized agencies or institutes would be created for particular spheres of activity in certain countries (European Labour Office, European Agricultural Institute etc.); these would be autonomous subject to general directives and tasks assigned by the Economic Congress or its Conferences. The purpose of the specialized agencies would be to collect and study relevant material, follow up new ideas, provide expert opinions and information, compile statistics etc.

VII. COMMUNICATIONS

The communications system of the Euro-African *Grossraum* will be similarly organized. For this purpose, however, it will suffice to create a permanent European Communications Conference with Committees for particular subjects (railways, waterways, autobahns, heavy goods traffic, canals, airways etc.). Here too it would be useful to set up specialized agencies and institutes for the different forms of transport.

VIII. CULTURAL COOPERATION

The promotion of culture is primarily a national affair and does not require so elaborate an organization as is envisaged for economics and communications. For the exchange of cultural values and experience it will suffice to have specialized agencies and institutes, perhaps also Chambers (e.g. a European Film Chamber) on which professionals from different countries would be directly represented. Conferences at government level are only necessary when European specialized conventions have to be drafted, e.g. in matters of copyright, translation rights etc.

IX. PRESS MATTERS

Given the great political importance of the press, this is primarily a matter of political organization. It is the duty of the political leadership in each country, arising from the political treaties and the principles of the European peace pact, to ensure that the press functions in the spirit of European solidarity and with respect for European obligations. Any disputes over the attitude of the press in particular countries should be dealt with under the procedure laid down in the peace pact. It would, however, also be desirable to have a specialized organization in the form of a European Press Institute, and perhaps a European Press Chamber as well.

X. EDUCATION

The education and training of youth in the new Europe will also be primarily a national matter, and can therefore not be the object of a Europe-wide organization. To see that it takes place in a spirit of European solidarity is, as in the case of the press, a matter of political concern first and foremost, to be regarded from the point of view of the political treaties and the peace pact. Here too, however, it would be useful to have a European specialized institute to exchange experience, statistics etc., and above all a general youth organization to work for understanding among European peoples in a spirit of European solidarity. [...]

CHAPTER II

EUROPE EMERGES

1944–1954

The construction of a new Europe began before the end of Hitler's war. During 1943 the leadership of most of the anti-fascist Resistance agreed to coordinate their struggle against the Nazis and to start planning for a democratic and united Europe. In spite of all the dangers, they established an international fraternity. The Resistance in northern Italy, for example, was frequently in contact with the *maquis* in France and with Tito's partisans in Yugoslavia. Everywhere in Europe, the Resistance were conscious of a common goal, the defeat of Nazism, and of a common vision, a postwar federation of states based on the rule of law.

In April and May of 1944, a number of the Resistance leaders managed to evade the Gestapo and travel to neutral Switzerland. Meeting in Geneva, they drafted two declarations on the future of Europe. The first recalled the years of 'sacrifices and suffering [which] have created ties of brotherhood ... and have given birth to a new awareness of solidarity among the free peoples'. The second declaration, also signed on 20 May, took the form of a manifesto (DOCUMENT 5). It said that only a federal union could put an end to Europe's wars and that states 'must irrevocably surrender to the Federation their sovereign rights in the sphere of defence, relations with powers outside the Union, international exchange and communications'. The Resistance leaders foresaw a Union open to all European states which were prepared 'to guarantee democratic institutions and the free development of the human personality'.[1]

These lofty expressions were eclipsed by the Allied landings in Normandy and southern France. The restoration of national governments in France and the Lowlands tended to discourage talk of European federalism.[2] Even so, the discussions which absorbed spokespersons of the Resistance were destined to revive in a few years. While there were few specific proposals for the structure of the Union or the nature of European federalism, there was nonetheless a strong and lasting consensus about the dangers of state sovereignty. The European system of national states had manifestly failed the supreme test of keeping the peace. By their aggressive policies and their prodigal waste of Europe's material resources, the Axis states had discredited the concept of nationhood. By their spineless policies of appeasement before 1939, the democratic states had actually encouraged violations of Europe's peace. Europe's future would be brighter only if states agreed to abridge sovereignty and to entrust the making of foreign policy to a new international authority.[3]

In the 1944 Geneva conference of Resistance spokespersons, we have a sort of theatre play which was destined to more than a generation of performances. The various roles have continued even if the actors have changed. Since 1944, the Italians have been among the most vocal enthusiasts of European federalism; Ernesto Rossi and Altiero Spinelli had already started the Movimento Federalista Europeo and at Geneva they boldly called for a United States of Europe. The French also supported a federal union, provided they received sufficient guarantees against future German expansion. The Danish and Norwegian representatives, by contrast, were extremely wary of any supranational authority in Europe and hoped for a looser confederation which did not erode national sovereignties. The communist Resistance representatives opposed a federal union. Mindful of Moscow's feelings on the subject, they insisted on the restoration of prewar states (apart from those annexed by the Soviet Union). They feared that European federalism would only destroy the new vitality which nations had gained by resisting Nazi tyranny. Not for them was the state to wither away in favour of a supranational and democratic Europe.

Finally, there was no British voice at the Geneva meetings. Axis forces had never generated a British Resistance movement by occupying the United Kingdom. The absence of British representation in Geneva in the spring of 1944 was prophetic of things to come: the British were absent from many postwar conferences as well, preferring to observe from a safe distance the discussions which eventually led to a united Europe.

Many Resistance leaders believed that the unity of postwar Europe would be achieved on two complementary levels. The first, of course, was some sort of federal union embracing all European states, perhaps including Russia. Inside this union, there was the potential for a second level of unity, involving regional confederations of two or more states of similar economic and political development. The Resistance movements imagined several such mergers. In south-eastern Europe, for example, they entertained the idea of combining Greece and Yugoslavia; in central Europe, there were advocates of a loose union of Poland and Czechoslovakia. These ideas never got very far. All four states had been victims of Axis aggression and they were reluctant to repeat the mistake of the 1920s by entering into unions or alliances which might prolong the status of the defeated Axis states (Hungary and Bulgaria) as the disgruntled pariahs of the region. Another reason for the early demise of these proposals was the clear and constant opposition of the Soviet Union, which realized that the political fragmentation of eastern and central Europe was very much to its advantage.

In another area of Europe, however, the prospects for regional unity were considerably brighter. The small states of Belgium, Luxembourg and the Netherlands, historically known as the Lowlands, agreed to a postwar union. The prime mover of this plan was the Belgian foreign minister, Paul-Henri Spaak. From his base in London, where he was the most influential of the exiled Belgian leaders, Spaak considered the role of small states in constructing a new Europe. As he tells us in his *Memoirs*, his faith in European federalism, as the only proper antidote to quarrelsome nation-states, dates from the early 1940s (DOCUMENT 6). He saw the formation of Benelux as the logical first step toward the integration of western

Europe. Several factors encouraged the Benelux experiment. The three small countries were all constitutional monarchies with long traditions of democratic politics and a regard for human rights. Most of the Resistance fighters had already declared their support for some kind of postwar unity.[4] Moreover, there was the 1922 Treaty which had brought together Belgium and Luxembourg in a customs union: their economic cooperation was now seen as a precedent for the broad integration of the three economies. But Liberation in the autumn of 1944 allowed for the return of old political rivalries and, as Spaak remarks, the politicians found reasons to postpone the implementation of the Benelux accord.

The agreement which finally came into force on 1 January 1948 was not as far-reaching as Spaak had hoped. It abolished some import duties in mutual trade relations and it established a common customs tariff vis-à-vis other countries. The strong economic recovery of Benelux by 1950 encouraged the three countries to take further steps: the coordination of social policies (1953), a liberalization of capital investment procedures (1954), the progressive harmonization of agricultural policies (1955) and the formation of a common labour market (1957), as well as the first meeting of the interparliamentary Council (February 1957). The momentum continued in 1960 with the abolition of all remaining internal customs duties and passport controls for Benelux citizens.

This impressive record of decisions, most of them taken even before the Treaty of Rome was signed in March 1957, made Benelux the first concrete initiative of European integration. Europeans were aware of Benelux as an integrated region, and its rapid progress inspired them to work harder for a larger union of states. The advocates of European integration attended the meetings which contributed to the formation of Benelux in the 1950s and they were impatient to imitate the same principles on a grander scale. At one 1955 Benelux meeting, for example, the European federalists (guided by Jean Monnet) circulated a memorandum urging the non-Benelux observers to coordinate their social, transport and energy policies with Benelux.

In many ways, Benelux reflected the hopes of Resistance movements in western Europe. The industrial workers, shopkeepers, peasants and intellectuals who came together in the Resistance wanted a more egalitarian society which recognized the dignity and talents of all people. Externally, the ideology of the Resistance meant a society which 'transcended old national boundaries' that now seemed 'discredited and artificial'.[5] Internally, the ideology of the Resistance required the mobility of labour, the harmonization of commercial and social policies, uniformly high standards of working and living conditions, and the coordination of monetary and economic policies. Benelux seemed to promise all those things. But the carefully measured federalism of Benelux was not everybody's model of the new Europe. The period from 1944 to 1948 saw the activity of many groups with different ideas of European unity. While these societies insisted on free and democratic institutions in Europe, they were decidedly more cautious about discarding the sovereign prerogatives of individual states. Their views were represented by a number of influential spokespersons, including Winston Churchill.

In the immediate postwar period, Churchill often spoke of his belief in a United

States of Europe. While some Europeans admired Churchill as a federalist, he was nothing of the sort. He welcomed the unity of Benelux but he never really understood the economic implications of their integration. The people who heard Churchill in Brussels in 1945 and in the Hague in 1946 were glad for his support: he was the only major wartime leader to declare himself a supporter of European unity.[6] Most of his speeches, however, offered only a vague idea of what this unity might mean. Usually Churchill's hopes were expressed in terms of justice, prosperity and security in Europe. He was slightly less ambiguous when he addressed a meeting at the University of Zurich in September 1947 (DOCUMENT 7). Paul-Henri Spaak thought this speech 'beautiful and passionate for its poetical language': it 'galvanized all those who believed in the need for a new Europe'.[7]

But as Spaak also noted, Churchill's definition of Europe did not include Britain. For Churchill, Europe was the continent, and its future rested on the friendship of France and Germany. Britain was ready to bless and praise European unity but saw no reason to be part of it. It had too many commitments elsewhere: the strong cultural ties to the independent dominions and the United States, the responsibilities of a large empire (most of which still existed) and the commercial connections with other European countries like Portugal, Greece and Norway. In spite of the new postwar realities, Churchill's view of Europe had not changed since he wrote for an American magazine seventeen years earlier.[8] Nor was he alone in his old-fashioned Tory opinions. Whether Labour, Conservative or Liberal, the vast majority of Britons agreed with him, and for decades to come they invoked Churchill's polite arguments for steering clear of European integration.

The British were not alone in rejecting integration. The French government, under Charles de Gaulle until January 1946, also scorned the idea of a close European union. The British and French governments wanted only military cooperation. They hoped that a number of intergovernment agreements, some bilateral and others multilateral, would produce a permanent military alliance of democratic states. Such an alliance would have virtually no role in forming economic or social policy and it would not imply the loss of national sovereignty. The reason for the British and French attitude may seem strange to us now, for their primary concern in the three years after VE Day was a resurgence of German military power. De Gaulle and his immediate successors hoped to minimize this danger in two ways. First they urged the territorial mutilation of Germany by giving the coal-rich area of the Saar to France, setting up a quasi-independent state in the Rhineland, and establishing a zone of 'international control' over the Ruhr Valley. The second strategy would complement the first: a special military alliance with Britain. The incoming Labour government in Britain shared France's assessment and her concern. The result was the bilateral alliance known as the Dunkirk Treaty (March 1947), expressly designed to meet future German aggression.

As Britain and France hoped, this Treaty served as the basis of an expanded alliance. With the signing of the Treaty of Brussels on 17 March 1948, Belgium, Luxembourg and the Netherlands joined Britain and France in a defensive military alliance (DOCUMENT 8). This Treaty was a mixture of diplomatic styles. On the one hand, it was the product of inter-governmental negotiations. It represented a

[margin handwritten note: Fr. + Br. plan for security against Ger.]

large measure of political trust on the part of similar states which identified another state, Germany, as a potential menace. The Treaty did not establish a supra-national authority. Even its provision for a permanent commission and secretariat did no more than many interwar treaties.

On the other hand, the expected life of the Treaty was extraordinary. The five states obviously assumed that it was necessary to take a long-term view of their commitments, and in this view they were wiser than they realized. Above all, the Treaty was remarkable for combining economic and social obligations with the arrangements for military cooperation. Indeed, the clauses on the 'economic recovery of Europe' and the 'attainment of a higher standard of living' preceded the clauses which dealt with military security.

The Brussels Treaty, or something very much like it, was probably inevitable in 1948, and it is usually explained as a response to developments in central Europe. On 13 March, the Czech communist party, with Soviet assistance, took control of the government in Prague. For the second time in a decade, the one viable democracy in central Europe was extinguished. The communist coup in Prague left governments in western Europe in a state of shock, and it no doubt sped the Brussels Treaty into existence. On 8 March, the Norwegian government revealed that it expected Soviet pressure to accept a treaty which would reduce Norway to the level of a Soviet satellite. The next month brought another shock. The Russians began their attempt to absorb West Berlin by denying the western Allies the use of certain highways across the Soviet zone to the city. These events helped western Europeans to understand two things about their own condition. First they realized that Europe's peace was not threatened by a vanquished and partitioned Germany but by the consolidation of Soviet military and political power. Secondly, they perceived the value of the timely commitments made in Brussels, but they also realized that the Brussels Treaty alone would not answer the Soviet challenge.

The western Europeans therefore sought a further extension of their alliance by including the United States. Thanks to the Vandenberg Resolution, passed in the US Senate in June 1948, the Americans found a way around their traditional dislike of entering entangling alliances in peacetime, and the expanded alliance was quickly arranged. The North Atlantic Treaty Organization (NATO) came into force in April 1949. Because it included Norway, Denmark, Iceland, Italy, Portugal, Canada and the United States, as well as the signatories of the Brussels Treaty, NATO virtually superseded the Brussels Treaty as the essential instrument of European security. Notwithstanding the occasional expression of neutralist sentiments in Norway and Denmark, and in spite of the vociferous opposition from the communist parties in France and Italy, NATO was welcomed by most Europeans as a necessary insurance policy. Military security, rather than economic and social integration, was their first priority in the late 1940s. But while it was their fear of Russia which caused western Europeans to form a military alliance, it was the pressure from the United States which put them on the road to integration.

Early in 1947 the American government decided that Europe's economy might not revive on its own. Food supplies were running out and the severe winter of

1946–47 aggravated problems of transport and communications. The Americans feared that Europe's economic misery would undermine democratic governments and leave them too feeble to deal with the well-organized local communist parties. In a speech at Harvard University in June 1947, the American Secretary of State observed that Europe's recovery was proving more difficult than most people had expected; he called for a united and conclusive effort to heal the wounds of war. What he proposed at Harvard was not a 'plan' as such; it was more a statement of America's intent (DOCUMENT 9). The Secretary of State offered a contract: if European governments decided, very quickly, to work with new financial agencies and to share the responsibilities of a comprehensive aid programme, the United States was ready to offer them 'substantial aid'. No one (including Secretary Marshall) had any clear idea how much money would be required; the total sum was inconceivable in June 1947. But it was clear that Marshall's address was an invitation to collective action rather than to a series of bilateral treaties, or aid 'on a piecemeal basis'.

If Marshall's speech at Harvard seems disjointed to us now, it is because it had 'many fathers'.[9] Marshall admitted this himself: in 1959 he confessed to composing the speech by putting together words and phrases from recent conversations with several of his advisors.[10] However clumsy the text, there is no doubting its impact. The Europeans were quick to realize its importance. The British foreign secretary, Ernest Bevin, and the French foreign minister, Georges Bidault, immediately consulted about the proposal and arranged for a European conference. Sixteen governments were represented at the Paris meeting of 12 July. In little more than three months, and in spite of some acrimonious debate, they established the Committee for European Economic Cooperation (CEEC) and they met the US government's request for a list of their urgent needs. Some Americans urged Europeans to consider entrusting sweeping powers to the CEEC; they wanted a large single market without internal frontiers. The idea was too utopian for the moment. The French and the British did not want the CEEC (or its successor, the OEEC) to become a mechanism for supranational decision-making. They much preferred the more traditional reliance on bilateral agreements, which the British saw as a guarantee of their own 'special relationship' with the United States.

The hostility of the Soviets was unmistakable. On 2 July 1947, the Soviet Foreign Minister, V. M. Molotov, rejected any notion of a collaborative plan for European reconstruction. He thought that any collective approach must be demeaning to the sovereignty of independent states. The next morning, he and his enormous delegation of interpreters, advisors and secretaries left Paris for Moscow. They set to work on an alternative system for the Soviet bloc, which was officially launched in September 1947 as the Communist Information Bureau (COMINFORM). This was Russia's answer to the 'European Recovery Programme', as the American-funded plan came to be called. COMINFORM united the large communist parties of France and Italy with the communist governments of Bulgaria, Poland, Yugoslavia, Hungary and the USSR in the name of 'national independence and the sovereignty of those states'. Their mandate was to confront and if possible to derail the Marshall Plan. The economic recovery of Europe thus became part of a much wider issue of Europe's postwar division into two spheres of influence.

Some historians have explained the Marshall Plan as an 'ornament of the Cold War' and as a conscious effort to undermine Russia's influence in Europe. They have doubted Marshall's sincerity in asking all European states, including Russia, to participate. It is true that Marshall did not really expect the USSR and its satellites to take part in the plan to rebuild Europe's economy; some weeks before the Harvard address, Marshall returned from a conference in Moscow pessimistic about Soviet cooperation. Pessimism increased during the next few months. The Harvard speech practically coincided with the final stitching of Hungary into the Soviet camp and the arrest of noncommunist politicians in Bulgaria. Some people explained Russia's negative attitude as one based on the assumption that the Plan would never be implemented and that 'isolationists' in the US Congress would permit only a meagre amount of aid, or that they would withhold aid altogether. More significant in terms of *realpolitik* was the Soviet pressure on Poland and Czechoslovakia to change their minds about joining the Recovery Programme. As the USSR and its satellites refused to participate, we cannot know how much they might have benefited from the Americans' largess. By excluding themselves, they never put the promises of US capital to the test.

The efforts of COMINFORM had little effect on those countries which agreed to apply American aid to 'the most appropriate objectives'. Their economies responded at once. The first major infusion of Marshall aid occurred in late 1948. Within three years, inflation was under control in most of the participating countries. By 1950, inter-European trade exceeded the prewar level, whereas in 1947 it was half that before the war. By 1952, agricultural production was more than 10 per cent higher than it was in 1939, and industrial output had increased by almost 40 per cent. The combined gross national product of these countries had risen by almost 30 per cent.[11]

In April 1948 the CEEC gave way to the Organization of European Economic Cooperation (OEEC), which oversaw the distribution of funds. The OEEC is not usually regarded as one of the milestones on the road to European integration. Spinelli and other dedicated federalists were contemptuous of the OEEC because it was, after all, an inter-governmental agency. (The British and the French would not have had it otherwise.) Its membership was too numerous and too diverse to allow it to decide on far-reaching policies.[12] Its mandate was too limited, and the French (who frequently complained of its reviving Germany at their expense) assumed that its proper function was to make France the centre of a union of western European states.

While the OEEC did not dispel the suspicions of the past, it nonetheless proved a modest success. The Europeans soon decided that it should continue after American aid had stopped. In July 1950 the OEEC sponsored another agency which the Americans had wanted since the beginning of the aid programme: the European Payments Union. More than just a clearing house, the EPU established credit margins for the participating states and signalled the elimination of quantitative restrictions on 60 per cent of their trade with each other. It allowed them to manage bilateral deficits without renewing or setting up trade restrictions: one country's deficit with another could be offset by a surplus with still other countries.[13] Many Europeans were at first sceptical about all these new arrangements. Like Mr Molotov, they were accustomed to bilateral agreements which solved specific economic or monetary problems for a given period of time and which gave every assurance of respecting their national sovereignties.

The OEEC and the EPU began a seachange in the economic mentality of European states by making the economies of those states more interdependent than ever. At the same time that they established the OEEC, Europeans created a permanent forum which was to provide a place for those states which did not join the OEEC. The Council of Europe began with the Hague Conference early in May 1948. Paul-Henri Spaak remembered it as a 'historic landmark in the annals of Europe'.[14] It was certainly an impressive occasion, with about 1,000 delegates from the democratic countries and refugee-observers from central and eastern Europe. The luminaries of European unity were there: Paul van Zeeland, Konrad Adenauer, Paul Reynaud, Alcide de Gasperi, Paul-Henri Spaak and Winston Churchill, who was by now regarded as the godfather of the 'European movement'. The Hague Conference served as the symbol rather than as the motor of European unity; the institutions which it created satisfied only those who believed in Europe as a 'family of nations' (DOCUMENT 10).

The Council of Europe was really composed of two bodies: one in favour of European integration and the other against it. The Consultative (or parliamentary) Assembly, which held its meetings in Strasbourg, was the first body. Its members were not directly elected but nominated by the national parliaments of the member states. All but the small splinter parties and the national communist parties could send representatives to Strasbourg in a system of proportional representation. The powers of the Assembly were limited to debate. The other organ of the Council, the Committee of Ministers, could override, ignore or destroy any recommendation which the parliamentarians had reached. The Assembly debates were public; the decisions of the Committee of Ministers were reached behind closed doors. It is not surprising that those who advocated a federal union or who wanted Europe to move more quickly towards economic integration were disappointed by the Council of Europe. The Council had no mandate to assume any supranational authority; its decisions were made by the Committee of Ministers, who reported to, and were directed by, their respective governments. As far as Britain and France were concerned, the Council of Europe was the tangible fulfilment of the nonmilitary provisions of the Treaty of Brussels, and they did not care to see it go any further.

In the summer of 1949 the Council of Europe began with ten member states. Over the years its membership grew until nearly all the noncommunist states had joined. By 1995 the Council of Europe claimed a membership of 35; the political structure of only a few states prevented their entry as 'democracies'.[15] Since its inception, the *raison d'être* of the Council has been more evocative of nineteenth-century liberalism than of twentieth-century federalism. According to Chapter I of its *Statute*, the Council's purpose is 'to safeguard the ideals and principles which are their common heritage' and 'to facilitate economic and social progress'. In practical terms, the Council's primary function has been to defend individual human rights in Europe. Spain and Portugal were denied membership of the Council as long as they had fascist governments which violated human rights; Greece was evicted from the Council in 1967 for its 'undemocratic and illiberal regime' and readmitted only when parliamentary democracy was restored in 1974. The Council of Europe always seemed tailor-made for Britain and the Scandinavian states, who made up almost half of its membership in its early years. It upheld the cultural integrity of Europe but it delayed (or opposed) any move which abridged the powers of national governments or harmonized industrial or monetary policies. The federalists who assisted at the birth of the Council were bound to be dissatisfied with it, for they wanted a constitutional structure for Europe's political and economic life. They were soon to seek this structure outside the Council.

Apart from the unwillingness of Britain and France to accept any measure which might diminish national sovereignty, there was another huge obstacle to the unity of Europe. Germany had lost her national sovereignty altogether and no longer existed as a political entity. Divided into four zones at the end of the war, Germany was under the military government of the victorious Allied powers. The Soviets occupied a large area of what used to be central Germany; the British took the north-west of the country; the Americans governed the south. The French were mollified (their status as a European power seemingly restored) by the concession of responsibility for an area in the south-west and the Rhineland.[16] The metropolitan area of Berlin was administered by all four powers, with the three western zones of the city a political island in the middle of the Soviet zone.

Was Germany ever to reappear as a single state? The Allies disagreed about its fate. During the war they contemplated various schemes for the permanent division of Germany into three or more states, in the hope of undoing the Prussian unification of the country in the nineteenth century.[17] These speculations continued after VE Day, as did the French desire to annex the Saar and much of the Rhineland. With their cities in ruin and every corner of their country under foreign occupation, the Germans themselves thought they had lost both the war and their national identity. + later French

The British and Americans, however, did not imagine that the zones of military government should continue indefinitely. In December 1946, they decided to administer their two zones as a single economic unit. It is unlikely that many people at the time realized that the creation of the so-called 'Bizonia' was the practical beginning of European as well as German integration. The French were at first reluctant to bring their zone into this unit, but they changed their minds when the Americans reminded them of the as yet undistributed aid of the Marshall Plan. During 1948 the Western allies made definite proposals for a united civilian government of their three zones. They wanted the new Germany to remain demilitarized and to pay war reparations; they also demanded the right to guide aspects of Germany's foreign policy and external trade. Above all, they insisted on a federal Germany in which the central government would lose considerable political influence to the governments of the constituent states (länder).

These guidelines were not very popular in Germany, but they were observed in the new federal constitution (basic law) of 1949. In the elections of that year, the government of the Bundesrepublik became the responsibility of the Christian Democratic Union (CDU) and its leader Konrad Adenauer. As federal chancellor from 1949 to 1963, Adenauer gained the respect and esteem of other European Christian Democrats, and his governments rebuilt Germany's identity as a stable, prosperous state, conscious of its historic connections with western Europe. In fact, it seemed to many of his contemporaries that Adenauer was more anxious to associate western Germany with the incipient union of European democratic states than he was to win Russian approval for the reunion of western and eastern Germany. In his *Memoirs*, Adenauer wrote that Germany had no choice at this point in its history (DOCUMENT 11). The history and culture of the country, he thought, were essentially 'western'. He believed that Germany was, in a very real sense, on probation. It had one last opportunity to prove its democratic credentials to its western neighbours and particularly to France, where there were still many advocates of Germany's dismemberment.

As a realist, Adenauer knew that the Russians were most unlikely to withdraw from their advanced positions in central Europe. Their response to the emergence of the German Federal Republic was to organize their zone as a separate German state, the German Democratic Republic (GDR). As the Cold War deepened in Europe (and erupted into hot war in Korea), Adenauer realized that the unification of his country lay far in the future. He undoubtably shared his compatriots' disdain for the naivety of the Western allies in dealing with the Soviets and he never forgave the British for certain administrative practices in their zone; he certainly felt that Germany had only narrowly escaped losing the Saar to France. But Adenauer knew that to save what remained of Germany he must align the country firmly with the West and secure a rapprochement with France.

The reappearance of Germany as a political entity helped the French to see Europe's future in a different light. Compared to the Germany established by the Versailles Treaty in 1919, the new Federal Republic must have seemed a weak rump state, with a sleepy Rhenish town as its 'provisional capital'. But France was nonetheless obliged to deal with it as an equal. The security of France now depended on the success of the new Germany. Robert Schuman, the French foreign minister, acknowledged that the peace and stability of both countries depended on the 'natural unity' of lands which they had long contested. On 9 May 1950, Schuman proposed an economic association which allowed France and Germany to share their joint production of coal (still important as a major source of energy) and steel (in great demand for the rebuilding of Europe's infrastructure) (DOCUMENT 12). Defending his proposal before the Consultative Assembly in Strasbourg on 13 August, Schuman admitted that there were many technical details to resolve before the two essential resources were 'pooled', and he acknowledged that the creation of a 'High Authority' would mean 'the renunciation of some sovereign rights'. But even with its inescapable implications for state sovereignty, the plan was, in his words, 'a necessity as the only means at our disposal to overcome national selfishness [and] the enmities and narrow-minded prejudices which are ruining us'.

While people hailed the French government's announcement of 9 May as brave and heroic, no one thought it original or particularly imaginative. For years successive French governments had been pushed in this direction. The Americans had preached tirelessly on the need to 'federate or perish'; in January 1947 John Foster Dulles and Secretary of State George Marshall urged the creation of a supranational agency to guarantee Germany and its neighbours 'equal access to certain resources', and they wanted to redefine the Ruhr as 'European' rather than as a 'national asset'.[18] In April 1949 the Westminster Conference of the European Movement passed a resolution calling for the coordination of western Europe's heavy industry, and in the autumn of 1949 the German Trade Union Federation (DGB) announced its support for international controls on major industrial areas in France and Germany. The negotiations between the French and German governments late in 1949 also pointed to an agreement on sharing the basic resources of heavy industry. With assurances from Adenauer on the likely nature of international controls and aware that Germany's constitution allowed it to transfer aspects of sovereignty to international agencies, the French felt they could safely propose a radically new relationship with their old enemy.

There were compelling economic reasons for France's decision to treat the Bundesrepublik as an equal. The French wanted a large and secure market for their steel products. But their supply of coking coal was inadequate and they had to rely on imports from the Ruhr. For the first two or three years after the war, when Germany was manifestly down and out, France and Belgium could talk bravely of taking all the coal they wanted from the Ruhr. But everyone knew this period was not to continue for long. The German economy would eventually bounce back. By 1949, German domestic steel consumption was a third higher than the French. French nationalist policies were increasingly inappropriate and dangerous. Schuman and Monnet knew that a much wiser policy was to enter an economic partnership with Germany. They wanted a policy which would insure France's expanded share of postwar steel production while it also guaranteed her security.

Schuman's announcement of 9 May 1950 marked the beginning of that policy and the end of the immediate postwar period. It foresaw a new age of cooperation in Europe and agreement on a new set of economic priorities beneficial to the consumer. Explicitly it recognized that the economic development of France was linked to that of neighbouring countries. In addition to its benign vision of a peaceful Europe, the Schuman Plan was calculated to make the world safer for France. It assumed that France's role in Africa might continue and prosper once a re-energized Europe was able to share in the development of the continent (of course, this hope predated the decision of France's African colonies to seek independence, and it also predated the agony of the Algerian war). In Europe, too, the Plan rested on the calculation that a partnership with Germany would be much more valuable to France than any other links it might forge, including the customs union with Italy (signed in March 1949) and the mooted customs union with Benelux.

The evolution of a democratic Germany, the influence of Europe overseas and the practical concerns of economic reconstruction were all important issues in

1950, but they were aspects of a much larger question. Was European integration really possible? The British and the Scandinavians saw the future of Europe in terms of free trade, peaceful relations and human rights; for them, the Council of Europe, representing a family of independent nations, was sufficient. This was the view of the European 'nationalists'. They distinguished themselves from the nationalists of the past by their dedication to peace and solidarity in Europe. They saw no need for any plan which might reduce the sovereignty of the nation state. On the other side of the spectrum were the European 'federalists'. They were disappointed with both the OECC and the Council of Europe. They wanted effective supranational institutions, independent of the national governments. They called for a 'constitutional convention' to devise a single constitution for all of democratic Europe. The federalists hoped to bury the concept of national sovereignty before it had the chance to grow once more into a dangerous form of nationalism.

Between the 'nationalists' and the 'federalists' were the 'functionalists'. Admitting Europe's diversity of customs, languages and vested interests, they conceded the danger of trying to integrate Europe too quickly. They thought it wiser for the states to move gradually by accepting a common responsibility in certain limited areas, one at a time. Theoretically, one advantage of this long-term strategy was that it made the grand objective of European union more palatable and more conceivable. The functionalists' approach was largely psychological: how could there be any harm in allowing Europeans gradually to trust one another by making collective decisions about their use of coal or their design of transport systems or their concern for working standards and the quality of life? And even if two or three of these issues were tackled at the same time, the effort would never be as momentous as deciding on a pan-European constitution or the sudden death of national sovereignty. Moreover, the functionalists expected that as Europeans enjoyed the material benefits of each step which their governments took, they would find the notion of integration increasingly attractive.

Schuman shared the beliefs of the functionalists and, as French foreign minister, he was well placed to speak on their behalf. His own background seemed to transcend nationality. Born in Luxembourg, Schuman served in the Kaiser's army in the Great War and became a French citizen in 1918. While he treated the political sensitivities of his compatriots with respect, Schuman also enjoyed the confidence of other Europeans. And although he did not draft the announcement of 9 May himself, he was fortunate to have the advice of those who did.

The most energetic of these advisors was Jean Monnet, now considered the father of European integration.[19] In French politics, Monnet was the 'great insider'. He never stood for election to any political office, nor did he care to: like de Gaulle, he was impatient with party politics. Unlike de Gaulle, he had no talent for public speaking and debate. But he knew most of Europe's leading politicians and even French politicians valued his worldwide connections. As a young man, Monnet represented his family's cognac business in Britain and North America. During the Great War he served with the inter-Allied Maritime Commission; thereafter he was deputy-secretary general with the League of Nations. When war came in 1939,

Monnet was busy as a supervisor of France's munitions programme and he became chairman of the Anglo-French coordinating committee. After the fall of France, Monnet spent much time in the United States. He was well acquainted with America's political leadership and with Wall Street. He admired the scope and success of Roosevelt's New Deal. It was probably inevitable that Charles de Gaulle would reproach Monnet as 'a great American'.

After the war, Monnet worked in Paris with the Commissariat du Plan de Modernization et d'Equipement. The 'Monnet Plan' which they devised for 1947–52 called for an immense increase in productivity, full employment and a much higher standard of living. Broadly speaking, the Plan aimed to modernize the French economy, not to build a healthier version of the lethargic economy which existed in the 1920s and 30s. Monnet assumed that western Europe could and should adopt the same goals. Like Schuman, Monnet wanted the process of integration to start before it was too late: he particularly feared that France and Germany might otherwise drift apart.[20] If Europe was to be 'constructed', France and Germany were the two essential building blocks of the edifice, and the 'High Authority' would serve as the first mortar to bind them together.

Almost everyone understood the radical implications of Monnet's plan as it was announced by Schuman. Predictably there was opposition from the communist parties of France and Italy and from the Social Democrats in Germany. The British were also negative; members of the Labour Party warned against 'a big business conspiracy', while Harold Macmillan spoke for many Conservatives when he declared that 'Our people will not hand over to any supranational authority the right to close our pits or our steel works'.[21] In August 1950 Macmillan brought an alternative plan before the Council of Europe: in place of the High Authority he proposed a committee of representatives from the coal and steel industries, with powers proportionate to the production of their respective industries, and a ministerial committee (representing the governments) with the right of veto.[22] This would have made a Coal and Steel Community in the image of the Council of Europe. Macmillan's suggestion was stillborn. In the end, the functionalists failed to win Britain's cooperation, but they decided to proceed with the Monnet–Schuman plan. For them, 'Little Europe' (the Six) was better than no Europe at all. Their assumption was that Britain and several other countries would join in a few years' time, and without too much difficulty.

Six countries were represented in the negotiations which began on 20 June 1950. Work on the treaty was finished in seven months and it was signed in April 1951. In July 1952 the European Coal and Steel Community came into existence (DOCUMENT 13). How much of Europe's economic activity in the next five years depended on this organization? Would the trade of the six states have flourished as much as it did, and would steel production have risen by over 40 per cent in the next five years, had there been no ECSC? There are only tentative answers to these questions. It must be said that the ECSC's objectives were laudable but limited. It was never intended as a mechanism to direct economic growth, nor did it create a strong pattern of social legislation. The ECSC did, however, give the Six the opportunity to coordinate two key industries and it gave them the institutional framework for economic planning and the management of resources. More important, the High Authority represented an executive economic power unparalleled in European history. It was entitled to issue reports and recommendations to all member states and, in times of shortage and surplus, it determined the prices and production of two basic industrial commodities.

The political image of the ECSC is more difficult to measure, at least in its early years. Few Europeans would have known (or understood) Monnet's comment that political unity was the real goal of the new organization. But in 1952, terms like 'political unity' and 'integration' had little meaning and almost no currency for the general public. The construction of Europe had only begun. Even after it had functioned for a few years, the ECSC gave Europeans only a glimpse of the future which they had to plan together. For the moment, however, the functionalists were satisfied. They had succeeded in persuading six European governments to accept a significant break with the past: the High Authority of the ECSC was Europe's first supranational institution. The six member states were to accept its decisions as binding. Because it included the High Authority, the ECSC started the process of redefining sovereignty just as much as it began the 'pooling' and distribution of certain resources.

What Europeans found easier to understand in 1952 was the ECSC's contribution to their political security. The ECSC assumed the reconciliation of two old enemies in a system which was invaluable to all countries of western Europe. For the French, the ECSC promised to 'contain Germany' inside a democratic Europe before the Bundesrepublik was tempted either to adopt aggressive nationalist policies or to seek German unification by becoming a client state of the USSR. For the Germans, the ECSC strengthened rather than subtracted from the sovereignty of the Bundesrepublik; the political status of the Rhine and the Ruhr was finally settled, and Germany was accepted as an equal partner in an association of democratic states. By achieving so much, the Coal and Steel Community was a pragmatic beginning of European integration. More pragmatic still, the articles of the ECSC Treaty took the place of the peace treaty which western Europeans had never written.

ENDNOTES

1 Article IV of the Geneva Conference Draft Declaration II on European Federalism (20 May 1944).
2 W. A. Visser 't Hooft: *Memoirs* (London: Westminster Press, 1973), p.180.
3 Walter Lipgens (ed.): *Documents on the History of European Integration* (Berlin: Walter de Gruyter, 1985), I, p. 18.
4 *Ibid.*, I, documents 55 and 67.
5 Derek Urwin: *Western Europe Since 1945: A Political History* (4th edn., London: Longman, 1989), p. 9.
6 During the war, neither Stalin nor de Gaulle ever expressed support for a federal union of European states. In March 1943, Count Coudenhove-Kalergi urged President Roosevelt to announce America's support for a federal Europe. Roosevelt replied that Soviet

demands for a sphere of influence in central Europe were more important and that any sort of federation would only upset the future relations of the USA and the USSR.

7 Paul-Henri Spaak: *The Continuing Battle: Memoirs of a European, 1936–1966* (trans. Henry Fox) (London: Weidenfeld and Nicolson, 1971), p. 200.

8 In an article for the *Saturday Evening Post* of 15 February 1930, Churchill wrote, 'We have our own dreams, and our own task ... We are with Europe, but not part of it. We are interested and associated, but not absorbed'.

9 Allen W. Dulles: *The Marshall Plan* (ed. Michael Wala) (Ann Arbor: Edwards Bros., 1993), p. 3.

10 Forrest Pogue: 'The Harvard Speech' (Chapter XII), in *George C. Marshall, Statesman* (New York: Viking, 1987), IV, pp. 209–10; Ed Cray: *General of the Army: George C. Marshall* (New York: Norton, 1990), p. 612.

11 A. S. Milward: *The Reconstruction of Western Europe 1945–51* (4th edn., London: Methuen, 1984), pp. 358–60, 472; John Llewellyn and Stephen Potter: 'Competitiveness and the Current Account', in *The European Economy, Growth and Crisis* (ed. Andrea Boltha) (Oxford: Oxford University Press, 1982), p. 135.

12 Canada and the United States were associate members of the OEEC.

13 Michael J. Hogan: *The Marshall Plan. America, Britain and the Reconstruction of Western Europe, 1947–1952* (Cambridge: Cambridge University Press, 1987), pp. 322–5.

14 Spaak (1966), *Continuing Battle*, pp. 201–2.

15 The Council of Europe now includes new or re-emerged states such as Slovenia, the Czech Republic and Slovakia, Estonia and Lithuania (all in 1993) and micro-states such as Lichtenstein (1978), and San Marino (1988). Russia gained membership in January 1996.

16 The French zone was carved out of the British and American zones. The Soviet Union opposed this as an unwarranted gift.

17 Roosevelt thought that Germany might be divided into as many as seven states, of which five would be self-governing. Churchill assumed that the division of Prussia into several federal states would be enough to tame the new Germany.

18 John Foster Dulles: 'Europe must federate or perish; America must offer inspiration and guidance', in *Vital Speeches of the Day*, 13 (1 February 1947), pp. 234–6.

19 The latest and best biography of Monnet is by François Duchene: *Jean Monnet, the First Statesman of Interdependence* (New York and London: W. W. Norton & Co., 1994).

20 Jean Monnet: *Memoirs* (trans. Richard Mayne) (London: Collins, 1978), Chapter 12.

21 Anthony Sampson: *Macmillan: A Study in Ambiguity* (London and New York: Allen Lane/Penguin Press, 1967), p. 86.

22 Monnet (1978), *Memoirs*, p. 315.

ADDITIONAL READINGS

A. Deporte: *Europe between the Superpowers: The Enduring Balance* (New Haven: Yale University Press, 1979).

W. Diebold: *The Schuman Plan* (New York: Prager, 1959).

D. Ellwood: *Rebuilding Europe: Western Europe, America and Postwar Reconstruction* (London: Longman, 1992).

E. Fursdon: *The European Defence Community: A History* (London: Macmillan, 1980).

J. Gillingham: *Coal, Steel and the Rebirth of Europe, 1945–1955* (Cambridge: Cambridge University Press, 1991).

A. Grosser: *The Western Alliance: European-American Relations since 1945* (New York: Vintage, 1982).

E. Haas: *The Uniting of Europe* (Stanford: University Press, 2nd edn., 1968).

W. Hallstein: *Europe in the Making* (London: Allen and Unwin, 1972).

F. Heller and J. Gillingham: *NATO: The Founding of the Atlantic Alliance and the Integration of Europe* (New York: St Martin's, 1992).

W. Lipgens: *A History of European Integration* (Oxford: Oxford University Press, 1981 and 1986).

L. Lister: *Europe's Coal and Steel Community* (New York: Twentieth Century Fund, 1960).

W. Loth: *The Division of the World, 1941–1955* (London: Routlege and Kegan Paul, 1988).

C. Maier (ed.): *The Marshall Plan and Germany* (New York: Berg, 1991).

J. Meade: *Negotiations for Benelux: An Annotated Chronicle, 1943–56* (Princeton: Princeton University Press, 1957).

A. S. Milward: *The Reconstruction of Western Europe, 1945–1951* (London: Methuen, 1984).

A. H. Robertson: *The Council of Europe* (London: Stevens, 1956).

K. Schwabe (ed.): *The Beginnings of the Schuman Plan* (Baden-Baden: Namos, 1988).

P. M. R. Stirk and D. Willis (eds): *Shaping Postwar Europe* (London: St Martin's, 1991).

T. Taylor: *European Defence Cooperation* (London: Routledge and Kegan Paul, 1984).

F. R. Willis: *France, Germany and the New Europe* (Stanford: Stanford University Press, 1968).

J. Young: *Britain, France and the Unity of Europe, 1945–1951* (Leicester: Leicester University Press, 1984).

———— (ed.): *The Foreign Policy of Churchill's Peacetime Administration, 1951–1955* (Leicester: Leicester University Press, 1988).

A WARTIME MANIFESTO

The anti-fascist resistance movements looked ahead to a postwar federation of democratic states. During their secret meetings in Switzerland in 1944, they drafted the following statement of their political aspirations. The draft of *Declaration II* (20 May 1944) is included in *Documents on the History of European Integration*, edited by Walter Lipgens, vol.I (Berlin: Walter de Gruyter, 1985), pp. 479–82.

Some active members of the resistance movements of Denmark, France, Italy, Norway, Holland, Poland, Czechoslovakia and Yugoslavia, and the representative of an active German anti-Nazi group, met in a town in occupied Europe on March 31, April 29, May 20, and July 7. They drafted the following declaration, which they have submitted for discussion and approval to their respective movements and to the other European resistance movements. They wish now to bring this draft to the notice of international public opinion. [...]

MANIFESTO

I

The peoples of Europe are united in their resistance to Nazi oppression. This common struggle has created among them a solidarity and unity of interests and aims which demonstrate their significance and value by the fact that the representatives of the European resistance movements have come together to draft this declaration expressing their hopes and aspirations regarding the future of peace and civilization.

The members of the resistance movements are well aware that their relentless struggle on the home front against the enemy's war machine is an important positive contribution towards the war effort of the United Nations; it gives their countries the right to participate in the reconstruction of Europe side by side with the other victorious powers.

They accept the essential principles of the Atlantic Charter and maintain that the life of their peoples must be based upon respect for the individual personality, security, the planned exploitation of economic resources for the benefit of the whole community and the autonomous development of national life.

II

These aims cannot be achieved unless the different countries are willing to give up the dogma of the absolute sovereignty of the State and unite in a single federal organization.

The lack of unity and cohesion between the different parts of the world make it impossible to tackle immediately the task of creating a federal world organization. At the end of this war we shall have to limit ourselves to the building up of a less ambitious world organization – which should however permit of development in a federal direction – in the framework of which the great powers will have the task of guaranteeing collective security. It will not be, however, an effective instrument of peace unless the great powers are organized in such a way that the spirit of peace and understanding can prevail.

It is for this reason that, within the framework of this world organization, a more radical and direct solution must be found for the European problem.

III

European peace is the keystone in the arch of world peace. During the lifetime of one generation Europe has twice been the centre of a world conflict whose chief cause was the existence of thirty sovereign States in Europe. It is a most urgent task to end this international anarchy by creating a European Federal Union.

Only a Federal Union will enable the German people to join the European community without becoming a danger to other peoples. ←— Solve Ger. ?

Only a Federal Union will make it possible to solve the problem of drawing frontiers in districts with mixed population. The minorities will thus cease to be the object of nationalistic jealousies, and frontiers will be nothing but demarcation lines between administrative districts.

Only a Federal Union will be in a position to protect democratic institutions and so prevent politically less developed countries becoming a danger to the international order.

Only a Federal Union will make possible the economic reconstruction of the Continent and the liquidation of monopolies and national self-sufficiency.

Only a Federal Union will allow a logical and natural solution of the problems of the access to the sea of those countries which are situated in the interior of the Continent, of a rational use of those rivers which flow through the several States, of the control of straits, and, generally, of most of the problems which during recent years have disturbed international relations.

IV

It is not possible at present to determine the geographical frontiers of a Federal Union which would guarantee peace in Europe. We must, however, state that from the outset such a Union must be strong enough to avoid the risk of either being used as a mere sphere of influence by a foreign State or of becoming the instrument of the political ambitions of one of its member States. Furthermore it must from the beginning be open to all countries which entirely or partly belong to Europe and which wish to join it and are qualified to do so.

The Federal Union must be based upon a declaration of civil, political and economic rights which would guarantee democratic institutions and the free development of the human personality, and upon a declaration of the rights of minorities to have as much autonomy as is compatible with the integrity of the national States to which they belong.

The Federal Union must not interfere with the right of each of its member States to solve its special problems in conformity with its ethnical and cultural pattern. But, in view of the failure of the League of Nations, the States must irrevocably surrender to the Federation their sovereign rights in the sphere of defence, relations with powers outside the Union, international exchange and communications.

The Federal Union must possess the following essential features:

1. A government responsible not to the governments of the various member States but to the peoples, who must be under its direct jurisdiction in the spheres to which its powers extend.
2. An army at the disposal of this government, no national armies being permitted.
3. A Supreme Court acting as authority in interpreting the Constitution and deciding cases of conflict between the member States or between the member States and the Union.

V

The peace which will follow this war must be based upon justice and progress and not upon vengeance and reaction. It should, however, treat the war criminals with ruthless severity; to let them escape their punishment would be an insult to all who have fallen in this war and especially to the unknown heroes of the resistance movements throughout Europe. Germany and her satellites must take part in the economic reconstruction of the regions they have devastated. But Germany must be helped and, if necessary, compelled to change her political and economic structure with a view to qualifying for membership of the Federal Union. For that purpose she must be completely disarmed and temporarily subjected to a Federal control, which will have in the main the following tasks:

- To entrust power to those truly democratic elements which have consistently fought against Nazism.
- To build up a decentralized democratic State free from the last trace of Prussian militarism and bureaucracy.
- To secure the liquidation of feudalism in the agricultural and industrial life of Germany.
- To integrate German chemical and heavy industries into the European industrial organization so as to prevent their use for German nationalistic ends.
- To prevent the education of German youth in accordance with Nazi, militaristic and totalitarian doctrines.

VI

The signatory resistance movements recognize that the <u>active participation</u> of the <u>United Nations is essential</u> for the resolution of the European problem, but they demand that all measures taken between the cessation of hostilities and the establishment of peace shall be in conformity with the requirements of a Federal organization.

They appeal to all the spiritual and political forces of the world and in particular to those of the United Nations to help them to attain the objectives indicated in this Manifesto.

They undertake to consider their respective national problems only as particular aspects of the general European problem, and they intend immediately to establish a permanent bureau with the function of co-ordinating their efforts on behalf of the liberation of their countries, the organization of a Federal Union of European peoples and the establishment of peace and justice throughout the world.

6

THE BENELUX PLAN

The first plan for European integration was devised before the Second World War had finished, and involved three small countries: Belgium, Netherlands and Luxembourg. Paul-Henri Spaak, then a minister in the exiled Belgian government, saw 'Benelux' as a first step to European unity. The following extract is from his book, *The Continuing Battle: Memoirs of a European, 1936–1966* (trans. Henry Fox) (London, Weidenfeld and Nicolson, 1971), pp.76–80.

THE BENELUX PLAN

We were quite busy in London. Governing several tens of thousands of Belgians presented the same problems as governing nine million, but, on the other hand, we were freed from certain peace-time chores. There were no sittings of Parliament, no Party meetings. This gave us time to consider the main problems in greater depth. As soon as military victory seemed certain, we began to think about the future.

I have found some of the notes written in those war years and can trace back to them the ideas which were to inspire me after the victory. Re-reading years later what one has written about oneself or about events is often a painful experience. One is surprised at oneself and saddened to have misjudged things so often. However, one is also pleased at one's insight when one has not been proved too wrong. My wartime predictions about the future have been largely justified. In a note written in 1941 to Miss Irene Ward, the Conservative MP, a note which, I believe, reached the Foreign Office, I said:

> Allow me to end with a few thoughts about the future. The events of the last twenty months in Europe have shown that its countries must unite. They have been shown to be dependent on each other for their security. After the war Europe will be glad to

unite behind Britain's victorious leadership, providing that (1) Britain remains strong, (2) Britain concerns herself with Europe. It will not be sufficient for Britain to establish, and try to maintain, a balance of power to offset a hegemony in Europe. She must herself assume the responsibilities born of her supremacy.

If Britain fails to recognize her duty to Europe, if she does not pursue a continental policy which makes her a strong leader of Europe, she must expect to be rapidly deprived of the fruits of her present efforts. Europe will organize against her, and I dare say that Germany, despite her defeat, will be the leader. The ideal solution would, of course, be a world organization, or failing this an organization embracing all Europe. But ideals are rarely compatible with political reality. After the war it will be essential to try and construct something solid, but to do this it may be necessary to sacrifice some of the more grandiose features of such an organization.

Naturally, the security and prosperity of Western Europe is Belgium's main preoccupation. The countries of Western Europe have their own peculiarities, but there are no territorial disputes which divide them. On the contrary, they share political, legal and moral standards as well as a broadly similar standard of living. They possess all that is necessary for close cooperation. A united or federated Western Europe must be the nucleus of post-war policy and reconstruction, and it is on this that Britain must lean.

By 1942, my thinking had become more specific.

There can be no political solution without an economic solution, and vice versa. In the world of tomorrow, especially the Europe of tomorrow and, more particularly, the small countries of Europe, the problems of security and prosperity will be inseparable. The formula 'United in war, but isolated in peace' did not apply yesterday and it will be completely inapplicable tomorrow. We must reconcile the rebirth of nationalism with an internationalism which will be essential. This can be done, and I believe we shall have to go a long way in this direction.

The principles of national sovereignty will have to be modified not only where the small countries are concerned but also in regard to the great ones. If we try to cling to old formulae we shall achieve nothing worthwhile. The experience of the League of Nations demonstrates this point. Its rule of unanimity, its deference to national sovereignty, was one of the principal reasons for its failure. Tomorrow there will be international, regional, European or world organizations, it does not matter which. But they are doomed to failure from the outset if their participants do not accept that the body must be superior to its individual members. No system is without its disadvantages. Order always involves some restriction of liberty. We must make our choice and, above all, having made it, accept the consequences.

Thus, in the middle of the war, long before the hour of decision had struck, I was thinking of the future, dreaming of a united or federated Europe. I wanted to see Britain leading a movement which would champion this idea. I refused to make a distinction between military alliances and economic agreements. I pleaded strongly against the absolute sovereignty of States, and for supra-nationalism, ideas for which I was to go on fighting for the next twenty years.

During my stay in Britain I had the opportunity, in laying the foundation of the Benelux plan, to participate in setting the first major example of European economic collaboration. On 11 June 1941 I received the following letter from Gutt:

My dear Spaak,

I have just received some routine papers which have arrived in the bag from America. Among them there is a record of a conversation I had over there with a M. Vandenbroek. He is the real leader of the Dutch delegation to the tin cartel. This cartel consisted essentially of Vandenbroek, Lyttleton, a top British civil servant, and myself. The negotiations were very tough, and because of this very fact they resulted in a fair measure of friendship and confidence between us. Vandenbroek is not a civil servant. He is an industrialist, but has a good deal of influence in Government circles. Basically, what he said was this: 'If we all take back to our respective countries the same ideas with which we left them, the economic war between Belgium and Holland will start up again. There is only one way of ending once and for all the 'war' over cauliflowers and sulphuric acid, and that is to create a complete customs union between our two countries. But if you suggest such a thing only two weeks after our return, all our industrialists will protest, and so will your farmers. We must go back to Holland and Belgium with the union already made.'

This of course, sounds very interesting, and from what I know of Belgium, it would, on the whole, be favourably received. How would the British react? If we did anything of the sort, could other countries invoke their commercial agreements with us, notably the most favoured nation clause? These are questions I cannot answer, but I thought it worth reporting this conversation to you so that you can act on it as you see fit.

11 June 1941. I will not go so far as to say this was the day Benelux was born, but it was certainly the day the good seed was sown in my own mind. The notion of a customs union between Holland, Belgium and Luxembourg was a bold one. It meant giving a new dimension to the relations between our three countries, shedding established traditions and upsetting important economic interests.

Vandenbroek's advice was excellent: 'Create an economic union at once, while the war is still on. If you wait for the liberation and your return to your respective countries, you will never do it.' I am sure he was right. Isolated as we were, and sheltered from the pressure groups which oppose revolutionary ideas of this sort, it still took us more than two years to give our idea concrete shape.

My colleague, M. Van Kleffens, the Dutch Foreign Minister – precise, prudent, opposed to romantic flights of fancy – at first did not appear to be enthusiastic. He favoured a military alliance which would encompass the principal countries of Western Europe. He was hostile to anything which might, even superficially, weaken the Netherlands' ties with Britain. In this respect, he was a resolute champion of a strong Dutch tradition.

The turning point in the long negotiations was the provisional monetary agreement, considered so vital by our financial experts. On 21 October 1943 we fixed the official exchange rate between the Dutch guilder and the Belgian franc. Having thus begun to resolve our economic problems, we were ready to take a much more important step.

On 5 September 1944, a few days after our return to Belgium, we issued a communiqué announcing that a customs union would be set up to include the Belgium–Luxembourg Economic Union and the Netherlands.

> This will be a temporary arrangement, intended to promote the restoration of economic activity and to create conditions which would favour the establishment of a more lasting union later on. It follows the monetary convention concluded by the three countries on 21 December 1943. The agreement, signed by the Ministers of Foreign Affairs and Finance of the three countries, provides for a customs union and will eliminate the levying of duties between Belgium, the Netherlands and Luxembourg. There will be joint arrangements governing the entry of goods from other countries, conceived along liberal lines. All essential commodities, materials and equipment for restoring production will be temporarily exempt from duty. These supplies will account for the bulk of the imports during the period of the agreement.

Some technical details followed, and the communiqué finished thus: 'The agreement will take effect provisionally as soon as the governments are once more installed in their liberated countries.' Clearly, we were not lacking in optimism or boldness.

In the first months after returning to our respective countries, our decisions came up against strong opposition. Many of our civil servants viewed our London agreement with slightly contemptuous scepticism. They tended to claim that the common tariff provided for in the agreement would be difficult to put into effect, that we had behaved like amateurs, barely aware of the real problems, and that we should now allow experts to reopen the issues we had settled. In fact, we were marking time. We let ourselves be impressed by the objections of the technicians. Contrary to our hopes, the London agreement was not implemented after the liberation of our countries. We had to wait until April 1946 before we could make any real progress.

7

United States
of Europe speech

CHURCHILL ON EUROPE

British hopes for European security and reconstruction were expressed by Winston Churchill at the University of Zurich on 19 September 1946. The text of his speech appears in *The Sinews of Peace: Postwar Speeches by Winston S. Churchill* (ed. Randolph S. Churchill) (London: Cassell, 1948), pp.198–202.

I wish to speak to you to-day about the tragedy of Europe. This noble continent, comprising on the whole the fairest and the most cultivated regions of the earth, enjoying a temperate and equable climate, is the home of all the great parent races of the western world. It is the fountain of Christian faith and Christian ethics. It is the origin of most of the culture, arts, philosophy and science both of ancient and modern times. If Europe were once united in the sharing of its common inheritance, there would be no limit to the happiness, to the prosperity and glory which its three or four hundred million people would enjoy. Yet it is from Europe that have sprung that series of frightful nationalistic quarrels, originated by the Teutonic nations, which we have seen even in this twentieth century and in our own lifetime, wreck the peace and mar the prospects of all mankind.

And what is the plight to which Europe has been reduced? Some of the smaller States have indeed made a good recovery, but over wide areas a vast quivering mass of tormented, hungry, care-worn and bewildered human beings gape at the ruins of their cities and homes, and scan the dark horizons for the approach of some new peril, tyranny or terror. Among the victors there is a babel of jarring voices; among the vanquished the sullen silence of despair. That is all that Europeans, grouped in so many ancient States and nations, that is all that the Germanic Powers have got by tearing each other to pieces and spreading havoc far and wide. Indeed, but for the fact that the great Republic across the Atlantic Ocean *US saved Europe* has at length realized that the ruin or enslavement of Europe would involve their own fate as well, and has stretched out hands of succour and guidance, the Dark Ages would have returned in all their cruelty and squalor. They may still return.

Yet all the while there is a remedy which, if it were generally and spontaneously adopted, would as if by a miracle transform the whole scene, and would in a few years make all Europe, or the greater part of it, as free and as happy as Switzerland is to-day. What is this sovereign remedy? It is to re-create the European family, or as much of it as we can, and provide it with a structure under which it can dwell in peace, in safety and in freedom. We must build a kind of United States of Europe; in this way only will hundreds of millions of toilers be able to regain the simple joys and hopes which make life worth living. The process is simple. All that is needed is the resolve of hundreds of millions of men and women to do right instead of wrong and gain as their reward blessing instead of cursing.

Much work has been done upon this task by the exertions of the Pan-European Union which owes so much to Count Coudenhove-Kalergi and which commanded the services of the famous French patriot and statesman, Aristide Briand. There is also that immense body of doctrine and procedure, which was brought into being amid high hopes after the first world war, as the League of Nations. The League of Nations did not fail because of its principles or conceptions. It failed because these principles were deserted by those States who had brought it into being. It failed because the Governments of those days feared to face the facts, and act while time remained. This disaster must not be repeated. There is therefore much knowledge and material with which to build; and also bitter dear-bought experience.

I was very glad to read in the newspapers two days ago that my friend President Truman had expressed his interest and sympathy with this great design. There is no reason why a regional organization of Europe should in any way conflict with the world organization of the United Nations. On the contrary, I believe that the larger synthesis will only survive if it is founded upon coherent natural groupings. There is already a natural grouping in the Western Hemisphere. We British have our own Commonwealth of Nations. These do not weaken, on the contrary they strengthen, the world organization. They are in fact its main support. And why should there not be a European group which could give a sense of enlarged patriotism and common citizenship to the distracted peoples of this turbulent and mighty

Groups in the UN: US + West. hemi
Britain - Commonwealth
Europe

continent and why should it not take its rightful place with other great groupings in shaping the destinies of men? In order that this should be accomplished there must be an act of faith in which millions of families speaking many languages must consciously take part.

We all know that the two world wars through which we have passed arose out of the vain passion of a newly-united Germany to play the dominating part in the world. In this last struggle crimes and massacres have been committed for which there is no parallel since the invasions of the Mongols in the fourteenth century and no equal at any time in human history. The guilty must be punished. Germany must be deprived of the power to re-arm and make another aggressive war. But when all this has been done, as it will be done, as it is being done, there must be an end to retribution. There must be what Mr. Gladstone many years ago called 'a blessed act of oblivion'. We must all turn our backs upon the horrors of the past. We must look to the future. We cannot afford to drag forward across the years that are to come the hatreds and revenges which have sprung from the injuries of the past. If Europe is to be saved from infinite misery, and indeed from final doom, there must be an act of faith in the European family and an act of oblivion against all the crimes and follies of the past.

Can the free peoples of Europe rise to the height of these resolves of the soul and instincts of the spirit of man? If they can, the wrongs and injuries which have been inflicted will have been washed away on all sides by the miseries which have been endured. Is there any need for further floods of agony? Is it the only lesson of history that mankind is unteachable? Let there be justice, mercy and freedom. The peoples have only to will it, and all will achieve their hearts' desire.

I am now going to say something that will astonish you. The first step in the re-creation of the European family must be a partnership between France and Germany. In this way only can France recover the moral leadership of Europe. There can be no revival of Europe without a spiritually great France and a spiritually great Germany. The structure of the United States of Europe, if well and truly built, will be such as to make the material strength of a single state less important. Small nations will count as much as large ones and gain their honour by their contribution to the common cause. The ancient states and principalities of Germany, freely joined together for mutual convenience in a federal system, might each take their individual place among the United States of Europe. I shall not try to make a detailed programme for hundreds of millions of people who want to be happy and free, prosperous and safe, who wish to enjoy the four freedoms of which the great President Roosevelt spoke, and live in accordance with the principles embodied in the Atlantic Charter. If this is their wish, they have only to say so, and means can certainly be found, and machinery erected, to carry that wish into full fruition.

But I must give you a warning. Time may be short. At present there is a breathing-space. The cannon have ceased firing. The fighting has stopped; but the dangers have not stopped. If we are to form the United States of Europe or whatever name or form it may take, we must begin now.

In these present days we dwell strangely and precariously under the shield and protection of the atomic bomb. The atomic bomb is still only in the hands of a State and nation which we know will never use it except in the cause of right and freedom. But it may well be that in a few years this awful agency of destruction will be widespread and the catastrophe following from its use by several warring nations will not only bring to an end all that we call civilisation, but may possibly disintegrate the globe itself.

I must now sum up the propositions which are before you. Our constant aim must be to build and fortify the strength of U.N.O. Under and within that world concept we must re-create the European family in a regional structure called, it may be, the United States of Europe. The first step is to form a Council of Europe. If at first all the States of Europe are not willing or able to join the Union, we must nevertheless proceed to assemble and combine those who will and those who can. The salvation of the common people of every race and of every land from war or servitude must be established on solid foundations and must be guarded by the readiness of all men and women to die rather than submit to tyranny. In all this urgent work, France and Germany must take the lead together. Great Britain, the British Commonwealth of Nations, mighty America, and I trust Soviet Russia – for then indeed all would be well – must be the friends and sponsors of the new Europe and must champion its right to live and shine.

8

BRUSSELS TREATY

First proposed by the British Foreign Secretary, Ernest Bevin, this agreement was the first practical step towards a united Western Europe. It was signed on 17 March 1948 by the governments of Belgium, France, Great Britain, Luxembourg and the Netherlands. The text of the Treaty appears in E. J. Osmanczyk's *Encyclopedia of the United Nations and International Agreements* (New York: Taylor and Francis, 2nd edn., 1990), pp.113–14.

[The contracting parties . . .]

To reaffirm their faith in fundamental human rights, in the dignity and worth of the human person and in the other ideals proclaimed in the Charter of the United Nations;

To fortify and preserve the principles of democracy, personal freedom and political liberty, the constitutional traditions and the rule of law, which are their common heritage;

To strengthen, with these aims in view, the economic, social and cultural ties by which they are already united;

To cooperate loyally and to coordinate their efforts to create in Western Europe a firm basis for European economic recovery;

To afford assistance to each other, in accordance with the Charter of the United

Nations, in maintaining international peace and security and in resisting any policy of aggression;

To take such steps as may be held to be necessary in the event of a renewal by Germany of a policy of aggression;

To associate progressively in the pursuance of these aims other States inspired by the same ideals and animated by the like determination;

Desiring for these purposes to conclude a treaty for collaboration in economic, social and cultural matters and for collective self-defence [...]

Art. I.   Convinced of the close community of their interests and of the necessity of uniting in order to promote the economic recovery of Europe, the High Contracting Parties will so organize and coordinate their economic activities as to produce the best possible results, by the elimination of conflict in their economic policies, the coordination of production and the development of commercial exchanges.

The cooperation provided for in the preceding paragraph, which will be effected through the Consultative Council referred to in Article VII as well as through other bodies, shall not involve any duplication of, or prejudice to, the work of other economic organizations in which the High Contracting Parties are or may be represented but shall on the contrary assist the work of those organizations.

Art. II.   The High Contracting Parties will make every effort in common, both by direct consultation and in specialized agencies, to promote the attainment of a higher standard of living by their peoples and to develop on corresponding lines the social and other related services of their countries. The High Contracting Parties will consult with the object of achieving the earliest possible application of recommendations of immediate practical interest, relating to social matters, adopted with their approval in the specialized agencies. They will endeavour to conclude as soon as possible conventions with each other in the sphere of social security.

Art. III.   The High Contracting Parties will make every effort in common to lead their peoples towards a better understanding of the principles which form the basis of their common civilization and to promote cultural exchanges by conventions between themselves or by other means.

Art. IV.   If any of the High Contracting Parties should be the object of an armed attack in Europe, the other High Contracting Parties will, in accordance with the provisions of Article 51 of the Charter of the United Nations, afford the Party so attacked all the military and other aid and assistance in their power.

Art. V.   All measures taken as a result of the preceding Article shall be immediately reported to the Security Council. They shall be terminated as soon as the Security Council has taken the measures necessary to maintain or restore international peace and security.

The present Treaty does not prejudice in any way the obligations of the High

Contracting Parties under the provisions of the Charter of the United Nations. It shall not be interpreted as affecting in any way the authority and responsibility of the Security Council under the Charter to take at any time such action as it deems necessary in order to maintain or restore international peace and security.

Art. VI. The High Contracting Parties declare, each so far as he is concerned, that none of the international engagements now in force between him and any other of the High Contracting Parties or any third State is in conflict with the provisions of the present Treaty.

None of the High Contracting Parties will conclude any alliance or participate in any coalition directed against any other of the High Contracting Parties.

Art. VII. For the purpose of consulting together on all the questions dealt with in the present Treaty, the High Contracting Parties will create a Consultative Council, which shall be so organized as to be able to exercise its functions continuously. The Council shall meet at such times as it shall deem fit.

At the request of any of the High Contracting Parties, the Council shall be immediately convened in order to permit the High Contracting Parties to consult with regard to any situation which may constitute a threat to peace, in whatever area this threat should arise; with regard to the attitude to be adopted and the steps to be taken in case of renewal by Germany of an aggressive policy; or with regard to any situation constituting a danger to economic stability.

Art. VIII. In pursuance of their determination to settle disputes only by peaceful means, the High Contracting Parties will apply to disputes between themselves the following provisions:

The High Contracting Parties will, while the present Treaty remains in force, settle all disputes falling within the scope of Article 36, paragraph 2, of the Statute of the International Court of Justice by referring them to the Court, subject only, in the case of each of them, to any reservation already made by that Party when accepting this clause for compulsory jurisdiction to the extent that Party may maintain the reservation.

In addition, the High Contracting Parties will submit to conciliation all disputes outside the scope of Article 36, paragraph 2, of the Statute of the International Court of Justice. In the case of a mixed dispute involving both questions for which conciliation is appropriate and other questions for which judicial settlement is appropriate, any Party to the dispute shall have the right to insist that the judicial settlement of the legal questions shall precede conciliation.

The preceding provisions of this Article in no way affect the application of relevant provisions or agreements prescribing some other method of pacific settlement.

Art. IX. The High Contracting Parties may, by agreement, invite any other State to accede to the present Treaty on condition to be agreed between them and the State so invited. Any State so invited may become a Party to the Treaty by depositing an instrument of accession with the Belgian Government. The Belgian Government will inform each of the High Contracting Parties of the deposit of each instrument of accession.

Art. X.   The present Treaty shall be ratified and the instruments of ratification shall be deposited as soon as possible with the Belgian Government.

It shall enter into force on the date of the deposit of the last instrument of ratification and shall thereafter remain in force for fifty years.

After the expiry of the period of fifty years, each of the High Contracting Parties shall have the right to cease to be a party thereto provided that he shall have previously given one year's notice of denunciation to the Belgian Government. The Belgian Government shall inform the Governments of the other High Contracting Parties of the deposit of each instrument of ratification and of signing the present Treaty and each notice of denunciation.

9

THE MARSHALL PLAN

The address given at Harvard University by the American Secretary of State, General George Marshall, on 5 June 1947, was published in the *New York Times* on 6 June 1947.

I need not tell you, gentlemen, that the world situation is very serious. That must be apparent to all intelligent people. I think one difficulty is that the problem is one of such enormous complexity that the very mass of facts presented to the public by press and radio make it exceedingly difficult for the man in the street to reach a clear appraisement of the situation. Furthermore, the people of this country are distant from the troubled areas of the earth and it is hard for them to comprehend the plight and consequent reactions of the long-suffering peoples, and the effect of those reactions on their governments in connection with our efforts to promote peace in the world.

In considering the requirements for the rehabilitation of Europe, the physical loss of life, the visible destruction of cities, factories, mines and railroads was correctly estimated, but it has become obvious during recent months that this visible destruction was probably less serious than the dislocation of the entire fabric of European economy. For the past ten years conditions have been highly abnormal.

The feverish preparation for war and the more feverish maintenance of the war effort engulfed all aspects of national economies. Machinery has fallen into disrepair or is entirely obsolete. Under the arbitrary and destructive Nazi rule, virtually every possible enterprise was geared into the German war machine. Long-standing commercial ties, private institutions, banks, insurance companies and shipping companies disappeared, through loss of capital, absorption through nationalization or by simple destruction.

Economic System Not Working

In many countries, confidence in the local currency has been severely shaken. The breakdown of the business structure of Europe during the war was complete. Recovery has been seriously retarded by the fact that two years after the close of hostilities a peace settlement with Germany and Austria has not been agreed upon. But even given a more prompt solution of these difficult problems, the rehabilitation of the economic structure of Europe quite evidently will require a much longer time and greater effort than had been foreseen.

There is a phase of this matter which is both interesting and serious. The farmer has always produced the foodstuffs to exchange with the city dweller for the other necessities of life. This division of labor is the basis of modern civilization. At the present time it is threatened with breakdown. The town and city industries are not producing adequate goods to exchange with the food-producing farmer. Raw materials and fuel are in short supply. Machinery is lacking or worn out.

The farmer or the peasant cannot find the goods for sale which he desires to purchase. So the sale of his farm produce for money which he cannot use seems to him an unprofitable transaction. He, therefore, has withdrawn many fields from crop cultivation and is using them for grazing. He feeds more grain to stock and finds for himself and his family an ample supply of food, however short he may be on clothing and the other ordinary gadgets of civilization. Meanwhile, people in the cities are short of food and fuel. So the governments are forced to use their foreign money and credits to procure these necessities abroad. This process exhausts funds which are urgently needed for reconstruction. Thus a very serious situation is rapidly developing which bodes no good for the world. The modern system of the division of labor upon which the exchange of products is based is in danger of breaking down.

The truth of the matter is that Europe's requirements for the next three or four years of foreign food and other essential products – principally from America – are so much greater than her present ability to pay that she must have substantial additional help, or face economic, social and political deterioration of a very grave character.

The remedy lies in breaking the vicious circle and restoring the confidence of the European people in the economic future of their own countries and of Europe as a whole. The manufacturer and the farmer throughout wide areas must be able and willing to exchange their products for currencies, the continuing value of which is not open to question.

Aside from the demoralizing effect on the world at large and the possibilities of disturbances arising as a result of the desperation of the people concerned, the consequences to the economy of the United States should be apparent to all. It is logical that the United States should do whatever it is able to do to assist in the return of normal economic health in the world, without which there can be no political stability and no assured peace.

Cold War Context

Our policy is directed not against any country or doctrine but against hunger, poverty, desperation and chaos. Its purpose should be the revival of a working economy in the world so as to permit the emergence of political and social conditions in which free institutions can exist. Such assistance, I am convinced, must not be on a piecemeal basis as various crises develop. Any assistance that this Government may render in the future should provide a cure rather than a mere palliative.

Any government that is willing to assist in the task of recovery will find full cooperation, I am sure, on the part of the United States Government. Any government which maneuvers to block the recovery of other countries cannot expect help from us. Furthermore, governments, political parties or groups which seek to perpetuate human misery in order to profit therefrom politically or otherwise will encounter the opposition of the United States.

European Agreement Needed

It is already evident that, before the United States Government can proceed much further in its efforts to alleviate the situation and help start the European world on its way to recovery, there must be some agreement among the countries of Europe as to the requirements of the situation and the part those countries themselves will take in order to give proper effect to whatever action might be undertaken by this Government. It would be neither fitting nor efficacious for this Government to undertake to draw up unilaterally a program designed to place Europe on its feet economically. This is the business of the Europeans. The initiative, I think, must come from Europe. The role of this country should consist of friendly aid in the drafting of a European program and of later support of such a program so far as it may be practical for us to do so. The program should be a joint one, agreed to by a number, if not all European nations.

An essential part of any successful action on the part of the United States is an understanding on the part of the people of America of the character of the problem and the remedies to be applied. Political passion and prejudice should have no part. With foresight, and a willingness on the part of our people to face up to the vast responsibility which history has clearly placed upon our country, the difficulties I have outlined can and will be overcome.

—————————————— 10 ——————————————

COUNCIL OF EUROPE

The Statute of the Council of Europe was signed on 5 May 1949 by the foreign ministers of ten states. The principal articles of the Statute are published in Keesing's Reference, *Treaties and Alliances of the World* (3rd edn., 1981), Section 8, pp. 105–06.

[Representatives of the governments of Belgium, Denmark, France, Ireland, Italy, Luxembourg, the Netherlands, Norway, Sweden and the United Kingdom. . . .]

Convinced that the pursuit of peace based upon justice and international co-operation is vital for the preservation of human society and civilization;
Reaffirming their devotion to the spiritual and moral values which are the common heritage of their peoples and the true source of individual freedom, political liberty and the rule of law. [. . .]

[. . . have adopted the following STATUTE]

CHAPTER I

Aim of the Council of Europe

Article 1. (a) The aim of the Council of Europe is to achieve a greater unity between its members for the purpose of safeguarding and realizing the ideals and principles which are their common heritage and facilitating their economic and social progress.

(b) This aim shall be pursued through the organs of the Council by discussion of questions of common concern and by agreements and common action in economic, social, cultural, scientific, legal and administrative matters and in the maintenance and further realization of human rights and fundamental freedoms. [. . .]

CHAPTER II

MEMBERSHIP
[. . .]

Article 3.   Every member of the Council of Europe must accept the principles of the rule of law and of the enjoyment by all persons within its jurisdiction of human rights and fundamental freedoms, and collaborate sincerely and effectively in the realization of the aim of the Council as specified in Chapter I.

Article 4.   Any European state which is deemed to be able and willing to fulfil the provision of Article 3 may be invited to become a member of the Council of Europe. [...]

Article 8.   Any member of the Council of Europe which has seriously violated Article 3 may be suspended from its rights of representation and requested by the Committee of Ministers to withdraw. [...]

CHAPTER III

[Articles 10–12 establish the seat of the Council of Europe at Strasbourg and provide for a Committee of Ministers and a Consultative Assembly]

[...]

CHAPTER IV

Committee of Ministers

Article 14.   Each member state shall be entitled to one representative and that representative shall be entitled to one vote.

Article 15.   On the recommendation of the Consultative Assembly or on its own initiative, the Committee of Ministers shall consider the action required to further the aim of the Council of Europe, including the conclusion of conventions or agreements and the adoption by governments of a common policy with regard to particular matters. [...]

Article 16.   The Committee of Ministers shall ... decide with binding effect all matters relating to the internal organization and arrangements of the Council of Europe. For this purpose, the Committee of Ministers shall adopt such financial and administrative regulations as may be necessary.

Article 17.   The Committee of Ministers may set up advisory and technical committees for such specific purposes as it may deem desirable. [...]

Article 21.   Unless the Committee decides otherwise, meetings of the Committee of Ministers shall be held
(i)   in private, and
(ii) at the seat of the Council.

CHAPTER V

Consultative Assembly

Article 22.   The Consultative Assembly is the deliberative organ of the Council of Europe. It shall debate matters within its competence under this Statute and present its conclusions, in the form of recommendations, to the Committee of Ministers. [...]

—————————————————— 11 ——————————————————

GERMANY'S IDENTITY

West Germany's role in the integration of Europe was guided by the first Chancellor of the Federal Republic, Konrad Adenauer. His view of Germany's place is taken from his *Memoirs, 1945–1953* (trans. Beate Ruhm von Oppen) (London: Weidenfeld and Nicolson, 1965), pp. 35–7, 78–9.

Now I had time and leisure to read newspapers thoroughly, to listen to the radio, and most important to hold long and detailed conversations with my old friend von Weiss, the Swiss Consul-General, about world events. A letter I wrote to the then Oberbürgermeister of Duisburg, Herr Weitz, on 31 October 1945, shows my assessment of the political situation.

Russia holds the Eastern half of Germany, Poland, the Balkans, apparently Hungary, and a part of Austria. Russia is withdrawing more and more from cooperation with the other great powers and directs affairs in the countries dominated by her entirely as she sees fit. The countries ruled by her are already governed by economic and political principles that are totally different from those accepted in the rest of Europe. Thus the division of Europe into Eastern Europe, the Russian territory, and Western Europe is a fact.

Britain and France are the leading great powers in Western Europe. The part of Germany not occupied by Russia is an integral part of Western Europe. If it remains crippled the consequences for the whole of Western Europe, and that includes Britain and France, will be terrible. It is in the real interests not only of that part of Germany but also of Britain and France, to unite Europe under their leadership, and politically and economically to pacify and restore to health the part of Germany not occupied by Russia. The separation of the Rhineland and Westphalia from Germany does not serve this purpose; it would have the opposite effect. It would bring about a political orientation towards the East of the part of Germany not occupied by the Russians. *Germans unhappy will turn to Russia*

In the long run the French and Belgian demand for security can only be met by the economic integration of Western Germany, France, Belgium, Luxembourg and Holland. If Britain, too, were to decide to participate in this economic integration, we would be much closer to the ultimate goal of a Union of the States of Western Europe.

As for the constitution of the part of Germany not occupied by Russia: at the moment there is no sensible constitution and a constitutional structure must be found and restored. As the creation of a unitary centralized state will be neither possible nor desirable, the constitutional cohesion can be looser than before; it might take the form of a federal relationship.

I knew the anxieties of Germany's western neighbours. I understood and appreciated them fully in view of their experiences in the past hundred years. I thought it was wrong to try to calm their fears by pointing to the distribution of power in the Europe of 1945. Political history has shown that nothing ever stands still and that political circumstances can change very rapidly.

A solution to the German question had to be found that was organic and natural and that would therefore be durable; a solution which would reassure our western neighbours and give them a feeling of lasting security. I did not, however, regard an amputation of German territory, such as the Allies were planning – with France, for instance, wanting to detach the left bank of the Rhine – as such a solution. Also whoever undertook such a dismembering had to consider what was to become of the rest of Germany and whether it would not thereby become, as Churchill put it, a rotting corpse in the middle of Europe, which would present as deadly a danger to Europe as any victorious National Socialist Germany could have done. *divided + wasted Ger. just as bad as victorious Ger.*

I am a German, but I am also, and always have been, a European and have always felt like a European. I have therefore long advocated an understanding with France; I did so, moreover, in the 1920s, during the severest crises, and also in the face of the Reich Government. I always urged a reasonable understanding that would do justice to the interests of both countries. After the First World War I advocated a plan for an organic integration of the French, Belgian, and German economies for the safeguarding of a durable peace. In my view parallel, unified economic interests are and always will be the healthiest and most lasting foundation for good political relations between peoples. Despite the misery prevailing in Europe I saw great possibilities for the future of Western Europe. The unification of Europe seemed far more feasible now than in the 1920s. The idea of international cooperation between peoples must succeed.

I thought a great deal about the problem of a United States of Europe with Germany as a part. In a future United States of Europe I saw the greatest and most lasting security for Germany's western neighbours. The French fear of German resurgence which caused France to press for a policy of dismemberment of Germany seemed to be altogether exaggerated. After 1945 Germany lay prostrate – militarily, economically and politically – and in my opinion this condition was a sufficient guarantee that Germany could not again threaten France. In the future United States of Europe I saw great hope for Europe and thus for Germany. We had to try to remind France, Holland, Belgium, and the other European countries that they were – as we were – situated in Western Europe, that they are and will forever remain our neighbours, that any violence they do to us must in the end lead to trouble, and that no lasting peace can be established in Europe if it is founded on force alone. General de Gaulle had recognized this in his speech at Saarbrücken in August 1945: 'Frenchmen and Germans must let bygones be bygones, must work together, and must remember that they are Europeans.'

Ger. in ruin no need for Fri to be so afraid

These words gave me great hope for Germany and for the realization of my hopes for a united Europe.

I realized that we Germans could only engage in a very limited foreign policy at first. The aim of our foreign policy had to be to take part, as equals, in peaceful cooperation in the concert of nations. The burdens put on Germany vis-à-vis other countries as a result of a lost war should not exceed what Germany could bear and fulfil. Even the vanquished have a right to live and work. Bitter need without hope is the greatest obstacle to peaceful development. The victor, who has the power, also has obligations towards the vanquished under human and divine law.

I knew that a united Europe would only be possible if a community of the peoples of Europe could be restored in which every people made its irreplaceable and indispensable contribution to the European economy and civilization, to Western thought, writing, and creativeness. [...]

In my opinion the Western powers were not equal to the Russians politically. As far as I could see they lacked a clear and consistent understanding of the post-war situation. Their countries' people, especially those of the United States, were longing for peace and preferred not to see the growing communist danger. The Western countries had finally prevailed after bitter fighting. Political thought and public opinion were entirely concentrated on punishing Germany for what she had done and on rendering her powerless. There were not many who looked further into the future.

It is a true saying that geography, the geographic situation of a country, constitutes one of the essential factors in its historical development.

Germany lies at the heart of Europe. The Western powers were not clear in their minds about what was to be done with this country whose destiny was in any case bound to be of the greatest importance for the fate of Europe and thus for their own. There was no unity among the Western powers concerning policy towards Germany. This was the case, for instance, in the matter of the Ruhr and of the detachment of the left bank of the Rhine desired by France. The aim of the Russians was unambiguous. Soviet Russia had, like Tsarist Russia, an urge to acquire or subdue new territories in Europe. The policy of the Western Allies had allowed the Soviet Union to assume governmental power in a very large part of the former German Reich and had furthermore given the Russians a chance to install governments subservient to Moscow in a large part of Eastern Europe.

By our geographic position we found ourselves between two power blocs standing for totally opposed ideals. We had to join the one or the other side if we did not want to be ground up between them. I considered a neutral attitude between the two power groups unrealistic for our people. Sooner or later one or the other bloc was bound to try to get the German potential on its side. Soviet Russia was making it quite clear that for the time being she was not willing to release the German territory she had been allowed to take over, and that moreover she had every intention of gradually drawing the other part of Germany towards her as well.

There was only one way for us to save our political liberty, our personal freedom, our security, the way of life we had formed in many centuries and which was based on the Christian and humanistic ideology: we must form firm links with the peoples and countries that shared our views concerning the state, the individual, liberty and property. We must resolutely and firmly resist all further pressure from the East.

It was our task to dispel the mistrust harboured against us everywhere in the West. We had to try, step by step, to reawaken confidence in Germans. The fundamental precondition for this, in my view, was a clear, steady, unwavering affirmation of identity with the West. The orientation of our foreign policy had to be clear, logical and open.

12

SCHUMAN DECLARATION

The Declaration of the French government, concerning the joint authority for the production of coal and steel by France and Germany, was made on 9 May 1950. The following text of the Declaration was translated from that given by *Le Monde* on 11 May 1950.

World peace cannot be safeguarded without making efforts proportionate to the dangers which threaten it.

The contribution which an organized and active Europe can bring to civilization is indispensable to the maintenance of peaceful relations. For more than twenty years, France has acted as the champion of a united Europe, and has always had the defence of peace as an essential goal. When Europe has not shared this goal, we have had war.

Europe will not be made all at once, or according to a single, general plan. It will be built through definite achievements, first creating a solidarity in fact. The coming together of European nations requires that the age-old hostility between France and Germany be eliminated. The essential project ought therefore to affect France and Germany above all.

With this as our plan, the French government proposes to take action immediately in a limited but decisive area.

The French government proposes to place the whole of the French and German output of coal and steel under a joint High Authority in an organization open to the participation of other European countries.

Combining coal and steel production will immediately assure the setting up of common bases of economic development, the first step of a European federation, and will alter the destiny of regions so long devoted to the production of armaments of which they have been the most constant victims.

The fusion of production formed in this way will mean that any war between France and Germany will become not only unthinkable but materially impossible. The founding of this powerful manufacturing association, open to all countries who will wish to join it, will establish the true foundations of economic unification, by furnishing to all those countries the basic materials of industrial production under the same conditions.

This production will be offered to the whole world without distinction or exclusion in order to contribute to the raising of the standard of living and to the progress of peaceful enterprises. With ever-growing wealth, Europe will be able to pursue the realization of one of its essential tasks: the development of the African continent.

As the fusion of interests required for the establishment of an economic market will be easily and quickly achieved, it introduces the condition for a larger and broader community among nations long separated by bloody conflict.

By placing basic production under joint control and by the institution of a new High Authority, whose decisions will be binding for France, Germany and the countries who join it, this proposal will achieve the first definite stages of a European federation indispensable to the preservation of peace.

In order to reach the goals just defined, the French government is ready to begin negotiations on the following points:

The mission entrusted to the high economic authority will be to insure as quickly as possible the

- modernization of production and the improvement of quality,
- the provision of identical conditions of coal and steel in both the French and German markets, and in the markets of associated countries as well,
- the development of common export procedures to other countries, and
- the harmonization of living and working conditions in these countries.

To reach these goals from the very different conditions which actually exist in the production of the participating countries, certain arrangements will have to be made, including the adoption of a plan for production and investments, the institution of price mechanisms and adjustments, the creation of a redeployment fund facilitating the rationalization of production.

The movement of coal and steel supplies among the participating states will be immediately freed from all customs and will be unaffected by different transport tolls. Conditions spontaneously insuring the most rational distribution of high quality products will gradually prevail.

In contrast to an international cartel committed to distribution and exploitation of national markets by restrictive practices and the expectation of high profits, the projected organization will insure the fusion of markets and the growth of production.

The essential principles and commitments defined above will be the object of a treaty signed by the states and submitted to their parliaments for ratification. The important negotiations to specify the implementation procedures will be conducted with the assistance of an arbiter chosen by general agreement. He will have the responsibility for seeing that the agreements conform to the principles and, in the event of some unresolvable difficulty, he will determine the solution which will be adopted.

The common High Authority responsible for the working of the whole system will be composed of independent persons designated by the governments, with equal representation for all parties. A president will be chosen by general agreement of the governments; his decisions will be enforceable in France and Germany, and in the other participating states. Suitable arrangements will allow for any necessary appeals against decisions of the High Authority.

A United Nations representative attached to the High Authority will be expected to make a public report to the United Nations twice each year, providing an account of the working of the new organization, with special attention to those activities which concern the maintenance of peace.

The founding of the High Authority does not in any way prejudice the system of commercial properties. In the exercise of its mission, the common High Authority will recognize the powers conferred upon the International Authority of the Ruhr and obligations of every sort imposed on Germany, as long as these continue.

——————————— 13 ———————————

COAL AND STEEL COMMUNITY

The Schuman Plan led to the signing in April 1952 of a Treaty which was the first decisive step towards European union. By asserting the principle of supranational authority, the Coal and Steel Community promised more than cooperation in one key sector of the European economy. The following articles of the Treaty are taken from the original text, published by the ECSC High Authority (Brussels, 1953). Among the more accessible editions (incorporating subsequent amendments) is that published in Chapter 1 of Sweet and Maxwell's *European Community Texts*, 3rd edn. (London: Sweet and Maxwell, 1977).

TITLE ONE

THE EUROPEAN COAL AND STEEL COMMUNITY

Article 1

By this Treaty the HIGH CONTRACTING PARTIES establish among themselves a EUROPEAN COAL AND STEEL COMMUNITY, based on a common market, common objectives, and common institutions.

Article 2

The mission of the European Coal and Steel Community is to contribute to the expansion of the economy, the development of employment and the improvement of the standard of living in the participating countries through the creation, in harmony with the general economy of the member States, of a common market as defined in Article 4.

The Community must progressively establish conditions which will in themselves assure the most rational distribution of production at the highest possible level of productivity, while safeguarding the continuity of employment and avoiding the creation of fundamental and persistent disturbances in the economies of the member States.

Article 3

Within the framework of their respective powers and responsibilities and in the common interest, the institutions of the Community shall:

(a) ensure that the common market is regularly supplied, while taking into account the needs of third countries;
(b) assure to all consumers in comparable positions within the common market equal access to the sources of production;
(c) seek the establishment of the lowest possible prices without involving any corresponding rise either in the prices charged by the same enterprises in other transactions or in the price-level as a whole in another period, while at the same time permitting necessary amortization and providing the possibility of normal returns on invested capital;
(d) ensure that conditions are maintained which will encourage enterprises to expand and improve their ability to produce and to promote a policy of rational development of natural resources, while avoiding undue exhaustion of such resources;
(e) promote the improvement of the living and working conditions of the labour force in each of the industries under its jurisdiction so as to harmonize those conditions in an upward direction;
(f) foster the development of international trade and ensure that equitable limits are observed in prices charged in foreign markets;
(g) promote the regular expansion and the modernization of production as well as the improvement of quality, under conditions which preclude any protection against competing industries except where justified by illegitimate action on the part of such industries or in their favour.

Article 4

The following are recognized to be incompatible with the common market for coal and steel, and are, therefore, abolished and prohibited within the Community in the manner set forth in this Treaty:

(a) import and export duties, or taxes with an equivalent effect, and quantitative restrictions on the movement of coal and steel;
(b) measures or practices discriminating among producers, among buyers or among consumers, especially as concerns prices, delivery terms and transport rates, as well as measures or practices which hamper the buyer in the free choice of his supplier;
(c) subsidies or state assistance, or special charges imposed by the state, in any form whatsoever;
(d) restrictive practices tending towards the division or the exploitation of the market.

Article 5

The Community shall accomplish its mission, under the conditions provided for in this Treaty, with limited intervention.

To this end, the Community shall:

- assist the interested parties to take action by collecting information, organizing consultations and defining general objectives;
- place financial means at the disposal of enterprises for their investments and participate in the expenses of readaptation;
- assure the establishment, the maintenance and the observance of normal conditions of competition, and take direct action with respect to production and the operation of the market only when circumstances make it absolutely necessary;
- publish the reasons for its action and take the necessary measures to ensure observance of the rules set forth in this Treaty.

The institutions of the Community shall carry out these activities with as little administrative machinery as possible and in close cooperation with the interested parties.

Article 6

The Community shall be a legal person.

In its international relationships, the Community shall enjoy the legal capacity necessary to exercise its functions and to achieve its purposes.

In each of the member States, the Community shall enjoy the most extensive legal capacity pertaining to legal persons in that country. Specifically, it may acquire and transfer real and personal property, and may sue and be sued in its own name.

The Community shall be represented by its institutions, each one of them acting within the framework of its own powers and responsibilities.

TITLE TWO

THE INSTITUTIONS OF THE COMMUNITY

Article 7

The institutions of the Community shall be as follows:

- a HIGH AUTHORITY, assisted by a *Consultative Committee*;
- a COMMON ASSEMBLY, hereinafter referred to as "the Assembly";
- a SPECIAL COUNCIL, composed of MINISTERS, hereinafter referred to as "the Council";
- a COURT OF JUSTICE, hereinafter referred to as "the Court".

CHAPTER I

THE HIGH AUTHORITY

Article 8

The High Authority shall be responsible for assuring the achievement of the purposes stated in this Treaty within the terms thereof.

Article 9

The High Authority shall be composed of nine members designated for six years and chosen for their general competence.

A member shall be eligible for reappointment. The number of members of the High Authority may be reduced by unanimous decision of the Council.

Only nationals of the member States may be members of the High Authority.

The High Authority shall not include more than two members of the same nationality.

The members of the High Authority shall exercise their functions in complete independence, in the general interest of the Community. In the fulfilment of their duties, they shall neither solicit nor accept instructions from any government or from any organization. They will abstain from all conduct incompatible with the supranational character of their functions.

Each member State undertakes to respect this supranational character and not to seek to influence the members of the High Authority in the execution of their duties.

The members of the High Authority shall not exercise any business or professional activities, paid or unpaid, nor acquire or hold, directly or indirectly, any interest in any business related to coal and steel during their term of office or for a period of three years thereafter. [...]

Article 11

The President and the Vice President of the High Authority shall be appointed from among the membership of the High Authority for two years, in accordance with the procedure provided for the appointment of the members of the High Authority by the governments of the member States. They may be re-elected.

Except in the case of a complete renewal of the membership of the High Authority, the appointment of the President and Vice President shall be made after consultation with the High Authority. [...]

Article 14

In the execution of the tasks entrusted to it by this Treaty and in accordance with the provisions thereof, the High Authority shall take decisions, formulate recommendations and issue opinions.

Decisions shall be binding in every respect.

Recommendations shall be binding with respect to the objectives which they specify but shall leave to those to whom they are directed the choice of appropriate means for attaining these objectives.

Opinions shall not be binding.

When the High Authority is empowered to take a decision, it may limit itself to formulating a recommendation.

Article 15

The decisions, recommendations and opinions of the High Authority shall include the reasons therefore, and shall refer to the advice which the High Authority is required to obtain.

When such decisions and recommendations are individual in character, they shall be binding on the interested party upon notification. In other cases, they shall take effect automatically upon publication.

The High Authority shall determine the manner in which the provisions of the present article are to be carried out. [...]

Article 18

There shall be created a Consultative Committee, attached to the High Authority. It shall consist of not less than thirty and not more than fifty-one members, and shall include an equal number of producers, workers, and consumers and dealers.

The members of the Consultative Committee shall be appointed by the Council.

As concerns producers and workers, the Council shall appoint the representative organizations among which it shall allocate the seats to be filled. Each organization shall be asked to draw up a list comprising twice the number of seats allocated to it. Appointments shall be made from this list.

The members of the Consultative Committee shall be appointed in their individual capacity for a period of two years. They shall not be bound by any mandate or instruction from the organizations which proposed them as candidates.

A President and officers shall be elected for periods of one year by the Consultative Committee from among its own members. The Committee shall make its own rules of procedure. [...]

Article 19

The High Authority may consult the Consultative Committee on all matters it deems proper. It shall be required to do so whenever such consultation is prescribed by the present Treaty. [...]

The Consultative Committee shall be called together by its President, either at the request of the High Authority or at the request of a majority of its members, for the purpose of discussing a given question.

CHAPTER II

THE ASSEMBLY

Article 20

The Assembly, consisting of representatives of the peoples of the member States of the Community, shall exercise the supervisory powers which are granted to it by this Treaty.

Article 21

The Assembly shall consist of delegates whom the parliaments of each of the member States shall be called upon to appoint once a year from among their own membership, or who shall be elected by direct universal suffrage, according to the procedure determined by each respective High Contracting Party.

The number of delegates is fixed as follows:

Belgium 10
France 18
Germany 18
Italy 18
Luxembourg 4
Netherlands 10

The representatives of the people of the Saar are included in the number of delegates attributed to France.

Article 22

The Assembly shall hold an annual session. It shall meet regularly on the second Tuesday in May. Its session may not last beyond the end of the current fiscal year.

The Assembly may be called together in extraordinary session at the request of the Council in order to state its opinion on such questions as may be put to it by the Council. It may also meet in extraordinary session at the request of a majority of its members or of the High Authority. [. . .]

CHAPTER III

THE COUNCIL

Article 26

The Council shall exercise its functions in the cases and in the manner laid down by this Treaty, in particular with a view to harmonizing the action of the High

Authority and that of the government which are responsible for the general economic policy of their countries.

To this end, the Council and the High Authority shall exchange information and consult together.

The Council may request the High Authority to examine any proposals and measures which it may deem necessary or appropriate for the realization of the common objectives.

Article 27

The Council shall consist of representatives of the member States. Each State shall appoint thereto one of the members of its government.

The Presidency of the Council shall be exercised for a term of three months by each member of the Council in rotation in the alphabetical order of the member States.

Article 28

Meetings of the Council shall be called by its President at the request of a member State or of the High Authority.

When the Council is consulted by the High Authority, it may deliberate without necessarily proceeding to a vote. The minutes of its meetings shall be forwarded to the High Authority.

Wherever this Treaty requires the agreement of the Council, this agreement shall be deemed to have been given if the proposal submitted by the High Authority is approved:

- by an absolute majority of the representatives of the member States, including the vote of the representative of one of the States which produces at least twenty percent of the total value of coal and steel produced in the Community;
- or, in case of an equal division of votes, and if the High Authority maintains its proposal after a second reading, by the representatives of two member States, each of which produces at least twenty percent of the total value of coal and steel in the Community. . . .

CHAPTER IV

THE COURT

Article 31

The function of the Court is to ensure the rule of law in the interpretation and application of the present Treaty and of the regulations for its execution.

Article 32

The Court shall consist of seven judges, appointed for six years by agreement among the governments of the member States from among persons of recognized independence and competence.

A partial renewal of the membership of the Court shall occur every three years, affecting alternately three members and four members. The three members whose terms of office expire at the end of the first period of three years shall be designated by lot.

Judges shall be eligible for reappointment. [Their number may be increased by unanimous vote of the Council on proposal by the Court; the judges shall approve of one of their number as President for a period of three years.]

Article 33

The Court shall have jurisdiction over appeals by a member State or by the Council for the annulment of decisions and recommendations of the High Authority on the grounds of lack of legal competence, major violations of procedure, violation of the Treaty or of any rule of law relating to its application, or abuse of power. However, the Court may not review the High Authority's evaluation of the situation, based on economic facts and circumstances, which led to such decisions or recommendations, except where the High Authority is alleged to have abused its powers or to have clearly misinterpreted the provisions of the Treaty or of a rule of law relating to its application.

The enterprises, or the associations referred to in Article 48, shall have the right of appeal on the same grounds against individual decisions and recommendations affecting them, or against general decisions and recommendations which they deem to involve an abuse of power affecting them. [...]

Article 37

If a member State considers that in a given case an action of the High Authority, or a failure to act, is of such a nature as to provoke fundamental and persistent disturbances in the economy of the said State, it may bring the matter to the attention of the High Authority.

The High Authority, after consulting the Council, shall if it is appropriate recognize the existence of such a situation, and decide on the measures to be taken, under the terms of the present Treaty, to correct such a situation while at the same time safeguarding the essential interests of the Community. [...]

Article 38

At the request of a member State or of the High Authority, the Court may annul the resolutions of the Assembly or of the Council. [... Such an appeal may be made

only on the grounds of lack of legal competence or major violations of procedure.]

Article 40

Subject to [other provisions], the Court shall have competence to assess damages
against the Community, at the request of the injured party, in cases where injury
results from an official fault of the Community in execution of this Treaty.

It shall also have competence to assess damages against any official or employee
of the Community, in cases where injury results from a personal fault of such
official or employee in the performance of his duties. If the injured party is unable
to recover damages from such an official or employee, the Court may assess
equitable damages against the Community. [...]

Article 41

When the validity of resolutions of the High Authority or the Council is contested
in litigation before a national court, such issue shall be certified to the Court, which
shall have exclusive competence to rule thereupon.

Article 42

The Court shall exercise jurisdiction as may be provided by any clause to that effect
in a public or private contract to which the Community is a party or which is
undertaken on its behalf. [...]

TITLE THREE

ECONOMIC AND SOCIAL PROVISIONS

CHAPTER I

GENERAL PROVISIONS

Article 46

The High Authority may at any time consult the governments, the various
interested parties (enterprises, workers, consumers and dealers) and their associations, as well as any experts.

Enterprises, workers, consumers and dealers, and their associations, may
present any suggestions or observations to the High Authority on questions
affecting them.

In order to provide guidance for the action of all interested parties, taking
account of the purposes assigned to the Community, and in order to determine its
own action within the conditions laid down in this Treaty, the High Authority
shall, by means of the consultations mentioned above:

(1) carry on a permanent study of the development of the market and price trends;
(2) periodically draw up programmes giving forecasts, for guidance, of production, consumption, exports and imports;
(3) periodically set out the general objectives with respect to modernization, the long-term planning of production and the expansion of productive capacity;
(4) at the request of the interested governments, participate in the study of the possibilities of re-employing, either in existing industries or through the creation of new activities, workers unemployed by reason of the development of the market or technical changes;
(5) gather any information required to assess the possibilities of improving the living and working conditions of the labour force in the industries under its jurisdiction, and the risks menacing their living conditions.

It shall publish the general objectives and programmes after submitting them to the Consultative Committee. [It may publish the studies and information mentioned above.]

Article 47

The High Authority may gather such information as may be necessary to the accomplishment of its mission. It may have the necessary verifications carried out.

The High Authority shall not divulge information which by its nature is considered a trade secret, and in particular information pertaining to the commercial relations or the breakdown of the costs of production of enterprises. With this reservation, it must publish such data as may be useful to governments or to any other interested parties.

The High Authority may impose fines and daily penalty payments upon those enterprises which evade their obligations resulting from decisions made in application of the provisions of this Article, or which knowingly furnish false information. The maximum amount of such fines shall be one percent of the annual turnover and the maximum amount of such penalty payments shall be five percent of the average daily turnover for each day's delay.

Any violation by the High Authority of trade secrecy which has caused damage to an enterprise may be the subject of a suit for damages before the Court under the conditions provided for in Article 40.

Article 48

The right of enterprises to form associations is not affected by this Treaty. Membership in such associations must be voluntary. The associations may engage in any activity which is not contrary to the provisions of this Treaty or to the decisions or recommendations of the High Authority. [...]

INVESTMENTS AND FINANCIAL ASSISTANCE

Article 54

The High Authority may facilitate the carrying out of investment programmes by granting loans to enterprises or by giving its guarantee to other loans which they obtain.

With the unanimous agreement of the Council, the High Authority may by the same means assist the financing of works and installations which contribute directly and mainly to an increase of production or to lower production costs or which facilitate the marketing of products subject to its jurisdiction.

In order to encourage the co-ordinated development of investments, the High Authority may, in accordance with the provisions of Article 47, require enterprises to submit individual projects in advance, either by a special request addressed to the enterprise concerned or by a decision defining the nature and the size of the projects to be submitted.

Within the framework of the general programmes described in Article 46, the High Authority may, after giving the interested parties an opportunity to present their views, issue a reasoned opinion on such projects. It shall be obliged to issue such an opinion when requested by an enterprise. The High Authority shall notify the enterprise of its opinion and shall bring it to the attention of the government concerned. A list of the opinions shall be made public. [...]

The High Authority may impose on enterprises violating the provisions of the above paragraph fines not exceeding the sums improperly devoted to the carrying out of the project in question.

Article 55

1. The High Authority must encourage technical and economic research concerning the production and the development of consumption of coal and steel, as well as workers' safety in these industries. To this end, it shall organize all appropriate contacts among existing research organizations.
2. After consultation with the Consultative Committee, the High Authority may initiate and facilitate the development of research work:
   (a) by encouraging joint financing by the enterprise concerned; or
   (b) by earmarking for that purpose any grants it may receive [...]

CHAPTER IV

PRODUCTION

Article 57

In the field of production, the High Authority shall give preference to the indirect means of action at its disposal, such as:

- cooperation with governments to stabilize or influence general consumption, particularly that of the public services;
- intervention on prices and commercial policy as provided for in this Treaty.

Article 58

1. In case of a decline in demand, if the High Authority considers that the Community is faced with a period of manifest crisis and that the means of action provided for in Article 57 are not sufficient to cope with this situation, it must, after consulting the Consultative Committee and with the agreement of the Council, establish a system of production quotas [...]
   If the High Authority fails to act, one of the member States may bring the matter to the attention of the Council which, acting by a unanimous vote, may oblige the High Authority to establish a system of quotas.
2. The High Authority, basing its action on studies made in conjunction with the enterprises and their associations, shall establish quotas on an equitable basis, taking account of the principles defined in Articles 2, 3 and 4. The High Authority may in particular regulate the rate of operation of the enterprises by appropriate levies on tonnages exceeding a reference level defined by a general decision.
   The sums thus obtained will be earmarked for the support of those enterprises whose rate of production has dropped below the reference level with a view to ensuring as far as possible the maintenance of employment in those enterprises.
3. The system of quotas shall be automatically ended upon a proposal addressed to the Council by the High Authority after consulting the Consultative Committee, or by the government of one of the member States, unless the Council decides to the contrary; such a decision must be taken by unanimous vote, if the proposal originates with the High Authority, or by simple majority if the proposal originates with a government. The ending of the quota system shall be made public by the High Authority.
4. The High Authority may impose upon enterprises violating the decisions which it takes in application of this article, fines not to exceed a sum equal to the value of the irregular production.

Article 59

1. If, after consulting the Consultative Committee, the High Authority finds that the Community is faced with a serious shortage of certain or of all of the products subject to its jurisdiction, and that the means of action provided for in Article 57 do not enable it to cope with this situation, it shall bring it to the attention of the Council, and shall propose the necessary measures, unless the Council decides to the contrary by unanimous vote.
   If the High Authority fails to act, one of the member States may bring the matter

before the Council, which by unanimous decision may recognize the existence of the above-mentioned situation.

2. The Council, acting by a unanimous vote, shall on the basis of proposals made by the High Authority and in consultation with it, establish consumption priorities and determine the allocation of the coal and steel resources of the Community among the industries subject to its jurisdiction, exports, and other consumption.

   On the basis of the consumption priorities thus established, the High Authority shall, after consulting the enterprises concerned, draw up production programmes which the enterprises shall be obliged to carry out.

3. If the Council fails to reach a unanimous decision on the measures referred to in Section 2, the High Authority shall itself proceed to allocate the resources of the Community among the member States on the basis of consumption and exports and independently of the place of production.

   Within each of the member States the allocation of the resources assigned by the High Authority shall be carried out under the responsibility of the government. This allocation shall not affect prospective deliveries to other member States, and the governments shall consult with the High Authority concerning the portion of such resources to be assigned to export and to the operation of the coal and steel industries. [...]

4. In all cases, the High Authority, acting on the basis of studies undertaken jointly with the enterprises and their associations, shall be responsible for allocating equitably among enterprises the quantities earmarked for the industries under its jurisdiction. [...]

CHAPTER V

PRICES

Article 60

1. Pricing practices contrary to the provisions of Articles 2, 3 and 4 are prohibited, and in particular:
   - unfair competitive practices, in particular purely temporary or purely local price reductions the purpose of which is to acquire a monopoly within the common market;
   - discriminatory practices involving within the common market the application by a seller of unequal conditions to comparable transactions, especially according to the nationality of the buyer.

After consulting the Consultative Committee and the Council, the High Authority may define the practices covered by this prohibition. [...]

Article 61

On the basis of studies undertaken jointly with the enterprises and their associations ... and after consulting the Consultative Committee and the Council as to the advisability of these measures as well as concerning the price level which they determine, the High Authority may fix for one or more products subject to its jurisdiction:

(a) maximum prices within the common market, if it finds that such a decision is necessary to attain the objectives defined in Article 3 and particularly in paragraph (c) thereof;

(b) minimum prices within the common market, if it finds that a manifest crisis exists or is imminent and that such a decision is necessary to attain the objectives defined in Article 3;

(c) after consulting with the enterprises concerned or their associations, and acting in accordance with methods adapted to the nature of the export markets, minimum or maximum export prices, if such action can be effectively supervised and appears necessary either because of dangers to the enterprises resulting from the state of the market or to pursue in international economic relations the objective defined in Article 3 paragraph (f), [...]

If the High Authority should fail to act under the circumstances described above, the government of one of the member States may refer the matter to the Council, which may, by unanimous decision, request the High Authority to fix such maximum or minimum prices.

Article 62

If the High Authority considers such an action the most appropriate for preventing the price of coal from being established at the level of the production costs of the most costly mines to operate whose production is temporarily required to ensure the fulfilment of the objectives defined in Article 3, the High Authority may, after consulting the Consultative Committee, authorize compensation schemes:

– among enterprises of the same coalfield applying the same price-list;
– after consulting the Council, among enterprises situated in different coalfields.
   [...]

Article 63

1. If the High Authority finds that discrimination is being systematically practised by buyers, in particular discrimination resulting from clauses in contracts concluded by public services, it shall address the necessary recommendations to the governments concerned.

2. To the extent that it finds necessary, the High Authority may decide that:
   (a) enterprises shall establish their conditions of sale in such a way that their customers or their agents shall be obliged to conform to the rules established by the High Authority in application of the provisions of this Chapter;
   (b) enterprises shall be made responsible for violations committed by their direct agents or by dealers acting on behalf of such enterprises.

In case of a violation committed by a buyer against the obligations thus contracted, the High Authority may limit the right of enterprises of the Community to deal with the said buyer, to a degree which may temporarily deprive him of access to the market in case of repeated violations. In that case, and without prejudice to the provisions of Article 33, the buyer has the right of appeal to the Court. [...]

Article 64

The High Authority may impose upon enterprises which violate the provisions of this Chapter or the decisions taken in application thereof, fines not to exceed twice the value of the irregular sales. In case of a second offence, the above maximum may be doubled. [...]

Article 65

1. All agreements among enterprises, all decisions of associations of enterprises, and all concerted practices, tending, directly or indirectly, to prevent, restrict or distort the normal operation of competition within the common market are hereby forbidden, and in particular those tending: (a) to fix or determine prices; (b) to restrict or control production, technical development or investments; (c) to allocate markets, products, customers or sources of supply. [...]

EUROPEAN CONSTRUCTIONS

1954–1962

During the five years from VE Day to Robert Schuman's announcement, European unity belonged mostly to the realm of ideas. Europe's potential as a single cohesive unit in world affairs was a matter which intellectuals discussed; most people were busy clearing the rubble which had been their towns and cities. The professed advocates of European unity were, by and large, members of a political elite. Many of them did not identify with political parties and had never been elected to public office. Nationalists, federalists and functionalists, they spent these years trying to define (for themselves as much as for the general public) the new Europe. Their opinions found various sounding boards but only Benelux and the ECSC emerged as working champions of European integration.

In the early 1950s the military security of western Europe became a critical issue. Although thousands of miles away, the Korean War (June 1950–July 1953) profoundly frightened Europe and provoked nervous questions. If this distant war lasted a long time, would the Americans transfer some of their armies from Europe? If they did so, would the Russians race across Germany to the Rhine and to the Atlantic? Would the new and untried NATO alliance deter Soviet aggression? Europe's vulnerability was manifest, and it was not long before the Americans were urging their allies to assume more of the burden of Europe's defence. The European response centred on the proposal made in October 1950 by the French premier, Réné Pleven, for a European Defence Community (EDC). Two features of the Pleven Plan made it palatable to many Europeans. First it envisaged a supranational defence structure based on an integrated European army under permanent European (not American) command. This provision appealed to the federalists and functionalists, for whom it was an unexpected but welcome promotion of European unity. Second, the Plan promised to involve all armies, including the German. This feature appealed particularly to the French but also to 'nationalists' in all countries who were uneasy about the possibility of German rearmament on a national basis.[1]

The Pleven Plan eventually took the form of a treaty which, during 1952, was accepted by six western European governments. Confident of its ratification by the six parliaments, members of the six governments started planning for a European Political Community (EPC), which the EDC logically (and legally) required in order to function. Had the European Political Community come into existence, it would have done more than merely combine the ECSC and the EDC: it would have suddenly provided Europe with an institutional framework for political federation.

But the fate of the EPC depended entirely on that of the EDC, and the defence community was not to be. The plan was defeated where it began, in Paris. The French National Assembly rejected the EDC (and with it, the EPC) in August 1954, partly because many of the deputies thought that a more gentle Soviet foreign policy was about to follow the death of Stalin (March 1953) and the end of the Korean War (July 1953). With the new Soviet leadership hinting at an 'era of peaceful coexistence', there seemed less need for a supranational defence community. In retrospect, however, it is hard to see how the European defence and political communities could have got off the ground. Their birth in the early 1950s would have been decidedly and grotesquely premature, for there was no sufficient apparatus for collective decision-making. It would have been more realistic for the EDC and the EPC to 'come later in that chain of integrating communities envisaged by Schuman and Monnet.'[2]

The failure of the EDC enhanced the importance of existing defence organizations. The Brussels Treaty organization was enlarged by the membership of Italy and West Germany and was named in 1955 as the Western European Union (WEU). In the same year, West Germany's admission to NATO added to the strength of that organization. The expansion of these two overlapping military alliances seemed to offer some compensation for the failure of the EDC. Although they never attempted the integration of army units, NATO and the WEU nonetheless promoted a regime of close military consultation and cooperation.

The Benelux governments continued to regard military cooperation and economic integration as two sides of the same coin. In the negotiations which led in the late 1940s to the Brussels Treaty and the NATO pact, Benelux representatives argued for a community which was both a military alliance and a 'full economic and customs union'.[3] In the early 1950s they urged their partners in the Coal and Steel Community to adopt measures which Benelux had taken or was about to take. In November 1950, for example, when the negotiations for the ECSC were already under way, Sicco Mansholt, the Dutch minister of agriculture, presented a plan for a European organization of agricultural markets. This 'agricultural community' was to have a high authority similar to that contemplated for the ECSC. In 1952, the Dutch foreign minister, J. W. Beyen, suggested a still more comprehensive plan for a west European common market. Other countries gave polite replies but neither plan was put into operation. Finally, in May 1955, Benelux ministers succeeded in persuading their colleagues to discuss a customs union, with special attention to the needs of transport and energy.

The Six agreed to consider the 'Benelux Memorandum' at a special conference in Messina, on 1 and 2 June 1955. For the politicians and their advisors accustomed to meetings in Paris, Strasbourg and Brussels, the east coast of Sicily was rather a long journey. The conference site was the idea of the Italian foreign minister, Gaetano Martino, who was then campaigning for re-election in the district. No doubt he wanted to remind his constituents of his importance in European affairs just as much as he wanted his colleagues to enjoy the sights of

Taormina's classical ruins, the sparkling sea and Mt Etna in the distance. Spaak thought the conference a confused affair because of the many different reactions to the Memorandum.[4] The Conference communiqué itself was an agitated text, but at least it identified two broad objectives (DOCUMENT 14).

The first accepted the functionalists' strategy of concentrating on one or two key sectors of economic life. The ministers decided to focus on 'communications' (no small sector, for it embraced everything from canals to air-transport) and 'energy' (an area which complemented and expanded the ECSC's mandate for coordinating coal supplies). The enthusiasm for atomic energy reflected the hopes of some Benelux leaders (including Spaak) for a 'new industrial revolution'. The second objective expressed in the communiqué was more far-reaching. It looked to the establishment of a common market in trade and labour and to the harmonization of social policies. Taken together, the two objectives of the communiqué repre-sented a very ambitious – and startling – agreement. They committed the Six to the path which Benelux was already travelling. Those who composed a detailed agenda based on the communiqué were 'conscious of achieving nothing short of a revolution.'[5]

The report was the work of an intergovernmental committee. Spaak, who chaired these meetings, later said that they 'frequently came close to failure', so great was the acrimony and confusion.[6] The people charged with beginning the construction of Europe had little to guide them, apart from the Messina commu-niqué and the recent experiences of Benelux, the ECSC and the Nordic Council. There were no expressions of public opinion, no referenda and no elections on the subject of European integration. Most of the external pressures on the committee were positive: they came from the 'action committees for the United States of Europe' which Jean Monnet and his friends had recently sponsored in all member states of the ECSC. Composed of leading members of democratic political parties and trade unions, journalists and intellectuals, these societies lobbied government ministers of the Six. Ultimately their pressure helped to insure the acceptance of the Spaak Report, following its completion early in 1956.

Notwithstanding all the confusion about the meaning of integration, the Report was remarkably bold. It cast aside the notion of the sectoral approach to integration (as exemplified by the apparently successful ECSC) as too restrictive and too slow. The Report adopted the Benelux view that the time had come to abandon piecemeal integration in favour of an organization which promoted coordination in all sectors generally. But this did not mean anything like a United States of Europe. Instead, the Spaak Report proposed an economic community (beginning with a formal customs union) and a separate organization to develop nuclear energy. After another round of conferences from June 1956 to February 1957, two treaties were ready for the Six to sign in Rome.

The Treaty which established the Economic Community was certainly compre-hensive (DOCUMENT 15). It touched on almost every aspect of economic activity in western Europe. In some areas, the Treaty paved the way for a new economic regime: it prescribed the total (if phased) elimination of most trade barriers, the harmonization of social welfare policies, the free movement of labour, an investment policy for underdeveloped regions and the liberation of capital among the Six. It allowed states to form smaller and more cohesive customs unions within the Community in the belief that such regional organizations would, like Benelux, quicken the pulse of union. But the scope of the Treaty left little room for precision. There was, it is true, a timetable for the reduction of internal tariffs, and scales were proposed for contributions to the common budget and the social fund. There was also clarity on the number of representatives assigned to the various institutions of the Community. Apart from these details, the Treaty of Rome was not heavy with specific provisions. It was more a statement of principles about such matters as 'the coordination of efforts', the 'compatibility' of financial practices, the 'balanced and steady development of the community'. There were a number of areas which the Treaty left for future definition and development.

Agriculture was the first major subject left to the maturing Community. In the 1950s the agricultural population of western Europe was much larger than it is today and national governments were more careful not to antagonize the agricultural sector. Agriculture was a particularly sensitive problem in France, where the rural demagogue Pierre Poujade contributed to the political instability of the mid-1950s. If the Treaty of Rome was to mean anything as far as agriculture was concerned, it had to make at least a start at reconciling the different schedules of domestic prices and the different ideas of how much protection certain aspects of agriculture were likely to need. Not surprisingly, there was much hard bargaining before the Treaty of Rome sounded the right note on agriculture. The eventual outcome was the Common Agricultural Policy (CAP). Expressed in fairly general terms, the CAP created almost as many problems as it was supposed to solve. It very soon provoked agricultural producers outside the Six: they accused the Common Market of defending free trade when that meant the export of the market's industrial goods and restricting agricultural imports from other countries which had little else to sell. Indeed, it was not very long before the protectionist nature of CAP attracted foreign criticism; a committee of GATT in 1959 was only the first group to ask the Six to revise their Common Agricultural Policy.

While agricultural policies owed much to the historic strategies of protectionism, the Treaty of Rome neglected to give other areas any definite policies at all. The Treaty did not, for example, specify a common financial policy. There were broad provisions for a social fund and an investment bank, but (to the annoyance of the federalists) the Treaty did not allow for a reserve fund, a common monetary policy or a central bank. One explanation for these omissions is that there was no need for such things in 1957: the Bretton Woods system and the strong US dollar formed a strong platform for most international monetary activity.[7] For the first five or six years of the EEC, currencies were relatively stable and the balance of payments was not a major issue for the Six. The Treaty of Rome did not anticipate problems in these areas. But when rising inflation and an increase in currency speculation began to affect their economies after 1965, the Six realized the need for more definite regulations. Similarly, guidelines for a coordinated energy policy and aid to the 'developing regions' of the Community did not appear until 1964.

The imprecision of the Treaty of Rome did not embarrass the people who drafted it in 1957. They were more troubled by the large gaps which they perceived in the very structure of the Community. There was, for example, no strong supranational agency which might defend the Community as a whole against the petulant claims of the nation-state. The Commission of nine members enjoyed an important executive role, but there was nothing in the EEC comparable to the High Authority of the Coal and Steel Community. This omission made many people wonder whether the Community would ever develop the self-discipline needed to meet its obligations. Articles 5 and 6 suggested that the responsibility for fulfilling the Treaty rested with the Six as individual member states. There was no great confidence in 1957 that the Treaty's timetable could be kept. The structure of the Community also seemed incomplete because it embraced only the Six – 'Little Europe'. Britain's refusal to take part in the conferences leading to the Treaty of Rome undoubtably disappointed Monnet and Spaak, and the decision of several countries (Austria, Ireland, Switzerland and the Scandinavian states) to stand aloof with Britain was very disturbing to the cause of European unity.[8]

Even so, there was now a framework which allowed the Six to do more than they had in the EEC. It is unlikely that the Treaty of Rome would have allowed for so much, had the representatives of Britain and Scandinavia joined the Six at the conferences which began in Messina. Events moved very quickly after Messina. Public opinion was not an important factor: there was no coherent opposition to the formation of the EEC, nor was there an outpouring of public enthusiasm. In this near-vacuum of public expression, the makers of Europe saw their opportunity. Their decisions were probably accelerated by two major crises which exploded in late 1956: the Soviet suppression of a liberal government in Hungary and the disruption of oil deliveries caused by the Suez invasion. Both events raised the question of America's role in Europe and left many Europeans worried that they might be on their own. The signatories of the Treaty of Rome in March 1957 were acutely aware of Europe's vulnerability and they were ready to accept an affirmation of Europe's unity.

The treaty which established the European Atomic Energy Community (EURA-TOM) was also signed in Rome on 25 March 1957. It was more similar to the ECSC Treaty in that it concerned a single aspect of economic cooperation (DOCUMENT 16). The planners of EURATOM expected much of it. They believed, as Spaak did, that nuclear energy would free Europe from its dependence on imported oil. During the 1950s, the importance of coal to the economy of western Europe declined, in spite of the new and imaginative provisions of the ECSC. Oil, imported mostly from the Middle East via the Suez Canal, became ever more essential to western Europe. In the mid-1950s Arab nationalism seemed to endanger the oil supply and the Suez War of late 1956 left the Canal unusable for months. Many Europeans therefore welcomed the plan which they believed would bring them a relatively cheap and clean energy, the energy of the future which they could produce for themselves. Their faith in this new energy is manifest in the words of the EURATOM Treaty, just as it was in the molecular design of the huge atom which graced the Brussels World Fair in 1958.

During the negotiations of 1956, the proposals for EURATOM won more support from Europeans than those which concerned the Common Market. There was a general anxiety about the use of coal (unpopular because it was dirty and unhealthy) and oil (because its source and price were determined largely by the Arabs). As an alternative to these vulnerable sources of energy, nuclear power promised several advantages. The cost of research and of building power plants could be shared by a number of countries. The Germans would have no need to develop nuclear power on their own: their participation in a cooperative venture would be positive, peaceful and public. Once in operation, EURATOM would advance the cause of supranationalism by giving the Community, rather than the individual states, the responsibility for developing and regulating nuclear energy. Finally, EURATOM was expected to generate a number of distinctly European projects, including scientific research centres and at least one university (Articles 8 and 9). No wonder Monnet and Spaak saw EURATOM as the jewel of Europe's new crown: modern energy meant modern industry and modern organizations and a truly modern (i.e. collective) sense of responsibility.

Dazzled by the brilliant prospects of EURATOM, the supranationalists did not allow for the scepticism and the hostility of old-fashioned nationalists. In May 1958, General de Gaulle returned to power in France. The faction-ridden Fourth Republic (1944–58) gave way to the Fifth Republic and to a new constitution which enhanced the powers of the presidency. De Gaulle understood the political implications of EURATOM, and he did not like them. Almost immediately he decided to restrict the French cooperation with EURATOM. For de Gaulle, EURATOM was the wrong road for a great nation to take, and it was an obstacle to his own plan to give France an independent nuclear energy programme. More important still, de Gaulle hoped to restore France to its former greatness as a world power by providing it with its own nuclear weaponry (the *force de frappe*). As a consequence of his decisions, the French role in EURATOM was very limited, and EURATOM never achieved the importance it was supposed to have. As Spinelli has commented, the 'feverish haste' to research and develop safe, clean nuclear power in western Europe never occurred as a joint effort. The energy of tomorrow became the energy of the day after tomorrow. Even the project of the European University was postponed. Instead of a cluster of research centres, it eventually emerged as a scheme of graduate studies with Italy as the host country.[9]

Although EURATOM never got off the ground, the economic success of the EEC was soon obvious to all. With a total of about 160 million, the Community became the largest trading bloc in the world. 'It was the biggest exporter and buyer of raw materials ... [and] its steel production was second only to that of the United States.'[10] In the ten years from the beginning of the ECSC until 1962, there was a 70 per cent increase in the industrial output of the Six. In the first six years of the EEC, trade among the Six rose by 85 per cent and the total GNP by 33 per cent.[11] The surge in productivity was accompanied by a steady increase of public support. Unexcited by the EEC at its inception and indifferent to the vague notions of political unity, Europeans were soon won over to the programme of economic integration.

Nowhere was there more enthusiasm for the EEC than in Benelux. Since their economic union began in 1948, these three countries were well acquainted with the benefits of integration. Internal trade flourished as never before and industrial production soared. By 1960 the region's standard of living was among the highest in the world. The economy of Benelux saw a remarkable equalization. In 1945 Belgium and Luxembourg were more industrialized than the Netherlands, whose economy was mostly commercial and agricultural: in 1948 the share of industrial employment was 46 per cent in Belgium and 37 per cent in the Netherlands.[12] The Benelux Union made the relatively cheap labour of the Netherlands more attractive to industry and as early as 1953 the level of Dutch manufacturing approached that of Belgium. As the disparities of wealth became less pronounced across the whole of Benelux, the Dutch and Belgian governments became fearless promoters of European integration. At Messina, where the Six member states agreed to the principle of a common market, Benelux representatives urged their colleagues to subject the whole of the economy to the integrating process, rather than just parts of it.

With the headstart of almost a decade, Benelux was confident of the common market's success. Indeed, they had hoped for a somewhat more ambitious Treaty of Rome. Having won recognition in the Treaty as an integrated region, and the permission to advance more quickly if they wished, Benelux wasted no time in taking another step. Even before the Treaty of Rome was signed, Benelux representatives were at work on another treaty which ostensibly applied only to their region but was actually intended to encourage their partners in the EEC as well. This treaty was signed in the Hague early in 1958 (DOCUMENT 17). Its first purpose was to define more explicitly the conditions which identified Benelux as a region. It clarified long-standing goals in economic and social policy formation. It pointed to some of the issues which the EEC would inevitably have to face: the mobility of citizens (Article 2), the fixing of exchange rates and monetary stability (Articles 12 and 13), and the harmonization of social security and welfare benefits (Articles 60 and 70). Many areas, however, were left untouched. There was no hint of a system for common patents, and the attempt to unify contract law did not get very far. Moreover, the Treaty did not suggest a supranational agency for the whole of the Community and it did not even affect the political institutions of Benelux.

The late 1950s were remarkable in contemporary history for the number of attempts to bring European nations together. In the core of western Europe, as we have seen, there was the European Economic Community (the 'Common Market', as it was popularly known for its first two decades); this grouping included the Coal and Steel Community, which continued as a separate organization, and the more tightly knit region of the Benelux Economic union. Seven other states decided against joining the EEC and formed the European Free Trade Association, which in turn embraced yet another region group, the Nordic Council. To the east, countries of the Soviet bloc formed an organization, supposedly inspired by Marxist notions of national development. In very different ways, all these organizations responded to the challenges of postwar reconstruction. It is important to note, however, that they all began as instruments of economic development and not as mechanisms for the political unity of the continent.

After Benelux, the second oldest of these organizations had never wanted political integration. The Nordic Council, formally established in 1953, joined Denmark, Iceland, Norway and Sweden; Finland entered in 1955. The Council has a long prehistory, as it was first proposed as a bloc of neutral states in 1939. The Council built on a large legacy of nineteenth century Scandinavian cooperation, and its achievements in the 1950s included a single labour market, coordination of social security and health policies, relaxed passport controls and a system of transport and communications.

The Treaty signed in Helsinki in March 1962 was an affirmation of Nordic cooperation (DOCUMENT 18). As a résumé of historic and current agreements, the Treaty is often regarded as the basic constitution for a single Nordic state. The paradox of Nordic cooperation is that it does not formally encompass political institutions, even though the word 'Scandinavia' suggests a region whose culture, languages, religion and traditions presumably make it a supranational state.[13] But strong national sentiments and a general concern for state sovereignty have discouraged the political integration of Scandinavia. Notwithstanding the popular support for a common definition of social services, citizenship, working conditions and professional qualifications, the Nordic states are disinclined to share sovereignty. While the cultural homogeneity of this region may impress the outside world, it has not generated political unity.

External pressures have worked against supranationalism in the north. As relatively small states, the Scandinavian countries have always been vulnerable to the machinations of more powerful neighbours. Sweden, the largest of the Nordic states with a population of eight million (less than either Belgium or Portugal), is the only one to have escaped direct involvement in both world wars. Even so, Sweden's foreign policy (and to some extent its commercial connections) have been moulded by the expectations of the great powers. After German occupation during the war, Norway and Denmark tied themselves economically and politically to the West and joined the NATO alliance. Iceland, with a population of only 250,000, was occupied by British and American forces during the war and kept these partners after 1945. Sweden's status as a neutral country continued (at great cost) after 1945; to avoid offending the Soviet Union, Swedish governments carefully avoided close political links with other democratic states. Finland was in the most delicate position of all. The defeated ally of Nazi Germany, Finland paid war reparations to the Soviet Union until 1952; its external and domestic policies were generally designed to please the Soviet government and a large communist party at home.

Because of the value which they placed on national sovereignty and because of the many considerable differences in their domestic and foreign policies, the Nordic Council states were unable to form a single political unit. But they did share with other European states the hope of achieving a higher standard of living and they were not reticent about joining an association which promoted economic cooperation. Their needs were well served by the European Free Trade Association. The internal politics of the EFTA countries made them a curious league. Sweden and Switzerland were unwilling to compromise their status as neutral states. Austria had neutrality imposed upon it: the State Treaty of 1955 permitted the reemergence of Austria as an independent state, but it expressly forbade it to enter any political and economic union with Germany. EFTA included two other Nordic Council countries, Denmark and Norway, which were also members of NATO. Two very different states at opposite ends of Europe also joined EFTA: Portugal, a right-wing dictatorship with a limited role in NATO,[14] and Finland, whose neutrality in world affairs was defined and enforced by Moscow.

The leader of this odd assortment of states was the United Kingdom. With a population larger than that of all the other EFTA countries combined, Britain stood aloof from decision-making on the continent. It declined an invitation to Messina and to the conferences which followed. Britain's attitude was carefree, if not cavalier: it could not believe that its old friends (especially Benelux) would form an association without it. Almost before Britain knew what had happened, the Treaty of Rome and the Euratom Treaty were signed and Britain was on the outside of both. Even then, in the middle of 1957, Britain was not sure she wanted 'to go in'. Its ideal solution was an economic version of the Council of Europe: a large free trade area – the larger the better – an association which embraced virtually all the non-communist states of Europe. This solution meant a safe and very large market for British goods and the preservation of special links with the USA and Commonwealth countries. In effect, Britain saw EFTA as a weapon to force open the EEC and then to persuade the Six to abandon their interest in quasi-federalist schemes.

The desultory contacts which Britain entered with the EEC got nowhere. Even Britain's friends on the continent were embarrassed by its suggestion that they recast the EEC in a different form, renegotiate the Treaty of Rome and establish a huge free trade area in Europe. Britain's attitude outraged President de Gaulle, who brought the contacts to a close in November 1958. The British persisted in the attempt to refashion Europe. They instigated meetings of the 'Outer Seven' in Geneva in December 1958: these led to the conferences of government ministers in 1959 and to the formal recommendation to establish EFTA. In little more than twelve months, EFTA was conceived and rushed into existence: the Stockholm Convention was signed in January 1960.

The text of the Treaty reveals the reasons for EFTA's easy and early birth (DOCUMENT 19). Unlike the Treaty of Rome, the Stockholm Convention did not say much simply because EFTA was not expected to do much. The goal of the association was very limited: to create an international free trade area. EFTA's administrative machinery was modest in scale and traditional in function. A small secretariat was assigned a headquarters in Geneva, which had been the centre of intergovernmental diplomacy in the 1920s and 1930s. Each member state remained free to regulate its trade with countries outside EFTA; unlike the EEC, EFTA did not attempt a common external tariff. The basic difference between the EEC and EFTA was philosophical and involved ideas of what any national government, on its own or in combination with others, was entitled to do. The governments of the Six were ready (and historically disposed) to work together inside a preconceived structure of regulations and expectations; the Seven wanted almost no formal framework, as they attached great importance to the free play of national and regional economies. For this reason, there was never any possibility of the members agreeing to defer to a supranational agency.

All things considered, EFTA was the sort of association which de Gaulle would gladly have helped to build, had he returned to power two or three years earlier than he did. Because it depended entirely on intergovernmental agreements and never promised to do anything as rash as the coordination of monetary policies, EFTA would have been far preferable to de Gaulle than the EEC. But the EEC had developed first, France was in it, and de Gaulle was determined to keep Britain out.

EFTA proved successful largely because of its limited objectives. With few exceptions, the barriers which had formerly discouraged trade were removed by 1967 and commerce between EFTA members expanded considerably. Characteristic of EFTA were bilateral accords such as Britain's agreement to accept more imports of Danish butter and Norwegian fish. Inevitably, however, EFTA saw itself (and was perceived elsewhere in Europe) as a rival to the EEC. The two organizations were very different in their objectives and in the way they functioned, but they were conscious of being in a race to liberalize the internal trade of their respective blocs. They also competed for the support of uncommitted countries. This was a race which EFTA was destined to lose, as Greece, Turkey, Malta and Yugoslavia saw greater value in affiliation with the EEC.[15] In the short term, the two organizations divided non-communist Europe into two unequal halves, and there were times, particularly in the mid-1960s, when this division was keenly felt. On the other hand, no one expected the rivalry to last forever. Most Europeans saw EFTA as a temporary shelter for those countries excluded from the EEC by French policy. The applications of Britain, Norway, Denmark and Ireland to join the EEC in 1961 (and again in 1967) confirmed the general view of EFTA as an expendable feature of European relations.

EFTA could not last for a number of reasons. It was, first of all, too disparate in its membership and too eccentric in its geography: unlike the Six, the Seven did not form a compact geographical unit. The members of EFTA disagreed about their relationship with the EEC. Norway and Switzerland believed that EFTA should avoid intimate political connections with the Common Market, while Denmark and Britain (and Austria, who was reluctant to express it) all knew that their trading relations with the EEC would someday require a merger of the two blocs. Few Europeans ever doubted that the EEC was the more purposeful and dynamic of the two. EFTA never enjoyed a strong *raison d'être*, and it never managed to resolve its internal contradictions. Britain, the instigator and leader of EFTA, caused the most internal disruption when in 1964 it unilaterally imposed a 15 per cent surcharge on EFTA products. Those who believed in European unity and who regretted the division of non-communist Europe into two trading blocs were also exasperated by EFTA. In their opinion, the subdivision of Europe was beneficial only to the Soviet Union and they welcomed every sign of EFTA's impermanence.

While western Europeans were always apprehensive about the military prowess and the aggressive diplomacy of the Soviet Union, they had less to fear from the economic development of the Soviet bloc. In fact, it was the Soviets who worried that the economic integration of western Europe might prove too distracting to those states which were now in the Soviet sphere. At first Moscow hoped that the large communist parties of Italy and France might prevent, or at least postpone, each step which those two countries took on the road to European unity, but it was soon clear that the tactics of opposition by proxy would not succeed. Faced by the accelerating pace of moves to unity in the west, the Soviet Union sponsored its own organization as the framework for the economic coordination of Soviet bloc countries. Such was the purpose of the Council for Mutual Economic Assistance (CMEA), established in 1949 as the Soviet answer to the OEEC.

The CMEA served as a clearing house for economic information and expertise, and as an agency to encourage the sharing of raw materials, foodstuffs, machinery and equipment. The official reasons behind CMEA certainly appeared timely and generous in the early 1950s but they depended on an abundance which did not actually exist. The meagre supply of material goods could not generate much trade, nor did it ever allow for much 'fraternal aid'. There were no agricultural surpluses to sell or give away to other communist states. The road and rail systems did not cater to a community of consumers. Worst of all handicaps was the chronic lack of capital, which stunted the economic growth of all the CMEA states.

Political factors also retarded economic growth. For the leaders of the new communist regimes of central and eastern Europe, the postwar challenge was to create, rather than to rebuild: their goal was a political and social structure which bore little resemblance to that which existed before the war. But they knew that their resources were very limited and that they could accomplish little on their own. For a short time after the war, they were ready to cooperate with other states, even if that meant redefining the concept of state sovereignty. They were willing to imitate some of the unfolding experiments in the west. In December 1946, for example, Albania and Yugoslavia announced plans to establish a customs union and currency union; in January 1948 the Bulgarian leadership proposed a similar arrangement with Yugoslavia. It appeared that a federation of Balkan states was under way. Why did it not become the Balkan version of Benelux?

The opportunity was cut short. Economically, it is true, there was nothing to build on: the countries of south-east Europe did not boast anything comparable to the Benelux system of transport, communications, intensive agriculture and industrial development. Nor were the Balkan regimes likely to attract the capital which they desperately needed. The real obstacle, however, was political. The proposed federation was not to the liking of Marshal Stalin. He warned his Balkan comrades against making political commitments and entering interstate relation-ships which 'exceeded the interests of the Soviet government.'[16] His advice was intended primarily for the Yugoslav leader, Josef Tito, who had rather different ideas about the political latitude which socialist states might enjoy. Tito's political quarrel with Stalin early in 1948 led to Yugoslavia's excommunication as a 'renegade socialist state'. Yugoslavia then sought a happier relationship with western Europe, while the Soviet satellites became ever more attentive to Moscow. Political heresy in Yugoslavia therefore led to tighter Soviet control of other countries in the east, including Czechoslovakia. After 1948, the communist leaders of eastern Europe knew better than to indulge in wayward speculation about federations, customs unions and regional groupings.

Political stasis then overtook the Soviet satellites. The functions and institutions of the state were invested with an almost religious reverence. When they embarked on their ruthless policies of state-building, the communist governments did so in relatively new countries. The independence of Bulgaria and Rumania had taken place during the second half of the nineteenth century: the events had just receded from living memory. Poland and Czechoslovakia had appeared as recently as 1918, and the DDR emerged only in 1949. The boundaries of these countries were sacred as the visible definition of new geographical and political (communist) entities. Garnished with electric fences and border police, they were the first line of defence against the contagion of counter-revolution, such as the rebellions which convulsed Poland and Hungary in 1956. Given their obsession with political security and with the unchanging integrity of the state, the countries of the CMEA were unlikely to participate in any truly supranational experiment. Moreover, the stubborn and doleful realities of Soviet power in eastern Europe made anything like Benelux and the Nordic Council inconceivable.

Apart from the presence of Soviet troops and the loan of Russian military officers to the national armies, the best expression of Soviet power in eastern Europe was the Council for Mutual Economic Assistance (or COMECON, as it was known after 1960). Unlike the Schuman announcement of 1950, which promised 'federation' in Europe, COMECON's Charter of 1959 looked for 'unity and the co-ordination' of economic activity (DOCUMENT 20). The Charter repeatedly upheld the sovereignty and national interests of the member states. It recognized their equality in the organization and it even allowed for their withdrawal (only Albania did so, in 1961). The general purpose of COMECON was to encourage the exchange of services, resources and 'mutual aid'. COME-CON had almost no public persona. In its first five years, the Council met only once; its constitution (the Charter) was composed and signed only in 1959 and there was always much secrecy about its operation.[17] The directors of the Council were proud members of an international fraternity. Many of them had known one another since the war years, which they spent in Moscow. Now, as government ministers and bureaucrats in six satellite states, they presided over the meagre fortunes of a large part of Europe.

According to its Charter, COMECON set out to improve the economies of this portion of Europe through the 'international socialist division of labour'. Theoretically this principle recognized the historic strengths of each national economy. What each country had done well in the past, it was to continue doing well for the benefit of the international socialist community. At the same time, no one wanted to believe that specialization – the emphasis on traditional products – was enough. All the new communist governments esteemed heavy industry as the mark of a truly modern state. They were eager to imitate the development of industry along Russian lines, even if this were achieved at great cost to the environment – as it certainly was, in Poland, Slovakia and the DDR. The new regimes wanted both specialization (traditional products with a relatively secure market) and heavy industry (products new to their economies, in manufacture or in volume). They wanted a much wider variety of production, even if they lacked the raw materials and the capital to support it.

In almost all states, the result was severe and prolonged economic dislocation.[18] Agriculture suffered most. Poland, Hungary and Rumania, historically known for their relatively successful agriculture, now endured chronic shortages of foodstuffs. The equalization of living standards, promised by COMECON, never occurred. Czechoslovakia and eastern Germany remained richer than Hungary and Poland, who, in their turn, remained better off than Rumania and Bulgaria. All these states claimed that they had preserved every bit of their sovereignty because it was they (and not a High Authority) who were supposed to implement the recommendations of COMECON 'in conformity with their laws'. In reality, their attention to heavy industry (not always condoned by the Soviet Union) made them increasingly dependent on Russian technology and oil.

In 1962 the principles of COMECON were further defined by an article in *Pravda* (DOCUMENT 21). The article apparently represented the views of economists and 'workers' representatives', who regarded the socialist states as an 'economic and political commonwealth'. They praised COMECON for its support of economic coordination and they recognized the importance of the extractive industries. But they stopped short of proposing a formally instituted agency (such as the ECSC's High Authority) to coordinate the supply of certain minerals. It is interesting that the *Pravda* report eschewed empirical information. COMECON (or CMEA) had by now existed for more than a decade, but it was still difficult to assess publicly its performance in statistical terms. Instead, *Pravda* stressed COMECON's basic assumption, the international socialist division of labour. *Pravda* defined this principle as 'rational interstate specialization'. Upon it depended almost everything: full employment, high living standards, the process of economic decision-making and the self-respect of the member states of the communist commonwealth. Indeed, it was the Soviet government's view that without the international socialist division of labour (specialization in the national economies), there could be no communist commonwealth. Any state which did not abide by this basic principle risked losing its place in the 'historical epoch' which brought true communism to all the others.

Moscow's economic prescriptions were not always taken to heart. The rhetoric of national sovereignty, present in every treaty and audible in almost every official speech, had a much greater impact on the thinking of east European leaders. While they admired Russia as an industrial world power, they were often tempted to think that they were the better judges of their countries' economic potential. The result of these temptations was a lack of cohesion within the bloc. Bulgaria and the DDR remained the Soviet Union's most deferential apprentices, while other countries became increasingly vocal in their criticism of price structures and other guidelines decided in Moscow. The boldest mavericks were Rumania and Albania: determined to develop their own heavy industry, they rejected Russian advice to concentrate on other things. In fact, most of the COMECON states hoped, at one time or another, to gain the organization's support for projects which Moscow disapproved. There was always at least one member of COMECON whose procrastination or critical arguments undermined the USSR's direction of the bloc.

By the mid-1960s, Rumania led the way as the most intractable member of the group. While Bucharest denounced COMECON as an economic dictatorship, other countries held their breath, believing it only a matter of time before Soviet armies put an end to Rumania's complaints. But Rumania survived and contacts with the west multiplied. In practice, COMECON was a dead letter as early as 1970, because Poland, Hungary and Czechoslovakia also managed to ignore Soviet warnings and circumvent Soviet regulations. In little more than a decade, from 1958 to 1970, the imports and exports of all COMECON states with the EEC more than doubled; in the case of Poland and Hungary, trade was almost three times greater.[19]

Had they enjoyed more latitude in foreign and economic policy, the satellite states would probably have sought an accommodation with the Common Market even sooner than they did. For its part, the Soviet Union was for many years deeply suspicious, if not antagonistic, towards both the ECSC and the Common Market. As the guardian of communist orthodoxy, Russia denounced the EEC as 'a conspiracy of international monopolists' and forbade the satellite governments from having anything to do with it. As far as the Soviet Union was concerned, integration in western Europe was a sham and a nonsense; the word 'integration' invariably appeared in inverted commas and was pronounced with sneers. But as a new and curious phenomenon in the history of capitalism, integration was not easily ignored, and Marxists were compelled to explain what was going on in the west. One of the most comprehensive of these analyses appeared in *Pravda* in August 1962 (DOCUMENT 22).

The *Theses on Imperialist Integration* actually date from 1957, when the Institute for World Economy and International Relations commented on the Treaty of Rome. Their assessment was filled with ideological pitfalls. They had to explain how the great 'monopolies and trusts' in the west could abandon decades of vicious rivalry in favour of a coordinated economy; they also had to explain why communist states should worry about a scheme so unnatural to capitalist Europe that it could not possibly last. Part of their answer depended on the 'class unity' of the 'financial oligarchy' in the west and the dangerous overflow of surplus capital. However the explanation was expressed in *Pravda* (and elsewhere), criticism of integration always bore an element of irony. Marxists condemned the west for allegedly promoting 'international specialization' while the Soviet Union was urging its economic partners to adopt policies of 'rational interstate special-ization'.

The ideological attacks on western integration masked real anxieties. Although it was not always apparent, trade between the two halves of Europe slowly increased in the late 1950s and early 1960s. More flexible Soviet policies under Khrushchev meant a growing reliance on the west for credit and the supply of a limited range of commodities. Some of this trade was initiated by COMECON states acting as proxies for the Soviet Union, which was too embarrassed to indulge openly in such contacts. The rising importance of these exchanges raised difficult questions. What would happen to this limited but valuable trade if the EEC managed to impose common external tariffs? Would it not become harder for the Soviet Union to play off one western trading partner against another, when six (or more) of them adopted common policies on trade and credit?

The political dangers seemed even greater. According to Soviet commentators, the political goal of western integration was to produce an ever-stronger bloc of states dominated by reactionary governments. The Soviets never understood the new political psychology in western Europe: that six (and possibly more) states should be willing to accept international treaties and conventions as an integral part of their national legal codes was an unwanted puzzle in the development of the bourgeois democracies. The Marxist critique of western integration would not allow for the fact that bourgeois states might be so genuinely alarmed by the wastefulness of war that they could now 'cut off a whole dimension of destructive expectations in the minds of policy-makers.'[20] Inevitably there was also confusion about the nature of political unity in the west, partly because the EEC was so far from becoming a federation and partly because the USSR's experience of federation was so very different. There was, however, one great certainty in the Soviet analysis. The expansion of the EEC was something to be feared, as it would eventually bring more of Europe (including, perhaps, some neutral states) into a community which challenged the status quo of European politics. Such a development would only undermine the political stability of relatively new communist regimes.

The leading culprit of this anti-communist league was, of course, the Federal Republic of Germany. The accusations of the Soviet press and the warnings of Soviet leaders were continuous and unchanging: Germany was determined to dominate the Common Market politically and economically, and to equip a huge new army with nuclear weapons. Having created this criminal combination of political, economic and military power, Germany would then be able to reverse the verdict of war and establish a hegemony in Europe. Nor did the process end there. The Soviets perceived a scheme to extend the Common Market's influence beyond Europe by reviving many of the old colonial connections under a different guise. This much of the Soviet analysis was certainly plausible. Schuman's declaration in 1950 invited other European countries to share France's civilizing mission in Africa, and in 1957 France was so anxious to preserve its influence in Africa that it insisted on special trading arrangements for African states and colonies as a condition of signing the Treaty of Rome. It made no difference to the Soviet argument that France's partners were either indifferent or hostile (as Germany and the Netherlands were) to granting African states associate membership in the EEC, nor did the Soviets admit that this issue caused much debate among the Six. Instead, it was the Soviet strategy to exaggerate the political cohesion of the EEC in order to portray it as a new leviathan dangerous to the sovereignty of states on two continents.

Uncompromising at first, Soviet hostility to European integration later gave way to a more positive attitude. By 1968 the EEC had ceased to be an 'imperialist plot' and the Soviet press rarely bothered to identify the 'internal contradictions' of the Common Market. How do we account for the moderation? The rapidly expanding commerce between the EEC and several of the Soviet satellites was certainly a factor, particularly as there was little the Soviet Union could do to prevent this trade. Pressure on Moscow from the Italian communist party (which discerned much good in the Common Market) may have helped.[21] More basic perhaps was the Soviet government's conclusion that the Common Market was not going to collapse after all, but represented a significant and permanent expression of European cooperation. Whatever the reasons, a more pragmatic view gained ground among the member states of COMECON. By the late 1960s the Common Market was regarded as an 'economic reality' which COMECON could ill afford to ignore. Paradoxically, the same years which saw the revision of Marxist views witnessed a contest among the Six which apparently justified the earlier scepticism of Soviet critiques. The old rivalries of nations and the 'internal contradictions' of the Common Market threatened not only its expansion but its survival as a community of free and peaceful states.

ENDNOTES

1 The 'nationalists' ranged from Churchill, a conservative, to André Philip, a socialist who supported de Gaulle during the war.

2 Derek Urwin: *Western Europe since 1945: A Political History* (4th edn., London: Longman, 1989) p. 128.

3 Escott Reid: *Time of Fear and Hope* (Toronto: McClelland and Stewart, 1977), p. 39.

4 Paul-Henri Spaak: *The Continuing Battle: Memoirs of a European, 1936–1966* (trans. Henry Fox) (London: Weidenfeld and Nicolson, 1971) p. 228.

5 *Ibid.*, pp. 230–1.

6 *Ibid.*, p. 238.

7 John Pinder: *European Community: The Building of a Union* (Oxford: Oxford University Press, 1992), p. 114.

8 Peter Lane: *The Postwar World: An Introduction* (Chicago: Dorsey Press, 1987), p. 65.

9 Altiero Spinelli: *The Eurocrats: Conflict and Crisis in the European Community* (trans. C. G. Haines) (Baltimore: John Hopkins, 1966), pp. 44–5.

10 Walter Laqueur: *Europe in our Time* (London: Viking Penguin, 1992), p. 121.

11 E. Etzioni: *Political Unification* (New York: Holt, Rinehart and Winston, 1965), p. 231.

12 Willy van Rijekeghem: 'Benelux', in *The European Economy: Growth and Crisis* (ed. Andrea Boltho) (Oxford: Oxford University Press, 1982), p. 583.

13 Etzioni (1965), *Political Unification*, p. 231.

14 During the 1960s and early 1970s, Portugal's military efforts were devoted almost exclusively to the suppression of popular revolts in Angola and Mozambique. Portugal's importance to NATO (and particularly to the Americans) involved the use of the Azores Islands in the mid-Atlantic.

15 Greece gained associate status with the EEC in 1962 and Turkey in 1963; Yugoslavia and Malta signed special agreements in 1970.

16 Wilfried Loth, referring to Milivan Djilas, in *The Division of the World, 1941–55* (London: Routledge, 1988), p. 168.

17 Peter van Ham: *The European Community, Eastern Europe and European Unity: Discord, Collaboration and Integration since 1947* (London: Pinter, 1993), p. 36.

18 Arguably, the DDR and Czechoslovakia suffered less than the other new communist regimes of eastern Europe.

19 Van Ham (1993), p. 62. The figures are given in millions of ECU.

20 François Duchene, *Jean Monnet, the First Statesman of Interdependence* (Norton: New York and London: 1994) p. 405.

21 Van Ham (1993), p. 64.

ADDITIONAL READINGS

R. Aron and D. Lerner (eds): *France Defeats EDC* (London: Praeger, 1957).

B. Balassa: *The Theory of Economic Integration* (Illinois: Irwin Press, 1961).

M. Beloff: *The United States and the Unity of Europe* (London: Vintage, 1963).

E. Benoit: *Europe at Sixes and Sevens* (New York: Columbia University Press, 1961).

M. Bromberger: *Jean Monnet and the United States of Europe* (New York: Coward-McCann, 1969).

M. Camps: *Britain and the European Community, 1955–1963* (Princeton: Princeton University Press, 1964).

D. Coombes: *Politics and Bureaucracy in the European Communities* (London: Allen and Unwin, 1970).

V. Curzon: *The Essentials of Economic Integration: Lessons of EFTA Experience* (London: St Martins, 1974).

E. B. Haas: *Beyond the Nation State* (Stanford: Stanford University Press, 1964).

V. D. Hurd: *The Council of Europe* (New York: Manhattan Publishing, 1958).

U. Kitzinger: *The Politics and Economics of European Economic Integration: Britain, Europe and the United States* (New York: Praeger, 1963).

L. Lindberg: *The Political Dynamics of Economic Integration* (Stanford: Stanford University Press, 1963).

L. Lister: *Europe's Coal and Steel Community* (New York: Twentieth Century Fund, 1960).

R. Mayne: *The Community of Europe: Past, Present and Future* (New York: Norton, 1962).

—— : *The Recovery of Europe: From Devastation to Unity* (London: Weidenfeld and Nicolson, 1970).

F. V. Meyer: *The Seven* (London: Barrie and Rockliff, 1960).

T. Miljan: *The Reluctant Europeans* (Montreal: McGill-Queens University Press, 1977).

J. Pinder: *Europe Against De Gaulle* (London: Pall Mall Press, 1963).

—— : 'The case for economic integration', *Journal of Common Market Studies*, 3 (1964/65), pp. 246–59.

E. Solem: *The Nordic Council and Scandinavian Integration* (New York: Praeger, 1977).

F. R. Willis: *France, Germany and the New Europe 1945–1967* (Oxford: Oxford University Press, 1969).

MESSINA COMMUNIQUÉ

Building on the success of the Coal and Steel Community and aided by the leadership of Paul-Henri Spaak, representatives of the six member states of the ECSC met in Messina in June 1955. The communiqué of their conference appeared in *Le Monde* on 4 June 1955.

The governments of the Federal Republic of Germany, Belgium, France, Italy, Luxembourg and the Netherlands believe the time has come to take a new step on the road of European construction. They are of the opinion that this objective should be achieved first of all in the economic sphere.

They believe that the establishment of a united Europe must be achieved through the development of common institutions, the progressive fusion of national economies, the creation of a common market, and the gradual harmonization of their social policies.

Such an agenda seems indispensable to them if Europe is to preserve the standing which she has in the world, to restore her influence and her prestige, and to improve steadily the living standard of her population.

To these ends, the six ministers have agreed on the following objectives:

1. The growth of trade and the migration of the population require the joint development of the main channels of communication. To this end, a joint study will be undertaken of development plans oriented to establishing a European network of canals, motorways, electric rail lines, and for a standardization of equipment, as well as research for a better co-ordination of air-transport.
2. Putting more abundant energy at a cheaper price at the disposal of the European economies constitutes a fundamental element of economic progress. That is why all arrangements should be made to develop sufficient exchanges of gas and electric power capable of increasing the profitability of investments and reducing the supply costs. Studies will be undertaken of methods to co-ordinate development prospects for the production and consumption of energy, and to draw up general guidelines for an overall policy.
3. The development of atomic energy for peaceful purposes will very soon open up the prospect of a new industrial revolution beyond comparison with that of the last hundred years. The signatory states believe they must study the creation of a joint organization to which will be assigned the responsibility and the means to secure the peaceful development of atomic energy while taking into consideration the special commitments of certain governments with third parties.
These means should include:
(a) The establishment of a common fund supported by the contribution of each of the participating countries, and allowing for the financing of power plants and for current or future energy research;

(b) Free and adequate access to raw materials, the free exchange of information, by-products and special equipment, and the mobility of technicians;

(c) Making available any benefits and financial subsidies without discrimination, towards the development of energy sources;

(d) Co-operation with non-member states.

THE OBJECTIVE OF THE 'COMMON MARKET'

The six governments acknowledge that the constitution of a European Common Market free of internal duties and all quantitative restrictions is the goal of their action in the realm of economic policy. They believe that this market should be achieved in stages. The realization of this objective requires study of the following questions:

(a) The procedure and the pace of the gradual suppression of obstacles to trade in relations between the participating countries, as well as appropriate steps leading to the gradual standardization of tariffs applying to non-member states;

(b) The measures to be taken in order to harmonize general policy of the participating states in the financial, economic and social fields;

(c) The adoption of practical steps to insure an adequate co-ordination of monetary policies of the member-states, in order to allow for the creation and development of a common market;

(d) A system of escape clauses;

(e) The creation and operation of a currency re-adaptation fund;

(f) The gradual introduction of free circulation of labour;

(g) The development of rules assuring the free play of competition within the common market, particularly in such a way as to exclude all preferences of a national basis;

(h) The institutional agencies appropriate for the realization and operating of the common market.

The creation of a European investment fund will be studied. This fund should have as its object the joint development of European economic projects, and especially the development of the less favoured regions of the participating states.

As for the social field, the six governments believe it essential to study the progressive harmonization of regulations now in force in the different states, particularly those relating to the length of the work-day, and payment of additional benefits (overtime work, Sunday and holiday work, the length of vacations and vacation allowances).

The six governments have decided to adopt the following procedure:

1. Conferences will be called to work on the treaties or the conventions dealing with the matters under consideration;

2. The preparation of these reports and treaties will be entrusted to a committee of government representatives, assisted by experts, under the chairmanship of a political personality charged with co-ordinating the various tasks;

3. The committee will consult with the High Authority of the European Coal and Steel Community, and as well with the general secretariats of the Council of Europe and the European Committee of Transport Ministers, on necessary co-operation;

4. The full report of the committee will be submitted to the Ministers of Foreign Affairs by 1 October 1955 at the latest;

5. The Ministers of Foreign Affairs will meet again before this date in order to review the interim reports prepared by the committee and to give it any necessary instructions;

6. The government of the United Kingdom ... will be invited to take part in these sessions;

7. The Ministers of Foreign Affairs will decide at an agreed time on the invitations to send eventually to other states to take part in this conference or in any others forecast in the first paragraph.

—————————————————— 15 ——————————————————

TREATY OF ROME

Signed on 25 March 1957, the Treaty of Rome was immediately recognized as the basic document of European integration. The following version does not include those amendments necessitated by the accession of member states after 1957. Editions of the Treaty of Rome which incorporate amendments since 1957 can be found in: J. A. S. Grenville, *The Major International Treaties, 1914–1973. A History and Guide with Texts* (New York: Stein and Day, 1974) and J. A. S. Grenville and Bernard Wasserstein, *The Major International Treaties since 1945* (London: Methuen, 1987).

PART ONE

PRINCIPLES

Article 1

By this Treaty, the High Contracting Parties establish among themselves a EUROPEAN ECONOMIC COMMUNITY.

Article 2

The Community shall have as its task, by establishing a common market and progressively approximating the economic policies of Member States, to promote throughout the Community a harmonious development of economic activities, a continuous and balanced expansion, an increase in stability, an accelerated raising of the standard of living and closer relations between the States belonging to it.

Article 3

For the purposes set out in Article 2, the activities of the Community shall include, as provided in this Treaty and in accordance with the timetable set out therein:

(a) the elimination, as between Member States, of customs duties and of quantitative restrictions on the import and export of goods, and of all other measures having equivalent effect;

(b) the establishment of a common customs tariff and of a common commercial policy towards third countries;

(c) the abolition, as between Member States, of obstacles to freedom of movement for persons, services and capital;

(d) the adoption of a common policy in the sphere of agriculture;

(e) the adoption of a common policy in the sphere of transport;

(f) the institution of a system ensuring that competition in the common market is not distorted;

(g) the application of procedures by which the economic policies of Member States can be coordinated and disequilibria in their balances of payments remedied;

(h) the approximation of the laws of Member States to the extent required for the proper functioning of the common market;

(i) the creation of a European Social Fund in order to improve employment opportunities for workers and to contribute to the raising of their standard of living;

(j) the establishment of a European Investment Bank to facilitate the economic expansion of the Community by opening up fresh resources;

(k) the association of the overseas countries and territories in order to increase trade and to promote jointly economic and social development.

Article 4

1. The tasks entrusted to the Community shall be carried out by the following institutions: an ASSEMBLY, a COUNCIL, a COMMISSION, a COURT OF JUSTICE. [...]

Article 5

Member States shall take all appropriate measures, whether general or particular, to ensure fulfilment of the obligations arising out of this Treaty or resulting from action taken by the institutions of the Community. They shall facilitate the achievement of the Community's tasks.

They shall abstain from any measure which could jeopardise the attainment of the objectives of this Treaty.

Article 6

1. Member States shall, in close cooperation with the institutions of the Community, coordinate their respective economic policies to the extent necessary to attain the objectives of this Treaty.
2. The institutions of the Community shall take care not to prejudice the internal and external financial stability of the Member States.

Article 7

Within the scope of application of this Treaty, and without prejudice to any special provisions contained therein, any discrimination on grounds of nationality shall be prohibited.

The Council may, on a proposal from the Commission and after consulting the Assembly, adopt, by a qualified majority, rules designed to prohibit such discrimination.

Article 8

1. The common market shall be progressively established during a transitional period of twelve years [divided into three stages, each of four years]. [...]

PART TWO

FOUNDATIONS OF THE COMMUNITY

TITLE I

FREE MOVEMENT OF GOODS

Article 9

1. The Community shall be based upon a customs union which shall cover all trade in goods and which shall involve the prohibition between Member States of customs duties on imports and exports and of all charges having equivalent effect, and the adoption of a common customs tariff in their relations with third countries. [...]

Article 10

1. Products coming from a third country shall be considered to be in free circulation in a Member State if the import formalities have been complied with and any customs duties or charges having equivalent effect which are payable have been levied in that Member State, and if they have not benefited from a total or partial drawback of such duties or charges.
2. [...] Before the end of the first year after the entry into force of this Treaty, the Commission shall lay down the provisions applicable, as regards trade between Member States, to goods originating in another Member State in whose

manufacture products have been used on which the exporting Member State has not levied the appropriate customs duties or charges having equivalent effect, or which have benefited from a total or partial drawback of such duties or charges.

CHAPTER 1

THE CUSTOMS UNION

SECTION 1

ELIMINATION OF CUSTOMS DUTIES BETWEEN MEMBER STATES

Article 12

Member States shall refrain from introducing between themselves any new customs duties on imports or exports or any charges having equivalent effect, and from increasing those which they already apply in their trade with each other.

[**Article 13** provides for the progressive abolition of customs duties on imports between Member States.]

Article 13

1. Customs duties on imports in force between Member States shall be progressively abolished by them during the transitional period in accordance with Articles 14 and 15. [...]

[**Articles 14 and 15** provide a timetable for the reduction of duties.]

Article 15

1. Irrespective of the provisions of Article 14, any Member State may, in the course of the transitional period, suspend in whole or in part the collection of duties applied by it to products imported from other Member States. It shall inform the other Member States and the Commission thereof. [...]

Article 16

Member States shall abolish between themselves customs duties on exports and charges having equivalent effect by the end of the first stage at the latest. [...]

SETTING UP OF THE COMMON CUSTOMS TARIFF

Article 18

The Member States declare their readiness to contribute to the development of international trade and the lowering of barriers to trade by entering into agreements designed, on a basis of reciprocity and mutual advantage, to reduce customs duties below the general level of which they could avail themselves as a result of the establishment of a customs union between them.

Article 19

1. Subject to the conditions and within the limits provided for hereinafter, duties in the common customs tariff shall be at the level of the arithmetical average of the duties applied in the four customs territories comprised in the Community.
2. The duties taken as the basis for calculating this average shall be those applied by Member States on 1 January 1957. [...]

> [Articles 19–28: These determine the external trade barrier
> between the Common Market and the rest of the world – the
> Common External Tariff. The articles also establish detailed
> provisions of the tariffs.]

Article 29

In carrying out the tasks entrusted to it under this Section the Commission shall be guided by:

(a) the need to promote trade between Member States and third countries;
(b) developments in conditions of competition within the Community in so far as they lead to an improvement in the competitive capacity of undertakings;
(c) the requirements of the Community as regards the supply of raw materials and semi-finished goods; in this connection the Commission shall take care to avoid distorting conditions of competition between Member States in respect of finished goods;
(d) the need to avoid serious disturbances in the economies of Member States and to ensure rational development of production and an expansion of consumption within the Community.

CHAPTER 2

ELIMINATION OF QUANTITATIVE RESTRICTIONS BETWEEN MEMBER STATES

Article 30

Quantitative restrictions on imports and all measures having equivalent effect shall, without prejudice to the following provisions, be prohibited between Member States.

Article 31

Member States shall refrain from introducing between themselves any new quantitative restrictions or measures having equivalent effect. [...]

Article 32

In their trade with one another Member States shall refrain from making more restrictive the quotas and measures having equivalent effect existing at the date of the entry into force of this Treaty.

These quotas shall be abolished by the end of the transitional period at the latest. During that period, they shall be progressively abolished in accordance with the following provisions [...]

[**Articles 33 and 34** establish the nature and timing of the quotas.]

Article 35

The Member States declare their readiness to abolish quantitative restrictions on imports from and exports to other Member States more rapidly than is provided for in the preceding Articles, if their general economic situation and the situation of the economic sector concerned so permit. [...]

Article 36

The provisions of Articles 30 to 34 shall not preclude prohibitions or restrictions on imports, exports or goods in transit justified on grounds of public morality, public policy or public security; the protection of health and life of humans, animals or plants; the protection of national treasures possessing artistic, historic or archaeological value; or the protection of industrial and commercial property. Such prohibitions or restrictions shall not, however, constitute a means of arbitrary discrimination or a disguised restriction on trade between Member States.

Article 37

1. Member States shall progressively adjust any State monopolies of a commercial character so as to ensure that when the transitional period has ended no discrimination regarding the conditions under which goods are procured and marketed exists between nationals of Member States.

   The provisions of this Article shall apply to any body through which a Member State, in law or in fact, either directly or indirectly supervises, determines or appreciably influences imports or exports between Member States. These provisions shall likewise apply to monopolies delegated by the State to others.

2. Member States shall refrain from introducing any new measure which is contrary to the principles laid down in paragraph 1 or which restricts the scope of the Articles dealing with the abolition of customs duties and quantitative restrictions between Member States. [...]

TITLE II

AGRICULTURE

Article 38

1. The common market shall extend to agriculture and trade in agricultural products. 'Agricultural products' means the products of the soil, of stock-farming and of fisheries and products of first-stage processing directly related to these products. [...]

4. The operation and development of the common market for agricultural products must be accompanied by the establishment of a common agricultural policy among the Member States.

Article 39

1. The objectives of the common agricultural policy shall be:
   (a) to increase agricultural productivity by promoting technical progress and by ensuring the rational development of agricultural production and the optimum utilisation of the factors of production, in particular labour;
   (b) thus to ensure a fair standard of living for the agricultural community, in particular by increasing the individual earnings of persons engaged in agriculture;
   (c) to stabilise markets;
   (d) to assure the availability of supplies;
   (e) to ensure that supplies reach consumers at reasonable prices.
2. In working out the common agricultural policy and the special methods for its application, account shall be taken of:
   (a) the particular nature of agricultural activity, which results from the social structure of agriculture and from structural and natural disparities between the various agricultural regions;
   (b) the need to effect the appropriate adjustments by degrees;
   (c) the fact that in the Member States agriculture constitutes a sector closely linked with the economy as a whole.

Article 40

1. Member States shall develop the common agricultural policy by degrees during the transitional period and shall bring it into force by the end of that period at

the latest. [Depending on the product concerned, this organization will involve: (a) common rules on competition, (b) compulsory coordination of the various national market organisations, and (c) a European market organisation.]

Article 41

To enable the objectives set out in Article 39 to be attained, provision may be made within the framework of the common agricultural policy for measures such as:

(a) an effective coordination of efforts in the spheres of vocational training, of research and of the dissemination of agricultural knowledge; this may include joint financing of projects or institutions;
(b) joint measures to promote consumption of certain products. [...]

[**Article 42** authorises the Council to grant aid for the protection of enterprises handicapped by structural or natural conditions.]

Article 43

1. In order to evolve the broad lines of a common agricultural policy, the Commission shall, immediately this Treaty enters into force, convene a conference of the Member States with a view to making a comparison of their agricultural policies, in particular by producing a statement of their resources and needs. [...]

Article 44

3. As soon as this Treaty enters into force the Council shall, on a proposal from the Commission, determine objective criteria for the establishment of minimum price systems and for the fixing of such prices.
These criteria shall in particular take account of the average national production costs in the Member State applying the minimum price, of the position of the various undertakings concerned in relation to such average production costs, and of the need to promote both the progressive improvement of agricultural practice and the adjustments and specialisation needed within the common market. [...]

TITLE III

FREE MOVEMENT OF PERSONS, SERVICES AND CAPITAL

CHAPTER 1

WORKERS

Article 48

1. Freedom of movement for workers shall be secured within the Community by the end of the transitional period at the latest.

2. Such freedom of movement shall entail the abolition of any discrimination based on nationality between workers of the Member States as regards employment, remuneration and other conditions of work and employment.
3. It shall entail the right, subject to limitations justified on grounds of public policy, public security or public health;
   (a) to accept offers of employment actually made;
   (b) to move freely within the territory of Member States for this purpose;
   (c) to stay in a Member State for the purpose of employment in accordance with the provisions governing the employment of nationals of that State laid down by law, regulation or administrative action;
   (d) to remain in the territory of a Member State after having been employed in that State, subject to conditions which shall be embodied in implementing regulations to be drawn up by the Commission.
4. The provisions of this Article shall not apply to employment in the public service.

Article 49

As soon as this Treaty enters into force, the Council shall, acting on a proposal from the Commission and after consulting the Economic and Social Committee, issue directives or make regulations setting out the measures required to bring about, by progressive stages, freedom of movement for workers, as defined in Article 48, in particular:

(a) by ensuring close cooperation between national employment services;
(b) by systematically and progressively abolishing those administrative procedures and practices and those qualifying periods in respect of eligibility for available employment, whether resulting from national legislation or from agreements previously concluded between Member States, the maintenance of which would form an obstacle to liberalisation of the movement of workers;
(c) by systematically and progressively abolishing all such qualifying periods and other restrictions provided for either under national legislation or under agreements previously concluded between Member States as imposed on workers of other Member States conditions regarding the free choice of employment other than those imposed on workers of the State concerned;
(d) by setting up appropriate machinery to bring offers of employment into touch with applications for employment and to facilitate the achievement of a balance between supply and demand in the employment market in such a way as to avoid serious threats to the standard of living and level of employment in the various regions and industries.

Article 50

Member States shall, within the framework of a joint programme, encourage the exchange of young workers.

Article 51

The Council shall, acting unanimously on a proposal from the Commission, adopt such measures in the field of social security as are necessary to provide freedom of movement for workers; to this end, it shall make arrangements to secure for migrant workers and their dependants:

(a) aggregation, for the purpose of acquiring and retaining the right to benefit and of calculating the amount of benefit, of all periods taken into account under the laws of the several countries;
(b) payment of benefits to persons resident in the territories of Member States.

CHAPTER 2

RIGHT OF ESTABLISHMENT

Article 52

Within the framework of the provisions set out below, restrictions on the freedom of establishment of nationals of a Member State in the territory of another Member State shall be abolished by progressive stages in the course of the transitional period. Such progressive abolition shall also apply to restrictions on the setting up of agencies, branches or subsidiaries by nationals of any Member State established in the territory of any Member State.

Freedom of establishment shall include the right to take up and pursue activities as self-employed persons and to set up and manage undertakings ... under the conditions laid down for its own nationals by the law of the country where such establishment is effected, subject to the provisions of the Chapter relating to capital.

Article 53

Member States shall not introduce any new restrictions on the right of establishment in their territories of nationals of other Member States, save as otherwise provided in this Treaty. [...]

[**Articles 54, 55 and 56** establish procedures for implementation.]

Article 57

1. In order to make it easier for persons to take up and pursue activities as self-employed persons, the Council shall, on a proposal from the Commission and after consulting the Assembly, acting unanimously during the first stage and by a qualified majority thereafter, issue directives for the mutual recognition of diplomas, certificates and other evidence of formal qualifications. [...]

Article 58

Companies or firms formed in accordance with the law of a Member State and having their registered office, central administration or principal place of business within the Community shall, for the purposes of this Chapter, be treated in the same way as natural persons who are nationals of Member States.

CHAPTER 3

SERVICES

Article 59

Within the framework of the provisions set out below, restrictions on freedom to provide services within the Community shall be progressively abolished during the transitional period in respect of nationals of Member States who are established in a State of the Community other than that of the person for whom the services are intended.

The Council may, acting unanimously on a proposal from the Commission, extend the provisions of this Chapter to nationals of a third country who provide services and who are established within the Community.

Article 60

Services shall be considered to be 'services' within the meaning of this Treaty where they are normally provided for remuneration, in so far as they are not governed by the provisions relating to freedom of movement for goods, capital and persons.

'Services' shall in particular include: (a) activities of an industrial character; (b) activities of a commercial character; (c) activities of craftsmen; (d) activities of the professions.

CHAPTER 4

CAPITAL

Article 67

1. During the transitional period and to the extent necessary to ensure the proper functioning of the common market, Member States shall progressively abolish between themselves all restrictions on the movement of capital belonging to persons resident in Member States and any discrimination based on the nationality or on the place of residence of the parties or on the place where such capital is invested.

2. Current payments connected with the movement of capital between Member States shall be freed from all restrictions by the end of the first stage at the latest.

Article 68

1. Member States shall, as regards the matters dealt with in this Chapter, be as liberal as possible in granting such exchange authorisations as are still necessary after the entry into force of this Treaty.
2. Where a Member State applies to the movements of capital liberalised in accordance with the provisions of this Chapter the domestic rules governing the capital market and the credit system, it shall do so in a non-discriminatory manner.
3. Loans for the direct or indirect financing of a Member State or its regional or local authorities shall not be issued or placed in other Member States unless the States concerned have reached agreement thereon. [...]

Article 71

Member States shall endeavour to avoid introducing within the Community any new exchange restrictions on the movement of capital and current payments connected with such movements, and shall endeavour not to make existing rules more restrictive.

They declare their readiness to go beyond the degree of liberalisation of capital movements provided for in the preceding Articles in so far as their economic situation, in particular the situation of their balance of payments, so permits.

Article 72

Member States shall keep the Commission informed of any movements of capital to and from third countries which come to their knowledge. The Commission may deliver to Member States any opinions which it considers appropriate on this subject.

Article 73

1. If movements of capital lead to disturbances in the functioning of the capital market in any Member State, the Commission shall, after consulting the Monetary Committee, authorise that State to take protective measures in the field of capital movements, the conditions and details of which the Commission shall determine. [...]

TITLE IV

TRANSPORT

Article 74

The objectives of this Treaty shall, in matters governed by this Title, be pursued by Member States within the framework of a common transport policy.

Article 75

1. For the purpose of implementing Article 74, and taking into account the distinctive features of transport, the Council shall, acting unanimously until the end of the second stage and by a qualified majority thereafter, lay down, on a proposal from the Commission and after consulting the Economic and Social Committee and the Assembly:
   (a) common rules applicable to international transport to or from the territory of a Member State or passing across the territory of one or more Member States;
   (b) the conditions under which non-resident carriers may operate transport services within a Member State;
   (c) any other appropriate provisions. [...]

Article 76

Until the provisions referred to in Article 75 (1) have been laid down, no Member State may, without the unanimous approval of the Council, make the various provisions governing the subject when this Treaty enters into force less favourable in their direct or indirect effect on carriers of other Member States as compared with carriers who are nationals of that State. [...]

Article 78

Any measures taken within the framework of this Treaty in respect of transport rates and conditions shall take account of the economic circumstances of carriers.

Article 79

1. In the case of transport within the Community, discrimination which takes the form of carriers charging different rates and imposing different conditions for the carriage of the same goods over the same transport links on grounds of the country of origin or of destination of the goods in question, shall be abolished, at the latest, before the end of the second stage. [...]

Article 80

1. The imposition by a Member State, in respect of transport operations carried out within the Community, of rates and conditions involving any element of support or protection in the interest of one or more particular undertakings or industries shall be prohibited as from the beginning of the second stage, unless authorised by the Commission.
2. The Commission shall, acting on its own initiative or on application by a Member State, examine the rates and conditions referred to in paragraph 1, taking account in particular of the requirements of an appropriate regional economic policy, the needs of underdeveloped areas and the problems of areas

seriously affected by political circumstances on the one hand, and of the effects of such rates and conditions on competition between the different modes of transport on the other. [...]

Article 81

Charges or dues in respect of the crossing of frontiers which are charged by a carrier in addition to the transport rates shall not exceed a reasonable level after taking the costs actually incurred thereby into account.
Member States shall endeavour to reduce these costs progressively. [...]

Article 82

The provisions of this Title shall not form an obstacle to the application of measures taken in the Federal Republic of Germany to the extent that such measures are required in order to compensate for the economic disadvantages caused by the division of Germany to the economy of certain areas of the Federal Republic affected by that division. [...]

Article 84

1. The provisions of this Title shall apply to transport by rail, road and inland waterway.
2. The Council may, acting unanimously, decide whether, to what extent and by what procedure appropriate provisions may be laid down for sea and air transport.

PART THREE

POLICY OF THE COMMUNITY

TITLE I

COMMON RULES

CHAPTER 1

RULES ON COMPETITION

SECTION 1

RULES APPLYING TO UNDERTAKINGS

Article 85

1. The following shall be prohibited as incompatible with the common market: all agreements between undertakings, decisions by associations of undertakings and concerted practices which may affect trade between Member States and which have as their object or effect the prevention, restriction or distortion of competition within the common market, and in particular those which:

(a) directly or indirectly fix purchase or selling prices or any other trading conditions;
(b) limit or control production, markets, technical development, or investment;
(c) share markets or sources of supply;
(d) apply dissimilar conditions to equivalent transactions with other trading parties, thereby placing them at a competitive disadvantage;
(e) make the conclusion of contracts subject to acceptance by the other parties of supplementary obligations which, by their nature or according to commercial usage, have no connection with the subject of such contracts.
2. Any agreements or decisions prohibited pursuant to this Article shall be automatically void. [...]

Article 86

Any abuse by one or more undertakings of a dominant position within the common market or in a substantial part of it shall be prohibited as incompatible with the common market in so far as it may affect trade between Member States. Such abuse may, in particular, consist in:

(a) directly or indirectly imposing unfair purchase or selling prices or other unfair trading conditions;
(b) limiting production, markets or technical development to the prejudice of consumers;
(c) applying dissimilar conditions to equivalent transactions with other trading parties, thereby placing them at a competitive disadvantage;
(d) making the conclusion of contracts subject to acceptance by the other parties of supplementary obligations which, by their nature or according to commercial usage, have no connection with the subject of such contracts. [...]

Article 91

[Section 2, Article 91, prohibits the 'dumping' of products made or traded in the EEC at prices considerably lower than those established by the Market.]

SECTION 3

AIDS GRANTED BY STATES

Article 92

1. Save as otherwise provided in this Treaty, any aid granted by a Member State or through State resources in any form whatsoever which distorts or threatens to distort competition by favouring certain undertakings or the production of

certain goods shall, in so far as it affects trade between Member States, be incompatible with the common market.

2. The following shall be compatible with the common market:

(a) aid having a social character, granted to individual consumers, provided that such aid is granted without discrimination related to the origin of the products concerned;

(b) aid to make good the damage caused by natural disasters or exceptional occurrences;

(c) aid granted to the economy of certain areas of the Federal Republic of Germany affected by the division of Germany, in so far as such aid is required in order to compensate for the economic disadvantages caused by that division.

3. The following may be considered to be compatible with the common market:

(a) aid to promote the economic development of areas where the standard of living is abnormally low or where there is serious underemployment;

(b) aid to promote the execution of an important project of common European interest or to remedy a serious disturbance in the economy of a Member State. [...]

CHAPTER 2

TAX PROVISIONS

Article 95

No Member State shall impose, directly or indirectly, on the products of other Member States any internal taxation of any kind in excess of that imposed directly or indirectly on similar domestic products.

Furthermore, no Member State shall impose on the products of other Member States any internal taxation of such a nature as to afford indirect protection to other products. [...]

Article 96

Where products are exported to the territory of any Member State, any repayment of internal taxation shall not exceed the internal taxation imposed on them, whether directly or indirectly. [...]

Article 99

The Commission shall consider how the legislation of the various Member States concerning turnover taxes, excise duties and other forms of indirect taxation, including countervailing measures applicable to trade between Member States, can be harmonised in the interest of the common market. [...]

APPROXIMATION OF LAWS

Article 100

The Council shall, acting unanimously on a proposal from the Commission, issue directives for the approximation of such provisions laid down by law, regulation or administrative action in Member States as directly affect the establishment or functioning of the common market.

Article 101

Where the Commission finds that a difference between the provisions laid down by law, regulation or administrative action in Member States is distorting the conditions of competition in the common market and that the resultant distortion needs to be eliminated, it shall consult the Member States concerned.

If such consultation does not result in an agreement eliminating the distortion in question, the Council shall, on a proposal from the Commission, acting unanimously during the first stage and by a qualified majority thereafter, issue the necessary directives. The Commission and the Council may take any other appropriate measures provided for in this Treaty. [...]

TITLE II

ECONOMIC POLICY

CHAPTER 2

BALANCE OF PAYMENTS

Article 104

Each Member State shall pursue the economic policy needed to ensure the equilibrium of its overall balance of payments and to maintain confidence in its currency, while taking care to ensure a high level of employment and a stable level of prices.

Article 105

1. In order to facilitate attainment of the objectives set out in Article 104, Member States shall coordinate their economic policies. They shall for this purpose provide for cooperation between their appropriate administrative departments and between their central banks. The Commission shall submit to the Council recommendations on how to achieve such cooperation.
2. In order to promote coordination of the policies of Member States in the monetary field to the full extent needed for the functioning of the common

market, a Monetary Committee with advisory status is hereby set up. It shall have the following tasks:
- to keep under review the monetary and financial situation of the Member States and of the Community and the general payments system of the Member States and to report regularly thereon to the Council and to the Commission;
- to deliver opinions at the request of the Council or of the Commission or on its own initiative, for submission to these institutions.

The Member States and the Commission shall each appoint two members of the Monetary Committee.

Article 107

1. Each Member State shall treat its policy with regard to rates of exchange as a matter of common concern.
2. If a Member State makes an alteration in its rate of exchange which is inconsistent with the objectives set out in Article 104 and which seriously distorts conditions of competition, the Commission may, after consulting the Monetary Committee, authorise other Member States to take for a strictly limited period the necessary measures, the conditions and details of which it shall determine, in order to counter the consequences of such alteration.

Article 108

1. Where a Member State is in difficulties or is seriously threatened with difficulties as regards its balance of payments either as a result of an overall disequilibrium in its balance of payments, or as a result of the type of currency at its disposal, and where such difficulties are liable in particular to jeopardise the functioning of the common market or the progressive implementation of the common commercial policy, the Commission shall immediately investigate the position of the State in question and the action which, making use of all the means at its disposal, that State has taken or may take in accordance with the provisions of Article 104. The Commission shall state what measures it recommends the State concerned to take. [...]

Article 109

1. Where a sudden crisis in the balance of payments occurs and a decision ... is not immediately taken, the Member State concerned may, as a precaution, take the necessary protective measures. Such measures must cause the least possible disturbance in the functioning of the common market and must not be wider in scope than is strictly necessary to remedy the sudden difficulties which have arisen. [...]

CHAPTER 3

COMMERCIAL POLICY

Article 110

By establishing a customs union between themselves Member States aim to contribute, in the common interest, to the harmonious development of world trade, the progressive abolition of restrictions on international trade and the lowering of customs barriers.

The common commercial policy shall take into account the favourable effect which the abolition of customs duties between Member States may have on the increase in the competitive strength of undertakings in those States. [...]

[**Articles 111 and 112** detail provisions for implementation during the transitional period.]

Article 113

1. After the transitional period has ended, the common commercial policy shall be based on uniform principles, particularly in regard to changes in tariff rates, the conclusion of tariff and trade agreements, the achievement of uniformity in measures of liberalisation, export policy and measures to protect trade such as those to be taken in case of dumping or subsidies. [...]

TITLE III

SOCIAL POLICY

CHAPTER 1

SOCIAL PROVISIONS

Article 117

Member States agree upon the need to promote improved working conditions and an improved standard of living for workers, so as to make possible their harmonisation while the improvement is being maintained.

They believe that such a development will ensue not only from the functioning of the common market, which will favour the harmonisation of social systems, but also from the procedures provided for in this Treaty and from the approximation of provisions laid down by law, regulation or administrative action.

Article 118

Without prejudice to the other provisions of this Treaty and in conformity with its general objectives, the Commission shall have the task of promoting close cooperation between Member States in the social field, particularly in matters relating to: employment; labour law and working conditions; basic and advanced vocational training; social security; prevention of occupational accidents and diseases; occupational hygiene; the right of association, and collective bargaining between employers and workers.

To this end, the Commission shall act in close contact with Member States by making studies, delivering opinions and arranging consultations both on problems arising at national level and on those of concern to international organisations. [...]

Article 119

Each Member State shall during the first stage ensure and subsequently maintain the application of the principle that men and women should receive equal pay for equal work.

For the purpose of this Article, 'pay' means the ordinary basic or minimum wage or salary and any other consideration, whether in cash or in kind, which the worker receives, directly or indirectly, in respect of his employment from his employer.

Equal pay without discrimination based on sex means:

(a) that pay for the same work at piece rates shall be calculated on the basis of the same unit of measurement;
(b) that pay for work at time rates shall be the same for the same job. [...]

Article 120

Member States shall endeavour to maintain that existing equivalence between paid holiday schemes. [...]

CHAPTER 2

THE EUROPEAN SOCIAL FUND

Article 123

In order to improve employment opportunities for workers in the common market and to contribute thereby to raising the standard of living, a European Social Fund is hereby established in accordance with the provisions set out below; it shall have the task of rendering the employment of workers easier and of increasing their geographical and occupational mobility within the Community.

[**Article 124** authorises the Commission to administer the Social Fund, assisted by a Committee composed of representatives of Governments, trade unions and employers' organisations.]

Article 125

1. [The purposes of the Social Fund include:]
   (a) ensuring productive re-employment of workers by means of:
      vocational training;
      resettlement allowances;
   (b) granting aid for the benefit of workers whose employment is reduced or temporarily suspended, in whole or in part, as a result of the conversion of an undertaking to other production, in order that they may retain the same wage level pending their full re-employment.
2. Assistance granted by the Fund towards the cost of vocational retraining shall be granted only if the unemployed workers could not be found employment except in a new occupation and only if they have been in productive employment for at least six months in the occupation for which they have been retrained.

   Assistance towards resettlement allowances shall be granted only if the unemployed workers have been caused to change their home within the Community and have been in productive employment for at least six months in their new place of residence. [...]

TITLE IV

THE EUROPEAN INVESTMENT BANK

Article 129

A European Investment Bank is hereby established; it shall have legal personality.
   The members of the European Investment Bank shall be the Member States.
   The Statute of the European Investment Bank is laid down in a Protocol annexed to this Treaty.

Article 130

The task of the European Investment Bank shall be to contribute, by having recourse to the capital market and utilising its own resources, to the balanced and steady development of the common market in the interest of the Community. For this purpose the Bank shall, operating on a non-profit-making basis, grant loans and give guarantees which facilitate the financing of the following projects in all sectors of the economy:

(a) projects for developing less developed regions;
(b) projects for modernising or converting undertakings or for developing fresh activities called for by the progressive establishment of the common market, where these projects are of such a size or nature that they cannot be entirely financed by the various means available in the individual Member States;
(c) projects of common interest to several Member States which are of such a size

or nature that they cannot be entirely financed by the various means available in the individual Member States.

PART FOUR

ASSOCIATION OF THE OVERSEAS COUNTRIES AND TERRITORIES

Article 131

The Member States agree to associate with the Community the non-European countries and territories which have special relations with Belgium, France, Italy, and the Netherlands.

The purpose of association shall be to promote the economic and social development of the countries and territories and to establish close economic relations between them and the Community as a whole.

In accordance with the principles set out in the Preamble to this Treaty, association shall serve primarily to further the interests and prosperity of the inhabitants of these countries and territories in order to lead them to the economic, social and cultural development to which they aspire.

Article 132

Association shall have the following objectives:

1. Member States shall apply to their trade with the countries and territories the same treatment as they accord each other pursuant to this Treaty.
2. Each country or territory shall apply to its trade with Member States and with the other countries and territories the same treatment as that which it applies to the European State with which it has special relations.
3. The Member States shall contribute to the investments required for the progressive development of these countries and territories.
4. For investments financed by the Community, participation in tenders and supplies shall be open on equal terms to all natural and legal persons who are nationals of a Member State or of one of the countries and territories.

Article 133

1. Customs duties on imports into the Member States of goods originating in the countries and territories shall be completely abolished in conformity with the progressive abolition of customs duties between Member States in accordance with the provisions of this Treaty. [...]

[**Part Five** concerns the Institutions of the Community: the Assembly, the Council, the Commission, and the Court of Justice. It also provides for the Economic and Social Committee and, very generally, for the Budget and Revenue of these Institutions.]

PART SIX

GENERAL AND FINAL PROVISIONS

Article 210

The Community shall have legal personality.

Article 211

In each of the Member States, the Community shall enjoy the most extensive legal capacity accorded to legal persons under their laws; it may, in particular, acquire or dispose of movable and immovable property and may be a party to legal proceedings. To this end, the Community shall be represented by the Commission. [...]

Article 213

The Commission may, within the limits and under the conditions laid down by the Council in accordance with the provisions of this Treaty, collect any information and carry out any checks required for the performance of the tasks entrusted to it. [...]

Article 215

The contractual liability of the Community shall be governed by the law applicable to the contract in question.

In the case of non-contractual liability, the Community shall, in accordance with the general principles common to the laws of the Member States, make good any damage caused by its institutions or by its servants in the performance of their duties.

The personal liability of its servants towards the Community shall be governed by the provisions laid down in their Staff Regulations or in the Conditions of Employment applicable to them. [...]

Article 220

Member States shall, so far as is necessary, enter into negotiations with each other with a view to securing for the benefit of their nationals:

– the protection of persons and the enjoyment and protection of rights under the same conditions as those accorded by each State to its own nationals;
– the abolition of double taxation within the Community;
– the mutual recognition of companies or firms within the meaning of the second paragraph of Article 58, the retention of legal personality in the event of transfer of their seat from one country to another, and the possibility of mergers between companies or firms governed by the laws of different countries;
– the simplification of formalities governing the reciprocal recognition and

enforcement of judgments of courts or tribunals and of arbitration awards.
[...]

Article 222

This Treaty shall in no way prejudice the rules in Member States governing the system of property ownership.

Article 223

1. The provisions of this Treaty shall not preclude the application of the following rules:
   (a) No Member State shall be obliged to supply information the disclosure of which it considers contrary to the essential interests of its security;
   (b) Any Member State may take such measures as it considers necessary for the protection of the essential interests of its security which are connected with the production of or trade in arms, munitions and war material; such measures shall not adversely affect the conditions of competition in the common market regarding products which are not intended for specifically military purposes. [...]

Article 224

Member States shall consult each other with a view to taking together the steps needed to prevent the functioning of the common market being affected by measures which a Member State may be called upon to take in the event of serious internal disturbances affecting the maintenance of law and order, in the event of war or serious international tension constituting a threat of war, or in order to carry out obligations it has accepted for the purpose of maintaining peace and international security. [...]

Article 229

It shall be for the Commission to ensure the maintenance of all appropriate relations with the organs of the United Nations, of its specialised agencies and of the General Agreement on Tariffs and Trade.

The Commission shall also maintain such relations as are appropriate with all international organisations.

Article 230

The Community shall establish all appropriate forms of co-operation with the Council of Europe.

Article 231

The Community shall establish close cooperation with the Organisation for European Economic Co-operation, the details to be determined by common accord.

Article 232

1. The provisions of this Treaty shall not affect the provisions of the Treaty establishing the European Coal and Steel Community, in particular as regards the rights and obligations of Member States, the powers of the institutions of that Community and the rules laid down by that Treaty for the functioning of the common market in coal and steel.
2. The provisions of this Treaty shall not derogate from those of the Treaty establishing the European Atomic Energy Community.

Article 233

The provisions of this Treaty shall not preclude the existence or completion of regional unions between Belgium and Luxembourg, or between Belgium, Luxembourg and the Netherlands, to the extent that the objectives of these regional unions are not attained by application of this Treaty. [...]

Article 236

The Government of any Member State or the Commission may submit to the Council proposals for the amendment of this Treaty.

If the Council, after consulting the Assembly and, where appropriate, the Commission, delivers an opinion in favour of calling a conference of representatives of the Governments of the Member States, the conference shall be convened by the President of the Council for the purpose of determining by common accord the amendments to be made to this Treaty.

The amendments shall enter into force after being ratified by all the Member States in accordance with their respective constitutional requirements.

Article 237

Any European State may apply to become a member of the Community. It shall address its application to the Council, which shall act unanimously after obtaining the opinion of the Commission.

The conditions of admission and the adjustments to this Treaty necessitated thereby shall be the subject of an agreement between the Member States and the applicant State. This agreement shall be submitted for ratification by all the Contracting States in accordance with their respective constitutional requirements.

Article 238

The Community may conclude with a third State, a union of States or an international organisation agreements establishing an association involving reciprocal rights and obligations, common action and special procedures.

These agreements shall be concluded by the Council, acting unanimously after consulting the Assembly.

Where such agreements call for amendments to this Treaty, these amendments shall first be adopted in accordance with the procedure laid down in Article 236. [...]

[Articles 241–246 provide for the first meetings of the Council, the Assembly, the Commission and the Court of Justice.]

Article 240

This Treaty is concluded for an unlimited period.

[Signed by P. H. Spaak and J. Ch. Snoy et d'Oppuers (for Belgium), Konrad Adenauer and Walter Hallstein (for the Federal Republic of Germany), Christian Pineau and Edgar Faure (for France), Antonio Segni and Gaetano Martino (for Italy), Joseph Bech and Lambert Schaus (for Luxembourg), Joseph Luns and J. Linthorst Homan (for the Netherlands).]

_____ 16 _____

EURATOM

The Treaty establishing the European Atomic Energy Community was signed in Rome on 25 March 1957 and was published by the Commission of the European Communities.

[The nominated ambassadors have decided to create a European Atomic Energy Community (EURATOM).]

RECOGNISING that nuclear energy represents an essential resource for the development and invigoration of industry and will permit the advancement of the cause of peace,

CONVINCED that only a joint effort undertaken without delay can offer the prospect of achievements commensurate with the creative capacities of their countries,

RESOLVED to create the conditions necessary for the development of a powerful nuclear industry which will provide extensive energy resources, lead to the modernisation of technical processes and contribute, through its many other applications, to the prosperity of their peoples,

ANXIOUS to create the conditions of safety necessary to eliminate hazards to the life and health of the public,

DESIRING to associate other countries with their work and to cooperate with international organisations concerned with the peaceful development of atomic energy. [...]

TITLE ONE

THE TASKS OF THE COMMUNITY

Article 1

By this Treaty the High Contracting Parties establish among themselves a EUROPEAN ATOMIC ENERGY COMMUNITY (EURATOM).

It shall be the task of the Community to contribute to the raising of the standard of living in the Member States and to the development of relations with the other countries by creating the conditions necessary for the speedy establishment and growth of nuclear industries.

Article 2

In order to perform its task, the Community shall, as provided in this Treaty:

(a) promote research and ensure the dissemination of technical information;

(b) establish uniform safety standards to protect the health of workers and of the general public and ensure that they are applied;

(c) facilitate investment and ensure, particularly by encouraging ventures on the part of undertakings, the establishment of the basic installations necessary for the development of nuclear energy in the Community;

(d) ensure that all users in the Community receive a regular and equitable supply of ores and nuclear fuels;

(e) make certain, by appropriate supervision, that nuclear materials are not diverted to purposes other than those for which they are intended;

(f) exercise the right of ownership conferred upon it with respect to special fissile materials;

(g) ensure wide commercial outlets and access to the best technical facilities by the creation of a common market in specialised materials and equipment, by the free movement of capital for investment in the field of nuclear energy. [...]

(h) establish with other countries and international organisations such relations as will foster progress in the peaceful uses of nuclear energy.

Article 3

1. The tasks entrusted to the Community shall be carried out by the following institutions: an Assembly, a Council, a Commission, a Court of Justice.

   Each institution shall act within the limits of the powers conferred upon it by this Treaty.

2. The Council and the Commission shall be assisted by an Economic and Social Committee acting in an advisory capacity.

TITLE TWO

PROVISIONS FOR THE ENCOURAGEMENT OF PROGRESS IN THE FIELD OF NUCLEAR ENERGY

CHAPTER I

PROMOTION OF RESEARCH

Article 4

1. The Commission shall be responsible for promoting and facilitating nuclear research in the Member States and for complementing it by carrying out a Community research and training programme. [...]

Article 5

For purposes of co-ordinating and complementing research undertaken in Member States, the Commission shall, either by a specific request addressed to a given recipient and conveyed to the Government concerned, or by a general published request, call upon Member States, persons or undertakings to communicate to it their programmes relating to the research which it specifies in the request.

After giving those concerned full opportunity to comment, the Commission may deliver a reasoned opinion on each of the programmes communicated to it. The Commission shall deliver such an opinion if the State, person or undertaking which has communicated the programme so requests.

By such opinions the Commission shall discourage unnecessary duplication and shall direct research towards sectors which are insufficiently explored. The Commission may not publish these programmes without the consent of the State, person or undertaking which has communicated them.

The Commission shall publish at regular intervals a list of those sectors of nuclear research which it considers to be insufficiently explored. [...]

Article 6

To encourage the carrying out of research programmes communicated to it the Commission may:

(a) provide financial assistance within the framework of research contracts, without, however, offering subsidies;
(b) supply, either free of charge or against payment, for carrying out such programmes, any source materials or special fissile materials which it has available;
(c) place installations, equipment or expert assistance at the disposal of Member States, persons or undertakings, either free of charge or against payment;

(d) promote joint financing by the Member States, persons or undertakings concerned.

Article 7

Community research and training programmes shall be determined by the Council, acting unanimously on a proposal from the Commission, which shall consult the Scientific and Technical Committee.

These programmes shall be drawn up for a period of not more than five years.

The funds required for carrying out these programmes shall be included each year in the research and investment budget of the Community. [...]

Article 8

1. After consulting the Scientific and Technical Committee, the Commission shall establish a Joint Nuclear Research Centre.

   This Centre shall ensure that the research programmes and other tasks assigned to it by the Commission are carried out.

   It shall also ensure that a uniform nuclear terminology and a standard system of measurements are established. It shall set up a central bureau for nuclear measurements.

2. The activities of the Centre may, for geographical or functional reasons, be carried out in separate establishments.

Article 9

1. After obtaining the opinion of the Economic and Social Committee the Commission may, within the framework of the Joint Nuclear Research Centre, set up schools for the training of specialists, particularly in the fields of prospecting for minerals, the production of high-purity nuclear materials, the processing of irradiated fuels, nuclear engineering, health and safety and the production and use of radioisotopes.

   The Commission shall determine the details of such training.

2. An institution of university status shall be established; the way in which it will function shall be determined by the Council, acting by a qualified majority on a proposal from the Commission.

Article 10

The Commission may, by contract, entrust the carrying out of certain parts of the Community research programme to Member States, persons or undertakings, or to third countries, international organisations or nationals of third countries. [...]

CHAPTER II

DISSEMINATION OF INFORMATION

SECTION I

INFORMATION OVER WHICH THE COMMUNITY HAS POWER OF DISPOSAL

Article 12

Member States, persons or undertakings shall have the right, on application to the Commission, to obtain non-exclusive licences under patents, provisionally protected patent rights, utility models or patent applications owned by the Community, where they are able to make effective use of the inventions covered thereby.

Under the same conditions, the Commission shall grant sub-licences under patents, provisionally protected patent rights, utility models or patent applications, where the Community holds contractual licences conferring power to do so.

The Commission shall grant such licences or sub-licences on terms to be agreed with the licensees and shall furnish all the information required for their use. These terms shall relate in particular to suitable remuneration and, where appropriate, to the right of the licensee to grant sub-licences to third parties and to the obligation to treat the information as a trade secret. [...]

SECTION II

OTHER INFORMATION [...]

Article 14

The Commission shall endeavour, by amicable agreement, to secure both the communication of information which is of use to the Community in the attainment of its objectives and the granting of licences under patents, provisionally protected patent rights, utility models or patent applications covering such information. [...]

Article 16

1. As soon as an application for a patent or a utility model relating to a specifically nuclear subject is filed with a Member State, that State shall ask the applicant to agree that the contents of the application be communicated to the Commission forthwith.

   If the applicant agrees, this communication shall be made within three months of the date of filing the application. If the applicant does not agree, the Member State shall, within the same period, notify the Commission of the existence of the application.

   The Commission may require a Member State to communicate the contents of an application of whose existence it has been notified. [...]

2. Member States shall inform the Commission, within eighteen months of the

filing date, of the existence of any as yet unpublished application for a patent or utility model which seems to them, *prima facie*, to deal with a subject which, although not specifically nuclear, is directly connected with and essential to the development of nuclear energy in the Community. [...]

SECTION III

SECURITY PROVISIONS

Article 24

Information which the Community acquires as a result of carrying out its research programme, and the disclosure of which is liable to harm the defence interests of one or more Member States, shall be subject to a security system in accordance with the following provisions:

1. The Council shall, acting on a proposal from the Commission, adopt security regulations which, account being taken of the provisions of this Article, lay down the various security gradings to be applied and the security measures appropriate to each grading.
2. Where the Commission considers that the disclosure of certain information is liable to harm the defence interests of one or more Member States, it shall provisionally apply to that information the security grading required in that case by the security regulations.
It shall communicate such information forthwith to the Member States, which shall provisionally ensure its security in the same manner. [...]

SECTION IV

SPECIAL PROVISIONS

Article 28

Where, as a result of their communication to the Commission, unpublished applications for patents or utility models, or patents or utility models classified for defence reasons, are improperly used or come to the knowledge of an unauthorised person, the Community shall make good the damage suffered by the party concerned. [...]

Article 29

Where an agreement or contract for the exchange of scientific or industrial information in the nuclear field between a Member State, a person or an undertaking on the one hand, and a third State, an international organisation or a national of a third State on the other, requires, on either part, the signature of a State acting in its sovereign capacity, it shall he concluded by the Commission. [...]

HEALTH AND SAFETY

Article 30

Basic standards shall be laid down within the Community for the protection of the health of workers and the general public against the dangers arising from ionizing radiations. The expression 'basic standards' means:

(a) maximum permissible doses compatible with adequate safety;
(b) maximum permissible levels of exposure and contamination;
(c) the fundamental principles governing the health surveillance of workers.

Article 31

The basic standards shall be worked out by the Commission after it has obtained the opinion of a group of persons appointed by the Scientific and Technical Committee from among scientific experts, and in particular public health experts, in the Member States. The Commission shall obtain the opinion of the Economic and Social Committee on these basic standards.

After consulting the Assembly the Council shall, on a proposal from the Commission, which shall forward to it the opinions obtained from these Committees, establish the basic standards; the Council shall act by a qualified majority.

Article 33

Each Member State shall lay down the appropriate provisions, whether by legislation, regulation or administrative action, to ensure compliance with the basic standards which have been established and shall take the necessary measures with regard to teaching, education and vocational training.

The Commission shall make appropriate recommendations for harmonising the provisions applicable in this field in the Member States. [...]

Article 34

Any Member State in whose territories particularly dangerous experiments are to take place shall take additional health and safety measures, on which it shall first obtain the opinion of the Commission.

The assent of the Commission shall be required where the effects of such experiments are liable to affect the territories of other Member States.

Article 35

Each Member State shall establish the facilities necessary to carry out continuous monitoring of the level of radioactivity in the air, water and soil and to ensure compliance with the basic standards.

The Commission shall have the right of access to such facilities; it may verify their operation and efficiency.

Article 36

The appropriate authorities shall periodically communicate information on the checks referred to in Article 35 to the Commission so that it is kept informed of the level of radioactivity to which the public is exposed.

Article 37

Each Member State shall provide the Commission with such general data relating to any plan for the disposal of radioactive waste in whatever form as will make it possible to determine whether the implementation of such plan is liable to result in the radioactive contamination of the water, soil or airspace of another Member State.

The Commission shall deliver its opinion within six months, after consulting the group of experts referred to in Article 31.

Article 38

The Commission shall make recommendations to the Member States with regard to the level of radioactivity in the air, water and soil. [...]

CHAPTER VI

SUPPLIES

Article 52

1. The supply of ores, source materials and special fissile materials shall be ensured, in accordance with the provisions of this Chapter, by means of a common supply policy on the principle of equal access to sources of supply.
2. For this purpose and under the conditions laid down in this Chapter:
    (a) all practices designed to secure a privileged position for certain users shall be prohibited;
    (b) an Agency is hereby established; it shall have a right of option on ores, source materials and special fissile materials produced in the territories of Member States and an exclusive right to conclude contracts relating to the supply of ores, source materials and special fissile materials coming from inside the Community or from outside.

    The Agency may not discriminate in any way between users on grounds of the use which they intend to make of the supplies requested unless such use is unlawful or is found to be contrary to the conditions imposed by suppliers outside the Community on the consignment in question.

THE AGENCY

Article 53

The Agency shall be under the supervision of the Commission, which shall issue directives to it, possess a right of veto over its decisions and appoint its Director-General and Deputy Director-General. [...]

Article 59

If the Agency does not exercise its right of option on the whole or any part of the output of a producer, the latter

(a) may, either by using his own resources or under contract, process or cause to be processed the ores, source materials or special fissile materials, provided that he offers to the Agency the product of such processing;

(b) shall be authorised by a decision of the Commission to dispose of his available production outside the Community, provided that the terms he offers are not more favourable than those previously offered to the Agency. However, special fissile materials may be exported only through the Agency and in accordance with the provisions of Article 62.

The Commission may not grant such authorisation if the recipients of the supplies fail to satisfy it that the general interests of the Community will be safeguarded or if the terms and conditions of such contracts are contrary to the objectives of this Treaty.

Article 60

Potential users shall periodically inform the Agency of the supplies they require, specifying the quantities, the physical and chemical nature, the place of origin, the intended use, delivery dates and price terms, which are to form the terms and conditions of the supply contract which they wish to conclude.

Similarly, producers shall inform the Agency of offers which they are able to make, stating all the specifications, and in particular the duration of contracts, required to enable their production programmes to be drawn up. Such contracts shall be of not more than ten years' duration save with the agreement of the Commission. [...]

Article 62

1. The Agency shall exercise its right of option on special fissile materials produced in the territories of Member States in order
   (a) to meet demand from users within the Community in accordance with Article 60; or
   (b) to store such materials itself, or

(c) to export such materials with the authorisation of the Commission. [...]

ORES, SOURCE MATERIALS AND SPECIAL FISSILE MATERIALS COMING FROM OUTSIDE THE COMMUNITY

Article 64

The Agency, acting where appropriate within the framework of agreements concluded between the Community and a third State or an international organisation, shall, subject to the exceptions provided for in this Treaty, have the exclusive right to enter into agreements or contracts whose principal aim is the supply of ores, source materials or special fissile materials coming from outside the Community. [...]

Article 66

Should the Commission find, on application by the users concerned, that the Agency is not in a position to deliver within a reasonable period of time all or part of the supplies ordered, or that it can only do so at excessively high prices, the users shall have the right to conclude directly contracts relating to supplies from outside the Community, provided that such contracts meet in essential respects the requirements specified in their orders.

This right shall be granted for a period of one year; it may be extended if the situation which justified its granting continues. [...]

Article 69

The Council may fix prices, acting unanimously on a proposal from the Commission. [...]

PROVISIONS RELATING TO SUPPLY POLICY

Article 70

Within the limits set by the budget of the Community, the Commission may, on such conditions as it shall determine, give financial support to prospecting programmes in the territories of Member States.

The Commission may make recommendations to the Member States with a view to the development of prospecting for and exploitation of mineral deposits.

The Member States shall submit annually to the Commission a report on the development of prospecting and production, on probable reserves and on investment in mining which has been made or is planned in their territories. The reports shall be submitted to the Council, together with an opinion from the Commission which shall state in particular what action has been taken by Member States on recommendations made to them under the preceding paragraph.

If, when the matter has been submitted to it by the Commission, the Council finds by a qualified majority that, although the prospects for extraction appear economically justified on a long-term basis, prospecting activities and the expansion of mining operations continue to be markedly inadequate, the Member State concerned shall, for as long as it has failed to remedy this situation, be deemed to have waived, both for itself and for its nationals, the right of equal access to other sources of supply within the Community. [...]

Article 72

The Agency may, from material available inside or outside the Community, build up the necessary commercial stocks to facilitate supplies to or normal deliveries by the Community. [...]

CHAPTER VII

SAFEGUARDS

Article 77

In accordance with the provisions of this Chapter, the Commission shall satisfy itself that, in the territories of Member States,

(a) ores, source materials and special fissile materials are not diverted from their intended uses as declared by the users;
(b) the provisions relating to supply and any particular safeguarding obligations assumed by the Community under an agreement concluded with a third State or an international organisation are complied with.

Article 78

Anyone setting up or operating an installation for the production, separation or other use of source materials or special fissile materials or for the processing of irradiated nuclear fuels shall declare to the Commission the basic technical characteristics of the installations, to the extent that knowledge of these characteristics is necessary for the attainment of the objectives set out in Article 77.

The Commission must approve the techniques to be used for the chemical processing of irradiated materials, to the extent necessary to attain the objectives set out in Article 77.

Article 79

The Commission shall require that operating records be kept and produced in order to permit accounting for ores, source materials and special fissile materials used or produced. The same requirement shall apply in the case of the transport of source materials and special fissile materials. [...]

Article 80

The Commission may require that any excess special fissile materials recovered or obtained as by-products and not actually being used or ready for use shall be deposited with the Agency or in other stores which are or can be supervised by the Commission.

Special fissile materials deposited in this way must be returned forthwith to those concerned at their request.

Article 81

The Commission may send inspectors into the territories of Member States. Before sending an inspector on his first assignment in the territory of a Member State, the Commission shall consult the State concerned; such consultation shall suffice to cover all future assignments of this inspector. [...]

Article 84

In the application of the safeguards, no discrimination shall be made on grounds of the use for which ores, source materials and special fissile materials are intended.

The scope of and procedure for the safeguards and the powers of the bodies responsible for their application shall be confined to the attainment of the objectives set out in this Chapter.

The safeguards may not extend to materials intended to meet defence requirements which are in the course of being specially processed for this purpose or which, after being so processed, are, in accordance with an operational plan, placed or stored in a military establishment. [...]

CHAPTER VIII

PROPERTY OWNERSHIP

Article 86

Special fissile materials shall be the property of the Community.

The Community's right of ownership shall extend to all special fissile materials which are produced or imported by a Member State, a person or an undertaking and are subject to the safeguards provided for in Chapter VII.

Article 87

Member States, persons or undertakings shall have the unlimited right of use and consumption of special fissile materials which have properly come into their possession, subject to the obligations imposed on them by this Treaty, in particular those relating to safeguards, the right of option conferred on the Agency and health and safety.

Article 88

The Agency shall keep a special account in the name of the Community, called 'Special Fissile Materials Financial Account'. [...]

Article 91

The system of ownership applicable to all objects, materials and assets which are not vested in the Community under this Chapter shall be determined by the law of each Member State.

CHAPTER IX

THE NUCLEAR COMMON MARKET [...]

Article 93

Member States shall abolish between themselves, one year after the entry into force of this Treaty, all customs duties on imports and exports or charges having equivalent effect, and all quantitative restrictions on imports and exports, in respect of: [...]

[the Article proposes two lists of products useful to atomic energy production]

Article 96

The Member States shall abolish all restrictions based on nationality affecting the right of nationals of any Member State to take skilled employment in the field of nuclear energy, subject to the limitations resulting from the basic requirements of public policy, public security or public health. [...]

Article 97

No restrictions based on nationality may be applied to natural or legal persons, whether public or private, under the jurisdiction of a Member State, where they desire to participate in the construction of nuclear installations of a scientific or industrial nature in the Community.

Article 98

Member States shall take all measures necessary to facilitate the conclusion of insurance contracts covering nuclear risks.

Within two years of the entry into force of this Treaty, the Council acting by a qualified majority on a proposal from the Commission, which shall first request the opinion of the Economic and Social Committee, shall, after consulting the Assembly, issue directives for the application of this Article. [...]

CHAPTER X

EXTERNAL RELATIONS

Article 101

The Community may, within the limits of its powers and jurisdiction, enter into obligations by concluding agreements or contracts with a third State, an international organisation or a national of a third State.

Such agreements or contracts shall be negotiated by the Commission in accordance with the directives of the Council; they shall be concluded by the Commission with the approval of the Council, which shall act by a qualified majority.

Agreements or contracts whose implementation does not require action by the Council and can be effected within the limits of the relevant budget shall, however, be negotiated and concluded solely by the Commission; the Commission shall keep the Council informed.

Article 102

Agreements or contracts concluded with a third State, an international organisation or a national of a third State to which, in addition to the Community, one or more Member States are parties, shall not enter into force until the Commission has been notified by all the Member States concerned that those agreements or contracts have become applicable in accordance with the provisions of their respective national laws. [...]

——————————— 17 ———————————

BENELUX TREATY

Although they had already become members of the European Economic Community, Belgium, Luxembourg and the Netherlands decided in 1958 to formalize the regional identity which they had been building since 1945. Their Economic Union Treaty is published in the *United Nations Treaty Series*, vol. 380–381, no. 5471 (New York: United Nations [by authority of the Secretariat], 1960).

[Representatives of the Governments of Belgium, Luxembourg and the Netherlands have agreed to the following Treaty]

PART 1

BASIC PROVISIONS

Article 1

1. An Economic Union is established between the Kingdom of Belgium, the Grand Duchy of Luxembourg and the Kingdom of the Netherlands, entailing free movement of persons, goods, capital and services.
2. This Union implies:
   a) the co-ordination of economic, financial and social policies;
   b) the pursuit of a joint policy in economic relations with third countries and regarding payments related thereto.

Article 2

1. The nationals of each High Contracting Party may freely enter and leave the territory of any other Contracting Party.
2. They shall enjoy the same treatment as nationals of that State as regards:
   a) freedom of movement, sojourn and settlement;
   b) freedom to carry on a trade or occupation, including the rendering of services;
   c) capital transactions;
   d) conditions of employment;
   e) social security benefits;
   f) taxes and charges of any kind;
   g) exercise of civil rights as well as legal and judicial protection of their person, individual rights and interests.

Article 3

1. Goods traffic between the territories of the High Contracting Parties, irrespective of origin, last exporting country or destination of the goods, shall be free of

import and excise duty and any other duties, charges, imposts or dues of whatsoever kind.

2. It shall likewise be free from all prohibitions or restrictions of an economic or financial nature, such as quotas, restrictions applying to certain types of goods or currency restrictions.

3. Goods originating from the territory of one of the High Contracting Parties shall receive in the territories of the other Contracting Parties the same treatment as national products.

Article 4

There shall be no prohibition or restriction for transfers of capital between the territories of the High Contracting Parties.

Article 5

1. The rendering of services between the territories of the High Contracting Parties shall be free of taxes, charges, imposts or dues of whatsoever kind.

2. It shall likewise be free from all prohibitions or restrictions of an economic or financial nature, such as quotas, restrictions applying to certain types of goods or currency restrictions.

Article 6

Without prejudice to the provisions of Articles 2 to 5 above, the High Contracting Parties shall jointly ensure that no law or regulation, in particular public health regulations, should unduly hinder freedom of movement.

Article 7

The High Contracting Parties shall jointly ensure that no law or regulation has the effect of disturbing competitive conditions in their territories.

Article 8

1. The High Contracting Parties shall, in close consultation, pursue a co-ordinated policy in the economic, financial and social fields.

2. The High Contracting Parties shall co-ordinate their policies in respect of private commercial agreements of abuses arising from the dominant position of one or more concerns; they shall take steps to prevent the abuse of economic power.

Article 9

In so far as the attitude they may wish to adopt, or the commitments they wish to undertake, either in their relations with third countries or *vis-à-vis* or within the framework of international institutions or conferences, affect the aims of the Union, the High Contracting Parties shall hold consultations in order that these attitudes and commitments may be conducive to the realisation of these aims.

Article 10

In their relations with third countries the High Contracting Parties shall:

a) accept and pursue a joint policy in the field of foreign trade and of payments related thereto;

b) jointly conclude treaties and conventions regarding foreign trade and the customs tariff;

c) conclude, either jointly or concurrently, treaties and conventions regarding payments in connection with foreign trade.

Article 11

1. As regards goods coming from or destined for third countries, import duties and excise duties as well as all other taxes, imposts or dues whatsoever, to be imposed on account of imports, exports or transit traffic shall be fixed in accordance with a common tariff with identical rates, the regulations for levying the same being co-ordinated.

2. The procedure in the matter of licences and quotas with regard to imports, exports and transit shall be identical.

3. The High Contracting Parties shall co-ordinate all regulations, either legal or executive, and other stipulations of public law of an economic or financial nature regarding imports, exports or transit traffic, which are not covered by the first and second paragraphs of this Article.

Article 12

1. As regards the rate of exchange between the Netherlands guilder and the Belgian and the Luxembourg franc, the High Contracting Parties shall determine their policies by mutual agreement. Likewise, by mutual agreement they shall fix their exchange rates in relation to the currencies of third countries.

2. In particular, they shall not effect any alteration of rates of exchange except by mutual agreement.

Article 13

Measures taken by the High Contracting Parties in carrying into effect the joint and co-ordinated policy covered by this Treaty should take account of the necessity of ensuring monetary stability and may not entail for a High Contracting Party the necessity of sustaining losses in foreign currency reserves which are incompatible with its responsibility for its national currency; nor should they involve the necessity of accepting inconvertible foreign currencies or of granting credits, unless previous agreement has been reached as to the limits permitted.

Article 14

1. In the event of the vital interests of one of the High Contracting Parties being endangered, the Committee of Ministers, after advice has been sought from the Consultative Interparliamentary Council and from the Economic and Social Advisory Council, may decide what measures may be taken in derogation of the stipulations of this Treaty during a certain period, the length of which is to be fixed simultaneously. [...]

> [**Part 2** concerns the various INSTITUTIONS of the Benelux
> Union, their memberships and responsibilities: the Committee
> of Ministers; the Consultative Interparliamentary Council; the
> Council of the Economic Union; the Committees and the Special
> Committees; the General Secretariat; Joint Services; the College
> of Arbitrators; the Economic and Social Advisory Council.]

PART 3

SOCIAL PROVISIONS REGARDING CERTAIN ASPECTS OF THE ECONOMIC UNION

CHAPTER 1

NATIONAL TREATMENT, FREEDOM OF MOVEMENT AND THE EXERCISE OF ECONOMIC AND PROFESSIONAL ACTIVITIES

Article 55

The High Contracting Parties shall conclude a convention determining, in the interests of public order, public security, public health or morality, such provisions which may be applied to nationals of a High Contracting Party in the territory of another High Contracting Party with regard to their entering or leaving its territory, to their freedom of movement, of sojourn and of establishment therein, and to their expulsion.

Article 56

The High Contracting Parties shall, as far as may be required, conclude a convention determining the treatment of nationals of a High Contracting Party in the territory of another Contracting Party with regard to legal and judicial protection of their person, and their rights and interests.

Article 57

In so far as house-rents are governed by regulations laid down by legal or administrative authorities, the nationals of each High Contracting Party shall enjoy the same treatment in the territories of the other Contracting Parties as apply to their own nationals.

Article 58

1. The activities of companies established under the legislation of one of the High Contracting Parties shall be made subject to the national law of the other Contracting Party in whose territory they perform their activities either directly or through the medium of branch-establishments or agencies.
2. These activities may not be subjected to stricter conditions than those applied to national companies. Albeit, the companies of one of the High Contracting Parties may not enjoy more rights in the territory of another Contracting Party than similar national companies of the latter Party.
3. Inasmuch as any departure from the rules will have as its principal object the protection of insured persons, insurers, depositors with a building society and financially injured persons, the High Contracting Parties may depart from the second paragraph of this Article in the field of insurances, capital issues and mortgage arrangements. Any such derogations shall be specified in a convention.
4. Companies within the meaning of the present Article are companies according to civil and commercial law including co-operative societies and other legal persons in accordance with civil law. Albeit, as regards the application of this Article, legal persons in civil law, not seeking profit, are considered companies only with regard to their activities in the field of insurances, tontine or mortgage societies. Luxembourg agricultural associations shall also be considered as companies in the sense of this Article.

Article 59

1. Companies established according to the legislation of a High Contracting Party and having their fiscal domicile within the territory of one of the High Contracting Parties shall not be subjected to higher fiscal charges in the territory of the other Contracting Parties than those borne by similar national companies, irrespective of the fact whether the former companies have one or several branch-establishments or agencies in the territory of the other Contracting Parties. [...]

Article 60

The High Contracting Parties shall conclude a convention determining the treatment of nationals of the Contracting Parties with regard to their employment as wage-earners in the service of a private employer and to their enjoying social security benefits.

Article 61

1. Contrary to the provisions of Article 2, paragraph 2 (b) of the present Treaty each High Contracting Party shall remain entitled to reserve the exercise of the following economic and professional activities for its own nationals:
   a) officials posts, public functions or professions, including those of notary public, solicitor and bailiff;
   b) the profession of lawyer;
   c) the medical profession and related occupations in the Grand Duchy of Luxembourg;
   d) fisheries in inland waterways, pilotage and inland harbour-services.
2. The provisions of Article 2, paragraph 2 (b) of the present Treaty shall not affect national regulations concerning the qualifications required for exercising certain professions.

Article 62

In the field of public contracts and tenders, the authorities of a High Contracting Party may not discriminate in any way whatsoever in favour of national products or of their nationals and to the detriment of products or nationals of other High Contracting Parties. [...]

CHAPTER 2

COORDINATION OF POLICY

Article 64

1. In the field of investments the Committee of Ministers shall decide as to the expediency of accepting general or special objectives for a co-ordinated investment policy which may cover the entire economy or only one or several parts.
2. In establishing such objectives the Committee of Ministers shall simultaneously determine the methods appropriate for realising this co-ordinated policy; these methods may involve harmonising legislations concerning investments.

Article 65

In the field of agricultural policy the High Contracting Parties shall undertake:

a) to advance systematically technical progress.
b) to take measures as may make it possible to harmonise production and the sale of agricultural products and to secure farmers and farm labourers of the three countries a safe existence in well-managed and economically and socially warranted enterprises; these measures should also make it possible to develop

productivity and to maintain agricultural cost prices at the lowest possible level required fully to satisfy home demand and to build up the strongest possible position in foreign markets.

Article 66

1. If one of the High Contracting Parties ascertains that the situation in a certain field of agriculture, food supply or fisheries is developing in such a way that a serious crisis is to be feared, the Committee of Ministers may take the necessary decisions to prevent or remedy such a crisis, after previously obtaining an advisory opinion from the Consultative Interparliamentary Council and the Economic and Social Advisory Council. These decisions may temporarily derogate from the provisions of the present Treaty. [...]

Article 67

When applying the provisions of Article 66 of the present Treaty the High Contracting Parties shall take into account the special situation of Luxembourg agriculture as long as the latter is determined by less favourable natural factors of production.

Article 68

In the field of transport the coordinated policy, provided for in Article 8 of the present Treaty, shall rest on the following basic principles:

a) the harmonising of competitive conditions between the various media of inland transport within the territory of each High Contracting Party by the abolition of charges imposed on transport undertakings and advantages granted to the same.
b) the profitable operation of public and private transport undertakings.

Article 69

The High Contracting Parties shall undertake to direct their joint policy towards the promotion of a harmonious development of, and active cooperation between, their seaports.

Article 70

In the field of social policy the High Contracting Parties shall pursue a co-ordinated policy in consultation with corporate organisations of trade and industry which aims at the advancement of social progress and at the introduction of social welfare measures providing a maximum of protection and of social security to their people.

Article 71

In the monetary field and in respect of international payments the High Contracting Parties shall authorise their National Banks to participate in the elaboration of their co-ordinated and their joint policies, in particular by securing these banks an adequate representation in the Committee for monetary and financial questions.

CHAPTER 3

ECONOMIC AND FINANCIAL RELATIONS WITH THIRD COUNTRIES

Article 72

1. The Committee of Ministers shall determine a joint trade policy in economic relations with third countries and shall establish measures for its application.
2. In particular, the Committee will fix joint import and export quotas.

Article 73

The Committee of Ministers shall decide as to the expediency:
a) of all negotiations with third countries directed to the conclusion of treaties and agreements concerning foreign trade and payments related to same, and regarding the customs tariff;
b) of joint participation in international economic conferences and organisations.
    [...]

———————————————— 18 ————————————————

NORDIC COOPERATION

The Treaty of Cooperation between Denmark, Finland, Iceland, Norway and Sweden was signed in Helsinki on 23 March 1962. The following text includes amendments made in 1971 and 1974. This translation was issued by the Nordic Council in 1976. Much of the Treaty also appears in T. B. Millar (ed.), *Current International Treaties* (London: Croom Helm, 1984), pp. 259–63.

[Preambulary paragraphs omitted.]

INTRODUCTORY PROVISION

Article 1

The Contracting Parties shall endeavour to maintain and further develop cooperation between the countries in the juridical, cultural, social and economic fields as well as in regard to matters concerning transport and communications and the protection of environment.

JURIDICAL COOPERATION

Article 2

The Contracting Parties shall continue the work to attain the highest possible degree of juridical equality between nationals of any Nordic country, resident in a Nordic country other than his own, and the citizens of his country of residence.

Article 3

The Contracting Parties shall endeavour to facilitate the acquisition of citizenship by nationals of one Nordic country in another Nordic country.

Article 4

The Contracting Parties shall continue legislative cooperation in order to attain the greatest possible uniformity in Private Law.

Article 5

The Contracting Parties should strive to create uniform provisions regarding crime and the consequences of crime.

The investigation and prosecution of a crime committed in one Nordic country should, to the greatest possible extent, be pursued also in another Nordic country.

Article 6

The Contracting Parties shall strive to achieve mutual coordination of other legislation than that defined above in any fields where this proves to be appropriate.

Article 7

Each Contracting Party should work for the creation of such rules that a sentence passed by a court or other authority in another Nordic country can be executed also within the territory of the Party in question.

CULTURAL COOPERATION

Article 8

In every Nordic country, education and training given at school shall include, in a suitable degree, instruction in the language, culture and general social conditions of the other Nordic countries.

Article 9

Each Contracting Party should maintain and extend the opportunities for a student from another Nordic country to pursue studies and graduate in its educational establishments. It should also be possible, to the greatest possible extent, to count a part examination passed in any Nordic country towards a final examination taken in another Nordic country.

It should be possible to receive economic assistance from the country of domicile, irrespective of the country where the studies are pursued.

Article 10

The Contracting Parties should coordinate public education qualifying for a given profession or trade.

Such education should as far as possible, have the same qualifying value in all the Nordic countries. Additional studies necessary for reasons connected with national conditions can, however, be required.

Article 11

In the fields where cooperation is expedient, the development of educational establishments should be made uniform through continuous cooperation over development plans and their implementation.

Article 12

Cooperation in the field of research should be so organized that research funds and other resources available will be coordinated and exploited in the best possible way, among other things by establishing joint institutions.

Article 13

In order to support and strengthen cultural development the Contracting Parties shall promote free Nordic popular education and exchange in the fields of literature, art, music, theatre, film and other fields of culture: among other things, the possibilities provided by radio and television should be borne in mind.

SOCIAL COOPERATION

Article 14

The Contracting Parties shall strive to preserve and further develop the common Nordic labour market along the lines drawn up in earlier agreements. Labour exchanges and vocational guidance shall be coordinated. The exchange of trainees shall be free.

Efforts should be made to achieve uniformity in national regulations on industrial safety and other questions of similar nature.

Article 15

The Contracting Parties shall strive for arrangements whereby it will be possible for the nationals of one Nordic country, while staying in another Nordic country, to receive, as far as possible, the same social benefits as are offered to the citizens of the country of residence.

Article 16

The Contracting Parties shall further develop cooperation in public health and medical care, temperance work, child welfare and youth welfare.

Article 17

Each one of the Contracting Parties shall strive to have medical, technical or other similar safety controls carried out in such a way that the examination certificate issued will be acceptable in the other Nordic countries.

ECONOMIC COOPERATION

Article 18

The Contracting Parties shall, in order to promote economic cooperation in different fields, consult one another on questions of economic policy. Attention shall be devoted to the possibilities of coordinating measures taken to level out cyclical fluctuations.

Article 19

The Contracting Parties intend, in so far as possible, to promote cooperation between their countries in production and investment, striving to create conditions for direct cooperation between enterprises in two or more Nordic countries. In the further development of international cooperation, the Contracting Parties should strive to achieve an appropriate division of labour between the countries in the fields of production and investment.

Article 20

The Contracting Parties shall work for the greatest possible freedom of capital movement between the Nordic countries. In other payments and currency questions of common interest joint solutions shall be sought.

Article 21

The Contracting Parties shall seek to consolidate the cooperation started earlier to remove barriers to trade between the Nordic countries and, to the greatest extent possible, to strengthen and further develop this cooperation.

Article 22

In issues of international commercial policy the Contracting Parties shall endeavour, both separately and jointly, to promote the interests of the Nordic countries and, with this purpose in view, to consult one another.

Article 23

The Contracting Parties shall strive for coordination of technical and administrative customs regulations and for simplification of customs procedure in order to facilitate communications between the countries.

Article 24

The regulations governing frontier trade between the Nordic countries shall be formulated in such a way as to cause a minimum of inconvenience to the inhabitants of frontier districts.

Article 25

When the need and the necessary conditions exist for joint economic development of adjoining parts of the territories of two or more Contracting Parties, these Parties shall jointly endeavour to promote such development.

[Other articles deal with cooperation in the field of transport and communications, protecting the environment, etc. The work of the Nordic Council is discussed in Articles 44–59, and of the Nordic Council of Ministers in Articles 60–70.]

19

EFTA

The European Free Trade Association (EFTA) was officially established by the Stockholm Convention of 1960. Led by Britain, the 'Outer Seven' did not share the Common Market's ambitious hopes for economic integration, but it was not long before the two organizations regarded each other as rivals. This edition of the Stockholm Convention is taken from the unamended text which appeared in the *United Nations Treaty Series*, vol. 370, no. 5266, (New York: United Nations [by authority of the Secretariat], 1960), pp. 5–28.

[On 4 January 1960, representatives of Austria, Denmark, Norway, Portugal, Sweden, Switzerland and the United Kingdom signed a 'convention' at Stockholm to establish a 'Free Trade Association']

[...] Article 2

OBJECTIVES

The objectives of the Association shall be

(a) to promote in the Area of the Association and in each Member State a sustained expansion of economic activity, full employment, increased productivity and the rational use of resources, financial stability and continuous improvement in living standards,

(b) to secure that trade between Member States takes place in conditions of fair competition,

(c) to avoid significant disparity between Member States in the conditions of supply of raw materials produced within the Area of the Association, and

(d) to contribute to the harmonious development and expansion of world trade and to the progressive removal of barriers to it.

Article 3

IMPORT DUTIES

1. Member States shall reduce and ultimately eliminate, in accordance with this Article, customs duties and any other charges with equivalent effect, except duties notified in accordance with Article 6 and other charges which fall within that Article, imposed on or in connection with the importation of goods which are eligible for Area tariff treatment in accordance with Article 4. Any such duty or other charge is hereinafter referred to as an 'import duty'.

2. (a) [a timetable for the gradual reduction of import duties]

   (b) On and after 1st January, 1970, Member States shall not apply any import duties. [...]

4. Each Member State declares its willingness to apply import duties at a level below that indicated in paragraph 2 of this Article if it considers that its economic and financial position and the position of the sector concerned so permit.

5. The Council may at any time decide that any import duties shall be reduced more rapidly or eliminated earlier than is provided in paragraph 2 of this Article. [...]

Article 4

AREA TARIFF TREATMENT

1. For the purposes of Articles 3 to 7, goods shall ... be accepted as eligible for Area tariff treatment if [goods have been wholly produced within the Area of the Association or are included in lists later attached to the Treaty] [...]

Article 6

REVENUE DUTIES AND INTERNAL TAXATION

1. Member States shall not
   (a) apply directly or indirectly to imported goods any fiscal charges in excess of those applied directly or indirectly to like domestic goods, nor otherwise apply such charges so as to afford effective protection to like domestic goods, or
   (b) apply fiscal charges to imported goods of a kind which they do not produce, or which they do not produce in substantial quantities, in such a way as to afford effective protection to the domestic production of goods of a different kind which are substitutable for the imported goods, which enter into direct competition with them and which do not bear directly or indirectly, in the country of importation, fiscal charges of equivalent incidence [...]

2. Member States shall not introduce new fiscal charges which are inconsistent with paragraph 1 of this Article [...]

3. (a) In the case of any internal tax or other internal charge, Member States shall eliminate any effective protective element on or before 1st January, 1962.
   (b) In the case of any revenue duty, Member States shall either
      (i) progressively eliminate any effective protective element in the duty by successive reductions corresponding to those prescribed for import duties in Article 3, or
      (ii) eliminate any effective protective element in the duty on or before 1st January, 1965 [...]

4. Each Member State shall notify to the Council all fiscal charges applied by it where the rates of exchange, or the conditions governing the imposition or collection of the charge, are not identical in relation to the imported goods and to the like domestic goods [...]

5. Each Member State shall notify to the Council the revenue duties to which it intends to apply the provisions of this Article.
6. For the purpose of this Article:
    (a) 'fiscal charges' means revenue duties, internal taxes and other internal charges on goods;
    (b) 'revenue duties' means customs duties and other similar charges applied primarily for the purpose of raising revenue;
    (c) 'imported goods' means goods which are accepted as being eligible for Area tariff treatment in accordance with the provisions of Article 4. [...]

Article 8

PROHIBITION OF EXPORT DUTIES

1. Member States shall not introduce or increase export duties, and, on and after 1st January, 1962, shall not apply any such duties.
2. The provisions of this Article shall not prevent any Member State from taking such measures as are necessary to prevent evasion, by means of re-export, of duties which it applies to exports to territories outside the Area of the Association.
3. For the purposes of this Article, 'export duties' means any duties or charges with equivalent effect, imposed on or in connection with the exportation of goods from the territory of any Member State to the territory of any other Member State. [...]

Article 10

QUANTITATIVE IMPORT RESTRICTIONS

1. Member States shall not introduce or intensify quantitative restrictions on imports of goods from the territory of other Member States.
2. Member States shall eliminate such quantitative restrictions as soon as possible and not later than 31st December, 1969.
3. Each Member State shall relax quantitative restrictions progressively and in such a way that a reasonable rate of expansion of trade as a result of the application of Articles 3 and 6 is not frustrated and that no burdensome problems are created for the Member State concerned in the years immediately preceding 1st January, 1970.
4. Each Member State shall apply the provisions of this Article in such a way that all other Member States are given like treatment [...]
11. For the purposes of this Article:
    (a) 'quantitative restrictions' means prohibitions or restrictions on imports from the territory of other Member States whether made effective through quotas, import licences or other measures with equivalent effect, including administrative measures and requirements restricting import; [...]

Article 11

QUANTITATIVE EXPORT RESTRICTIONS

1. Member States shall not introduce or intensify prohibitions or restrictions on exports to other Member States, whether made effective through quotas or export licences or other measures with equivalent effect, and shall eliminate any such prohibitions or restrictions not later than 31st December, 1961.
2. The provisions of this Article shall not prevent any Member State from taking such measures as are necessary to prevent evasion, by means of re-export, of restrictions which it applies to exports to territories outside the Area of the Association.

Article 12

EXCEPTIONS

Provided that such measures are not used as a means of arbitrary or unjustifiable discrimination between Member States or as a disguised restriction on trade between Member States, nothing in Articles 10 and 11 shall prevent the adoption or enforcement by any Member State of measures

(a) necessary to protect public morals,
(b) necessary for the prevention of disorder or crime,
(c) necessary to protect human, animal or plant life or health,
(d) necessary to secure compliance with laws or regulations relating to customs enforcement, or to the classification, grading or marketing of goods, or to the operation of monopolies by means of state enterprises or enterprises given exclusive or special privileges,
(e) necessary to protect industrial property or copyrights or to prevent deceptive practices,
(f) relating to gold or silver,
(g) relating to the products of prison labour, or
(h) imposed for the protection of national treasures of artistic, historic, or archaeological value. [...]

Article 15

RESTRICTIVE BUSINESS PRACTICES

1. Member States recognise that the following practices are incompatible with this Convention in so far as they frustrate the benefits expected from the removal or absence of duties and quantitative restrictions on trade between Member States:
    (a) agreements between enterprises, decisions by associations of enterprises and

concerted practices between enterprises which have as their object or result the prevention, restriction or distortion of competition within the Area of the Association;

(b) actions by which one or more enterprises take unfair advantage of a dominant position within the Area of the Association or a substantial part of it. [...]

Article 16

ESTABLISHMENT

1. Member States recognise that restrictions on the establishment and operation of economic enterprises in their territories by nationals of other Member States should not be applied, through accord to such nationals of treatment which is less favourable than that accorded to their own nationals in such matters, in such a way as to frustrate the benefits expected from the removal or the absence of duties and quantitative restrictions on trade between Member States. [...]
3. Member States shall notify to the Council, within such period as the Council may decide, particulars of any restrictions which they apply in such a way that nationals of another Member State are accorded in their territories less favourable treatment in respect of the matters set out in paragraph 1 of this Article than is accorded to their own nationals. [...]

Article 17

DUMPED AND SUBSIDISED IMPORTS

1. Nothing in this Convention shall prevent any Member State from taking action against dumped or subsidised imports consistently with its other international obligations.
2. Any products which have been exported from the territory of one Member State to the territory of another Member State and have not undergone any manufacturing process since exportation shall, when re-imported into the territory of the first Member State, be admitted free of quantitative restrictions and measures with equivalent effect. They shall also be admitted free of customs duties and charges with equivalent effect, except that any allowance by way of drawback, relief from duty or otherwise, given by reason of the exportation from the territory of the first Member State, may be recovered.
3. If any industry in the territory of any Member State is suffering or is threatened with material injury as the result of the import of dumped or subsidised products into the territory of another Member State, the latter Member State shall, at the request of the former Member State, examine the possibility of taking such action as is consistent with its international obligations to remedy the injury or prevent the threatened injury.

Article 18

SECURITY EXCEPTIONS

1. Nothing in this Convention shall prevent any Member State from taking action which it considers necessary for the protection of its essential security interests, where such action
   (a) is taken to prevent the disclosure of information,
   (b) relates to trade in arms, ammunition or war materials or to research, development or production indispensable for defence purposes, provided that such action does not include the application of import duties or the quantitative restriction of imports except in so far as such restriction is permitted in accordance with Article 12 or is authorised by decision of the Council,
   (c) is taken to ensure that nuclear materials and equipment made available for peaceful purposes do not further military purposes, or
   (d) is taken in time of war or other emergency in international relations.
2. Nothing in this Convention shall prevent any Member State from taking action to carry out undertakings into which that Member State has entered for the purpose of maintaining international peace and security.

Article 19

BALANCE OF PAYMENTS DIFFICULTIES

1. Notwithstanding the provisions of Article 10, any Member State may, consistently with its other international obligations, introduce quantitative restrictions on imports for the purpose of safe-guarding its balance of payments. [...]

Article 20

DIFFICULTIES IN PARTICULAR SECTORS

1. If, in the territory of a Member State,
   (a) an appreciable rise in unemployment in a particular sector of industry or region is caused by a substantial decrease in internal demand for a domestic product, and
   (b) this decrease in demand is due to an increase in imports from the territory of other Member States as a result of the progressive elimination of duties, charges and quantitative restrictions in accordance with Articles 3, 6 and 10, that Member State may, notwithstanding any other provisions of this Convention,
      (i) limit those imports by means of quantitative restrictions to a rate not less than the rate of such imports during any period of twelve months which ended within twelve months of the date on which the restrictions

come into force; the restrictions shall not be continued for a period longer than eighteen months, unless the Council, by majority decision authorises their continuance for such further period and on such conditions as the Council considers appropriate [...]

Article 22

AGRICULTURAL POLICIES AND OBJECTIVE

1. In regard to agriculture, Member States recognize that the policies pursued by them are designed
   - (a) to promote increased productivity and the rational development of production,
   - (b) to provide a reasonable degree of market stability and adequate supplies to consumers at reasonable prices, and
   - (c) to ensure an adequate standard of living to persons engaged in agriculture. In pursuing these policies, Member States shall have due regard to the interests of other Member States in the export of agricultural goods and shall take into consideration traditional channels of trade.
2. Having regard to these policies, the objective of the Association shall be to facilitate an expansion of trade which will provide reasonable reciprocity to Member States whose economies depend to a great extent on exports of agricultural goods. [...]

Article 24

EXPORT SUBSIDIES ON AGRICULTURAL GOODS

1. A Member State shall not cause damage to the interests of other Member States by granting directly or indirectly any subsidy on a product [listed in Annex D] which results in an increase of that Member State's exports of that product compared with the exports which that Member State had in the product in question in a recent representative period.
2. It shall be the object of the Council, before 1st January, 1962, to establish rules for the gradual abolition of subsidised exports detrimental to other Member States. [...]

Article 26

FISH AND OTHER MARINE PRODUCTS

1. The provisions in all the foregoing Articles of this Convention shall not apply in relation to the fish and other marine products [listed in Annex E]. [...]

Article 27

OBJECTIVE FOR TRADE IN FISH AND OTHER MARINE PRODUCTS

Having regard to the national policies of Member States and the special conditions prevailing in the fishing industry, the objective of the Association shall be to facilitate an expansion of trade in fish and other marine products which will provide reasonable reciprocity to Member States whose economies depend to a great extent on exports of those products. [...]

Article 29

INVISIBLE TRANSACTIONS AND TRANSFERS

Member States recognise the importance of invisible transactions and transfers for the proper functioning of the Association. They consider that the obligations with regard to the freedom of such transactions and transfers undertaken by them in other international organisations are sufficient at present. The Council may decide on such further provisions with regard to such transactions and transfers as may prove desirable, having due regard to the wider international obligations of Member States.

Article 30

ECONOMIC AND FINANCIAL POLICIES

Member States recognise that the economic and financial policies of each of them affect the economies of other Member States and intend to pursue those policies in a manner which serves to promote the objectives of the Association. They shall periodically exchange views on all aspects of those policies. In so doing, they shall take into account the corresponding activities within the Organisation for European Economic Cooperation and other international organisations. The Council may make recommendations to Member States on matters relating to those policies to the extent necessary to ensure the attainment of the objectives and the smooth operation of the Association.

Article 31

GENERAL CONSULTATIONS AND COMPLAINTS PROCEDURE

1. If any Member State considers that any benefit conferred upon it by this Convention or any objective of the Association is being or may be frustrated and if a satisfactory settlement is not reached between the Member States concerned, any of those Member States may refer the matter to the Council. [...]

Article 34

ADMINISTRATIVE ARRANGEMENTS OF THE ASSOCIATION

The Council should take decisions for the following purposes:

(a) to lay down the Rules of Procedure of the Council and of any other bodies of the Association, which may include provision that procedural questions may be decided by majority vote;

(b) to make arrangements for the secretariat services required by the Association;

(c) to establish the financial arrangements necessary for the administrative expenses of the Association, the procedure for establishing a budget and the apportionment of those expenses between the Member States [. . .]

Article 36

RELATIONS WITH INTERNATIONAL ORGANIZATIONS

The Council, acting on behalf of the Association, shall seek to establish such relationships with other international organisations as may facilitate the attainment of the objectives of the Association. It shall in particular seek to establish close collaboration with the Organisation for European Economic Cooperation. [. . .]

───────────── 20 ─────────────

COMECON

The Charter of the Council for Mutual Economic Assistance was signed in 1959. Known as CMEA or COMECON, this agreement was the basis of economic cooperation in the Soviet bloc. The original signatories included Albania, Bulgaria, Hungary, the German Democratic Republic, Romania, the USSR and Czechoslovakia. Albania withdrew from the Treaty in 1961. This text appeared in the *United Nations Treaty Series*, vol. 368, no. 5245, (New York: United Nations [by authority of the Secretariat], 1959) p. 253.

Article I

PURPOSES AND PRINCIPLES

1. The purpose of the Council for Mutual Economic Assistance is to promote, by uniting and coordinating the efforts of the member countries of the Council, the planned development of the national economies and the acceleration of the economic and technical progress of those countries, the raising of the level of industrialization of the countries with a less-developed industry, and a continual growth in the productivity, together with a steady increase in the well-being of the peoples, of the member countries of the Council.

2. The Council for Mutual Economic Assistance is based on the principle of the sovereign equality of all the member countries of the Council.

   Economic and scientific-technical cooperation between the member countries of the Council shall take place in accordance with the principles of complete equality of rights, respect for sovereignty and national interest, mutual advantage and friendly mutual aid.

Article II

MEMBERSHIP

1. The original members of the Council for Mutual Economic Assistance shall be the countries which have signed and ratified the present Charter.
2. Membership in the Council shall be open to other countries which subscribe to the purposes and principles of the Council and declare that they agree to accept the obligations contained in the present Charter.

   New members shall be admitted by a decision of the Session of the Council, on the basis of official requests by countries for their admission to membership in the Council.
3. Any member country of the Council may leave the Council, after notifying the depositary of the present Charter to that effect. Such notice shall take effect six months after its receipt by the depositary. Upon receiving such notice, the depositary shall inform the member countries of the Council thereof.
4. The member countries of the Council agree:
   (a) To ensure implementation of the recommendations, accepted by them, or organs of the Council;
   (b) To render to the Council and its officers the necessary assistance in the execution of the duties laid upon them by the present Charter;
   (c) To make available to the Council the material and information essential to the fulfilment of the tasks entrusted to it;
   (d) To keep the Council informed of progress in the implementation of the recommendations adopted in the Council.

Article III

FUNCTIONS AND POWERS

1. In conformity with the purposes and principles mentioned in Article 1 of the present Charter, the Council for Mutual Economic Assistance shall:
   (a) organize all-round economic, scientific and technical cooperation of the Council's member countries in the most rational use of their natural resources and acceleration of the development of their productive forces;
   (b) foster the improvement of the international socialist division of labour by coordinating national economic development plans, and the specialization and cooperation of production in the Council's member countries;
   (c) take measures to study economic, scientific and technical problems which are of interest to the Council's member countries;

(d) assist the Council's member countries in elaborating and carrying out joint measures for:
  - the development of the industry and agriculture of the Council's member countries;
  - the development of transport with a view to ensuring first priority for increasing export, import and transit shipments of the Council's member countries;
  - the most efficient use of principal capital investments allocated by the Council's member countries for the development of the mining and manufacturing industries and for the construction of major projects which are of interest to two countries or more;
  - the development of trade and exchange of services between the Council's member countries and between them and other countries;
  - the exchange of scientific and technical achievements and advanced production experience. [...]

Article IV

RECOMMENDATIONS AND DECISIONS

1. Recommendations shall be adopted on questions of economic and scientific-technical cooperation. Such recommendations shall be communicated to the member countries of the Council for consideration.
   Recommendations adopted by member countries of the Council shall be implemented by them through decisions of the Governments or competent authorities of those countries, in conformity with their laws. [...]
3. All recommendations and decisions of the Council shall be adopted only with the consent of the member countries concerned, each country being entitled to state its interest in any question under consideration by the Council.

Article V

ORGANS

[The Charter establishes four 'principal organs': the Session of the Council, the Conference of representatives of the countries in the Council, the standing Commissions, and the Secretariat.]
  [Articles VI–IX describe the role and functions of the four organs.]

Article X

PARTICIPATION OF OTHER COUNTRIES

The Council may invite countries which are not members of the Council to take part in the works of the organs of the Council. The conditions . . . shall be determined by the Council in agreement with the countries concerned. [...]

Article XIII

MISCELLANEOUS PROVISIONS

1. The Council for Mutual Economic Assistance shall enjoy, on the territories of all member countries of the Council, the legal capacity essential to the performance of its functions and the achievement of its purposes.
2. The Council, as also the representatives of the member countries ... and officers of the Council, shall enjoy, on the territory of each of those countries, the privileges and immunities which are necessary for the performance of the functions and the achievements of the purposes set forth in the present Charter.
3. The legal capacity, privileges and immunities mentioned in this Article shall be defined in a special Convention. [...]

Article XIV

LANGUAGES

The official language of the Council for Mutual Economic Assistance shall be the languages of all the member countries of the Council. The working language of the Council shall be Russian.

———————————————— 21 ————————————————

THE COMMUNIST COMMONWEALTH

The Council of Mutual Economic Aid (COMECON) met in Moscow in June 1962. Their recommendations appeared under the title of 'Basic Principles of the International Socialist Division of Labour' and were published in *Pravda* on 17 June 1962. The following translation appeared in the *Current Digest of the Soviet Press* XIV, no. 24, pp. 3–8.

1. *The Commonwealth of Socialist Countries and the International Socialist Division of Labor.* – The world socialist system is a social, economic and political commonwealth of free, sovereign peoples following the path of socialism and communism, united by a community of interests and goals and by indestructible ties of international socialist solidarity.

The need for close unity of the socialist countries in a single system is based on objective laws of economic and political development.

The commonwealth of socialist states is based on an economic foundation that is the same in each country – public ownership of the means of production; on the same system of government – the rule of the people headed by the working class; and on a single ideology – Marxism–Leninism. [...]

The commonwealth of socialist countries realizes its goals through comprehensive political, economic and cultural cooperation. In this all socialist countries are strictly guided by the principles of full equality, mutual respect for independence and sovereignty, fraternal mutual aid and mutual advantage. In the socialist camp no one has or can have any special rights or privileges. The observance of the principles of Marxism–Leninism and socialist internationalism is an indispensable condition for the successful development of the world socialist system. [...]

Each socialist state works out national plans for economic development proceeding from the specific conditions in the country and the political and economic tasks posed by the Communist and Workers' Parties, taking into account the needs and potentialities of all the socialist countries. The new social system permits the organic combination of the development of the national economies with the development and strengthening of the world economic system of socialism as a whole. The success of the entire world socialist system depends on the contribution of each country.

The socialist countries see it as their international duty to bend their efforts toward ensuing high rates of growth of industrial and agricultural production in each country in accordance with existing potentialities, toward gradually evening the levels of economic development, and toward the successful accomplishment of the task of surpassing the world capitalist system in absolute volume of industrial and agricultural output and then overtaking the most highly developed capitalist countries in per capita production and in the living standards of the working people.

The accomplishment of these tasks will require the maximum development of the creative capacities and initiative of the peoples in each socialist country, the industrial development of all socialist countries, a comprehensive rise in the productivity of social labor, continuous technical progress, steady improvement in the practice of economic planning, the use of collective experience, and the expansion and strengthening of economic cooperation between the socialist countries. The combination of efforts to develop the national economy of each socialist country with joint efforts to strengthen and expand economic cooperation and mutual aid is the highroad toward a further rise in the world socialist economy.

Various forms of economic cooperation and mutual aid among the socialist countries have been developed and are being perfected: the coordination of national economic plans, the introduction of production specialization and co-operation, international socialist trade, the granting of credits, technical aid and scientific and technical cooperation, cooperation in the construction of economic objectives and in the exploitation of natural resources, and others. Constant improvements are also being made in the organizational bases of economic cooperation between the socialist countries; the collective agency for the organization of this cooperation – the Council on Mutual Economic Aid – has been strengthened. [...]

In the process of economic, scientific and technical cooperation among the socialist countries, a new type of international division of labor is being formed.

As distinct from the international capitalist division of labor, which expresses the relations of the exploitation of the weak by the strong, is formed spontaneously in the course of the sharp competitive struggle and expansion of the capitalist monopolies, increases the distance between levels of economic development and leads to the formation of an abnormal, one-sided economic structure in the underdeveloped countries, the international socialist division of labor is implemented purposefully and according to plan, in accordance with the vital interests and tasks of harmonious and comprehensive development of all socialist countries, and leads to stronger unity among them.

The planned international socialist division of labor aids in making maximum use of the advantages of the world socialist system, establishing the proportions in the national economy of each country, rationally distributing productive forces on the scale of the world socialist system, using material and manpower resources effectively and strengthening the defensive power of the socialist camp. The division of labor must reliably provide each socialist country with a market for specialized types of products and make it possible for each country to obtain the necessary raw and other materials, equipment and other goods. [...]

2. [...] The coordination of plans is a voluntary joint planning activity undertaken by the socialist states and is directed toward the maximum utilization of the political and economic advantages of the socialist system in the interests of achieving the most rapid victory of socialism and communism. It aids in implementing the policies of the Communist and Workers' Parties, which are based on the scientific principles of Marxism–Leninism and on a profound analysis of the potentials and requirements of economic development. [...]

The coordination of plans will assume greater and greater importance for the expansion and strengthening of ties among the national economies of the socialist countries, for achieving planned expansion of reproduction in individual countries and thus in the world socialist system as a whole. The interrelation between the economies of the individual countries, following from the division of labor, must be strong and stable, since violation of them by even one country would inevitably lead to the disruption of the economic rhythm in the socialist countries as well. [...]

3. *Basic Trends in the Rational Division of Labor in Major Branches of Production.* – Further improvement of the international socialist division of labor on the basis of the coordination of plans presupposes accelerated development of such advanced forms as production specialization and cooperation in the socialist camp. Interstate specialization means the concentration of the output of one type of product in one or several socialist countries in order to satisfy the requirements of the interested countries, and in this connection raising the technical and organizational level of production and establishing firm economic ties and production cooperation between the countries. International production specialization leads to expanded output of products, reduced production costs, higher labor productivity and improved quality and technical characteristics.

Acting as active factors in technical progress, international specialization and cooperation of production contribute to the more rapid industrial development of all socialist countries. International specialization and cooperation are of great economic importance for the development of all branches of the national economy, particularly machine-building, the chemical industry and ferrous and nonferrous metallurgy. Through specialization it is possible to achieve the rapid introduction of new products linked with modern trends in technical progress.

An important basis for the further extension of specialization and cooperation is the broad application of uniform norms, types and standards, both within each country and on an international scale, in the first place for those materials, parts, units and finished articles the manufacture of which is best organized as mass or large-scale series production, in order to satisfy the needs of a number of countries.

The following are highly important conditions, for the most rational development of the international division of labor in the raw materials, fuel and power industries and for achieving high rates of development in them:

> the expansion by each country of its raw materials and power base first of all by intensifying and heightening the efficiency of geological prospecting work, conducted where necessary through the joint efforts of several countries on large promising areas;
> the comprehensive development of the extraction in all the socialist countries, taking natural and economic conditions into account, of raw materials that are in short supply in the socialist camp;
> the exchange of advanced technical experience in the field of the extraction and economical use of certain types of raw materials, and higher coefficients of extraction of minerals from deposits now being worked and of useful components from the raw materials mined;
> joint aid in the expansion of the raw material branches of industry, specifically through the financial participation of the states interested in obtaining the products of these branches;
> the development of technology in the field of the extraction of fuel and raw materials, and also in the production of building materials, in order to reduce operating expenditures and to increase the quality of existing fuels and materials and introduce new ones, particularly synthetic types;
> the integrated operation of the water resources of the countries in order to develop power production and water transport, as well as irrigation and reclamation. [...]

In coordinating plans for the development of the major branches of the national economies of the countries, it is also advisable to proceed from the following:

(a) The international socialist division of labor in the fuel and power fields will be increasingly expanded and will play a growing role in satisfying the power requirements of the socialist countries. This involves:
the development of power production throughout the socialist camp at high rates, greater than the rates of development of industry;

the development of power-consuming branches of industry chiefly near the sources of cheap power, in order to reduce power losses and to save the cost of power-line construction;

the reduction of shipments of coal for power production to the extent that such shipments can be profitably replaced by direct power-line transmission;

the gradual conversion to integrated power systems embracing groups of countries; this is one of the chief progressive tendencies in the division and cooperation of social labor in the socialist camp. The integration of power systems in the socialist countries calls for broader cooperation in mutual deliveries of power and also in the construction of large power-generating units and transmission lines.

The direction of the international socialist division of labor in this field may change as a result of the discovery of new types or sources of power available to all countries, and also as the result of radical changes in the methods of utilizing the so-called classical power sources.

(b) The development of the international socialist division of labor in the field of metallurgy must contribute to the greatest possible extent to the rapid growth of production of ferrous and nonferrous metals in the variety needed to satisfy the growing needs of the countries, and also to reducing expenditures for the production of metal.

The division of labor in the metallurgical industry is based on the need to develop this branch in all the socialist countries in accordance with the availability of raw materials, industrial fuel and power sources or with the possibility of the expedient importation of raw materials from other countries. It would be advisable to develop metallurgy with a complete production cycle chiefly in those countries that are fully or almost fully supplied with ore and industrial fuel, or with at least one of these basic raw materials. [. . .]

(c) The output of chemical products, particularly plastics and other synthetic materials and also mineral fertilizers, should be developed at accelerated rates in all the socialist countries.

Each country should develop its chemical industry chiefly from local raw materials. In addition, there will be an expansion of production from raw materials the use of which is profitable in spite of the need for long-distance hauling, and the processing of which ensures its complete utilization.

Expansion of the variety of the products of the chemical industry and the need for large production units presupposes an extension of international special- ization and economic cooperation in this field, in the first place in branches requiring large capital expenditures and special equipment, and also the exchange of products (dyes, chemical reagents, pharmaceutical preparations and others).

(d) The machine-building industry is being developed in all the socialist countries with utilization of the advantages of international specialization and coopera- tion. In carrying out specialization, account must be taken of the need for rapid growth of the machine-building industry in countries where it is relatively less developed.

Expansion of the output of the machine-building industry with appearance of new branches and types of production, the constant expansion of the range of products and the raising of the technical standard of output requires constant extension of international specialization and cooperation in this branch. Specialization and cooperation are important factors in the rapid introduction of new technology, the full mechanization and automation of production, and the mastering by the socialist camp of the entire range of modern machines and their constant technical improvement. [...]

Countries that do not have a large enough metallurgical base should concentrate mainly on the development of production that requires small amounts of metal but relatively large amounts of labor. In countries that do have a highly developed metallurgical base, it would be advisable to develop types of machine-building production that require large amounts of both metal and labor. At the same time the specialization of machine-building in each country, particularly the production of industrial equipment, should take into account the branch structure of the countries' national economies and the planned progressive changes in this structure. [...]

(e) Specialization of the production of consumer goods is advisable only when the total demand for individual varieties or models in a given country is and will remain for the next few years below the optimum rational output at the given level of technology. [...]

The food industry of each country in the socialist camp should be developed and specialized so as to provide the fullest processing of local agricultural raw materials.

(f) The further development of agriculture in the socialist countries is determined by the necessity of increasing in every way possible the output of food and agricultural raw materials in order to provide the world's highest standard of living for the working people.

Owing to the unequal amounts of farmland per capita in the socialist countries and to differences in soil and climatic conditions, the practice of exchanging farm products among these countries will continue and will be developed further. This raises the necessity for coordinating plans with consideration of the possibilities for the further development of specialization among the socialist countries in the field of agricultural production, based on the interests and potentials of the countries. The problem of agricultural specialization must be solved on the basis of the maximum possible increase in the output of grain and livestock products in each socialist country.

An increase in the output and efficiency of agriculture also calls for coordination of plans and production cooperation among the socialist countries in the manufacture of farm machinery, agricultural chemical and synthetic fodders, an expanded program for the exchange of high-grade seed, etc.

4. *Achieving High Economic Effectiveness in the International Socialist Division of Labor.* – The international socialist division of labor increases the effectiveness of social production and thus contributes to the successful performance of the

economic and political tasks posed by the Communist and Workers' Parties at each stage of historical development.

The effectiveness of social production in the world socialist system manifests itself in the high and steady rates of growth of output of products, which make it possible to satisfy more fully the growing requirements of the people in all the socialist countries and steadily to overcome the differences in their economic levels.

One condition for high economic effectiveness of the international division of labor in the world socialist system is the attainment of rational proportions in production by coordinating the plans of the countries, including the best distribution of production capacity for the manufacture of similar or interchangeable products. [...]

Along with calculating economic effectiveness, it is necessary in improving the international socialist division of labor to consider the need for ensuring full employment of the labor force, an even balance of payments, the role of a given industry in increasing the productivity of social labor in the whole of the national economy and in attaining an equal level of economic development for all countries, the strengthening of defense capabilities, and other factors. [...]

6. *Overcoming the Historically Formed Differences in the Levels of Economic Development of the Socialist Countries.* – The countries in the world socialist system have begun the construction of a socialist society at a time when there are still differences in the levels of development of productive forces. It follows logically from the very nature of socialism that their economic levels must be equalized. It is possible to attain the highest living standard in the world for all the peoples in the socialist states and to bring about a more or less simultaneous transition of all countries to communism only if the production conditions necessary for this are created. The material prerequisites for building communism are formed on the basis of the creative labor of the people in every country and a constant increase in their contribution to the common cause of strengthening the socialist system. [...]

The basic differences in the levels of development of productive forces, which are related to the countries' historical development under capitalism, will be eliminated in the course of building socialism and communism. The socialist countries will come closer to each other in volume of per capita national income and industrial production, in the efficiency of agricultural production, in level of labor productivity and in the most important indices of the living standard of the population. In the long run this means that the countries with a lower economic level as compared with other socialist countries will develop faster.

At the same time, equalization of the levels of economic development does not mean the elimination of all differences resulting from specific features having to do with natural resources, climatic conditions and national characteristics of the consumption structure and way of life of the population. [...]

[...] socialist countries can aid in increasing the effectiveness of the efforts made by these countries to develop their national economies rapidly by:

- sharing the latest achievements of science and technology;
- assisting in the design of technically advanced enterprises, in geological prospecting and in the training of skilled cadres;
- supplying industrial equipment, particularly complete sets of equipment for enterprises, and helping to install and adjust this equipment;
- granting credits and other forms of aid.

This end will also be served by cooperation in the construction of industrial installations, the exploitation of natural resources and the provision of raw materials, fuel and electric power.

Socialist industry, which calls for the preponderant development of heavy industry and its core, machine building, is the principal path toward overcoming technical and economic backwardness, and it is a path that has been tested by the experience of the Soviet Union and the other socialist states. Industrialization is much faster and easier if the advantages of the international socialist division of labor are utilized. [...]

_____ 22 _____

SOVIET REACTION

On 26 August 1962, *Pravda* printed the 'Theses on Imperialist Integration', prepared by a group of Russian political economists. The following translation appeared in the *Current Digest of the Soviet Press*, XIV (1962), no. 34, pp. 9–16. This document does not include all of the theses.

Introduction. – Problems of the so-called 'integration' (i.e., unification) of Western Europe have recently occupied a large place in the policies of the Western powers. [...]

V. I. Lenin foresaw that the international unification of monopoly capital, after it had divided up the world economically, might occur not only in the form of international monopolies but also as agreements between entire states. 'Of course,' Lenin wrote, '*temporary* agreements between capitalists and between powers are possible. In this sense a United States of Europe is a possibility as an agreement among *European* capitalists – but on what? Only on jointly suppressing socialism in Europe, on jointly guarding stolen colonies.' This Leninist principle provides the key to understanding the essence of the processes of modern West European 'integration'.

The Common Market reflects the class unity of the imperialists, who, in spite of their mutual hostility, are seeking to unite, attempting to strengthen the positions of capitalism through international state-monopoly alliances, and to cure, or at least relieve, the ulcers and vices of capitalism [...] The financial oligarchy hopes to discover in the development of 'integration' an 'answer' of sorts to the growing might of world socialism, which is becoming the decisive factor in the development of mankind; it is seeking with the help of the Common Market to keep the old colonial and semicolonial world within the orbit of imperialism, to reduce the competitive struggle in world markets and to achieve consolidation of the imperialist camp. But all these efforts are in vain. As is pointed out in the Party Program, the principal contradiction in the modern world – the contradiction between socialism and imperialism – does not remove the profound contradictions rending the capitalist world.

The uneven development of capitalism changes the alignment of forces in the world capitalist market and intensifies the struggle over the redivision of that market among international alliances of the monopolists. The European Economic Community, which is a new form of agreement between state-monopoly groupings, is at the same time a new form of the most intense kind of competition for a redivision of the world capitalist market in accordance with the present alignment of forces in the imperialist camp, a new form of penetration by the powerful monopolies of the imperialist states into the economies of their weaker partners.

The Common Market is a new phenomenon in the development of the capitalist economy. In the contemporary epoch, the epoch of the transition from capitalism to socialism, the social and economic contradictions of capitalism have become much sharper. [. . .]

The acceleration of technical progress and the introduction of methods of mass production and automation require an enormous expansion of markets, intensify the tendency toward the internationalization of economic life and further the development of international specialization of production. Under the conditions of imperialism these processes take on monstrous, reactionary forms. One of these forms is imperialist 'integration', in the development of which an important role is played by the international interweaving of finance capital and, specifically, the creation of international cartel associations of a new type based on production-specialization agreements between the largest concerns and trusts. The desire of the monopolies to take advantage of the fruits of technical progress and international specialization in order to increase their superprofits is the basis of the measures for economic integration and gives rise to a tendency toward the reduction of customs duties. [. . .]

Problems connected with the Common Market are of vital importance to the broad masses of working people in Western Europe. Making use of the Common Market, finance capital is striving to organize a new offensive against the working class in the economic, political and ideological spheres. The monopolies have actually gone so far as to mount a united front of struggle against the working class in Western Europe; they are striving at the working people's expense to overcome the profound contradictions of contemporary capitalism. The Common Market is also fraught with grave negative consequences for the peasantry, artisans and small and middle tradesmen and manufacturers. The European Economic Community is a conspiracy of the monopolies behind the backs of the peoples and against their fundamental interests.

The leaders of the imperialist powers are attempting to transform 'integration' into some sort of 'holy alliance' of reaction in the struggle against socialism, against the workers, national liberation and general democratic movements, and for the strengthening of the economic base of the aggressive North Atlantic bloc in Europe. West European 'integration' operates as a weapon of the imperialist policy of the 'cold war,' of increasing international tension.

2. [...] the creation of the Common Market was by no means the basis of the growth of production and trade. When this association was formed, it was joined by countries (the F.R.G., France and Italy) whose economies were already developing at relatively high rates. The expansion of production in West European countries was based on such factors as the mass renovation of fixed capital in the prevailing conditions of a world scientific and technological revolution, changes in the structure of the economy and the creation of new branches of production. The rates of economic development in West Germany, Italy and some other countries of the 'six' were high also, in part, because these countries had the opportunity to utilize the large accumulations resulting from the relatively low wages paid to workers, especially during the periods of extensive unemployment. Until recently West Germany was not burdened with large military expenditures. In addition, the United States has invested enormous sums in these countries. This is the basis of the growth of industrial production in Western Europe in the postwar years.

The Common Market has to a certain extent operated along the same lines, furthering the expansion of production. The implementation of the Rome Treaty, which has proceeded in conditions of sharpening competitive struggle in the Common Market, has aided in increasing capital investments, accelerated the modernization of enterprises and brought with it a certain amount of economic and organizational reconstruction of the monopolies. The lowering of customs barriers has stimulated the transition to mass production on a greater scale. The Common Market is not simply the arithmetical sum of the markets of the countries in the European Economic Community. Even in its degenerate capitalist forms, economic 'integration' can provide an impetus to increasing the volume of production and of domestic and foreign trade. But the importance of this factor should not be exaggerated. It is significant that Japan, which has no relationship with the Common Market, is considerably ahead of the countries in the European Economic Community in the rates of increase of its production and exports.

3. Thus far only the part of the Common Market program entailing relatively minor difficulties has gone into effect. However, the implementation of even this, the easiest, part of the 'integration' program has run into sharp contradictions. The European Economic Community has not only failed to form a harmoniously developing economic complex but on the contrary has become the source of an intensified competitive struggle for markets. New contradictions have been added to the old ones. The historically formed economic structure of the six West European countries has made them natural competitors for the sale of the same types of industrial output: products of the general machine-building industry, chemicals, electrical equipment, automobiles, textiles. [...]

In the near future, when the Common Market countries begin the implementation of the other, more complex measures set forth in the Rome Treaty, still greater contradictions and impediments will arise. Moreover, the strength of the Common Market has not yet been subjected to the test of an economic crisis. [...]

5. The Common Market was the result of the operations of the financial oligarchy in the new stage of the crisis of world capitalism. 'Integration' has in no degree altered the nature of contemporary monopoly capitalism, as the bourgeois ideologists assert. The Common Market is a 'Europe of trusts', an empire of giant monopolies exploiting millions upon millions of working people. Of the 200 largest monopolies in the world, in which are concentrated almost one-third of the world's capitalist production, 43 are leading trusts in the countries of the European Economic Community.

The concentration and centralization of production and capital has proceeded on an unprecedented scale in the six Common Market countries in recent years. While in 1954 joint-stock companies in the F.R.G. with assets of more than 100,000,000 marks each held 34 per cent of the country's stock capital, in 1961 they held more than 52 per cent. The lowering of customs barriers and the new conditions in the competitive struggle in the Common Market have brought on a new wave of mergers of large companies and also the swallowing of small and middle-sized enterprises by the gigantic trusts. In France, for instance, 310 mergers were registered in the period 1946–1956, while in 1959 there were 931 and in 1960 there were 1,000. The power of the monopolies over the life of the nations has been enormously strengthened. [...]

6. The alliance of the reactionary, imperialist bourgeoisie of the countries united in the Common Market has led to further intensified exploitation of the working class, to an offensive against the living standard of the working people, against the workers' and democratic movement.

The agencies of the European Economic Community – the so-called Assembly ('European Parliament'), whose duty it is to control the work of the community; the Council, which is the highest policy-making body of the Common Market; the Commission, which is the highest executive body of the community; and the Court – are made up of persons who were appointed with the full approval of the monopolies and who act in the interests of the monopolies.

In their attempts to secure for themselves a more favorable position in the Common Market system, the monopolies are implementing measures directed toward reducing wages and social benefits to the workers and are everywhere intensifying the labor of the workers. The gap between labor productivity and wages is becoming wider and wider; the monopolies gain from this, and the working class loses.

The Rome Treaty stipulates a gradual 'equalization' of wages and working conditions in the Common Market countries. The monopolies are attempting to 'equalize' wages and social benefits at the lowest level and to 'freeze' them there. [...]

In the majority of Common Market countries, the chief obstacle to the reduction of real wages has been the heightened strike struggle undertaken by the working class. As industrial production has increased, the working class in a number of countries has been able through stubborn struggle to achieve a certain increase in wages. In these conditions, opposition to increased wages has been proclaimed as a guiding principle of the government policies of Common Market countries.

7. West European 'integration' intensifies the process of expropriation of small producers. The lowered customs barriers and the eased restrictions on the movement of capital within the Common Market have forced small enterprises to face competition from foreign monopolies as well as domestic ones.

The monopolies are ruining tens and hundreds of thousands of artisans, small entrepreneurs and merchants. In France in the past four years 20 per cent of the small textile enterprises have been closed and the number of small mercantile enterprises has been reduced by 27 per cent, while the share of large enterprises in domestic trade has increased 50 per cent. In the F.R.G. the number of artisan enterprises declined by more than 20,000 from 1957 to 1960.

The ruin of the peasantry has assumed enormous proportions in the Common Market countries. In the postwar years several West European governments have begun to carry out plans for the 'modernization' and 'reorganization' of agriculture, directed toward the creation of large capitalist agricultural enterprises through accelerated expropriation of small and medium-sized peasant farms. In the conditions of the Common Market these processes have been intensified. In Italy more than 500,000·peasants and farmhands have been forced to leave agriculture during the past five years. At least 100,000 people have forsaken agriculture in the F.R.G. annually in recent years. [...]

Thus 'integration', which itself arose from the process of monopolization and the economic division of the capitalist world among the large trusts, has in its turn given a powerful impetus to the further development of the concentration and centralization of capital, to the still greater concentration of economic and financial power in the hands of a few giant monopolies. It has intensified the contradiction of interests not only between the monopoly bourgeoisie and the working class but also between the monopolies on the one hand and the petty and middle bourgeoisie of the cities and the countryside on the other.

8. The alliance between Adenauer's clerical–militaristic dictatorship and General de Gaulle's authoritarian regime has become the backbone of 'integration'. The already limited bourgeois democracy is being further curtailed, national sovereignty is being increasingly restricted and the rights of elected parliamentary institutions are being reduced to nothing and transformed into a fiction. West European 'integration' is accompanied by intensified political reaction and by the transfer of state power to authoritarian regimes. [...]

The schemes for establishing in one form or another a 'suprastate' political association of the Common Market countries with corresponding 'supranational' agencies poses a great danger for the democratic rights of the working people, for the vital interests of the peoples of Western Europe. The imperialists are striving for its organization in order to strengthen their aggressive military-political blocs. The efforts of the most reactionary circles of finance capital in the West European countries to join forces to impede nationalization and other democratic reforms plays an important role in the attempts to hammer this association together. The plans for political 'integration' are a serious threat to the independent national existence of the peoples of Western Europe. [...]

9. The Common Market has not led and cannot lead to the formation of a 'conflictless', 'harmonious' Western Europe. It is still an arena of sharp economic and political friction, contradictions and conflicts. The monopolies of West Germany and France occupy leading positions in the Common Market, and the position of the West German monopolies is growing constantly stronger. At present the F.R.G. accounts for almost half of the industrial output of all the countries in the European Economic Community. The economic superiority of the F.R.G. over France has increased considerably as compared with the prewar period. Eight of the ten biggest trusts in 'integrated' Europe are West German. The monopolies of the F.R.G. are striving to establish their economic domination in Western Europe and to achieve by 'peaceful' means such a redivision of 'spheres of influence' as German imperialism could not win by force of arms. The Bonn leaders are striving, under the European 'cover', to carry out their revanchist and aggressive plans, to broaden their economic expansion. On the other hand, the present rulers of France are making claims on the leadership of 'integrated' Europe. The bitter disputes about the forms and methods of political 'integration' and the talks about the creation of 'supranational' agencies that are being conducted without the consent of the peoples and behind their backs reflect the ineradicable contradictions that exist among the imperialist powers.

10. [...] The question of Britain's entry into the Common Market has become the subject of a sharp political struggle. Progressive organizations, the majority of trade unions, many Labor Party politicians and a number of farmers' unions are actively opposing Britain's participation in European 'integration'. They emphasize that membership in the Common Market would have a ruinous effect on the standard of living of British workers, would do serious harm to the country's agriculture and would impede the struggle of the working people for full employment and expansion of the social security system. A number of influential members of the Conservative Party and representatives of business circles have also come out against Britain's entry into the Common Market because they fear a weakening of Britain's position in the Commonwealth countries. Business circles in Australia, Canada, New Zealand and other countries of the British Commonwealth are also protesting against British participation in the Common Market because they fear the loss of their British market.

In their turn, the participants in the European Free Trade Association, abandoned by Britain, are feeling growing pressure from the large Common Market powers. For the small West European states, entry into the Common Market would mean serious infringements on their national, economic and political interests. The danger for the small countries is all the greater because the principle of unanimity in decisions on important problems by the Common Market agencies is being replaced by the majority principle.

11. The political tendency of the European Economic Community makes it impossible for Common Market members to maintain a neutral status. Therefore the attempts to draw Sweden, Switzerland and Austria into the Common Market are actually aimed at dragging these countries into the system of aggressive military-political blocs.

The encroachment on the neutrality of these countries has run into the opposition of their peoples, who consider neutrality to be one of their major accomplishments. Therefore some members of the ruling circles of these countries, under pressure from the USA and the F.R.G., are seeking roundabout paths toward union with the European community that take the form of so-called association and are attempting to veil the Common Market's political and military-strategic significance. They cherish the illusion that it is possible to find a form of association with the Common Market that would enable them to solve their own economic problems and would at the same time permit them to keep their neutrality. [...]

13. With the establishment of two mutually opposed trade blocs of capitalist countries, the economic division of Western Europe was intensified. What happened was not a relaxation but a deepening of the interimperialist struggle; this struggle was carried over into a wider arena. The imperialists fear that this could increase the political disarray within the aggressive North Atlantic bloc. The new phase in the development of 'integration' is related to the desire of imperialism to overcome the economic division of Western Europe. Throughout the postwar period monopolist 'integration' has been an integral part of the 'grand strategy' of American imperialism. Now, trying to bolster the military-political alliance of the West, the United States is unceremoniously prodding Britain and a number of other West European countries into joining the Common Market. It is thus trying to reduce the centrifugal tendencies in the North Atlantic bloc, to strengthen the cabal bond of the bloc members, and at the same time to take advantage of the contradictions among them in the interests of the United States. [...]

14. [...] The United States ruling circles emphasize the interdependence of the USA and Western Europe, as though the nature of the alliance they propose with the Common Market were one of equality. This is because of the bankruptcy of previous American plans. The doctrine of American 'world leadership' has collapsed ignominiously. Washington can no longer impose its will on Western Europe in the same way it used to. The balance of economic forces in the camp of imperialism has changed to America's disadvantage. The language of unconcealed diktat that was used in the days of the Marshall Plan and the Truman Doctrine is no longer suitable in present circumstances. The United States is, moreover, trying to shift to Western Europe an ever greater part of the burden of military expenditures connected with participation in military blocs. [...]

16. If the planned enlargement of West European 'integration' is carried out, it would consolidate the economic division of the imperialist system of states into three mutually opposed parts.

First, the United States. It will not, of course, join the Common Market, but, wishing to preserve its leadership, it is prepared to cooperate with the Common Market on special conditions. The ruling circles of Canada take approximately the same stand.

Second, an 'integrated Europe of the trusts', headed by the leading imperialist countries of Europe–Britain, the FRG and France.

Third, Japan, which would like to unite around itself some of the capitalist countries of Asia in order to fight more successfully for markets against its European and American competitors.

These rival forces cannot fail to maneuver; individual agreements and compromises among them are possible. But the logic of the struggle will have its way. Economic friction among the imperialist states is ineradicable. 'There are two trends objectively at work and intertwined in the camp of imperialism: one is toward the rallying of all its forces against socialism, and the other is toward mounting contradictions between the imperialist powers themselves and also between them and the other states in the capitalist world,' Comrade N. S. Khrushchev said at the 22nd Party Congress. 'The United States has been unable, and will be unable, to overcome this latter trend. The US financial oligarchy lacks the power and means to make good its claim to the role of savior of capitalism, much less its claim to world domination.'

17. The leaders of West European 'integration', while declaring it to be peaceful in nature, have in fact transformed the Common Market into an instrument of the 'cold war'. They stubbornly oppose any European or world measures that might lead to an easing of international tension and the establishment of a lasting peace. They resist the conclusion of a German peace treaty, the cessation of nuclear weapons tests and the achievement of general and complete disarmament, and they are striving for nuclear armaments in one form or another. [...]

18. With the creation of the Common Market, the militarization of the economic and public life of the countries of the 'six' was intensified. These countries are striving to create independent nuclear striking forces and to organize the mass production of various types of atomic weapons. Even now within the framework of the Common Market the production of several types of missiles, military aircraft, a 'European tank,' etc., is being pushed. Thus the European Economic Community is in fact becoming a 'European arsenal' of the North Atlantic bloc, supplying the latter's armed forces with important types of military equipment. [...]

The territory of the Common Market countries has been turned into a military base in which military construction is being developed intensively and the so-called 'infrastructure' program is being carried out. On the principal routes in the Western part of the European continent strategic highways, railroads, pipelines and power networks are being built, seaports and waterways are being enlarged and reconstructed and air and missile bases, military warehouses and dumps, etc., are under construction.

19. German militarism, which is playing a more and more sinister role in the

military preparations of the Common Market countries, represents the greatest danger for the peoples of Europe. The German militarists and revanchists began by importing arms and then set about organizing and speeding up their own arms production. The Bonn government is demanding 'equal rights' in the production and possession of nuclear weapons. The F.R.G. is conducting intensive preparations for the development of its own atomic industry. The West German militarists are demanding training sites, military bases, ports and storage facilities for their armed forces in various West European countries, and they are getting them. Under the banner of European 'integration' and the need for 'cooperation in matters of the defense of the West', the F.R.G. is not only borrowing the scientific and technical experience of other imperialist powers in the field of the development and production of modern weapons but is also trying to seize leading positions in the 'integrated' organizations that are directly or indirectly connected with the arms race (Euratom, the European Space Research Organization and others).

The 'integration' policy has become a major element in the aggressive military plans of German imperialism, which is striving to make use of American support to seize command positions in the NATO armed forces and to place the military-economic and manpower resources of Western Europe in the service of their revanchist, aggressive schemes.

20. The Common Market is a tool of imperialism's strategy and policy aimed against the young sovereign states that have won national independence. With the help of 'integration', the monopolies are seeking not only to preserve their old colonial privileges but to obtain new privileges, to organize joint exploitation of the economically underdeveloped countries. The European Economic Community is a new form of collective colonialism.

21. Proposing outwardly tempting conditions, the imperialists are trying to drive an ever greater number of economically underdeveloped countries into the Common Market trap. This question arises particularly acutely for the former colonies of France and Britain in Africa, the economies of which depend heavily on the former metropolitan countries. This is a matter of a modified 'Euro-African' plan, that is, a plan for preserving and strengthening the positions of West European imperialism on this continent, of providing it with the raw materials and manpower of the African countries. The so-called 'collective approach' of the colonial powers to African problems signifies nothing but an attempt to coordinate their actions in the struggle against the national-liberation movement of the peoples of Africa.

The Rome Treaty places the underdeveloped countries that decide to join the Common Market in a subordinate status. The treaty provides that these countries be admitted to the Common Market with the status of so-called 'associated' members. Such countries are granted the right to export their agricultural products to the Common Market states at preferential duties. But at the same time the 'associated' countries are obliged to reduce their own customs tariffs. Thus a number of countries of West Africa that have associated themselves with the

Common Market have already reduced tariff rates 30 per cent in 1962 on goods imported from Common Market countries.

Through having linked their destinies with the Common Market, the under-developed countries will continue to be agrarian-raw material appendages, and now appendages to the economy not of any one power but of an entire coalition of imperialist powers. At the same time, the import of manufactured goods from the highly developed capitalist states will sap at the roots the already weak national industry, will deprive the 'associated' countries of the possibility of carrying out a policy of industrialization. [...]

24. Marxist–Leninists are consistent proponents of economic and political co-operation and of bringing the peoples closer together in every possible way. In full accordance with historical experience, they proceed from the idea that the unification of the European countries on the basis of free choice, equality and brotherhood is possible only under socialism. They contrast the 'Europe of the trusts and NATO' with the socialist brotherhood of European peoples that has already come into being on a large part of the European continent. [...]

All the healthy forces of the West European countries have an urgent stake in frustrating the criminal conspiracy that a handful of trusts have mounted against the vital interests of the overwhelming majority of the people. This provides favorable conditions for the formation of a broad antimonopoly alliance uniting the working class, the peasantry and the urban middle strata.

CHAPTER IV

GROWTH AND PARALYSIS

1963–1983

The 1950s and early 1960s saw unprecedented economic growth in western Europe. The rationing of food and fuel during the immediate postwar years gave way to a seemingly endless period of prosperity. A higher standard of living was evident almost everywhere. High levels of employment and low rates of inflation prevailed across western Europe and by 1960 most currencies had achieved a remarkable stability. Europe was then overtaken by an embarrassment of riches. Such were the agricultural surpluses in countries of the Common Market that people spoke of a new economic topography whose principal features were 'mountains of butter and grain' and 'lakes of wine'.[1]

A sense of well-being also pervaded the external relations of western Europe. It is true, of course, that a number of very serious crises erupted during the second postwar decade: the Suez debacle and the Hungarian Revolution of 1956 proved the impotence of western Europeans to act on their own. They felt helpless, too, during the appearance of the Berlin Wall in 1961, the Cuban missile crisis of 1962 and postcolonial upheavals in Africa (especially the Congo) in the early 1960s. In spite of these alarms, however, western Europeans in 1963 were tempted to think that they were safer than they had been fifteen years earlier. With the departure of Russian troops from Austria (1955), the apparent consolidation of democracy in Greece and the emergence of reformist governments in Hungary and Poland, it seemed that the menace of Soviet communism might diminish after all. Cordial relations with Yugoslavia, the treaty banning atmospheric nuclear testing (1963) and the development of 'Eurocommunism' (with its own critique of Soviet society) also added to Europe's sense of relief. Above all, their successful efforts in collective decision-making made western Europeans more confident about the future. Their shared experience of economic coordination (in the EEC) and military planning (in NATO) encouraged them to feel less vulnerable to external pressures.

More damaging to the cause of European unity were the tensions between western states. The decade was filled with bitter disputes among the Six about political integration, supranational authority and the expansion of the Community. The Treaty of Rome allowed for the enlargement of the EEC, whose economic vitality proved irresistible to some of the countries which had remained outside. In 1961, four of these states (Denmark, Ireland, Norway and the United Kingdom) decided to join the Community. Their applications received strong support from the Benelux governments, which were ready to welcome Britain as a counterweight to the influence of France and Germany. But the outcome of the negotiations was never clear. Not everyone in the EEC appreciated the lofty British argument that Europe could never really unite without Britain and that Britain's world role would somehow insure Europe's future success. There remained, moreover, deep suspicions in the EEC about Britain's reasons for organizing EFTA and its willingness to adopt the EEC's standards in industry, agriculture and commerce.[2]

The negotiations came to an abrupt end in January 1963. During one of his carefully managed press conferences in the Elysée Palace, President de Gaulle delivered what amounted to a French veto of the applications (DOCUMENT 23). Neglecting the fate of the other applicants, de Gaulle spoke only of Britain: he professed admiration for the British people and their role in defeating Hitlerism. He had kind words for the Prime Minister, Harold Macmillan. But de Gaulle did not think Britain was ready to enter Europe. He believed the British were too distracted by their historic ties to other English-speaking nations, the vestiges of their maritime empire and their dependence on distant trading partners.

De Gaulle concluded his remarks with the polite but vague prediction of Britain joining a united Europe some day. Privately, however, he hoped that this would never happen. He had good reason to count on British indecisiveness: he knew that Macmillan had not convinced the Conservative Party and British agriculturalists to embrace the EEC, and he also knew that the Foreign Office remained sceptical about European unity.[3] He was aware of the growing hostility to the EEC in the ranks of the British Labour Party, who he expected to form the next government. There was therefore a callous simplicity to de Gaulle's attitude: why offer a place in Europe to a country whose government was so reluctant to accept it and whose people were likely to reject it?

Even more important to de Gaulle was the issue of military security. A week after pronouncing his veto, he told visitors that Britain had virtually 'disqualified itself as a European power' by agreeing to subordinate its nuclear defence capacity to American control. De Gaulle regarded the recent Nassau Conference (Macmillan's meeting with Kennedy) as another sign of Britain's loss of sovereignty to the USA. Soon, he warned, the only role open to Britain would be that of travelling salesman for American rockets and defence systems.

De Gaulle's distrust of the British and Americans dated from the inglorious years of the Nazi occupation, when he believed that his allies in London and Washington treated France ungenerously. He now saw Britain's approach to Europe as the Trojan horse of Anglo-Saxon cultural and military influence. He was determined to forestall this intrusion and to divide those who might challenge the political hegemony which France (with Germany's tacit approval) hoped to enjoy inside the EEC. Days after rejecting Britain's application, de Gaulle unilaterally offered Denmark membership of the EEC.[4] It was a gesture born of malice and calculated to disturb Britain's relations with one of her closest trading partners. It was fresh evidence of de Gaulle's contempt, not only for the British but also for the negotiation procedures ordained by the EEC.

The French veto of 1963 left the EEC in a state of shock. The smaller countries were angered by the French government's refusal to consult them and they were dismayed by Germany's passive acceptance of de Gaulle's opinions. Tensions and rancour deepened inside the EEC over a number of long-standing issues. Among these problems was the slowly evolving Common Agricultural Policy (CAP): how were grain prices to be determined and how were price supports (subsidies) to be financed? Once again, most member states hoped for open discussion and consensus, but the French government resorted to high-handed tactics and threats. In 1964 de Gaulle went so far as to say that France would have to consider leaving the Community if the CAP did not meet with its approval.

The real issue in the 1960s went well beyond the ingredients of agricultural policy. At the heart of the question was the political nature of the Community itself. For de Gaulle (and the French government as long as he led it), Europe was a league of friendly nations, *l'Europe des Patries*, in which the traditional forms of national authority remained virtually intact and unchallenged. De Gaulle wanted no further moves in the direction of a supranational authority in Europe: he did not want the Community to have its own budgetary resources and he did not want the Commission to acquire control over foreign and financial policies.[5] He knew that most of the British, Danes and Norwegians shared his apprehensions of a federal union which could only reduce the sovereignty of states. It is ironic that the countries that wished to join the EEC in 1961–62 would almost certainly have supported de Gaulle's notions of a confederal Europe, if only he had not barred their way.[6] As it was, he now had to contend with the stiffening opposition of 'the Five' – Germany included, as the dutiful Adenauer had been succeeded by the more outward-looking Ludwig Erhard. After months of dark words about the 'technical but temporary value' of the EEC, de Gaulle decided to sabotage the organization by boycotting it.

For seven months, from July 1965 to January 1966, France sent no one to the meetings of the Council of Ministers. The so-called 'empty chair crisis' was a serious blow to the European federalists and to their plans for political integration. De Gaulle complained more than ever about the 'technocratic body of elders' and the 'stateless, irresponsible men' who supposedly ran the EEC, and he urged revisions of the Treaty of Rome as the price of French cooperation. Embarrassed by election results in France, however, the General sent his men back to Brussels to arrange a truce (rather than a peace) with the Five.

The result was the 'Luxembourg Compromise' of January 1966 (DOCUMENT 24). This expedient of diplomacy recognized what both sides considered important principles. To placate the French, the Compromise upheld the right of all member states to use the veto in Council, 'when very important [national] issues are at stake'. To placate the Five, the Compromise insisted that important questions required the full consultation of all member states. It also reiterated those provisions of the Treaty of Rome which called for majority voting in the Council (an end to the effective veto) beginning in 1967. Generally speaking, the Compromise maintained (and in some respects increased) the authority of national governments vis-à-vis the Council. It left unresolved the thorny question of who controlled the Community's budget and it denied the Community a truly supranational role in financial matters. The federalist ambitions of the Council were checked for some years to come. The Luxembourg Compromise was a tacit recognition by the Six that their Community was essentially one of independent states brought together by national governments which remained very powerful.[7]

In spite of the tensions of the mid-1960s, the period was not a complete wasteland for European integration. The economies of the Six became increasingly interdependent. Many of the objectives prescribed by the Treaty of Rome were achieved ahead of time. The Six gained some experience as a common market. There was even a measure of administrative streamlining, in the form of the Merger Treaty. Agreed in April 1965 and taking effect in July 1967, the Treaty combined the administrative functions of three organizations (the ECSC, Euratom, and the EEC), and it established a single legal entity, the European Community (EC). While the Merger did nothing to advance the cause of federalism as such, it helped to clarify the identity of the Community and its place in world affairs.

The internal crises of the 1960s entered a diplomatic dénouement at Luxembourg, and the issue of authority in the Community remained. Who or what determined the direction of the EC? The parliament at Strasbourg enjoyed very little influence, for it was not yet the product of direct elections; until the 1980s, its role was largely advisory. Nor did the Commission exert continuous leadership, although it was supposed to be the executive arm of the Community. De Gaulle denounced the Commission for its 'excessive power', and its first president, Walter Hallstein, liked to describe himself as the 'President of Europe'. But the Commission was never as strong as its detractors and admirers liked to think; actually it was the unwieldy Council which assumed the greatest responsibilities. The presence in the Council of representatives (often ministers) of the member governments emphasized the continuing importance of decision-making at governmental (rather than Community) level. 'Intergovernmentalism' remained the basis of authority in the Community.

The smaller member states feared 'intergovernmentalism' because of its tendency in the 1960s to give a certain advantage to France and Germany, the two countries with the most powerful governments. The result of 'intergovernmentalism' was not a Franco-German hegemony as such, but a Community of unequal states.[8] The smaller member states often felt left out, bypassed by the decisions which the French and German governments reached privately. The 'empty chair crisis' demonstrated the peril to the Community of any one national government's refusal to consult with its partners, and the smaller countries remained vigilant critics of France and the failure to make decisions collectively. One such criticism came with the speech given in 1969 by the foreign minister of the Community's smallest member state, Gaston Thorn of Luxembourg (DOCUMENT 25).

Thorn spoke of a directorate or 'inner circle' of countries which he did not identify. The principal target of his remarks, however, was France; it had refused to join its partners in discussions about the Middle East. To Thorn this seemed a denial of the principle of continuous and full consultation involving all member states. Although the Treaty of Rome did not require the adoption of a common foreign policy, Thorn's concern was not misplaced: everyone admitted that the integration of Europe should enhance Europe's moral authority in the world at large. Of course, Thorn could not know in March 1969 that French obstructionism was soon to end. De Gaulle's defeat in a referendum the next month forced his retirement and the beginning of greater cooperation with France's five partners and with countries (like Britain) who wished to enter the Community. The change in French policy meant that the recourse to the WEU (which Thorn admitted as a possible strategy of dealing with France) was never used.

On the other hand, complaints of an 'inner circle' have persisted in one form or another. With the expansion of the Community, many disparities have become more pronounced: there remains a strong sense of the 'haves' and 'have-nots'. In the 1980s and 1990s, expressions such as 'fast track' and 'two tiers' were used to define possible solutions for various problems which apparently distinguished member states (e.g., levels of debt and unemployment, costs of social services and the timing of the monetary union). The 'political directorate' which Thorn feared has not yet appeared, but there is no denying that, as in 1969, the political weight of the Community's pace-setters (Germany, Netherlands, France and Sweden) is greater than that of other states (Greece, Portugal and Ireland).

Nine months after Thorn's speech, in December 1969, the Community's summit meeting in The Hague inaugurated a new stage in the integration of Europe. The leaders (including Willy Brandt of Germany and Georges Pompidou, the newly elected president of France) agreed on the necessity of two general developments: 'broadening' (expanding the membership of the Community) and 'deepening' (monetary union as a means of integrating the national economies).[9] To work out the details of this double mandate, two committees were established. The first, under the direction of Pierre Werner, Prime Minister of Luxembourg, advocated the free movement of capital and the replacement of all the national currencies by a single Community currency by 1980. The French were very reluctant about these proposals (notably that of a single currency) and the Werner Report languished as a list of possibilities rather than a practical plan.

The other committee, chaired by Étienne Davignon, addressed issues which had worried Gaston Thorn. The Davignon Report of October 1970 considered political harmony and political institutions essential to the process of European integration (DOCUMENT 26). The Report recommended that Europe's political unity begin with the coordination of foreign policy. The objective was a single foreign policy rather than six different ones: Europe was to speak to the world with one voice. In 1957 such a goal would have seemed overly ambitious, if not naive; in 1970, when the superpowers were exploring the parameters of détente and America's authority was tarnished by the experience of Vietnam, a common foreign policy for western Europe had become more conceivable and desirable. Moreover, it was now apparent that the EC's power as a world trading bloc meant that it could no longer afford the luxury of responding to serious international crises with different policies. And as far as the 'Five' were concerned, there was every reason to bring an end to the frustrations of trying to reconcile Gaullist foreign policies with their own.

The Davignon Report therefore specified a number of new procedures. First of all, it urged regular consultation to insure the accessibility of information and the full participation of all member states. The Council of the EC accepted the Report's proposal for regular meetings of the foreign ministers and senior officials of the foreign ministries of the member states. A 'Political Committee' was established, comprising officials and experts from the six foreign ministries, to prepare reports and recommendations on specific international problems. Ambassadors sent by EC member states to foreign capitals were to receive common instruction and were to keep in contact with one another. All these procedures, known collectively as European Political Cooperation (EPC), were implemented very quickly and with an ease which surprised the six foreign ministries.

The apparent success of EPC guaranteed its continuation, advised by the second Davignon Report in 1973. But the work of EPC only began with its redefinition of diplomatic procedures. As do so many other functions of European integration, EPC has depended on intergovernmental cooperation, and there have been times when, in spite of regular meetings and shared information, the cooperation of the national foreign ministries is not entirely whole-hearted. There was some discomfort, for example, when the Germans tried to use EPC as a support-mechanism for their diplomatic overtures to COMECON states in 1970–73. During the oil embargo of 1973–74, Germany and the Netherlands objected to what they considered excessively pro-Arab opinions on the part of France and Britain. And almost all the member states were suspicious of French demands in the 1980s for a permanent EPC secretariat.[10] More acceptable was the encouragement given by EPC in the 1970s to a critical discussion of human rights, not only in the member states but elsewhere in Europe and overseas. This concern was relatively new business for some foreign ministries, but the Community saw it as an aspect of its democratic mission and its 'responsibility to the world of tomorrow'.

In 1973 the Six became the Nine, as Denmark, Ireland and the United Kingdom joined the Community. In retrospect, this enlargement signalled the end of two dangers: the Gaullist scheme for a 'little Europe' guided by France, and the division of democratic Europe into two rival economic blocs. The more flexible French government under Georges Pompidou insisted on its Gaullist credentials while at the same time it supported the expansion of the Community and new moves to integrate Europe.[11] Meanwhile, the remaining members of EFTA saw every reason to draw closer to the Community. Once the defection of Britain and Denmark had reduced the importance of EFTA as an international organization, several of its members (Sweden, Austria, Portugal and Switzerland) sought bilateral agreements with the EC. They could not as yet offer to harmonize their legislation with that of the Community – their fear of the loss of sovereignty had not diminished – but they did hope for more economic cooperation, particularly with respect to 'sensitive products' such as foodstuffs and fisheries. The pragmatic new partnership of EFTA and the EC, coinciding as it did with the expansion of the Community itself, breathed new life into the cause of European unity.

Confidence in Europe's future was evident in a speech which the German Chancellor gave in Strasbourg at the end of 1973 (DOCUMENT 27). In his address to the European Parliament, Willy Brandt said that the process of European integration was both gradual and irreversible and that a new political organization must someday replace the old nation-state. At the same time, Brandt did not imagine that European unity was a mystical event: it would not depend on a single treaty or a revolutionary movement. Accepting the arguments of the European functionalists, Brandt believed that unity in Europe must be the cumulative result of decisions carefully considered and willingly accepted. The new Europe would succeed only if its new institutions were wholly responsible to the needs of Europe's citizens. Mindful of the criticism which the British and Scandinavians had for 'Eurocrats in Brussels', Brandt insisted on a lean and efficient European bureaucracy. He wanted to assure the new member states that the Community belonged to all Europeans and not to a distant, anonymous and unelected elite in Brussels.

Brandt's definition of the new Europe went beyond the role of its bureaucracy and the unity of the Nine. It was his hope that the Community would continue to expand and he saw the possibility of gaining the good will (if not the adhesion) of the communist countries in the East. Since 1949 Germany's attitude toward these states had been negative and disdainful; the Hallstein Doctrine obliged Germany to refuse contacts with any state which recognized the government in East Germany. In 1969 Brandt's government reversed this policy.[12] A series of diplomatic and commercial initiatives, collectively known as *Ostpolitik*, now assured the East of Germany's determination to be a peaceable and cooperative neighbour. One assumption of *Ostpolitik* was that the self-interests of European states must erode the differences between capitalism and communism and gradually bring states into a relatively benevolent partnership. *Ostpolitik* also assumed that Germany was the essential bridge linking East and West: only Germany could induce eastern Europeans to regard the Community as a timely and legitimate expression of European progress.[13]

Brandt was to prove a shrewd judge of Germany's central role in Europe and the eventual impact of *Ostpolitik*. But he was much too optimistic about the timetable for European integration. Conditions after 1973 would leave little room for confidence or achievement. For more than a decade it seemed that perhaps de Gaulle had been right in saying that the enlargement of the Community would aggravate many of its long-standing problems. The Community's budget, for example, acquired a fearful complexity in the 1970s. Britain's anxiety that its contribution to the budget was too large and that it must be renegotiated certainly did not add to the fiscal stability of the Community. Moreover, the entry of the three newcomers practically coincided with the first Arab oil embargo (1973–74). High rates of inflation occurred everywhere in Europe and the Community could do little more than wait out the economic storm.

In fact, the decade following the Community's first enlargement was one of economic confusion. The dislocation caused by rising oil prices, inflation and currency speculation seemed almost to arrest the development of the Community. The resolution of economic questions depended, as it always had, on securing the agreement of national governments, and the expansion of the Community did not make this task any easier.[14] On the other hand, the accession of three states in 1973 obliged the Community to consider the prospect of further expansion and the meaning of membership to other European countries. The economic crises of the 1970s did not detract from the Community's promise to promote a more equitable distribution of wealth in Europe and a uniformly high standard of living in all member states. To achieve these goals, however, the Community had to contend with local economies long known for their underdevelopment and poverty.

The Development Fund of 1975 was the first serious attempt to correct 'regional imbalances' in the Community (DOCUMENT 28). The Treaty of Rome had acknowledged the disparity of wealth among the Six; it urged a review of transport policies and aid programmes in the hope of improving regional economies (Articles 80 and 92). The Treaty of Rome also established an Investment Bank to help finance projects in 'less developed areas' (Article 130). These provisions were insufficient. In fact, the Community's record on regional development was (apart from the Italian Mezzogiorno) quite disappointing. Underemployment persisted through the 1960s and 1970s, particularly in regions where agriculture had exhausted the land.

The timing of the Regional Development Fund – almost twenty years after the Treaty of Rome – might be explained by two factors. The first is the gravity of the recession, arguably the worst economic shock western Europe had known since the early 1950s. As the recession became a major issue in the domestic politics of all member states, their governments became more disposed to Community action on regional development. The second factor was the recognition that 'regional imbalances' were likely to continue and multiply with the admission of new member states. Indeed, the Irish and British governments were ready to nominate a number of their own 'less developed areas' worthy of Community help, and the Development Fund was calculated, in part, to win greater public support for the Community in these countries.

The *Regulation* which set up the European Regional Development Fund (ERDF) was careful not to tread on the prerogatives of member states. It was the national governments which continued to identify the 'regions'; what constituted a region differed considerably from one member state to another. The national governments also designated 'priority areas' for investment programmes. Assistance from the ERDF was not meant as a substitute for the help which national governments gave to their regions; it was designed instead to supplement the help already promised by the national governments.[15]

The total amount which each state could claim from the ERDF depended on a system of national quotas. The poorer countries were entitled to receive the larger quotas. During the first decade of the ERDF, almost all of the development monies went to Britain, France, Ireland and Italy (and Greece, after it joined the Community in 1981). But the assistance did not always benefit the poorest regions of these countries, and the Commission frequently complained that better guidelines were necessary if the ERDF was to operate properly. It was also soon apparent that more monies were needed, too. Until the ERDF was reformed in 1984, its monies amounted to only 5 per cent of the Community's budget.[16]

Although its resources were limited and income levels in the Community remained very disparate, the ERDF was a necessary step in the direction of a federal Europe. By defining poverty as a problem which overlaps national frontiers, the *Regulation* required the combined intervention of member states and it provided a special agency to coordinate their efforts. The ERDF enhanced the powers of the Commission, which received the duty of determining the extent of aid and the continuity of contributions (Article 5). Moreover, the *Regulation* asserted the federalist notion that a more equitable distribution of the Community's wealth was not the final goal but a precondition of full economic and monetary union.

Another precondition was a truly federal budget. The 'general budget' of the Community was unlike the national budgets: it could not, on its own, undertake macroeconomic tasks such as promoting high levels of employment and welfare services, nor could it redistribute the wealth of the Community. It was instead an exercise in 'accounting': revenue and expenditure were supposed to balance. The needs of regional development pushed the Community towards a redefinition of the budget and the economic crises of the 1970s had much the same effect. Indeed, the impact of inflation and deficits was so different across western Europe that virtually all aspects of financial planning at Community level were frustrated. Economic confusion combined with political uncertainty (caused largely by Britain's wavering commitment to the EC) to produce a sort of paralysis which continued into the 1980s. During this period of 'Eurosclerosis', the Community avoided new initiatives and postponed indefinitely the inauguration of other projects.[17] Such was the fate of monetary union, which federalists had predicted so confidently in 1969–71. The elaborate plans for currency stability (known as the Snake in the Tunnel) were also put off; unilateral floating exchange rates took the place of a Community-based system.

To restore order to Europe's financial activity, the Commission began with the Community's budget. In 1974 they appointed a committee, led by Sir Donald MacDougall, to determine how public finance at Community level would relate to the future economic integration of Europe. In April 1977 the MacDougall Committee published their *Report* (DOCUMENT 29). It supported the Commission's idea that the budget should be more than just a routine statement of accounts: it must promote the 'cohesion' of the Community and prepare it for monetary union. The proper role of the budget (as both the Commission and the MacDougall Committee saw it) was to encourage the redistribution of the Community's wealth. To do this effectively, a much larger budget was necessary. The *Report* proposed that the budget amount to about 2.5 per cent of the Community's GNP. Only then would the budget become an instrument of 'fiscal federalism', and only then would the Community begin to enjoy the political and economic 'cohesion' of federal states like Canada, Australia and the USA.[18]

The fiscal system prescribed by the MacDougall Report was cautious in one respect. It did not advise (indeed, it hardly considered) a budget as large as those of Germany and the United States (20–25 per cent of the GNP). Instead, the *Report* assumed that a budget based on a smaller percentage of the Community's GNP would be quite adequate – particularly as it was not supposed to provide for defence (military) spending, as federal budgets in Germany and the USA had to do.

The *Report* proposed that Community budgets be financed largely by sharing the revenue raised by the value added taxes (VAT) imposed by most west European states. The contributions of member states to the budget would be progressive, with the richer states giving the Community a larger proportion of their VAT revenues.

While larger budgets might allow the Community to support regional development more generously, the European Monetary System (EMS) was designed to give all European states a more stable monetary environment (DOCUMENT 30). The *Commentary* on the EMS, published by the Commission in 1979, began with a clear description of a decade of hopes and frustrations, as major currency upheavals, the oil crisis and the demise of the postwar monetary system (symbolized by the Bretton Woods Agreement) undermined the Community's self-confidence and forced the postponement of the EMU project. After providing the historical background, the *Commentary* then presented the features of what became a fairly successful system.

The most important achievement of the EMS was to restore stability to currency exchanges. This it did by sponsoring the Exchange Rate Mechanism (ERM), which established 'margins of fluctuation' in which currencies were allowed to move. The ERM combined the virtues of discipline and flexibility: the margins were 'fixed' but could be 'adjusted'. The mechanism was pragmatic. The basic margins (2.25 per cent) accommodated most currencies, while a special margin (6 per cent) guided the Italian *lira*. The EMS was realistic in its general view of monetary conditions: it recognized the strength of the German mark and it accepted implicitly the priorities which the Germans attached to macroeconomic policies.[19]

Inevitably, the inauguration of the EMS was accompanied by much scepticism. The first few years were difficult, as inflationary pressures and the divergent monetary policies of the member states continued to work against the system. Gradually, however, EMS gained in strength. The 1983 realignment of the currencies (wisely provided for by the EMS) was one sure indication of its usefulness, as was the entry of other European states and a more cooperative role on the part of France.

The novelty of the EMS lay not in its attempt to guide the value of a number of currencies but in its creation of the European Currency Unit, the ECU. The ECU is an amalgam or 'basket' of EC currencies, the strength of each currency determining its 'weight' in the basket. European federalists have long hoped that the ECU will bring the Community at least three related advantages. The first is that the general use of the ECU will in effect immunize the national currencies against many of the maladies which afflicted them in the past. Another benefit, widely hoped for, is that the ECU might overshadow the overwhelming role of the Deutschmark vis-à-vis other European currencies. Finally, the federalists cherish the hope that the ECU might soon become a truly international currency in its own right, enjoying the sort of influence which the American dollar once had.[20]

By the mid-1990s, Europeans could open bank accounts in ECUs and buy ECU bonds. A few countries (such as Spain and Belgium) had begun to mint ECU coins. But the ECU has yet to fulfil the expectations of its creators. There are probably still too many restrictions on its use (even within the Union) and its changing value (revised every three months) has given it a structural instability. The inescapable fact is that the adoption of the ECU as the working currency is too great a step for most member states to contemplate. As long as these states are reluctant to participate fully in all the mechanisms of the European Monetary System (the United Kingdom and Greece, for example, refused to join the exchange rate mechanism), there will not be one 'system' in Europe, but several. For that matter, most member states are still too attached to traditional fiscal policies and too fond of the national currencies to be willing to lift the ECU, the keystone in the arch of monetary union, into place. It will be some time before the ECU is a fully fledged currency, a symbol of Europe's prestige as a monetary power in the brave new world of economic regional associations.[21]

The tensions which accompanied European integration in the 1970s were largely internal. Recession, inflation and the unsteady adjustment of new member states all contributed to the Community's paralysis. The pace of integration slowed and there were many studies (and opinion polls) to suggest a widespread disenchantment with the goals of European unity. Externally, the political climate was more relaxed. In international relations, the 1970s was the decade of détente. The antagonisms of the Cold War seemed to diminish as both East and West saw more advantage in talking about commercial contracts and cultural exchanges. The Berlin Wall remained in place, as did the great military alliances, but conflict seemed less likely in 1975 than at any time since 1945. Western Europeans were distracted by 'economic performance indicators'; eastern Europeans were increasingly interested in western trade and credit; the Soviet Union was tempted to think that a rash of revolutions in the Third World (e.g. Angola, Mozambique, Ethiopia, Nicaragua) might have the effect of outflanking western Europe, thereby leaving it more vulnerable to future pressure. Détente depended very much on new distractions and new opportunities.

The high point of détente came with the Helsinki Conference of 1975. The Soviet Union had for some years urged western Europeans to make a formal commitment to the 'security' of the whole continent. More precisely, the USSR wanted a conference of major political importance, one which brought together the members of the Warsaw Pact and those of NATO, including the USA, Canada and all the neutral states of Europe. The main aim of this conference, as the Russians saw it, was to extract from the West a promise to respect the sovereignty (i.e. the ideology) of European communist states. The Soviets had never felt entirely secure in their control of eastern Europe; the reforms of a liberal regime in Czechoslovakia (1968) and the beguiling offers of German friendship (through *Ostpolitik*) were only the most recent challenges to Soviet hegemony. The Russians therefore hoped to steer a grand conference into accepting the political status quo. What they wanted was a treaty which perpetuated the outcome of the Second World War by giving the regimes of eastern Europe a legitimacy and a respectability which they had never gained on their own.

There was much opposition in the West to this definition of 'security'. Whatever their different interpretations of the political and military realities of Europe, western states were reluctant to condone the division of the continent. The Germans nursed their own suspicions about the security conference: they feared it might signal the general acceptance of East Germany as a completely sovereign state and prevent forever the reunification of their country. On the other hand, most western governments saw some advantage in the sort of conference which the Soviet Union desired. The conference sessions therefore occurred, in Helsinki and Geneva, during the summer of 1975. The result was a treaty (the *Final Act*) which both sides thought imperfect but which they both felt they must accept.

There were four general categories or 'baskets' of agreements. The first 'basket' contained the most substantial decisions on security: affirmations of the inviolability and sovereignty of all participating states, the promise to inform other states of any major military exercise, and the pledge to respect human rights. 'Basket Three' concerned cooperation in humanitarian and other fields, while 'Basket Four' dealt with a variety of subjects, including future conferences. 'Basket Two' may not have meant a great deal in 1975, but such was the range of its agreements and its generous view of 'cooperation' that it implied a start to the integration of the continent (DOCUMENT 31).

'Basket Two' was a genuine expression of détente in Europe. It accepted, while at the same time it overlooked, the profound political differences between East and West and it assumed that all states saw the merit of peaceful exchanges. The nature of these exchanges was largely intellectual: ways of conducting business negotiations, the dissemination of statistics and commercial information, industrial research, legal protection for joint ventures, identifying and harmonizing technical regulations: 'Basket Two' seemed to promise an endless programme of seminars. Obviously these were basic concerns in a continent so long divided. The Soviets regarded 'Basket Two' as a politically safe way to modernize commercial, technological and environmental standards; for the West, 'Basket Two' was a confidence-building exercise which might someday turn rivals into partners.

There were not many Europeans in 1975 who imagined that the 'megasummitry' of Helsinki would produce long-term benefits. But in its capacity as a major, continuing forum, the Conference in Security and Cooperation in Europe (CSCE) soon acquired considerable significance. The Conference itself was important to the European Community: its representatives came from nine different countries but acted as one, even though the Conference rules did not officially allow for the representation of blocs and alliances. When Aldo Moro signed the Helsinki Final Act, he did so with the words 'for Italy, and in the name of the European Community'. Far from being a gesture of diplomatic bravado, Moro's action reminded all Europeans of the development of political consensus in the Community. The procedures ordained a few years earlier by EPC brought very visible results in Helsinki.

The CSCE added little to Europe's sense of military security. The Helsinki Conference did not reduce the troops and armaments based in Europe, although European states promised to consult about military issues. Nor was the CSCE able, as an ongoing feature of European relations, to prolong the delicate life of détente. Less than five years after the meetings in Helsinki, it was clear that nothing more could be expected of détente as an interlude in postwar European relations. The Soviet invasion of Afghanistan, the renewed attempts to curb political unrest in east-central Europe and the advent of a new generation of weapons for NATO and the Warsaw Pact confirmed not only the demise of détente but the continuity of Cold War antagonisms.

Other aspects of the Final Act proved more durable and practical. The basic notion of the CSCE was that European nations faced a number of issues which they had to discuss regularly among themselves; such consultations explicitly respected the wholeness of Europe. Whatever its political complexion or its military commitments, no state could be barred from the CSCE process. No country was regarded as a pariah, except Albania, which refused to take part. Helsinki led not so much to an era of good feelings as it did to a time of expectations – a period characterized by a cautious faith in the value of regular political and diplomatic discussions across the whole of Europe.

In addition to promoting a cordial and productive form of interstate relations ('low-level diplomacy'), the CSCE gained a limited role as the monitor of civil liberties. When the western democracies agreed to the Soviet demand for a security conference, they managed to secure discussions on human rights as well as trade and security. The communist states probably hoped to disregard Helsinki's words on human rights as empty rhetoric, but the strictures of 'Basket Three' were not easily ignored. Europeans increasingly perceived the CSCE as the first agency ever to serve as the forum of European opinion. For all its imperfections (and its reluctance to do very much after 1980), the CSCE was nevertheless the first pan-European institution entitled to monitor policies affecting European citizens. By subscribing to the Final Act, European states assumed a collective responsibility for both the international tranquillity and the internal harmony of their continent.

It is not difficult to exaggerate the success of the EC's external relations during these years. There were many crises, particularly in the Middle East (the Yom Kippur War and the Iranian Revolution) which revealed deep divisions among the Nine. Besides, the assertiveness of the Nine in dealing with other European states at Helsinki was no consolation for the multiple internal failures of the Community. The long years of paralysis meant that the 'deepening process', taken for granted at The Hague summit in 1969, was not taking place. The close partnership of France and Germany, symbolized by the personal friendship of Giscard d'Estaing and Helmut Schmidt, seemed to ensure the stability of the Community from 1974 to 1982. But d'Estaing and Schmidt were less interested in the EC as a whole than they were in preserving the relative importance of their countries in certain EC institutions. Their reluctance to increase the 'federal' powers of the EC Commission helped to prolong the Community's drifting from one crisis to another.

The changes which did occur in the late 1970s and early 1980s were half-hearted or counter-productive: they were no tonic for the Community's malaise. Three such changes illustrate the limited 'progress' of these years. The first took place in 1979 when direct elections for the European Parliament were held for the first time. Many Europeans welcomed these elections as a commitment to democracy in the Community. Others (particularly in Denmark and the UK) believed that supranationalism had taken a giant step; they saw direct elections to Strasbourg as a direct challenge to the authority of their own national parliaments. In the event, they had no cause for alarm. As the newly elected members of the European Parliament soon learned, direct elections did little to enhance the powers and the influence of their institution.

The second change came in 1981 with the accession of Greece as the tenth member of the Community. This was a very singular enlargement: virtually the whole of Greece was classified as a poor region deserving development aid from the rest of the Community. In return for their generosity, Greece immediately became the spoiled child of Europe, consistently opposing proposals for closer security cooperation and political integration.[22] It clung to old xenophobic attitudes vis-à-vis other Balkan and Mediterranean countries (notably Turkey). The admission of Greece to the Community in 1981 was not then regarded as one of the great and welcome milestones in the history of European integration, nor is it at the present time (1996).

The third event was the so-called 'Solemn Declaration on European Union'. This grandiose and extremely general statement was the outcome of protracted efforts by the foreign ministers of Germany and Italy, Hans-Dietrich Genscher and Emilio Columbo, beginning in 1981 and culminating with the meeting of the European Council in Stuttgart in June 1983. The Genscher–Columbo plan was a scatter-shot, designed to revive, redefine and energize the Community. They wanted, among other things, to clarify the relationship of the Council to the rest of the EC, to strengthen the powers of the Parliament in Strasbourg and, above all, to speed the integration of Europe by coordinating political decision-making and foreign policy. The Community was not ready to implement any of these ideas. The Genscher–Columbo plan became little more than a statement of intent; it never acquired the procedural studies and timetables required of any major community development. It was instead a marvellous act of faith in a Europe which was yet to be built.

ENDNOTES

1 W. Laqueur: *Europe in Our Time* (London: Viking Penguin, 1992), p. 415.

2 Derek Urwin: *The Community of Europe: A History of European Integration since 1945* (London: Longman, 1991), pp. 97–9.

3 In *Riding the Storm: 1956–1959* (London: Macmillan, 1971), p. 83, Macmillan admitted that the EC 'made little appeal to the imagination of our people'. Also see D. Sanders: *Losing an Empire, Finding a Role: British Foreign Policy since 1945* (London: Macmillan, 1990).

4 Michael Curtis: *Western European Integration* (New York: Harper and Row, 1965), p. 27.

5 Philip Cerny: *The Politics of Grandeur* (Cambridge: University Press, 1980), p. 135; Sean Greenwood: *Britain and European Cooperation since 1945* (Oxford: Blackwell, 1992), pp. 83–6.

6 Susanne J. Bodenheimer: *Political Union: a Microcosm of European Affairs, 1960–1966*

(Leyden: A. W. Sijthoff, 1967), pp. 141–4; John Pinder: *European Community: The Building of a Union* (Oxford: Oxford University Press, 1991), p. 47.

7 Urwin: *The Community of Europe*, pp. 114–15.

8 Allan Williams: *The European Community: The Contradictions of Integration* (Oxford: Blackwell, 1991), pp. 11, 51, 150–1; also P. Taylor: *The Limits of European Integration* (London: Croom Helm, 1983).

9 Urwin: *The Community of Europe*, p. 149.

10 *Ibid.*, pp. 85, 121.

11 Pinder: *European Community*, p. 146.

12 Josef Korbel: *Détente in Europe: Real or Imaginary?* (Princeton: Princeton University Press, 1972), chapter on 'Brandt's Détente'.

13 Lawrence L. Whetten: *Germany's Ostpolitik* (Oxford: Oxford University Press, 1971), chapter 6; also Wolfram F. Hanrieder: *Germany, America, Europe: Forty Years of German Foreign Policy* (New Haven: Yale University Press, 1989), chapter 7.

14 D. C. Kruse: *Monetary Integration in Western Europe: EMU, EMS and Beyond* (London: Butterworths, 1980), pp. 192–4.

15 Clive Archer and Fiona Butler: *The European Community: Structure and Process* (London: Pinter, 1992), pp. 82–3.

16 *Ibid.*, also Loukas Tsoukalis: *The New European Economy. The Politics and Economics of Integration* (Oxford: Oxford University Press, 1993), p. 238.

17 Urwin: *The Community of Europe*, pp. 156–63.

18 Michael Shackleton: 'The budget of the European Community', in J. Lodge (ed.) *The European Community and the Challenge of the Future* (London: Pinter, 1989), pp. 147–8.

19 Tsoukalis: *The New European Economy*, pp. 53, 184.

20 Supplement to Bulletin, 5–1975, in *Report on European Union* (Brussels: EC Commission, 1975).

21 Stefan Collingnon, Peter Bolinger, Christopher Johnson and Bertrand de Maigret: *Europe's Monetary Future* (London: Pinter, 1994), pp. 16–19.

22 Desmond Dinan: *Ever Closer Union? An Introduction to the European Community* (London: Macmillan, 1994), p. 122.

ADDITIONAL READINGS

P. Coffey: *The External Economic Relations of the EEC* (London: Macmillan, 1976).

B. Cornelius: *Managing Transnationalism in Northern Europe* (Boulder, Colorado: Westview, 1978).

D. Dosser: 'A federal budget for the Community?', in B. Burrows, G. Denton and G. Edwards (eds): *Federal Solutions to European Issues* (London: Macmillan, 1978).

K. Dyson (ed.): *European Détente* (London: St Martins, 1986).

S. George: *An Awkward Partner: Britain in the European Community* (Oxford: Oxford University Press, 1990).

——— : *Britain and European Integration Since 1945* (Oxford: Blackwell, 1991).

——— : *Politics and Policy in the European Community* (Oxford: Oxford University Press, 1991), chapter 11: 'Regional Policy'.

F. Giavazzi, S. Micossi and M. Miller (eds): *The European Monetary System* (Cambridge: Cambridge University Press, 1989).

J. Harrop: *The Political Economy of Integration in the European Community* (Aldershot: E. Elgar, 1989).

C. Hill (ed.): *National Foreign Policies and European Political Cooperation* (London: Allen and Unwin, 1983).

L. Hurwitz and C. Lequesne (eds): *The State of the European Community: Policies, Institutions and Debates in the Transition Years* (London: Longman, 1991).

R. Jenkins (ed.): *Britain and the EEC* (London: Macmillan, 1983).

P. Ludlow: *The Making of the European Monetary System* (London: Butterworth, 1982).

E. Neville-Rolfe: *The Politics of Agriculture in the European Community* (London: European Centre for Political Studies, 1984).

W. Nicol and D. Yuill: 'Regional problems and policy' in A. Boltho (ed.): *The European Economy* (Oxford: Oxford University Press, 1982).

J. Pelkmans: 'Economic theories of integration revisited', *Journal of Common Market Studies* 18 (June 1980), pp. 333–54.

K. Perry: *Britain and the European Community* (London: Heinemann, 1984).

J. Ravenhill: *Collective Clientism: The Lomé Conventions and North–South Relations* (New York: Columbia University Press, 1985).

A. Robinson: *The EP in the EC Policy Process* (London: Policy Studies Institute, 1985).

H. Simonian: *The Privileged Partnership: French–German Relations in the European Community* (Oxford: Oxford University Press, 1985).

V. Sobell: *The Red Market Industrial Cooperation and Specialisation in COMECON* (Aldershot: Gower, 1984).

C. Stevens (ed.): *The EEC and the Third World* (New York: Holmes and Maier, 1981).

D. Swann: *The Economics of the Common Market* (London: Penguin, 1988).

P. Taylor: *The Limits of European Integration* (London: Croom Helm, 1983).

J. Vandamme (ed.): *New Dimensions in European Social Policy* (London: Croom Helm, 1985).

W. Wallace (ed.): *Britain in Europe* (London: Heinemann, 1980).

P. Williams and M. Harrison: *Politics and Society in De Gaulle's Republic* (London: Longman, 1971).

23

A DEFINITION OF EUROPE AND BRITAIN'S PLACE

On 14 January 1963, President de Gaulle made use of one of his rare press conferences in the Elysée Palace to express his opinions of what the European Community was all about. His remarks had the effect of terminating the negotiations on Britain's membership of the EEC. The whole of the press conference was reported on 16 January 1963 in *Le Monde*, from which the following section has been taken.

GREAT BRITAIN MUST ACCEPT THE TREATY OF ROME WITHOUT RESERVE AND RESTRAINT

(*Question*) Would you be able to define clearly France's position on the entry of England into the Common Market and the political evolution of their role?

(*Answer*) That's a straight-forward question which I am going to try to answer clearly.

When people talk about economics and, even more so, when people construct the economy, what they say about it and what they do about it must be consistent with realities, because without this, they will get into difficulties and sometimes even into ruin.

In this great project of the European Economic Community, and also in this matter of Great Britain's eventual membership, there are realities which we must recognize from the beginning. No matter how favourable they might be, or how favourable they actually are, good feelings cannot be invoked to erase the given realities. What are these given realities?

The Treaty of Rome was concluded by six continental states. States which are, strictly speaking, all of the same sort. Whether it's a question of their industrial or agricultural production, their foreign trade, their customs and their commercial ties, or their living and working conditions, they have many more similarities than they do differences. Moreover, they are contiguous states; they network with one another, and they are all connected by their communications. The fact of grouping them together and binding them to each other in such a way that what they have to manufacture, to buy, to sell, to consume, all this conforms to the realities of what they produce, buy, sell and consume with preference to their own group. Moreover, we must add that from the point of view of their economic development, their social progress, their technological capability, they are decidedly in step, and they march at very much the same pace. Besides, we find that there is no sort of political grievance amongst them, no boundary disputes, no rivalry or hegemony or undue influence. To the contrary, they are united first of all by the conviction that together they represent an important part of the well-springs of our civilization. And as far as their security is concerned, they face as continental states the same threat across their common territory.

So they are bound together by the fact that none of them is obligated to the outside world by any particular political or military agreement. It was therefore psychologically and materially possible to establish the economic community of the Six. And even that was not achieved without pain. When the Treaty of Rome was signed in 1957, it was only after long negotiations, and in order for it to achieve anything once it was concluded, we French had to put our own house in order, economically, financially, monetarily and so on. And that was done in 1959.

AGRICULTURE AND THE COMMON MARKET

From that moment on, the Community was viable in principle, but we still had to apply the Treaty. As it happens, this Treaty was rather precise, fairly thorough, on the subject of industry, but was not at all that way on the subject of agriculture. However, for our country, this was an issue which had to be resolved. It is surely apparent that agriculture is an essential part of the whole of our national activity. We cannot imagine a common market in which French agriculture would not find outlets proportionate to its production, and among the Six we are agreed that we are the country which feels this necessity most acutely. That is why, when people were thinking of putting the second phase of the Treaty into operation – in other words, a practical beginning of the membership – we were led to place the introduction of agriculture as a formal condition in the Common Market.

This was finally accepted by our partners, but some very difficult and complex arrangements about agriculture were necessary. In fact, certain regulations are still being discussed. I note in passing that, in this great undertaking, all the decisions have been made by the various governments, because apart from them there is no other authority or responsibility. But I must say that, when it comes to preparing and clarifying business, the Commission in Brussels has worked in a very objective and practical way.

And so Great Britain has made its application to the Common Market. It has done so after refusing to join the Community when it was being built not very long ago, after having created a sort of free-trade arrangement with six other countries, and – now, I can say this because people recall the negotiations which dragged on so long on this subject – after they had exerted pressure on the Six to prevent the actual inauguration of the Common Market, finally, after all this, England asked in its own good time to enter it, but according to its own conditions.

Without doubt, this presents some huge problems to each of the Six, just as it does to England itself.

In reality, England is insular, maritime, connected by its trade, its sales and its food supplies, to very different and often very distant countries. It follows an essentially industrial and commercial activity, with very little agriculture. Across the whole of its experience, it has very conspicuous, very special, customs and traditions.

In short, the nature, the structure and the attitudes which are appropriate to England differ from those of the continentals.

For England living as it does, producing as it does, trading as it does, how can it be incorporated into the Common Market which has been conceived and functions as it does?

For example, the way that the people of Great Britain feed themselves – that is, in fact, by importing food-stuffs bought cheaply in the Americas or in the old Dominions, while at the same time giving large subsidies to English farmers – that procedure is obviously incompatible with the system which the Six have established so naturally among themselves.

The system of the Six consists of making a commonality of all the agricultural products of the whole Community, of rigorously determining their prices, of forbidding the subsidizing of prices, of monitoring consumption among all the member countries, and of requiring each one of these countries to pay to the Community all the savings realized by consuming foodstuffs supplied internally by the Common Market.

Once again, how can England enter this system, such as it is now?

On occasion, it is possible to believe that our English friends, in putting forward their application for the Common Market, realize they are to change themselves to the point of accepting all the conditions which are accepted and practised by the Six. But the question is to know whether Great Britain can align itself with the continent, and, like the continent, place itself within a tariff which will be truly common, whether it can give up Commonwealth preference entirely, whether it can cease claiming that its agriculture is privileged, and, again, whether it can regard as null the commitments which it has made with the countries which constitute the Free Trade Area. That question: that's the whole question.

We cannot say that this question has now been resolved. Will it be, some day? Obviously, only England can answer that.

In addition to England, this question applies to the other states which (again, I refer to this) are with England in the Free Trade Area for the same reasons as Great Britain, who would wish, or will wish, to enter the Common Market.

A PROPERLY EUROPEAN CONSTRUCTION

We must realize that the entry first of Great Britain, and then later of the other states, will change completely the structure of the agreement about definitions, compensations and regulations which have already been reached by the Six, because all those states, like England, have very important special interests. This would have to be a different sort of Common Market; we would have to think about a different structure. The structure we would build for eleven, and then for thirteen, and then maybe even for eighteen, that would no doubt hardly resemble the one which the Six have built.

Moreover, this Community, growing in this way, would be confronted with all the problems of economic relations with a multitude of states, and first of all with the United States.

It is foreseeable that the membership of all these states, who would be very numerous and very diverse, would not resist it for very long, for there would undoubtedly appear a vast Atlantic community, under American tutelage and direction, which would soon swallow up the European Community.

This is an assumption which might be perfectly justified in the eyes of some, but it is not at all what France wanted to do and is doing now, which is a strictly European construction.

Therefore, it is possible that some day England will manage to change itself sufficiently to become part of the European Community without limitation and without reserve. In that case, the Six will open the door to it, and France would not object, although obviously the mere inclusion of England in the community would considerably alter its nature and size.

It is also possible that England is not yet ready, and that is certainly what seems to come out of the long, so very long, negotiations in Brussels. But if that is the case, there is nothing so terrible about that.

First of all, whatever decision England takes in this matter, there is no reason to alter relations with it, as far as we are concerned. The courtesy, the respect, which are due to that great country, to that great people, will not be changed in the least.

What England has achieved through the centuries and around the world is recognized as great, even though it has often had disputes with France. The glorious participation of Great Britain in the victory which crowned the First World War: this, we French, will admire for ever. As to the role that England played in the most dramatic and decisive moment of the Second World War, no one has the right to forget it.

Truly, the fate of the free world – our own, above all, but even that of the United States and Russia – have depended to a great degree on the determination, on the solidarity, and on the courage of the English people, as Churchill knew how to motivate them. Even today, no one can challenge British ability and valour.

And so, I repeat, if the negotiations in Brussels should not succeed now, nothing would prevent an agreement of association being concluded between the Common Market and Great Britain, such as to guarantee trade. Nor would anything prevent close relations being maintained between England and France, and the continuation of their direct co-operation in all fields, especially those of science, technology and industry – as the two countries have just proved by deciding to build the supersonic airliner Concorde together.

Finally, it is very possible that the path suitable to Great Britain and the road taken by all the others will lead the English to the continent, whatever might be the delays encountered on the way. That is what I believe very willingly myself, and that is why, in my opinion, at any rate, this will be a great honour for the British Prime Minister, for my friend Harold Macmillan, and for his government, for having understood all this so soon, and for having had the courage to state it, and for having led their country to take the first steps on the path which, some day perhaps, will lead them to the continent.

24

LUXEMBOURG COMPROMISE

The impasse which developed between France and other members of the EEC was papered over by the agreement of the EEC Council of Ministers, meeting in Luxembourg in January 1966. The following text of the Agreement was published by the Western European Union, in *The Political Year in Europe* (1966).

[The Agreement primarily involved (a) the issue of majority voting by the Council of Ministers, and (b) the sharing of certain responsibilities by the Council and the Commission.]

(a) Application of the majority voting rule by the EEC Council of Ministers

1. When issues very important to one or more member countries are at stake, the members of the Council will try, within a reasonable time, to reach solutions which can be adopted by all the members of the Council, while respecting their mutual interests, and those of the Community, in accordance with Article 2 of the treaty.
2. The French Delegation considers that, when very important issues are at stake, discussion must be continued until unanimous agreement is reached.
3. The six delegations note that there is a divergence of views on what should be done in the event of a failure to reach complete agreement.
4. However, they consider that this divergence does not prevent the Community's work being resumed in accordance with the normal procedures.

(b) Cooperation between the Council of Ministers and the EEC Commission

Close cooperation between the Council and the Commission is essential to the functioning and development of the Community.

In order to improve and further intensify this cooperation at all levels, the Council considers that the following practical cooperation measures should be decided on by common agreement ... but that these measures should not affect the respective competence and duties of the two institutions.

1. It is desirable that the Commission, before adopting a proposal of particular importance should, through the Permanent Representatives, make appropriate contacts with the governments of the member States, without this procedure affecting the right of initiative which the Commission derives from the treaty.
2. Proposals and all other official acts which the Commission addresses to the Council and the member States shall only be made public after the latter have formally taken cognisance of them and have the texts in their possession.

The Official Gazette should be arranged so that legislative acts having a binding force are published distinctly as such. [...]

3. The credentials of Heads of Mission of non-member States accredited to the Community shall be presented to the President of the Council and the President of the Commission, meeting together for this purpose.

4. The Council and the Commission will inform each other rapidly and fully of any approaches relating to fundamental questions made to either institution by non-member States.

5. Within the scope of the application of Article 162, the Council and the Commission will consult together on the advisability of, the procedure for, and the nature of any links which the Commission might establish, under Article 229 of the treaty, with international organisations.

6. Cooperation between the Council and the Commission on the Community's information policy, which was examined by the Council on 24th September 1963, will be strengthened so that the programme of the Press and Information Service shall be drawn up and carried out jointly, in accordance with procedures to be defined later and which might include an ad hoc body.

7. Within the framework of the financial regulations for drawing up and putting into effect the Communities' budgets, the Council and the Commission will define methods of increasing the efficiency of control over the acceptance, authorisation and execution of the Communities' expenditures.

_____ 25 _____

EUROPE'S 'INNER CIRCLE'

Expressing the fears of the smaller member states of the EEC, the Luxembourg Foreign Minister, Gaston Thorn, spoke against the emergence of an 'inner circle'. This extract is taken from the *Bulletin de documentation*, No. 3 (20 March 1969).

[...] Without going into the details of any particular version of the talks which took place some four or five weeks ago between the President of the French Republic and the British Ambassador, I merely note with great concern that following these talks there was mention in the international press of large and small European countries, certain countries which qualified to belong to an 'inner circle' or political directorate, and other countries which according to some sources did not have the necessary qualifications and which, if necessary, would not be consulted beforehand on Europe's political course but informed *a posteriori* of such consultations.

I was very happy to hear from the very mouth of Mr Debré during my recent visit to Paris that, whatever the origin of these rumours which caused us concern, the French Government intended to respect scrupulously the spirit and the letter of the Rome and Paris Treaties and that it did not consider there were any privileged partners. I note with equal satisfaction that the British Government still wishes to enter the Community in its present form and is at present acting in such a way as not to jeopardise the institutions and principles which govern Community life.

[. . .]

Europe's weakness and paralysis will last until our countries agree on the political aims of the future organisation of our continent and on the guidelines of a European foreign policy. These are two aspects of the same problem, which is an essentially political one, and which must be solved before any substantial and lasting progress can be made in the building of Europe in other fields as well.

The resumption of the political dialogue between the European governments concerned, which has been interrupted for so long, might seem to be a first step towards enabling our countries to overcome their differences and Western Europe to resume its authority and influence on our continent and throughout the world.

To this end, Western European Union, with its political aims, the flexibility of its organisation and its membership, offered the most appropriate framework among the existing international organisations. In fact, the seven countries grouped in WEU, the Six of the Common Market and Britain, may be considered as the hub, the centre of gravity of Western Europe because of their geographical position, their economic strength, their history and their political rôle.

At the meeting of the WEU Council of Ministers in Rome last October, the Belgian Minister for Foreign Affairs therefore submitted proposals to his colleagues on the organisation of compulsory consultations on a list of subjects on which the member governments would undertake not to take any further decision or action without prior consultation with their partners.

Mr Harmel's proposals were welcomed warmly by most countries, but because of French reticence no decision was taken in Rome. The Italian Government then agreed to submit further proposals at the Council meeting in Luxembourg in February. It will be recalled that differences of views between the various delegations prevented agreement being reached on an exact agenda for the Luxembourg meeting. In spite of this and thanks to the goodwill and conciliatory spirit of all, the meeting eventually took place in a relaxed atmosphere and, after a very full discussion, the Council reached the following conclusions.

All the delegations showed their willingness to improve foreign policy consultations in the WEU framework. There was unanimity on the principle of holding emergency meetings whenever necessary, and restricted meetings to make the discussions more effective. Moreover, the Benelux States decided at this meeting that, prior to any decision on a list of foreign policy questions, they would consult their WEU partners, either at the level of the Council of Ministers or at the level of permanent representatives, with a view to encouraging the adoption of jointly-agreed positions, harmonised as far as possible. The British, Italian and German Delegations associated themselves with this proposal. The French Delegation reserved its position on all the fundamental and procedural aspects of the Benelux proposal and would make known its position at the latest during the next ministerial meeting.

The Permanent Council was instructed to work out procedure for the emergency convening of meetings and for restricted meetings, and, apart from the proposals made, to give further and wider consideration to any other proposals likely to improve consultations in the foreign policy field in the framework of WEU.

In view of the initially different positions of the various delegations, this result could be considered very satisfactory and there was a possibility of finding a consultation procedure acceptable to all the governments.

But a week later, further difficulties arose between France and its six partners when the British Secretary of State for Foreign Affairs convened an emergency meeting to discuss the Middle East problem. France opposed this meeting, which it considered pointless since the problem had already been amply discussed in Luxembourg and no new factors had arisen since. It invoked the unanimity rule which, according to its interpretation of Article VIII of the [WEU] treaty, required unanimity for the convocation of a meeting as well as for the preparation of the agenda. At the same time, the French representative to WEU stated that his government would no longer take part in the activities of the Council so long as it had not received assurances that the unanimity rule would henceforth be fully respected. Since then, the French representative has not attended Council meetings.

In opposition to the French interpretation, there are the various interpretations of the other countries, including that of Luxembourg, which considers that as Article VIII specifically lays down that the Council 'shall be so organised as to be able to exercise its functions continuously' the Secretary-General has no need for the unanimous agreement of all the members to convene a Council meeting or draw up an agenda.

In addition, although Council decisions have to be unanimous, the absence or abstention of one member does not in itself imply an absence of unanimity, this interpretation is based on normal procedure in the Security Council. This being so, we for our part can give France the most formal assurance that we do not in any way wish to make WEU a court of appeal for the European Communities, or make use of it as an indirect way of setting aside the obstacle of French opposition to British accession to the Common Market, and I am convinced that this is also the position of our other partners. [...]

26

DAVIGNON REPORT

The Davignon Report on European political unification was adopted by the Ministers for Foreign Affairs in Luxembourg, on 27 October 1970. The text is taken from *European Documents*, No. 593, 14 September 1970.

FIRST PART

1. The Ministers of Foreign Affairs of the member States of the European Communities were instructed by the Chiefs of State and of Government who

met at The Hague on 1st and 2nd December 1969 'to study the best way to bring about progress in the area of political unification, in the perspective of the enlargement' of the European Communities.

2. In carrying out this mandate, the Ministers took care to remain faithful to the spirit which governed the drafting of the Hague communiqué. The Chiefs of State and Government in particular noted that the construction of Europe has arrived, with the beginning of the definitive phase of the Common Market, 'at a turning point in its history'; they affirmed that 'the European Communities remain the original basis on which it has arisen'; finally, they expressed their determination to 'prepare the way of a united Europe capable of assuming its responsibilities in the world of tomorrow, and of making a contribution which corresponds to its tradition and its mission'.

3. The Chiefs of State and Government were determined to express 'the common conviction that a Europe – which groups together States which, in their national diversity, are united in their essential interests, assured of their own cohesion, faithful to their external friendships, aware of the rôle which they have to play to facilitate international détente and the rapprochement of all peoples and, above all, of those of the entire European continent – is indispensable for the preservation of an exceptional centre of development, of progress and of culture, for the stability of the world, and for the protection of peace'.

4. United Europe, aware of the responsibilities which it has by reason of its economic development, its industrial power and its standard of living, intends to increase its efforts with regard to developing countries in an effort to establish relations of confidence among peoples.

5. United Europe must be founded on a common patrimony of respect for liberty and for the rights of man, and must bring together democratic States endowed with a freely-elected parliament. This united Europe remains the fundamental goal which must be attained as soon as possible, thanks to the political will of the people and the decision of their governments.

6. The Ministers therefore considered that, in order to respect continuity and to be consistent with the political finality of the European design, as the conference of The Hague so strongly emphasised, their proposals should be based on three premises.

7. The first is that it is desirable, in the spirit of the preambles of the Treaties of Paris and Rome, to give form to the desire for political union which has never ceased to underlie the progress of the European Communities.

8. The second is that, as common policies – both those already established and those that are being proposed – are put into effect, corresponding developments should take place in the purely political domain, in order to bring nearer the moment when Europe can express itself with a single voice. This is why it is important that the construction of Europe should be pursued in successive steps, and that the most appropriate method and instruments for allowing common political action should develop in a gradual manner.

9. The last, finally, is that Europe must prepare itself to carry out the responsi-

bilities which, because of its greater cohesion and its growing rôle, it has the duty and necessity to assume in the world.

10. The present developments in the European Communities impose on the member States the need to increase their political cooperation and, in a first stage, to give themselves the means to harmonise their points of view with regard to international politics.

It thus appeared to the Ministers that it is in the area of the concertation of foreign policy that it would be best to make the first concrete efforts to make clear to all that Europe has a political vocation. In effect, the Ministers are convinced that progress in this area would benefit the development of the Communities and would give to Europeans a more active awareness of their common responsibility.

SECOND PART

The Ministers propose the following:
Desirous of making progress in the area of political unification, the governments decide to cooperate on foreign policy matters.

I. GOALS

The goals of this cooperation are the following:

- to assure, by information and regular consultation, better mutual comprehension on the major problems of internal politics;
- to strengthen solidarity by promoting the harmonisation of points of view, the concerting of attitudes and, when it seems possible and desirable, common actions.

II. MINISTERIAL MEETINGS

1. On the initiative of the President *pro tempore*, the Ministers for Foreign Affairs shall meet at least every six months:
   - If they consider that the gravity of the circumstances or the importance of the subjects to be treated so justify, their meeting can be replaced by a conference of Chiefs of State or of Government.
   - In case of grave crisis or particular urgency, a special consultation will be organised by the governments of the member States. The president *pro tempore* will contact his colleagues to ensure this consultation.
2. The Minister for Foreign Affairs of the State which has the presidency of the Council of the European Communities will preside over the meetings.
3. The ministerial meetings shall be prepared by a committee made up of the Directors for Political Affairs.

III. POLITICAL COMMITTEE

1. A committee made up of the Directors for Political Affairs shall meet at least four times per year in order to prepare the ministerial meetings and to carry out tasks which will be assigned to it by the Ministers.

   Besides, the President *pro tempore* can, on an exceptional basis and after consulting his colleagues, convoke the committee, either on his own initiative or at the request of one of the members.
2. The presidency of the committee follows the same rules as those of the ministerial meetings.
3. The committee can create working groups charged with particular tasks.

   It can instruct a group of experts to assemble the facts relating to a given problem and to present the different possible options.
4. All other forms of consultation can be envisaged as the need arises. [...]

V. THE COMMISSION OF THE EUROPEAN COMMUNITIES

In cases where the work of the Ministers would have an effect on the activities of the European Communities, the Commission would be invited to make known its opinion.

VI. EUROPEAN PARLIAMENTARY ASSEMBLY

In order to give a democratic character to the building of political union, it is necessary to associate public opinion and its representatives with it.

A semi-yearly meeting will bring together the Ministers and the members of the Political Committee of the European Parliamentary Assembly in order to discuss the questions which will be the subject of the consultations in the framework of cooperation on foreign policy matters. This meeting will be held in an informal manner in order to permit the parliamentarians and ministers to express their opinions freely.

VII. GENERAL PROVISIONS

1. Meetings will normally be held in the State whose representative is President *pro tempore* of the meetings.
2. The host government will make the necessary arrangements for the secretariat and the administrative details of the meetings.
3. Each State will designate within its Ministry of Foreign Affairs an official who will correspond with his counterparts in the other States. [...]

_____ 27 _____

A GERMAN VIEW OF EUROPE

Reflecting the optimism generated by the recent expansion of the Community, Chancellor Brandt addressed the European Parliament in Strasbourg, 13 November 1973. The following extracts are taken from the *Official Journal of the European Communities*, No. 168 (ANNEX), November 1973.

Let me now speak on European unification and say something I would not have said in this way ten years ago: we can, and we will, create Europe. (*Applause*)

We have had to put up with delays and set-backs. This has called for criticism, partly justified. Also from you, the members of the European Parliament. I understand that, and my government endeavours to follow your advice as much as possible.

Yet it is true when I say that we have without doubt made progress, thanks not least to the impulses provided by the two summit conferences at The Hague and Paris.

We can, if only we want to, now set out on a new phase of the European journey. I am certain that European union will come, which is why I time and again appeal to our partners throughout the world to regard this as a fact and in this way to anticipate Europe's future, to take it for granted as of now, so to speak.

The move towards European union is indispensable. It alone will offer our people the scope their political, economic, social and cultural energies require. The unification of Europe is not merely a question of the quality of our existence. It is a question of survival between the giants and in the rugged world of the young and the old nationalisms. Only in a Europe that has found its personality can we secure our national identities. The classical nation State belongs to yesterday. While – and maybe for long years to come we may have to move in narrow fields, our future no longer lies in the isolation of the nation State.

Naturally, European union will not be the outcome of a revolution, of a sudden leap from the nation State to supranationality, nor from an uprooting of boundary posts or from a constitution brilliantly put on paper overnight.

Instead, we have been speaking of the European evolution – the constant, energetic developments in all those spheres already incorporated in the process of integration, and in the other spheres that are not officially considered 'integrated'. The sum of these measures will one day – probably sooner than some people think – swing the pendulum from quantity to the new quality.

We should shorten the time limits we have set ourselves – be it for economic and monetary union, be it for what I have termed the social union, be it for political union. According to the Paris summit decision, the European union is to become a reality, within this very decade!

It is of decisive importance that on the road to European union we should have a proper sense of proportion. The proposal of the French President that the Heads of Government of the Community should meet at regular intervals to discuss the internal and external problems connected with the growing union intensively and without the burden of a 'machinery' certainly is in keeping with that sense of proportion.

This proposal concurs very opportunely, by the way, with the intentions of my government and with the suggestions of the British Prime Minister. I take this initiative to mean that this body can develop into a kind of regular presidential conference and become an accepted notion of, indeed, a decisive step towards political union.

Every step forward must be commensurate with the situation and with the necessities; it must equip the Community or the organs of political cooperation with the new powers needed for the fulfilment of the tasks which all agree must be fulfilled at the given time.

It is not so much a question of language than of concrete results. It is a matter of increasing the efficiency both within the Community and European political cooperation. The two must now work effectively together.

After twenty years of efforts to achieve European integration we should all by now have learned that the functional rather than the constitutional method is more likely to get us home. I do not mind if one calls this pragmatism. The goal is clear. It is, as I have put it from time to time, a sensibly organised European government which in the fields of common policies will be able to take the necessary decisions and will be subject to parliamentary control. (*Applause*)

The European States will transfer to that government those sovereign rights which in the future can only be effectively exercised together; the remaining rights will stay with the member States.

In this way we shall both preserve the national identity of our peoples, which is the source of their strength, and add the European identity from which fresh energies will ensue.

Such a European government will be in charge of the economic and monetary community, the social community, perhaps also the educational community, definitely the community of foreign affairs, and – certainly with a cogent logic one day – the community of a security administered under European sovereignty.

Once these spheres have become the responsibility of a European government, a basic law also will obviously be required which will have to be approved by our citizens.

Up to now we have given them little opportunity to feel themselves to be what they have largely been for some time: citizens of Europe. We know from opinion polls that many of them like us, regard European unity as the aim of political efforts. But we may have too rarely linked the European consciousness with their everyday lives. This I have pointed out time and again in recent years, if you permit me to say so.

It will be of vital importance for the Community to grow beyond economic cooperation and political organisation to become the socially progressive region in the world. European integration must serve the people directly.

I do not mean simply a vague concept of life. Our citizens should physically feel that Europe improves their working and living conditions, that it has an effect on their everyday life. Europe must at long last remove the barriers in the form of frontier checkpoints or aliens law for the many hundreds of thousands who within the Community travel from one country to the other or avail themselves of the right of establishment.

One should not accept the fact that whilst barriers are being reduced the number of customs officers is being increased instead of diminished (*Applause*), that customs regulations are becoming longer instead of shorter, more complicated instead of simpler. (*Applause*) If we give our national bureaucracies a European dimension then we shall be making a mistake. (*Applause*)

It certainly is not the will of our people that we create a Europe in which we wander about like citizen K in Kafka's *Schloss*.

This is where the political will should at long last carry the day over the many national administrative egoisms which may be justified individually but all in all can no longer be tolerated. What we want is a Europe of daily reason and of common sense and we must be prepared to state this and where necessary to act.

Mr President, my government hopes that at the end of this year a new and clear step forward will be taken along the road to a European government. This is what is required of us if we are to respect the decisions of the Paris Conference of October 1972.

The dramatic developments on the international scene of recent weeks have demonstrated the inability of the European States to serve as a factor of peace and stabilisation in the world as long as they are unable to act as one. People from other continents have felt perhaps more than we that in a world whose destiny cannot, and should not, be determined by two super powers alone, the influence of a united Europe has become indispensable.

In this 'year of Europe' the relationship between the Community and the United States should be defined, and after that, the relationship with Canada and Japan. At the same time the Comecon is seeking contact. A majority of African countries want association agreements, and considerable hopes are attached to European unification also in other parts of the world.

Special importance accrues to the definition of the relationship between uniting Europe and the United States of America. This will be a long-term process which will not come to an end before European union has been completed. We are linked by similar ideals. Our security interests are firmly interlocked through the Atlantic Alliance. America has always come out strongly in favour of European unification. Each of our nations will bring the experience of friendship into the Atlantic dialogue.

On the other hand, Europe has become self-confident and independent enough to regard itself as an equal partner in this relationship and it is as such that it must be accepted. Partnership cannot mean subordination. Partnership proves its value in the balance of interests, in their will jointly to settle their common problems, to fulfil their joint responsibilities by sensible agreement and in reliable mutual respect. [...]

_____ 28 _____

REGIONAL DEVELOPMENT

The European Regional Development Fund was established by Regulation of the Council (No. 724/75) on 18 May 1975. The following text of the Regulation was published in the *Official Journal of the European Communities*, No. L 73/1 (21 March 1975).

Whereas the Paris conference of Heads of State or of Government in October 1972, desirous of finding a Community solution to regional problems, invited the Community institutions to create a Regional Development Fund whose intervention, in conjunction with national aids, should permit, with the progressive realization of economic and monetary union, the correction of the main regional imbalances in the Community and particularly those resulting from the preponderance of agriculture and from industrial change and structural underemployment; [...]

Whereas the Treaty does not provide the necessary powers; whereas the Community should be granted such powers pursuant to Article 235 of the Treaty [of Rome];

Whereas an effective policy on regional structures is an essential prerequisite to the realization of economic and monetary union;

Whereas regional development requires investment in industrial or service activities ensuring that new jobs are created and existing jobs maintained on the one hand, and on the other, investment in infrastructures directly linked to the development of these activities; whereas it is necessary to contribute to the creation in certain less-favoured agricultural areas, of adequate, collective facilities to ensure that farming is continued and a minimum population maintained;

Whereas the principle should be adopted that the Fund's assistance should be allocated according to the relative severity of regional imbalances; whereas account should also be taken of other factors determining the interest of investments from the point of view of the region concerned as well as from that of the Community;

Whereas the management of the Fund should be the responsibility of the Commission assisted by a Fund Committee;

Whereas aid from the Fund will be effective only if investments benefiting from the Community's aid are included in regional development programmes; whereas the results obtained in each region from year to year should be monitored;

Whereas the Fund's assistance should not lead Member States to reduce their own regional development efforts but should complement these efforts;

Whereas the Commission should ensure, with the cooperation of Member States, the proper administration of investments receiving aid from the Fund and exercise effective control of the operation of the Fund;

Whereas the extent of the Community's activities requires specific information

to be provided to the Council and to the European Parliament in the form of an annual report.
HAS ADOPTED THIS REGULATION:

Article 1

A European Regional Development Fund is hereby established, hereinafter referred to as 'the Fund', intended to correct the principal regional imbalances within the Community resulting in particular from agricultural preponderance, industrial change and structural under-employment.

Article 2

1. For the period 1975 to 1977, financial assistance from the Fund shall be granted to the applicant Member States, subject to the conditions set out in this Regulation and within the limits of the following appropriations:

   300 million units of account in 1975,
   500 million units of account in 1976,
   500 million units of account in 1977. [...]

The resources of the Fund shall be distributed in accordance with the following table:

Belgium	1.5%
Denmark	1.3%
France	15.0%
Ireland	6.0%
Italy	40.0%
Luxembourg	0.1%
Netherlands	1.7%
Federal Republic of Germany	6.4%
United Kingdom	28.0%

Further, a sum of six million units of account shall be granted to Ireland, which shall be deducted from the share of other Member States with the exception of Italy. [...]

Article 3

Regions and areas which may benefit from the Fund shall be limited to those aided areas established by Member States in applying their systems of regional aids and in which State aids are granted which qualify for Fund assistance.
    When aid from the Fund is granted, priority shall be given to investments in

national priority areas, taking account of the principles for the coordination at Community level of regional aids.

Article 4

1. The Fund may contribute to the financing of investments which individually exceed 50 000 units of account, and come under any of the following categories:
   (a) Investments in industrial, handicraft, or service activities which are economically sound and which benefit from State regional aids, provided that at least 10 new jobs are created or that existing jobs are maintained. In the latter case, the investments should fall within the framework of a conversion or restructuring plan to ensure that the undertaking concerned is competitive. Preference shall, however, be given to operations which both maintain existing jobs and create new jobs.
   Service activities qualifying for assistance shall be those concerned with tourism and those which have a choice of location. Such activities should have a direct impact on the development of the region and on the level of employment. [...]
2. The amount of the Fund's contribution shall be:
   (a) In respect of investments covered by paragraph 1(a), 20 per cent of the investment cost without however exceeding 50 per cent of the aid accorded to each investment by public authorities under a system of regional aids, such contributions being limited moreover to that part of the investment which does not exceed 100 000 units of account per job created and 50 000 units of account per job maintained.
   The State aids to be taken into consideration in this connection shall be grants, interest rebates, or their equivalent where loans at reduced rates of interest are concerned, whether these aids are linked to the investment or to the number of jobs created. [...] The aid granted in the form of rent rebates or exemptions from payments of rents of factories may also be taken into account, provided that this form of calculation can be applied. [...]

Article 5

1. The Fund's assistance shall be decided by the Commission ... according to the relative severity of the economic imbalance of the region where the investment is made and the direct or indirect effect of the investment on employment. The Commission shall examine, in particular, the consistency of the investment with the range of actions undertaken by the relevant Member State in favour of the region concerned, as apparent from information supplied by Member States pursuant to Article 6 and taking special account of:
   (a) the investments contribution to the economic development of the region;

(b) the consistency of the investment with the Community's programmes or objectives;

(c) the situation of the economic sector concerned and the profitability of the investment;

(d) whether the investment falls within a frontier area, that is to say, within adjacent regions of separate Member States;

(e) other contributions made by Community institutions or by the European Investment Bank, either to the same investment or to other activities within the same region. Thus contributions from the Fund will be coordinated with other Community contributions, in such a way as to favour a range of converging and coordinated actions within a given region and to guarantee in particular consistency between regional policy and structural policy for agriculture. [...]

Article 6

1. Investments may benefit from the Fund's assistance only if they fall within the framework of a regional development programme, the implementation of which is likely to contribute to the correction of the main regional imbalances within the Community which are likely to prejudice the attainment of economic and monetary union. [...]

3. Member States shall notify the Commission of regional development programmes and alterations thereto as and when they are drawn up.

4. The programmes shall indicate the objectives and the means for developing the region. For this purpose, one of the priority tasks of the Committee for Regional Policy shall be to study the technical methods for preparing these programmes, so as to provide, by 31 December 1975 at the latest, an outline of the information to be included in these programmes.

5. The Committee for Regional Policy must be consulted about the programmes. The Commission shall examine them, having regard to the provisions of the Treaty and the decisions adopted by Community institutions.

6. Member States shall provide the Commission at the beginning of each year, and initially before the beginning of the third month following the entry into force of this Regulation, with all useful information concerning:

(a) the development of the economic and social situation of the regions referred to in Article 3;

(b) the resources which they have decided to allocate or which they proposed to allocate to the development of these regions;

(c) the measures envisaged in respect of infrastructure and the creation of economic activity, together with an implementation schedule;

(d) where applicable, the aid ceiling.

They also shall provide annually, at the latest by 1 April, an overall statistical summary indicating by region the results achieved during the previous year as a result of action taken in each region. Those results to which the Fund has contributed shall be indicated separately. [...]

Article 9

1. Where an investment which has been the subject of a contribution from the Fund has not been made as planned, or if the conditions of this Regulation are not fulfilled, the contribution from the fund may be reduced or cancelled, if the Commission so decides after consulting the Fund Committee.

   Any sums which have been paid in error shall be repaid to the Community by the Member State concerned or, where applicable, by the European Investment Bank, within 12 months following the date on which the relevant decision has been communicated.

2. Member States shall make available to the Commission all information required for the effective operation of the Fund and shall take all steps to facilitate such supervision as the Commission may consider useful in managing the Fund, including on-the-spot checks.

3. Notwithstanding verification carried out by Member States in accordance with national laws, regulations and administrative provisions ... at the request of the Commission and with the agreement of the Member State, the competent authorities of that Member State shall carry out on-the-spot checks or enquiries about operations financed by the Fund. Officials of the Commission may take part in these proceedings and the Commission may fix a time limit for carrying them out.

4. The objective of these on-the-spot checks or enquiries about operations financed by the Fund shall be to verify:
   (a) the conformity of administrative practices with Community rules;
   (b) the existence of supporting documentary evidence and its conformity with the operations financed by the fund;
   (c) conditions under which the operations financed by the Fund are executed and checked;
   (d) the conformity of projects implemented with the operations financed by the Fund.

5. The Commission may suspend payment of aid to a particular project if an inspection reveals either irregularities, or a substantial change in the character or conditions of the project for which the Commission's approval has not been sought.

6. If a project receiving aid from the Fund is not completed or is implemented in such a manner as no longer to justify payment of part of the aid from the Fund granted on behalf of that project, the outstanding part of the Fund's contribution shall be granted to another investment located in one of the eligible regions of the same Member State under the conditions laid down in this Regulation.

Article 10

1. The Fund may contribute part of its resources to finance studies which are closely related to the operations of the Fund and undertaken at the request of a Member State.

2. The Fund's contribution may not exceed 50 per cent of the cost of the study. [...]

——————————————— 29 ———————————————

MACDOUGALL REPORT

The expansion of the Community in the early 1970s obliged the member states to examine the role of public finance in European integration. The group of 'independent economists' (chaired by Sir Donald MacDougall) began their meetings in 1975; their *General Report* was published by the Commission of the European Communities (Brussels, April 1977).

INTRODUCTION AND SUMMARY

Free trade in goods and services within the Community of Nine has been largely achieved, although significant non-tariff barriers remain in both the industrial and the agricultural fields. Monetary union, on which much has been written, is – for reasons given by the Marjolin Committee[1] – a long way off and will probably have to await major developments in the political, monetary and fiscal fields. This report examines the third main element in economic union, largely neglected so far, namely the role of public finance, which we take to embrace not only taxation and public expenditure, but also the many regulatory, coordinating and non-budgetary activities in the economic field in existing economic unions.

A major part of our work has been a detailed and quantitative study of public finance in five existing federations (Federal Republic of Germany, USA, Canada, Australia, Switzerland) and three unitary states (France, Italy and the UK) – eight countries in all – and in particular the financial relationships between different levels of government and the economic effects of public finance on geographical regions within the countries. We have also studied a good deal of the voluminous theoretical literature on 'fiscal federalism'. The main purpose has been to see what light these studies throw on future developments in the public finances of the European Community. [...]

MAIN POINTS FROM STUDY OF EIGHT COUNTRIES [...]

The most relevant orders of magnitude and other facts are as follows:

1. Public expenditure by members of the Community in 1975 was about 45 per cent of the gross product of the area as a whole (this is the weighted average for the individual states). Expenditure by all Community Institutions is 0.7 per cent (10 billion units of account in 1977).
2. Although the statistical problems are considerable, it can be said with a fair

[1] Report of the Study Group *Economic and Monetary Union 1980*, Brussels, March 1975.

degree of certainty that per capita incomes are in general at least as unequal between the Nine Members of the Community (and between the 72 regions we have distinguished in the Community) as they are on average between the various regions of the countries we have studied, even *before* allowing for the equalising effects of public expenditure and taxation.

3. These reduce regional inequalities in per capita income by, on average, about 40 per cent in the countries studied (by more in Australia and France, by less in the USA and Germany). The redistributive power between member states of the Community's finances, by comparison, is – not surprisingly – very small indeed (1 per cent); partly because the Community budget is relatively so small, partly because the expenditures and revenues of the Community have a weak geographical redistributive power per unit of account.

4. The redistribution through public finance between regions in the countries studied tends to be reflected to a large extent (though not, of course, precisely because other factors are involved) in corresponding deficits in the balances of payments on current account of the poorer regions, with corresponding surpluses in the richer regions. These deficits and surpluses are of a continuing nature. Net flows of public finance in the range of 3–10 per cent of regional product are common for both relatively rich and relatively poor regions, but a few of the latter enjoy considerably higher net in-flows, up to around 30 per cent of regional product.

5. As well as redistributing income regionally on a continuing basis, public finance in existing economic unions plays a major role in cushioning short-term and cyclical fluctuations. For example, one-half to two-thirds of a short-term loss of primary income in a region due to a fall in its external sales may be automatically offset through lower payments of taxes and insurance contributions to the centre, and higher receipts of unemployment and other benefits. If only because the Community budget is so relatively very small there is no such mechanism in operation on any significant scale as between member countries, and this is an important reason why in present circumstances monetary union is impracticable.

6. The importance of the various instruments which effect inter-regional redistribution varies. On the tax side, personal income tax is, in most countries, the predominant instrument. The main public expenditure programmes and social security systems also tend to have substantial redistributive effects.

    In unitary states a large part of the total redistribution between regions arises automatically in these ways and is in a sense 'invisible'; high incomes go with high tax payments and low incomes with high receipts of centrally provided services and transfer payments. (Regional policy narrowly defined is relatively unimportant.)

    In federal countries inter-governmental grants and tax-sharing play a much more important part. These achieve relatively large redistributive results with relatively small amounts of federal expenditure, because the net inter-regional transfers are to a smaller extent than elsewhere the result of differences between large payments in opposite directions.

7. In the federal countries, leaving aside defence and external relations including aid, which are always a federal responsibility, as much as one-half to two-thirds of civil expenditure is left in the hands of lower levels of government, sometimes including most expenditure on education, health, houses and roads, although social security is normally a predominantly federal responsibility. On the other hand, the financing of the expenditure is much more a federal responsibility – to the extent of one-half to four-fifths. [...]

IMPLICATIONS FOR THE FUTURE ROLE OF PUBLIC FINANCE IN THE COMMUNITY

It is possible to conceive, presumably at some distant date, a Federation in Europe in which federal public expenditure is around 20–25 per cent of gross product as in the USA and the Federal Republic of Germany.

An earlier stage would be a federation with a much smaller federal expenditure of the order of 5–7 per cent of gross product, or roughly $7\frac{1}{2}$–10 per cent if defence were included. An essential characteristic of such a federation would be that the supply of social and welfare services would nearly all remain at the national level. Such an arrangement could provide sufficient geographical equalisation of productivity, living standards and cushioning of temporary fluctuations to support a monetary union. But there are various degrees of confidence as to whether this would in practice be feasible.

In our Report we have tended to concentrate more on what we call 'pre-federal integration', a period during which it is assumed that the Community's political structure is being gradually built up, partly with the direct election of the European Parliament. We can envisage public expenditure at Community level rising to around, say, 2–$2\frac{1}{2}$ per cent of gross product during this period.

In considering which expenditure functions might be carried out to a greater extent at Community level we have taken account, in addition to the experience of the eight countries studied, and political realities as we assume them to be, the following criteria.

First, the case for Community involvement where this can achieve 'economies of scale', including greater bargaining power *vis-à-vis* third countries. This applies mainly to external relations (where it is a reality in external trade; a partial reality, which might be extended, in aid to developing countries; a possibility in energy and political cooperation; not at present a possibility as regards the supply of the defence services, although this does not rule out *ad hoc* cooperation between individual members). There are also possible economies of scale in Community action on advanced technology, industrial and technical standards, etc.

Secondly, there is a case for Community involvement when developments in one part of the Community 'spill over' into other parts of it. [...] Several of the external functions already referred to as economies of scale also have major spillover effects. An important example, internal to the Community, during the 'pre-federal integration' stage will, in our view, be Community action in the areas of structural and cyclical policies (regional, manpower, unemployment) to ensure so far as possible that the benefits of closer integration are seen to accrue to all, that there is growing convergence – or at least not widening divergence – in the economic performance and fortunes of member states. Those measures should make a start in reducing the inequalities in per capita incomes between the various parts of the area; the situation in the eight countries studied tends to confirm that this is a necessary part of economic union.

Thirdly, we assume that most member governments are reluctant at the present time to see any significant increase in total public expenditure at all levels – Community, national, state and local – as a percentage of gross product. This means that, besides curbing our ambitions for the Community, we must look for transfers of expenditure from national to Community levels, especially where economies of scale can be achieved; for savings where possible in existing Community expenditures (for example agriculture, which at present comprises two-thirds of the Community budget) . . . and avoidance of regulations, harmonisation, etc. which are not worth-while in terms of the extra bureaucratic and other costs involved.

CHANGES IN THE COMMUNITY'S EXPENDITURE

In the light of these various considerations, and to provoke discussion by those responsible for action, we would suggest the following main directions in which the Community's expenditure might be changed during the 'pre-federal integration' phase.

(a) The Community is already, and will increasingly on present plans become, involved in development aid. There is scope for transfers from national to Community level of some 2–4 billion units of account. This could achieve economies of scale by reducing administrative costs for recipient and donor countries and increasing the value of aid received by spreading the choice of procurement over a wider area.

(b) We would not see a case at this stage – though circumstances may change – for significant Community involvement in social and welfare services, which make up well over one-half of member states' total public expenditure, except for unemployment and vocational training. The Community has an interest in such matters as standards of teaching of European languages, mutual recognition of examination standards and reciprocity in health services and social security, but these will not involve large amounts of public money.

(c) We would look for savings wherever possible, for example, in agriculture and, less important quantitatively, through economies of scale in, for example, advanced technology, common political representation in smaller third countries, etc.

(d) In industrial sectors other than agriculture, for which Community intervention is established or plausible (e.g. steel, fisheries, energy, certain declining industries), the amount of direct budgetary subsidies should not tend to become large. But, not to be confused with budgetary expenditure, much larger sums of parallel loan financing, borrowed by the Community on capital markets or under Community guarantee, might be appropriate in some cases.

(e) It is in the area of structural, cyclical, employment and regional policies that we see the main need for substantial expenditure at Community level. The purpose of these measures is mainly to help to reduce inter-regional differences in capital endowment and productivity. Our general report sets out a 'menu' of six possibilities.

(i) More Community participation than at present in regional policy aids (employment or investment incentives, public infrastructure, urban re-development).

(ii) More Community participation than at present in labour market policies (including vocational training and other employment measures).

(iii) A Community Unemployment Fund on the lines suggested in the Marjolin Report under which part of the contributions of individuals in work would be shown as being paid to the Community and part of the receipts of individuals out of work as coming from the Community. This need not necessarily involve any increase in total public expenditure or contributions in the Community as a whole. Apart from the political attractions of bringing the individual citizen into direct contact with the Community, it would have significant redistributive effects and help to cushion temporary setbacks in particular member countries, thereby going a small part of the way towards creating a situation in which monetary union could be sustained.

(iv) A limited budget equalisation scheme for extremely weak member states to bring their fiscal capacity up to, say, 65 per cent of the Community average and so ensure that their welfare and public service standards are not too far below those of the main body of the Community.

(v) A system of cyclical grants to local or regional governments that would depend upon regional economic conditions.

(vi) A 'conjunctural convergence facility' aimed at preventing acute cyclical problems for weak member states leading to increasing economic divergences.

We judge that a selection from these six possibilities, or variants of them, involving budgetary expenditure of the order of 5–10 billion units of account per annum on average could be regarded as beginning to be economically significant. A 10 billion unit of account packet could reduce inequalities in living standards between member states by about 10 per cent, compared with the average of about 40 per cent in the countries studied, and might be judged an acceptable start.

Where grants are involved in the above possibilities (other than the suggested Unemployment Fund) they should be made as cost-effective as possible. This could involve, for example, the use of specific purpose matching grants (the Community providing a share of the total cost); having variable matching ratios, e.g. between

80 per cent and 20 per cent for poorer and richer states or regions so that the money went where it was most needed; and possibly the attachment of macro-economic performance conditions (on inflation, monetary policy, etc.) to some of the grants, to increase the likelihood that they would increase economic convergence.

The net cost of the suggestions under (a)-(e) above, allowing for savings, economies of scale, and mere transfers of expenditure from national to Community level, as well as for the hopefully favourable effects on the growth and stability of the Community's gross product, should not increase total public expenditure in the Community at all levels as a proportion of real product by much more than a percentage point. Allowing for the transfer of expenditure from national to Community level, the Community budget might rise from 0.7 per cent to around 2–2½ per cent. [...]

30

THE EUROPEAN MONETARY SYSTEM (EMS)

To promote monetary stability in Europe, the European Monetary System (EMS) was organized in the 1970s. The following *Commentary* on the history and operation of the EMS was prepared by the Directorate-General for Economic and Financial Affairs in Brussels. It was published by the Commission of the European Communities in 1979 under the title *European Economy* (offprint of Number 3, July 1979). In this version, the footnotes found in the original text have been omitted.

The purpose of the EMS is to create a zone of monetary stability in Europe, through the implementation of certain exchange rate, credit and resource transfer policies backed up and guided by a new policy of coordination aimed at prompting the convergence of economic policies and performances. The main concern here was to ensure that monetary instability did not jeopardize the process of genuine integration within the Community, thereby undermining the well-being of this economic area, which over the years has enjoyed an increasingly closer measure of interdependence. More immediately, the establishment of the EMS is part of a strategy for 'pulling out of the crisis' and for achieving economic recovery within the Community. A variety of jointly agreed measures and Community initiatives has been taken recently, notably in the budgetary and financial fields, and form the first part of this strategy.

On 13 March 1979, the EMS embarked on its 'initial' phase of implementation, during which a review of its operation will be conducted. In this connection, the relevant texts stipulate that, not later than two years after the start of the system, the arrangements concluded and the existing institutions will be consolidated into a European Monetary Fund which will replace the EMCF; the definitive system will entail not only the creation of this Fund but also full utilization of the ECU as a reserve asset and a means of settlement. [...]

I BACKGROUND

In order to assess more effectively the scope of the venture described in this commentary, it is important to see it in its historical context by tracing the pattern of ideas and events that have marked monetary developments and notably the lessons drawn from the achievements of the first attempt at institutional monetary organization in Europe, as defined in the Council Resolution of 22 March 1971.

This resolution was adopted following presentation to the Council and to the Commission of the report on the realization by stages of economic and monetary union (EMU) in the Community, also known as the 'Werner Report', which was drawn up in accordance with the instructions issued by the Conference of Heads of State or Government held on 1 and 2 December 1969 in The Hague. It has adopted against a general background of exchange rate stability a system of 'stable but adjustable' parities subject to narrow margins of fluctuation (in theory, 1 per cent; 0.75 per cent as applied by central banks) either side of each currency's parity against the US dollar and was based on the universalist view of international economic and monetary relationships as reflected in the initial Articles of the International Monetary Fund (IMF). The agreement reached at the Smithsonian Institute in December 1971 introduced wider margins of fluctuation (plus or minus 2.25 per cent against the dollar or, as practised under the Bretton Woods system, plus or minus 4.50 per cent between two European currencies). In response, the EEC governments set up a separate exchange rate scheme for the EEC currencies which limited the margins of fluctuation between European currencies to the permissible margin of fluctuation against the dollar. This scheme, endorsed by the Basle Agreement of April 1972, is known as 'the Snake in the Tunnel'.

This action was deemed necessary in order to mitigate the impact of the upheavals affecting the international monetary system. More important, it reflected the determination to press ahead with common policies, which were increasingly hampered by disruptions on foreign exchange markets. Under the circumstances, European monetary union – where the key features were to be a narrowing of margins and, ultimately, their abolition as well as the transfer of some decision-making powers with regard to economic policy to Community bodies – was regarded as one of the steps that needed to be taken.

In retrospect, this may seem surprising but the general climate and views that prevailed at the time, coupled with the exchange rate stability of the first decade of the Common Market's existence, explain why it was felt that this objective was attainable. Where the gradual narrowing of the margins of fluctuation was concerned, the feeling was that it would be sufficient to comply with somewhat stricter obligations than those applied within the IMF while at the same time benefiting from the implementation of common policies and the smooth functioning of the European economies. It was soon to become evident just how inadequate were the measures taken to achieve the convergence of policies – the key to the success of this venture – at a time when the growing instability of the dollar, the gradual undermining of the Bretton Woods system and, lastly, the oil crisis swept away the existing structure of relations between European economies and had repercussions, albeit in differing ways, on their currencies. And so it proved impossible to embark on the second stage of the construction of EMU and, the Snake itself, after the pound sterling, the lira and the French franc withdrew in turn, was to be whittled down to a group of currencies dominated by the German mark.

In the late 1960s, the world entered a period of major currency upheavals and, after a succession of shocks marked in particular by various fits of weakness on the part of the dollar, embarked on a system of floating exchange rates which was endorsed a posteriori by the Second Amendment to the IMF Articles which took effect in April 1978. In the meantime, the doctrine that had been the mainstay of the system of exchange rate parities and the practice of 'stable but adjustable rates' had been seriously called into question by a widely supported school of thought in favour of 'fluctuating rates'. Such a system was thought to be a more effective means of resolving the problems posed by the process of adjustment to balance of payments disequilibria than the steps taken within the traditional framework of the IMF.

And so, for most of the 1970s, the Community developed against a background profoundly different from that which had marked its first ten years of existence and had to cope with serious difficulties that were holding back further progress towards monetary organization in Europe. However, sight was never lost of the political objective of this venture or of its economic justification, even at the most difficult times, as can be seen from the numerous reports and communications drawn up by the Community institutions, from the proposals presented by Mr Fourcade, the French Finance Minister, upon assuming the Presidency of the Council (Economic and Financial Affairs) on 16 September 1974 and by Mr Duisenberg, the Netherlands Finance Minister, under the same circumstances on 26 July 1976.

These reports and proposals were to set out new methods and techniques of monetary integration which were added to the common store of ideas that was to be drawn on in later years. Mention should here be made of the following: the analysis of the reasons for pooling part of Member States' foreign exchange reserves and the relevant technical arrangements proposed by the Commission, acting on a request from the Council, in its report dated 28 June 1973; the suggestion put forward by Mr Fourcade regarding the role of the EUA in a renovated Community exchange rate mechanism and the coordination of policies vis-à-vis the dollar; lastly, Mr Duisenberg's ideas on the ways and means of introducing a greater measure of stability in the exchange rate relationships between Member States' currencies and fresh attempts to achieve economic and monetary policy coordination.

The climate during this period was influenced by conflicting schools of thought and it was important to identify and examine their main arguments so as to draw on them fully in the process of economic and monetary construction in Europe. For instance, between 1970 and 1977, a number of study groups were set up comprising numerous academics and experts in all fields who submitted in-depth studies on the different aspects of the wide panorama afforded by the prospect of economic and monetary organization in Europe.

It is interesting to recall here that the theoretical debates conducted during this period were a powerful factor in highlighting the conditions on which a return to greater monetary stability depended and the forms it might take.

There was, for instance, a resurgence of interest during the 1960s in the links between money and the economy. In 1969, the Commission Communication to the Council (Barre Plan), which paved the way for the initial attempt at organizing policy coordination outside the framework of the Treaty, endorsed for the first time the idea that growth in the money supply at the European level must be controlled in such a way as not to exceed the expected or desired growth in nominal output (real growth plus price increases). These arguments were to surface again and be looked at more closely in the reports prepared by the 'Optimum currency area (Optica)' experts.

In addition, the idea gained ground that expansionary monetary policies essentially had a nominal effect and that the real long-term effects of exchange rate adjustments were virtually insignificant.

Further, the monetary theory of the balance of payments and the theory of purchasing power parity brought to light the links between exchange rate stability and consistency of monetary expansion in countries applying stable exchange rates as between one another. The need for coordination of domestic monetary policies is one of the matters examined in the report by the Study Group 'Economic and Monetary Union in 1980' (March 1975), chaired by Mr Marjolin, and in the two 'Optica' reports dated 1976 and 1977. [...]

For policy makers in Europe, the ineffectiveness and drawbacks of floating exchange rates when applied in a highly integrated area like the Community (where, after 1976, the snake comprised only five currencies and where three major currencies were floating independently) became increasingly evident, and the establishment of the EMS was the direct consequence of this realization. This was because currency floating had not fully come up to expectations where the adjustment process was concerned. More particularly the destabilizing nature of speculation was there for all to see as it accentuated exchange rate instability and very often entailed exchange rate adjustments over and beyond what would have been justified by underlying economic conditions. This produced a climate of uncertainty and distortions in competition that were damaging to trade and investment and made it more difficult to implement domestic economic policies, thereby bringing about a slowdown in growth. For, in the deficit countries, a falling exchange rate, often exaggerated by speculation, tended, via higher import prices and the adjustment of nominal wages and salaries, to exacerbate domestic inflation, and this in turn proved harmful to investment and growth in the medium and long term. This vicious circle had an all the more extensive and rapid impact in countries which pursued a more outward looking trade policy and where nominal incomes were more effectively safeguarded by indexation arrangements. The effects of a falling exchange rate on the competitiveness of products traded internationally were, therefore, short-lived. [...]

By contrast, the surplus countries, in which a 'virtuous circle' was at work in the opposite direction, saw their exports and growth curbed by the over-valuation of their currencies, caused among other things, by speculation, and thus were no longer in a position to impart the economic stimulus expected of them.

Last but not least, the process of genuine integration in Europe was jeopardized by monetary instability, as shown by the disruption caused to the common agricultural policy and, at a more general level, to intra-Community trade as a whole.

And so the idea began to gain ground that a return to greater monetary stability was an essential condition for a recovery in growth, especially in the Community, where the share of activity and investment dependent on intra-Community trade is extremely high, and where the degree to which the economies concerned are interdependent limits the effectiveness of economic policies formulated and implemented in a purely national framework and also the effectiveness of exchange rate adjustments. [...]

Such was the backcloth to the opening of the negotiations which were to result in the establishment of the EMS.

II THE APPROACH ADOPTED

1. Establishment of the EMS in two phases

The operating procedures of the system are to be implemented in two separate phases: the first phase began with the formal introduction of the system and the second phase is to start two years later. The intention is that, during the second phase:

(i)   the provisions and procedures of the transitional phase of the EMS will be consolidated into a final system;
(ii) 'the existing arrangements and institutions will be merged into a European Monetary Fund' (EMF), which will replace the EMCF;
(iii) a monetary system will be set up entailing not only the creation of such a fund but also 'the full utilization of the ECU as a reserve asset and a means of settlement'.

The decision to set up a transitional system (with certain aspects, relating in particular to the divergence indicator being revised after six months) was prompted by the need for rapid action in the monetary field dictated by political as well as economic considerations. At the economic level, the reduction in national inflation rates and in the divergences between net balance of payments positions indicated that conditions were favourable to an attempt at monetary stabilization, with there being a good chance that it would succeed. Moreover, there was a danger that the uncertainties stemming from the performance of the dollar might create disparities and strains between the Member States of the Community and this called for preventive measures.

The urgency of the matter meant the postponement of fundamental innovations, notably at the institutional level (e.g. the EMF), which have to be discussed in depth and also require parliamentary ratification in most countries. It was decided therefore to make provision for a two year period during which the experience acquired prior to establishment of the final EMS could be put to good account.

2. The course of the negotiations and the originality of the EMS

The EMS is, in essence, the result of a compromise on the issue of symmetry between the burdens and obligations incumbent on the participant countries. This compromise determined the choices made regarding the volume and duration of credits, the transfers of resources to the less prosperous countries and, above all, the exchange rate mechanism; should the Community confine itself to constructing a new snake or was it necessary to devise some other mechanism based on compliance with margins of fluctuation against the ECU, i.e. a basket of Community currencies?

The non-snake countries were opposed from the outset to a straightforward extension of the system based on a parity grid and compliance with bilateral margins of fluctuation. Their argument ran as follows; in such a system, responsibility for maintaining the margins and safeguarding the cohesion of the system lies, to a very large extent, with the countries that tend to find themselves near the bottom of the snake, regardless of the reason which forced two currencies to their opposing limits of intervention. In spite of the fact that, in a snake-type system, two currencies must reach their upper and lower limits of intervention before the two relevant central banks intervene simultaneously, the bank issuing the weakest currency is required, upon expiry of the period for which the credits were granted, to buy back whatever amounts of its currency the other bank purchased and to repay out of its own reserves whatever amounts of the strong currency it borrowed and then sold. This requirement is applicable even in the event of external strains (e.g. a temporary weakness of the dollar affecting the snake currencies in different ways), where the strong-currency EEC countries offer particularly attractive havens for capital flows, although countries with less attractive currencies cannot necessarily be accused of committing any mistake as regards economic policy. Because of the constraint imposed by the running down of reserves, the burden of adjustment thus falls to a very considerable degree and in an asymmetrical manner on the weaker-currency countries: to this extent, a snake-type system is imbued with a deflationary bias. A number of countries belonging to the snake counter these arguments with the assertion that intervention by the central banks of strong-currency countries also imposed constraints, namely a more rapid rate of monetary expansion and an upward movement of prices in those countries, and that the functioning of a snake-type system was thus broadly symmetrical and at the same time served to prevent an accentuation of inflationary tendencies in the Community. [...]

The major innovations in the EMS took shape as these problems were tackled and as the negotiations progressed. Moreover, the EMS, particularly where its initial phase is concerned, incorporates some of the positive aspects of the Community's achievement in the monetary field.

These innovations, which made the system quite different from the snake and account for its originality, are as follows:

(i)   introduction of the ECU in the Community exchange rate scheme, and its role in fixing central rates, thereby making it possible, among other things, to identify the currency which is tending to diverge from the others (principle of the divergence indicator);

(ii) the divergence indicator, which is designed to prevent strains appearing in the system by providing, for the first time, an objective basis on which to trigger consultations and by introducing, before the bilateral limits are reached, a 'presumption to act', i.e. to make adjustments, on the part of the different countries;

(iii) a substantial increase in the volume, and/or an extension of the duration of credits;

(iv) the possibility of wider margins (6 per cent) for the countries whose currencies were floating when the system was introduced. [...]

The EMS is thus the result of an approach linked to specific objectives and based on the need for parallelism between two interdependent factors, namely progress on the exchange rate front and progress with regard to economic convergence. The system is designed to be a balanced system and reflects the search for a suitable mix between rigidity (observance of margins) and flexibility (wider margins, changes in central rates); a symmetrical allocation of the adjustment burden acceptable to all the parties concerned and a measure of complementarity between domestic measures and external financing (in the form of credits and transfers). Lastly, the system is not an end in itself, but paves the way for further progress towards EMU.

III THE MAIN ELEMENTS OF THE EMS

General aspects [...]

The new system incorporates some of the operational and institutional features of the 'snake'. In addition, there are various new features, which are listed in Chapter II prominent among which is the ECU, which has been assigned a much more important role than the now defunct European Monetary Unit of Account (EMUA).

The ECU is a composite monetary unit consisting of a basket of the following amounts of each Community currency:

BFR	3.66	HFL	0.286	FF	1.15		
LFR	0.14	UKL	0.0885	DKR	0.217		
DM	0.828	LIT	109	IRL	0.00759		

The rate of the ECU in terms of any EEC currency is equal to the sum of the equivalents in that currency of the amounts of each of the EEC currencies making up the ECU. [...] In its present composition, the ECU is identical to the European unit of account (EUA), which has been used by the EEC in various fields since April 1975.

Unlike the EUA, there is provision for a revision procedure, the composition of the ECU being 're-examined and if necessary revised within six months of the entry into force of the system and thereafter every five years or, on request, if the weight of any currency has changed by 25 per cent'. Such revisions have to be mutually accepted; they will, by themselves, not modify the external value of the ECU. They will be made in line with underlying economic criteria.

The ECU thus defined performs four major functions:

(i)   that of *numéraire* for fixing central rates;
(ii)   that of reference unit for the operation of the divergence indicator;
(iii) that of denominator for operations in the intervention and credit mechanisms;
(iv)   that of a means of settlement between the monetary authorities of the EEC. [...]

1. The exchange rate and intervention mechanism

This mechanism is in two parts:

(i)   the first being based on the maintenance, by way of unlimited compulsory intervention on the exchanges, of bilateral limits of fluctuation between participating currencies;
(ii)   the second being based on the divergence indicator, the purpose of which is to establish a presumption to take action on the part of the authorities responsible for the currency whose rate exceeds certain limits which are fixed in terms of the ECU and which, generally speaking, since they are narrower than those demarcating the bilateral margins of fluctuation, will be reached before the latter:

(a) Central rates, bilateral limits and intervention obligations

All EEC currencies have an ECU-related central rate, with the exception of the pound sterling, which is not for the time being participating in the exchange rate mechanism. However, for the purposes of the operation of the divergence indicator (see (b) below), a notional central rate has been assigned to the pound sterling. The central rates are expressed as a certain quantity of currency per ECU, in accordance with the declarations made by the participating countries upon the entry into force of the system. [...]

Two currencies are in opposition to each other when one of them is at its intervention limit on the former's foreign exchange market and when the latter is thus at its reciprocal limit on the other's foreign exchange market. In such a situation, the issuing banks of the two 'opposing' currencies are required to intervene on their own markets to ensure that the currencies are kept within their respective margins. In other words, the issuing bank of the strong currency purchases the weak currency on its foreign exchange market while the issuing bank of the weak currency sells the strong currency (if need be, by first borrowing it from the issuing country). [...]

(b) The divergence indicator and the presumption of action

The divergence indicator makes it possible to trace the movement in the exchange rate of each EMS currency against the average movement and thereby to identify any currency deviating from that average.

This involves calculating for each currency the relationship between the appreciation or depreciation in the market rate of the ECU against the ECU-related central rate for this currency and the maximum percentage appreciation or depreciation which the rate of the ECU expressed in this currency may show against its ECU-related central rate. In a system where all the currencies maintain margins of plus or minus 2.25 per cent against one another, this maximum deviation is reached, in the case of a given currency, when the latter is standing at its bilateral limit of plus or minus 2.25 per cent against all the other currencies.

When the appreciation (premium) or depreciation (discount) in the market rate of the ECU in terms of a given currency reaches 75 per cent of this maximum spread, that currency is said to have reached its divergence threshold. [...]

If an EMS currency – say currency A – appreciates or depreciates by 2.25 per cent – the maximum amount permissible – against all other EEC currencies, the rate of the ECU in terms of currency A will tend to reflect this movement, but only in part. The variation in the rate of the ECU in terms of currency A will be less than 2.25 per cent because in that rate of the ECU the share accounted for by currency A represents a value which, by definition, does not vary, i.e. is equal to the number of units of currency A in the ECU. The ratio of this component to the rate of the ECU gives the weighting of currency A in the ECU basket. The larger the weighting of a currency in the ECU, the less the rate of the ECU in terms of that currency will be influenced by variations in the exchange rates of the other currencies making up the ECU.

This being so, the maximum possible divergence in the rate of the ECU will, for each EMS currency, be a function of its weighting in the ECU. It is this 'individualization' of spreads that gives each EEC currency an equal chance of reaching its divergence threshold.

As a general rule, the divergence threshold will be reached before the currency in question reaches its bilateral limit against another currency. As soon as the threshold is crossed, the currency in question will be in a position that may cause strains within the system. To prevent this, there is a presumption that the issuing country of the 'diverging currency' will act to remedy this situation. [...]

The divergence indicator mechanism thus adds important new features as compared with the system previously in force:

(a) it provides, for the first time, an objective basis for triggering consultations between competent authorities;

(b) by identifying the currency showing the greatest divergence from the average, it helps to pinpoint responsibilities more clearly and thus makes for a fairer allocation of the burden of adjustment.

This mechanism will be reviewed in the light of experience after six months.

2. The accounting and settlement mechanism

Purchases of Community currencies by a central bank represent for that bank an accumulation of claims on the EMCF. Conversely, sales of Community currencies by a central bank on its foreign exchange market represent an accumulation of debts with the EMCF. These debts and claims are recorded by the EMCF in the form of debits or credits in accounts denominated in ECU. The conversion of Community currencies into ECU are made at the rate obtaining on the day of intervention.

This accumulation of debts and claims represents very short-term financing facilities granted between the central banks. [...]

When a financing operation falls due and after all the debts and claims of a single central bank have been automatically offset, settlement by debtor central banks is made:

(i) in the first place, in assets denominated in the currency of the creditor central bank;

(ii) subsequently, in ECU, in whole or in part (created against the deposit of reserves, see below). However, the creditor central bank is not obliged to accept settlement in ECU of an amount of more than 50 per cent of its claim;

(iii) for any balance outstanding, as a rule, in accordance with the composition of the debtor central bank's reserves excluding gold.

The ECU here performs two important functions:

(i) that of the denominator for expressing debts and claims –
This means that both the creditor and the debtor central bank run something of an exchange risk in the event of an adjustment – something for which they are no longer solely responsible – in the rate of the ECU in terms of their currencies. This is because, if one central rate is adjusted, all the others follow suit; the rate of the ECU is also influenced by movements in the rate of the pound sterling, which is not, for the time being, taking part in the exchange rate mechanism. Previously, each country was responsible for its own actions as regards the conversion rate of its currency into EMUA. By denominating debt and claims in ECU, the system has introduced the concept of Community burden-sharing in respect of the exchange rate risk;

(ii) that of an instrument of settlement between Community central banks –

In the EMS, ECU are created by the EMCF against contributions of dollars and of gold by the participating central banks, thereby permitting activation of reserves hitherto difficult to mobilize. These contributions – which take the form of three-months revolving swaps renewable throughout the transitional period – represent 20 per cent of the central banks' gold holding and 20 per cent of their gross dollar reserves. In return, the central banks have been credited by the EMCF with an aggregate amount of 23 000 million ECU. [...]

4. Measures designed to strengthen the economies of the less prosperous Member States of the EMS

The durability of the EMS is linked to the convergence of Member States' economic performances; in the Resolution on the establishment of the EMS, the European Council stated that measures taken at Community level could and should serve a supporting role with regard to the less prosperous Member States' efforts to strengthen their economic potential and to facilitate convergence.

Measures will be taken to assist these Member States provided they participate fully and effectively in the exchange rate and intervention mechanism. Such measures will include the granting of 3 per cent interest rate subsidies for loans made available to the less prosperous countries by the Community institutions, which will be required to use the new financial facility and by the European Investment Bank. These loans may amount to 1 000 million EUA per year for a period of five years; the interest rate subsidies granted will amount to 200 million EUA per year for five years.

Member States which do not participate fully and effectively in the mechanisms of the EMS do not contribute to the financing of the system.

The funds provided are to be concentrated on the financing of selected infrastructure projects and programmes, on the understanding that any direct or indirect distortion of the competitive position of specific industries will have to be avoided.

5. The agri-monetary implications of the EMS

The purpose of the EMS is to create a zone of monetary stability within the Community and, in so far as this objective is achieved, it will have repercussions that should make for a simplification of the mechanisms applied under the common agricultural policy (CAP) precisely with a view to countering the effects of exchange rate instability. It will thus be possible, at some stage, to do away with 'monetary compensatory amounts', i.e. the intra-Community levies and subsidies designed to offset the impact of currency appreciation or depreciation on the price system. [...]

IV CONCLUSION AND PROSPECTS

1. The conditions determining the success of the system

The EMS can make a major contribution to a return to lasting growth in the Community especially if accompanied by progress in other fields (free movement of goods, services and factors of production; industrial, social and regional policies). It will safeguard and even give a fillip to the process of European integration and, in the more immediate future, will make for an expansion in investment, which is at present being held back by external and internal uncertainties on the monetary front. It will also increase and impart a more expansionary bias to the room for manoeuvre available to economic policy-makers since, for them, exchange rate fluctuations at present impose a constraint in that they either aggravate inflation via currency depreciation and accentuate the impact of 'vicious circles' or give rise to deflationary tendencies in countries with overvalued currencies.

It is important, therefore, that the EMS should succeed or, in other words, should be durable. The first problem here is how to define 'success'. Success must not be confused with an absence of changes in central rates. The snake survived ten parity adjustments (involving one or more currencies) between 1972 and 1978 and yet it was deemed to be a success by the participant countries until its replacement by the EMS. None the less, a system in which the central rates were adjusted by substantial amounts and at frequent intervals, in which the margins grew wider instead of narrower and in which instances of noncompliance with such limits proliferated for exceptional, albeit temporary reasons would be stable in name only and such a system might present more drawbacks – linked to speculation – than advantages. By contrast, if exchange rate adjustments became smaller and less frequent over time, the system could be regarded as a success. [...]

If the system is to be durable, it is important that it should be neither inflationary nor deflationary.

An inflationary bias would be imparted if the burden of adjustment was unduly weighted in favour of countries having to cope with rapid inflation. Such countries could delay implementing the policies that were essential, while stable-currency countries would have to intervene on foreign exchange markets to keep their currencies within the margins of 2.25 per cent, with all the attendant consequences for their domestic inflation. This would then tend to push up the average rate of inflation in the Community.

By contrast, a deflationary bias would be imparted if countries in which monetary depreciation tended to be most marked made the necessary adjustments in overhasty fashion.

If it was to be avoided, the first danger would seem to call for a vigilant attitude on the part of the countries in which inflation is currently running at a low level, with conditions being attached to the granting of credit. The second danger would probably be less difficult to avert in that exchange rate stability will tend to have expansionary effects while the possibility of adjusting central rates will enable the authorities to dispense with unduly harsh adjustment policies. The EMS will need to back up and cushion the impact of some countries' attempts to combat inflation.

Such attempts will, in any case, have to be made and are bound to have a positive impact on growth in the medium term. Nevertheless, the system's economic implications for each of the participating countries and for the Community as a whole will largely depend on how the system will function in practice. In this connection, the different countries' degree of commitment to the system and hence its chances of success will be dependent on the achievement of a satisfactory and balanced division of responsibilities and obligations. [. . .]

_____ 31 _____

CONFERENCE ON SECURITY AND COOPERATION IN EUROPE (HELSINKI CONFERENCE)

The Conference on Security and Cooperation in Europe (CSCE) held meetings in Helsinki and Geneva in the summer of 1975. The *Final Act* (or Treaty) involved four main sections or 'baskets'. 'Basket Two', which is given here, covers a wide range of agreements on cooperation in commercial exchanges, industrial cooperation, harmonization of standards, science, technology and the environment.

The full text or *Final Act* of the Treaty appears in section 12 of *Treaties and Alliances of the World* (ed. H. W. Degenhardt) for Keesing's References (Longman, 3rd edn., 1981), pp. 221–33.

BASKET TWO

COOPERATION IN THE FIELD OF ECONOMICS, OF SCIENCE AND TECHNOLOGY AND OF THE ENVIRONMENT

The participating states . . . have adopted the following:

1. Commercial Exchanges

General Provisions.

The participating states . . . are resolved to promote, on the basis of the modalities of their economic cooperation, the expansion of their mutual trade in goods and services, and to ensure conditions favourable to such development; recognize the beneficial effects which can result for the development of trade from the application of most-favoured-nation treatment; will encourage the expansion of trade on as broad a multilateral basis as possible, thereby endeavouring to utilize the various economic and commercial possibilities; recognize the importance of bilateral and multilateral intergovernmental and other agreements for the long-term development of trade; note the importance of monetary and financial questions for the development of international trade, and will endeavour to deal with them with a view to contributing to the continuous expansion of trade; will endeavour to reduce or progressively eliminate all kinds of obstacles to the development of trade; will foster a steady growth of trade while avoiding as far as possible abrupt fluctuations in their trade; [...]

Business Contacts and Facilities.

The participating states ... will take measures further to improve conditions for the expansion of contacts between representatives of official bodies, of the different organizations, enterprises, firms and banks concerned with foreign trade, in particular, where useful, between sellers and users of products and services, for the purpose of studying commercial possibilities, concluding contracts, ensuring their implementation and providing after-sales service; will encourage organizations, enterprises and firms concerned with foreign trade to take measures to accelerate the conduct of business negotiations; will further take measures aimed at improving working conditions of representatives of foreign organizations, enterprises, firms and banks concerned with external trade, particularly as follows:

By providing the necessary information, including information on legislation and procedures relating to the establishment and operation of permanent representation by the above-mentioned bodies; by examining as favourably as possible requests for the establishment of permanent representation and of offices for this purpose, including, where appropriate, the opening of joint offices by two or more firms; by encouraging the provision, on conditions as favourable as possible and equal for all representatives of the above-mentioned bodies, of hotel accommodation, means of communication, and of other facilities normally required by them, as well as of suitable business and residential premises for purposes of permanent representation;

Recognize the importance of such measures to encourage greater participation by small and medium-sized firms in trade between participating states.

Economic and Commercial Information.

The participating states ... will promote the publication and dissemination of economic and commercial information at regular intervals and as possible, in particular: Statistics concerning production, national income, budget, consumption and productivity; foreign trade statistics drawn up on the basis of comparable classification, including breakdown by product with indication of volume and value, as well as country of origin or destination; laws and regulations concerning foreign trade; information allowing forecasts of development of the economy to assist in trade promotion, for example, information on the general orientation of national economic plans and programmes; other information to help businessmen in commercial contacts, for example, periodic directories, lists, and where possible, organizational charts of firms and organizations concerned with foreign trade;

Will in addition to the above encourage the development of the exchange of economic and commercial information through, where appropriate, joint commissions for economic, scientific and technical cooperation, national and joint chambers of commerce, and other suitable bodies; will support a study, in the framework of the UN Economic Commission for Europe [ECE], of the possibilities of creating a multilateral system of notification of laws and regulations concerning foreign trade and changes therein; will encourage international work on the harmonization of statistical nomenclatures, notably in the ECE. [...]

2. Industrial Cooperation and Projects of Common Interest
Industrial Cooperation.

The participating states ... propose to encourage the development of industrial cooperation between the competent organizations, enterprises and firms of their countries; consider that industrial cooperation may be facilitated by means of intergovernmental and other bilateral and multilateral agreements between the interested parties; note that in promoting industrial cooperation they should bear in mind the economic structures and the development levels of their countries; note that industrial cooperation is implemented by means of contracts concluded between competent organizations, enterprises and firms on the basis of economic considerations; express their willingness to promote measures designed to create favourable conditions for industrial cooperation; recognize that industrial co-operation covers a number of forms of economic relations going beyond the framework of conventional trade, and that in concluding contracts on industrial cooperation the partners will determine jointly the appropriate forms and conditions of cooperation, taking into account their mutual interests and capabilities;

Recognize further that, if it is in their mutual interest, concrete forms such as the following may be useful for the development of industrial cooperation: joint production and sale, specialization in production and sale, construction, adaptation and modernization of industrial plants, cooperation for the setting up of complete industrial installations with a view to thus obtaining part of the resultant products, mixed companies, exchanges of 'know-how', of technical information, of patents and of licences, and joint industrial research within the framework of specific cooperation projects;

Recognize that new forms of industrial cooperation can be applied with a view to meeting specific needs; consider it desirable to improve the quality and the quantity of information relevant to industrial cooperation, in particular the laws and regulations, including those relating to foreign exchange, general orientation of national economic plans and programmes as well as programme priorities and economic conditions of the market; and to disseminate as quickly as possible published documentation thereon;

Will encourage all forms of exchange of information and communication of experience relevant to industrial cooperation, including through contacts between potential partners and, where appropriate, through joint commissions for economic, industrial, scientific and technical cooperation, national and joint chambers of commerce, and other suitable bodies; consider it desirable, with a view to expanding industrial cooperation, to encourage the exploration of cooperation possibilities and the implementation of cooperation projects and will take measures to this end, inter alia, by facilitating and increasing all forms of business contacts between competent organizations, enterprises and firms and between their respective qualified personnel; note that the provisions adopted by the conference relating to business contacts in the economic and commercial fields also apply to foreign organizations, enterprises and firms engaged in industrial cooperation, taking into account specific conditions of this cooperation, and will endeavour to ensure, in particular, the existence of appropriate working conditions for personnel engaged in the implementation of cooperation projects; [...]

Recommended further the continued examination – for example within the framework of the ECE – of means of improving the provision of information to those concerned on general conditions of industrial cooperation and guidance on the preparation of contracts in this field; consider it desirable to further improve conditions for the implementation of industrial cooperation projects, in particular with respect to: the protection of the interests of the partners in industrial cooperation projects, including the legal protection of the various kinds of property involved; the consideration, in ways that are compatible with their economic systems, of the needs and possibilities of industrial cooperation within the framework of economic policy and particularly in national economic plans and programmes;

Consider it desirable that the partners, when concluding industrial cooperation contracts, should devote due attention to provisions concerning the extension of the necessary mutual assistance and the provision of the necessary information during the implementation of these contracts, in particular with a view to attaining the required technical level and quality of the products resulting from such cooperation; recognize the usefulness of an increased participation of small and medium-sized firms in industrial cooperation projects.

Projects of Common Interest.

The participating states ... regard it as necessary to encourage, where appropriate, the investigation of competent and interested organizations, enterprises and firms of the possibilities for the carrying out of projects of common interest in the fields of energy resources and of the exploitation of raw materials, as well as of transport and communications; regard it as desirable that organizations, enterprises and firms exploring the possibilities of taking part in projects of common interest exchange with their potential partners, through the appropriate channels, the requisite economic, financial and technical information pertaining to these projects;

Consider that the fields of energy resources, in particular, petroleum, natural gas and coal, and the extraction and processing of mineral raw materials, in particular, iron ore and bauxite, are suitable ones for strengthening long-term economic cooperation and for the development of trade which could result; consider that possibilities for projects of common interest with a view to long-term economic cooperation also exist in the following fields: Exchanges of electrical energy within Europe with a view to utilizing the capacity of the electrical power stations as rationally as possible; cooperation in research for new sources of energy and, in particular, in the field of nuclear energy; development of road networks and cooperation aimed at establishing a coherent navigable network in Europe; cooperation in research and the perfecting of equipment for multimodal transport operations and for the handling of containers;

Recommend that the states interested in projects of common interest should consider under what conditions it would be possible to establish them, and if they so desire, create the necessary conditions for their actual implementation.

3. Provisions concerning Trade and Industrial Cooperation
Harmonization of Standards.

The participating states ... reaffirm their interest to achieve the widest possible international harmonization of standards and technical regulations; express their readiness to promote international agreements and other appropriate arrangements on acceptance of certificates of conformity with international cooperation on standardization, in particular by supporting the activities of intergovernmental and other appropriate organizations in this field. [...]

4. Science and Technology
Possibilities for Improving Cooperation.

[The participating states] recognize that possibilities exist for further improving scientific and technological cooperation and, to this end, express their intention to remove obstacles to such cooperation, in particular through: the improvement of opportunities for the exchange and dissemination of scientific and technological information among the parties interested in scientific and technological research and cooperation, including information related to the organization and implementation of such cooperation; the expeditious implementation and improvement in organization, including programmes, of international visits of scientists and specialists in connection with exchanges, conferences and cooperation; the wider use of commercial channels and activities for applied scientific and technological research and for the transfer of achievements obtained in this field while providing information on and protection of intellectual and industrial property rights.

Fields of Cooperation.

[The participating states] consider that possibilities to expand cooperation exist within the areas given below as examples, noting that it is for potential partners in the participating countries to identify and develop projects and arrangements of mutual interest and benefit:

Agriculture
Energy
New Technologies, Rational Use of Resources
Transport Technology
Physics
Chemistry
Meteorology and Hydrology
Oceanography
Seismological Research
Research on Glaciology, Permafrost and Problems of Life under Conditions of Cold
Computer, Communications and Information Technologies
Space Research
Medicine and Public Health
Environmental Research.

Forms and Methods of Cooperation.

The document enumerated a wide range of forms and methods by which scientific and technological cooperation should be promoted, including the exchange of publications, exchange of visits, international conferences and seminars, joint programmes, use of commercial channels and more effective use of existing international organizations.

5. Environment

Aims of Cooperation.

[The participating states] agree to the following aims of cooperation, in particular:

To study, with a view to their solution, those environmental problems which, by their nature, are of a multilateral, bilateral, regional or sub-regional dimension; as well as to encourage the development of an interdisciplinary approach to environmental problems; to increase the effectiveness of national and international measures for the protection of the environment by the comparison and, if appropriate, the harmonization of methods of gathering and analysing facts, by improving the knowledge of pollution phenomena and rational utilization of natural resources, by the exchange of information, by the harmonization of definitions and the adoption, as far as possible, of a common terminology in the field of the environment; to take the necessary measures to bring environmental policies closer together and, where appropriate and possible, to harmonize them; to encourage, where possible and appropriate, national and international efforts by their interested organizations, enterprises and forms in the development, production and improvement of equipment designed for monitoring, protecting and enhancing the environment. [...]

6. Cooperation in Other Areas

Development of Transport.

The document outlined various ways in which the participating states would seek to develop cooperation in the field of transport, including the simplification of frontier formalities, the harmonization of safety provisions, the elimination of disparities arising from the legal provisions applied to traffic on inland waterways subject to international conventions and the improvement of international rail transport.

Promotion of Tourism.

The participating states expressed their intention 'to encourage increased tourism on both an individual and group basis', the document specifying a number of ways to achieve this end.

Economic and Social Aspects of Migrant Labour.

The participating states ... are of the opinion that the problems arising bilaterally from the migration of workers in Europe as well as between the participating states should be dealt with by the parties directly concerned in order to resolve these problems in their mutual interest, in the light of the concern of each state involved to take due account of the requirements resulting from its socio-economic situation, having regard to the obligation of each state to comply with the bilateral and multilateral agreements to which it is party, and with the following aims in view:

To encourage the efforts of the countries of origin directed towards increasing the possibilities of employment for the nationals in their own territories, in particular by developing economic cooperation appropriate for this purpose and suitable for the host countries and the countries of origin concerned; to ensure through collaboration between the host country and the country of origin the conditions under which the orderly movement of workers might take place, while at the same time protecting their personal and social welfare and, if appropriate, to organize the recruitment of migrant workers and the provision of elementary language and vocational training; to ensure equality of rights between migrant workers and nationals of the host countries with regard to conditions of employment and work and to social security, and to endeavour to ensure that migrant workers may enjoy satisfactory living conditions, especially housing conditions;

To endeavour to ensure, as far as possible, that migrant workers may enjoy the same opportunities as nationals of the host countries of finding other suitable employment in the event of unemployment; to regard with favour the provision of vocational training to migrant workers [...]

CHAPTER V

A WORLD POWER

1984–1996

Most Europeans have always been prepared to see the Community become an economic power, competing with the industrial giants (Japan and the USA) and with other regional groups of states. They have long been eager for Europe to secure its place as one of the world's three or four major trading blocs and they believe that Europe should, whenever possible, address the world with one voice. But many Europeans have not wanted the Community's internal powers to be as formidable as its external influence. They have opposed the further development of those mechanisms (notably the Commission and the European Parliament) which might soon challenge the authority of their own national political institutions. They have doubted the value (and the practicability) even of modest plans to harmonize European working conditions and they are hostile to most notions of 'fiscal federalism'. In fact, the 'Eurosceptics' contributed mightily to the 'Euro-sclerosis' of the 1970s and to the stasis of Europe as a semi-developed world power.

The transformation of the Community's fortunes in the mid-1980s put the Eurosceptics on their guard. It seemed to them that the advocates of European federalism were planning once again to push the Community in the direction of a closely integrated union whose executive powers would grow only at the expense of the parliaments and financial institutions of the member states. Always suspicious of the Commission, the Eurosceptics were disturbed by the election in January 1985 of Jacques Delors as the new Commission President. Formerly the finance minister in France, Delors was known to favour European monetary union, and so were three of the incoming commissioners (also once ministers of finance). In the event, the Commission adopted a less alarming set of priorities during 1985 and postponed questions of political integration in favour of the single market programme – an aspect of European cooperation which most nationalists and Eurosceptics could accept.

The federalists were fortunate with Delors. He was an extremely able organizer of people, resources and ideas in Brussels, and he was also a confident and very public champion of European integration. His nemesis in London was less successful in working with her colleagues and her knowledge of European economic conditions was imprecise. But Margaret Thatcher's energy in expressing the doubts of European nationalists made her a constant opponent of Euro-federalism and of course she was never bashful about sharing her criticisms of Brussels with the public. During her long tenure as British Prime Minister

(1979–90), Thatcher frequently attacked what she saw as the construction of a European superstate and she particularly enjoyed battling against the plans of the Delors' Commission in the mid- and late 1980s. In September 1988, she carried her attack to the Belgian city of Bruges, one of the chief commercial centres of the late Middle Ages and, in the 1980s, 'a citadel of Eurofederalism'.[1] In a famous speech at the College of Europe in Bruges, Thatcher warned against the Commission's design for a 'European conglomerate' (DOCUMENT 32).

The speech is interesting to us as a definition of the Community's role in the world. Thatcher did not require Europe to act as a single player in global commerce; her chief concern was that European nations be allowed to trade freely among themselves and to forge their own commercial ties with other countries in the world. Neither the interstate commerce of the Community nor the overseas trade of European countries should, in her view, be constrained by 'more and more detailed regulation'. Trade policy was a matter to be left where it had always been, with national governments and foreign trade companies. Thatcher looked at Europe's military defence in a similar way. She urged a greater degree of coordination, planning and more spending on defence, but she saw no reason for Europe to establish its own defence organization, based on the WEU or any other agency. Like all other British prime ministers since 1949, she was content with the transatlantic connections of NATO.

Central to Thatcher's opinions was her belief in the almost sacred qualities of the nation state. Europe was special because it was home to a great number of very different nations whose experience of two world wars brought them together in an association which was unique in the world. Their trust and cooperation, their security and their prosperity, did not depend on the submersion of their national institutions; their long histories and their variety of cultures meant that they were very different from the thirteen miniature republics which long ago became the United States of America. A United States of Europe was inconceivable to Margaret Thatcher and it remains inconceivable to the Eurosceptics. Their vision of Europe is not that of Monnet, Spaak and Spinelli but that of de Gaulle, Macmillan and the founders of EFTA almost forty years ago: a confederation of states for whom 'arcane institutional debates' are a waste of time. Eurosceptics gladly countenance an array of intergovernmental agreements on interstate trade, investment, banking and transport, and they can be quite optimistic about Europe's potential as the world's leading consumer of goods and services. But for them the peculiar functions of national parliaments and other sovereign institutions are timeless, natural, and basic to the relationships which exist among European states and should not disappear in an artificial federal union.

Thirteen months after Thatcher's speech, Jacques Delors also addressed the College of Europe in Bruges. On this occasion he reasserted the federalist goal of European Political Union (EPU) – the very concept which Thatcher had decried. The contrast between the two speeches was unmistakable not only because the arguments ran in opposite directions but because of European conditions generally. Thatcher's remarks fit comfortably into the familiar postwar context of issues and solutions, while Delors spoke at a time of dramatic change in east-central Europe. There was no telling what might follow the chaos of the communist regimes or what political emergency might overtake the whole of Europe. In this context, Delors' arguments for improving the decision-making processes in Brussels and for enhancing the powers of the Community to deal with new international conditions made sense and, notwithstanding the complaints of the Eurosceptics, the way seemed clear for more centralization of political authority.

The updating of the Community's structures was well under way before the political cataclysms of the late 1980s. Delors wisely decided to gain the confidence of the member states by scrutinizing the most basic structures of the Community before going on to tackle the really contentious issues of monetary policy and monetary union. At the Milan Summit of 1985, Delors won the support of Community leaders for the most extensive revision of the original treaties which had yet occurred.[2] The Single European Act (SEA) of 1986 was the result. A relatively short treaty, it was acceptable even to the nationalists and Eurosceptics (like Margaret Thatcher) who thought it tidied up old formulas and insured the advent of a truly common market (which the Treaty of Rome had promised for 1970). In some respects, therefore, the SEA was not a revolutionary document.[3]

But the SEA did much more than promote the market liberties of the Community (DOCUMENT 33). By touching on almost every aspect of the Community's existence, the SEA made the entire integrative process more dynamic. Politically it insisted on 'legislative cooperation' and enhanced the authority of the European Parliament; decision-making in the Council of Ministers became quicker and easier because ministers were now entitled to vote by qualified majority rather than unanimity. The subsection on the Environment was one of the strongest statements ever made on that subject by the Community. In foreign affairs the SEA demanded still more coordination of national policies, particularly relating to matters of European security. It required member states to defer to the processes of EPC and it warned them against indulging in any foreign policy which might undermine the unity of the Community's external relations. The SEA also looked to the 'convergence of economic and monetary policies' as a necessary ingredient of European unity – an ominous prediction as far as the nationalists were concerned. Equally significant were the new powers of review accorded to the Commission, which expected member states to identify all national laws and regulations which did not embrace Community standards by 1992.

There were, of course, problems in the SEA's ratification and implementation. Italy and Greece held out for a time, waiting for Denmark to submit the question to a national referendum. And in spite of the snappy clear language of the SEA, the revision of the Treaty of Rome did not prove a neat and easy business. Delors thought the Act fell well short of its goal; it is probably revealing that Thatcher (and the Eurosceptics) were on the whole more pleased with the SEA than Delors and the Eurofederalists were.[4] On the other hand, the SEA was another of those limited but essential triumphs of European integration. Certainly its consequences were far more immediate (and visible) than those generated by other treaties. During 1987 and 1988 a 'merger mania' occurred almost everywhere in the

Community as companies recognized the opportunities of joining larger networks of production and distribution. The 'single market' of SEA was not legally expected until 1992, but its practical meaning translated at once into Europe-wide economies of scale.[5]

The SEA had an immediate effect on that part of democratic Europe which still lay outside the EC. The EFTA countries (Norway, Sweden, Austria, Switzerland and Finland) did not care to see their companies and citizens at a disadvantage when dealing with the Community; they decided to accelerate the harmonization of production and commercial standards with those of the EC. They believed they could join the 'Europe without borders' while sidestepping the old political issues of sovereignty and neutrality. The outcome was the all-embracing European Economic Area (EEA), the de facto union of EFTA with the EC and the consolidation of the world's largest trading bloc.

It is not surprising that the SEA gave so much attention to issues of social policy. Delors regarded this as one of the three major areas for development (along with monetary union and the budget). There are many historic hints of the Community's intention to harmonize social policies. The ECSC supported research into safety regulations for coal and steel workers; the Treaty of Rome pressed for the free mobility of labour, equality of women in the workplace and the standardization of social security in member states. The European Social Fund (established by the Treaty of Rome) was designed to promote work retraining, and during the recession of the 1970s its mandate was extended to help special groups (e.g. unemployed under-25s).[6] But the Social Fund was always handicapped by insufficient resources and Europeans were increasingly critical of the Community as a guarantor of employment security, training and safe working conditions. By the mid-1980s it was no longer possible to ignore Willy Brandt's warning (made at The Hague Summit of 1969) that the social policies of the Community must keep pace with its economic development: the integration of Europe must mean a better life for Europeans.

The Community charter of the Fundamental Social Rights of Workers was adopted by the Community's heads of government in December 1989 (DOCUMENT 34). Its wording was influenced by years of declarations of the Council of Europe, by information from the International Labour Organization and by the recent enactment of a social charter in Belgium. A comprehensive statement of workers' rights seemed the logical corollary to the arrangements for a single market, the social dimension of economic activity. The brevity of the Charter did not detract from its scope: there are twelve categories of 'fundamental social rights' affecting millions of people in the Community. On its own, however, the Charter could not deal with the continuing high levels of unemployment in the 1980s, nor could it do much about the disaffection of untrained (and probably unemployable) legions of migrant workers. There were problems, too, in dealing with atypical forms of employment (e.g. temporary and part-time jobs) and no one was anxious to define 'equitable wage' and 'minimum wage' in a Community where wages were so varied. In the end, the implementation of the Charter would depend on both Brussels and the twelve national governments with the Commission assigned the task of devising an 'action programme' for social legislation at the Community level.

The Delors Commission wanted the Charter to fulfil Willy Brandt's hopes for a 'People's Europe' – a community whose citizens shared the benefits of economic progress. The social rights were described as 'fundamental' and accepted as such by eleven of the twelve national governments. The British government under Margaret Thatcher opposed them, just as it opposed almost every Community initiative in the field of social legislation. In 1986, for example, the British rejected an EC proposal to harmonize maternity rights in the Community.[7] When work on the Charter began and the Commission consulted with employers, trade unions and other national governments, Thatcher branded the whole idea of a Social Charter as 'Marxist' and claimed it pushed the Community towards 'Eurosocialism'. In her speech at Bruges, the British Prime Minister had the Charter in mind when she warned against centralization's tendency to discourage European business and make it more expensive.

The British government remained recalcitrant. In the 1990s it opposed Community/Union definitions of the minimum wage, social security, the protection of young workers, employment contracts and collective redundancies. Given the disdain of the British government for the Charter and for the Community's efforts in the realm of social legislation, it is not surprising that so many British citizens have brought appeals to the European Court of Justice in recent years. The decisions of the ECJ have gradually amplified the Charter which, like so many other milestones of European integration, is a rather general statement of principles. The Commission has also joined the process by occasionally adding more detailed guidelines in social policy (e.g. the definition of living standards in the 'Decency Threshold' of 1992). The SEA also gave a green light to social legislation and the 'health and safety of workers' (Article 118a) has promoted a good deal of legislative attention since 1988.[8]

The implementation of the SEA brought a new confidence to European integration in the late 1980s. Indeed, it is possible to speak of a brief period of 'Europhoria' generated not only by the favourable reception of the SEA but also by a significant expansion of the Community itself. The long delayed accession of Spain and Portugal in 1986 added almost fifty million citizens to the Community and contributed to the reality of a Single Market. On the other side of the Community, the demise of communist regimes in east-central Europe (late 1989 and 1990) presented a host of exciting opportunities and challenges. And in the very centre of Europe, the unification of Germany (October 1990) obliged the Community to refocus its attention on political union (EPU) as the best way of insuring European security. Just as it had been important for western Europeans in the 1950s to harness Germany's resources and ambitions by knitting the Federal Republic into the fabric of the ECSC, NATO and the EEC, so too was it essential for the Community in the 1990s to keep an enlarged and populous (80 millions) Germany firmly connected to a democratic integrated Europe.[9]

With the addition of Spain, Portugal and eastern Germany, and following the agreements for a European Economic Area, the Community's credentials as a world power were confirmed. Its internal structures, however, were far from complete, as political union and monetary union both remained on the Community's agenda. Intergovernmental conferences and 'summit meetings' addressed these two enormous issues during 1990 and 1991 and their first conclusion was that agreement would not come as easily as it had for the SEA. Some member states favoured a major step toward EPU but not EMU; Germany insisted on both and Britain wanted neither. Italy, the Netherlands and Belgium were ready for a federal political structure; Denmark, Britain and Greece raised a 'storm of protest' against any use of the word 'federal' in the draft treaty.[10] In the event, almost no progress was made toward EMU. Debate continued over the desirability of a 'two-speed system' (should it be 'explicit' or 'implicit'?). As for a single European currency, the principal (and not very daring) decision was that everything depended on the economic conditions and political will of individual member states.

Eventually a rough consensus on most of the Union Treaty's 'chapters' emerged. Long and fierce bargaining led to an agreement on the 'deepening' of the internal structures of the Community. But even during the final negotiations in Maastricht in December 1991 the whole process came close to collapse: the British rejected proposals to give the Community a stronger role in social policy. As hosts of the conference, the Dutch solved this problem simply by deleting the chapter on social policy from the Treaty. Otherwise, many opponents of the Treaty were relieved by its schedules: these obviously permitted some latitude for revision and review (e.g. the inauguration of the common currency during 1998 and 1999). But in spite of distant deadlines, the Treaty on European Union (TEU) immediately acquired a legal status superseding that of the Treaty of Rome. In fact, it promised to guide European integration well beyond all previous treaties and conventions.[11] The scope of the Treaty is certainly apparent in its 'Common Provisions' and in the sections on Citizenship, Environment and Foreign Policy (DOCUMENT 35).

The Community did not adopt the environment as a major concern of policy-making until the 1980s. Environmental Action Programmes (EAPs) turned only gradually from remedial to preventive measures and tried during the 1980s to link the care of the natural environment with the creation of new forms of employment. The SEA gave environmental policy a much higher priority and urged member states to make strict environmental standards part of their adjustment to the single market. The Community (and national governments) used the 'European Year of the Environment' (1987) to bring various environmental issues before the public and into other areas of legislation (agriculture, transport, energy, industry). Aware of the serious environmental problems in east-central Europe, the TEU regarded environmental degradation as a concern of all Europeans and provided poorer countries help from the Cohesion Fund in tackling expensive environmental projects. Overseas, the European Union's assistance programmes have increasingly insisted on the protection of ecosystems and wildlife, with the environmental language of the TEU carrying into treaties with Third World countries.

Foreign and security policy did not present huge problems to the negotiators of the draft treaty. Events in east-central Europe and in the Gulf reminded them of the desirability of a common foreign policy. On the very doorstep of the Union, the breakup of Yugoslavia was an unwelcome advertisement for Europe's foreign policy confusion and a strong inducement to coordinate policies, particularly when they related to European issues. The fact that the TEU had to repeat the demands of earlier agreements (including those of the SEA) for a 'spirit of loyalty' and 'consultation' indicates that member states were still attempting 'diplomatic initiatives' of their own and that they were often tempted (presumably for reasons of national prestige) to bypass or pre-empt policies decided by the Union. The TEU entrusts the Council with considerable authority as the guardian of a common foreign policy but it remains to be seen whether all fifteen member states will always accept the Union's policy guidelines.

The Maastricht Treaty broke new ground in defining citizenship of the Union (Part 2). The text itself was not particularly controversial because so much of it did little more than elaborate on the Treaty of Rome concerning the mobility and employment opportunities of citizens in the member states. At the same time, the TEU added to the importance of the European Parliament as the forum of all Union citizens. Moreover, all member states were henceforth to share the responsibility of assisting Union citizens beyond the borders of the Union; the availability of EU passports strengthened the common identity of Union citizens among themselves and in the eyes of the rest of the world.

As the world's largest trading bloc, the European Union has developed an intricate web of external economic relationships. The most complex of these relations are those which link the Union to former colonies in the Third World. When the Treaty of Rome was signed in 1957, France and Belgium were still colonial powers and governed most of western and central Africa. At the same time, however, the political fragility of the Fourth Republic weakened the authority of France in Europe. To overcome this handicap, the French reminded their prospective partners in the EEC of the influence which France still enjoyed outside Europe. By 'associating' the colonial territories and emerging nations of French Africa with the EEC, France hoped to gain recognition as the indispensable member of the new Europe. In spite of opposition from Germany and the Netherlands, France succeeded in securing for many African states a special relationship with the EEC. While the seventeen states of AASM (the Association of African States and Madagascar) welcomed their economic affiliation with the Six, the partnership was bound to be uncomfortable.

The most basic problem concerned the economies of AASM. These countries were agricultural and likely to remain so; even after fifteen years of trading with the EC, more than 80 per cent of their exports to the Community were agricultural or semi-agricultural products. At the same time, the Community was determined to guarantee its own farmers a sufficient income by implementing a Common Agricultural Policy. How generous could the Community be toward AASM, once the CAP was in operation? The question became more pressing when statistics revealed (in the early 1960s) that the EC's trade with the 'associated states' was actually declining in comparison with the Community's trade with other states.[12]

Another problem developed with the growth in the number of associated states. During the 1970s, British ex-colonies, now independent members of the Commonwealth, sought close economic ties with the EC. In 1975, Nigeria, with a population equal to that of twelve of the AASM countries, became an associate state of the Community. For the original members of AASM, the more was not the merrier: they disliked having to share the European market with more competitors from Africa, the Caribbean and the Pacific. Even so, the list of 'associated states' continued to grow. The two Yaoundé Conventions (1963 and 1969) guided relations between the Community and AASM; the four Lomé Conventions (1975, 1980, 1985 and 1990) saw the creation of a global system of sixty-nine associated states with a population of almost 470 million. The much-expanded group became known as ACP (Africa, Caribbean and Pacific); it absorbed the AASM and provided a framework for almost all the economic contacts between ACP and the EC.

At first glance, the cumulative effect of the four Lomé Conventions is impress-ive. Each of these agreements, signed in the capital of one of Africa's poorest states, increased aid from the European Development Fund, the European Investment Bank and several special funds (such as STABEX, a mechanism designed to guarantee export prices for certain ACP products). The fourth Lomé Convention committed the EC still further to the development of ACP countries (DOCUMENT 36). Lomé IV prescribed an aid programme of 12 billion ECU for the years 1990–95; it urged progress on sustainable economic growth, the 'rational manage-ment of the environment', the improvement of working conditions for immigrants and the recognition of human rights (particularly those of women). More basic, perhaps, to the anxieties of ACP states, there were also generous trading arrange-ments. ACP products, whether agricultural or semi-agricultural, manufactured or semi-manufactured, could now be exported to the EC free of custom duties and levies (Article 25).

It remains to be seen, however, whether Lomé IV represents a 'new deal' for the ACP countries. It is true that the Convention has reassuring words about the 'equality of partners' (Article 2). But old tensions cloud the new provisions. Unfortunately the ex-colonial powers and their ex-colonies have inherited many suspicions and antagonisms. The ACP states admire the results of integration in Europe but they believe that wealthy, integrated Europe can – and should – do more for them. They have long felt that their status as 'associated states' makes them appendages of Europe, with almost no voice in decision-making. Indeed, they dislike the word 'associated' because it implies a continuation of the colonial donor–recipient relationships. For their part, the Europeans have grown increas-ingly impatient with the political instability of ACP states, particularly those in Africa. They have also become less reticent about condemning some ACP govern-ments for their alleged waste of development aid. Even more important to Europeans are the problems which confront them on their own continent: high rates of unemployment, standards of education, the presence of millions of immigrants and refugees, the commitment to help Bosnia and other Balkan states and of course the perennial question of monetary policy (not to mention the challenge of monetary union). All these European problems await solutions and none will be solved cheaply. Given the need for huge expenditures in Europe, the

EU is unlikely to support the economic development of ACP states (and other Third World countries) as generously as it used to.

In fact, the Lomé Convention contains a strong hint of Europe's attitude in the 1990s. Articles 7 and 16 insist on the principle of self-help through economic integration. The ACP states are expected to imitate Europe's example by forming 'regional groupings'; they are urged to create wider systems of labour, energy and mining. The message is clear: if the ACP states do not cooperate among themselves, if they make no effort to pool resources or share energy and communications, they can expect little help from the EU. Developing countries may well resent this condition as another example of European pressure and they may not care to abridge, even slightly, the political sovereignty which they have recently gained. On the other hand, they must know that the EU's largesse is not boundless, especially in times of economic recession. They are also aware that, with the end of the Cold War, the attention of the European Union has shifted to new geopolitical realities elsewhere.

This is certainly true of the Union's concern for central and eastern Europe, where the ferment of communism presented the West with opportunities unknown since the late 1940s. While few persons on either side of the Iron Curtain realized in 1985 that the disintegration of the communist commonwealth was at hand, the course of events seems prophetic enough in retrospect. Probably the most telling sign was the labour unrest in Poland, suppressed but not extinguished by the imposition of martial law in 1981. Communist regimes elsewhere feared the Solidarity movement as a contagion which could in no time wreck the economy of the state and complete the disaffection of the people with their government.

While Poland's economy deteriorated gravely, those of other communist states languished. Cautious reforms were attempted here and there: some countries encouraged smaller-scale enterprises while others tried to reduce the role of central planning or liberalize the foreign trade monopolies. Everywhere the results were disappointing. The countries of the Soviet bloc were still plagued by serious shortages of raw materials, energy, consumer goods, grain and even labour. They were increasingly addicted to infusions of credit from the West. Even East Germany (the DDR), long regarded as the industrial powerhouse of communist Europe, depended on the liberality of the Federal Republic (and special provisions in the Treaty of Rome) to keep going.

Insolvent and bewildered, the communist states of central Europe spent the 1980s seeking ever more help from the EC. With the exception of Albania, which saw no reason to change anything, these states promised to adopt more flexible economic policies and to respect human rights. They trimmed their ideological sails and drifted west. But their movement occurred separately and not as a bloc; so anxious were they for an accommodation with the EC that they now had less to do with one another than with the West. As Walter Laqueur has remarked, COMECON had virtually ceased to exist.[13] The diplomatic and political solidarity of the East, hailed in the 1960s as a triumph of fraternal socialism, was now a dead letter. So too was the COMECON concept of cooperation in economic development. For the countries to the east of the European Community, the status as 'associated states' would not have been as distasteful as it was for some ACP states.

What focused the Community's attention on eastern Europe was the huge question of Russia's political leadership. Three aged leaders in the space of four years left the Soviet government almost paralysed: there was little sign of the energy, ideas or even the ruthlessness needed to revive the Soviet state. The emergence of Mikhail Gorbachev in 1984 promised a new chapter, not only in Soviet political life but also in the way the two halves of Europe dealt with each other.

Unlike any of his predecessors, Gorbachev realized the need for a thorough, honest and public assessment of Soviet institutions. The goal of this 'rethinking', or *Perestroika*, was nothing less than a redefinition of the Soviet state and its economic and social priorities. For Gorbachev and his colleagues, the conduct of foreign policy was emphatically placed at the service of domestic policies.[14] This did not imply that the Soviet Union would cease to be a superpower. Gorbachev obviously believed in Russia's global mission in science, technology and trade. But his vision of the new Russia did not encompass the use of coercive diplomacy and military force. He suspected that the client states and foreign bases acquired during the Cold War were actually liabilities for the Soviet state. He concluded that the civilized world needed tranquillity, common ventures (such as space and medical research) and an end to superpower rivalries. Indeed, as Gorbachev explained in his book *Perestroika* (a best seller in the West in 1987 and 1988), the 'internal progress' of the Soviet Union depended on 'external peace and cooperation'.[15]

What did this mean to the process of integration in Europe? Gorbachev answered the question by saying that Europe was 'our common home' (DOCU-MENT 37). The word 'home' was, as Gorbachev admitted, his favourite metaphor. He used it often: Russia's east coast was 'our Asia-Pacific home'; the UN was the 'home of peace'; the earth was 'our planetary home'. Applied to Europe, 'home' meant to Gorbachev a region of the world familiar to its inhabitants for its material progress and its enormous political and cultural diversity. The home was 'common' because it was a single historical entity which Europeans had always shared. Since the Helsinki Conference of 1975 (which Gorbachev regarded as the turning point in modern history), Europeans had become increasingly aware of their security and well-being as a continental concern. For Gorbachev, the Final Act in Helsinki was the first step toward a new Europe: it asserted the wholeness of Europe, a principle neglected by all other postwar conferences. The supporters of *perestroika* thought it affirmed and revived the 'spirit of détente'. They did not imagine that *perestroika* would lead to the demise of communism in eastern Europe and the collapse of the Soviet Union. Instead, they expected *perestroika* to promote the interdependence of European states by encouraging trade, joint ventures and common humanitarian policies.

Perestroika contributed to the transformation of relations between the two halves of Europe. In the past, the Soviet Union refused to grant formal recognition to EC institutions and did what it could to prevent the member states of COMECON from negotiating with the European Community. (There were fewer

Soviet objections to the satellite states dealing with governmental agencies – or the banks – of individual member states of the EC.) For its part, the Community saw COMECON as the instrument of Soviet hegemony in eastern Europe and insisted on the right to negotiate directly with the member states of COMECON. In the late 1980s the Soviet Union reversed its policy and allowed COMECON states to contact Brussels and conduct negotiations on their own.

To mark the new age of economic dialogue, the European Community and COMECON issued the Joint Declaration of June 1988 (DOCUMENT 38). This brief statement did not announce any particular decision about tariffs or joint projects or investment, nor did it suggest guidelines for the cooperation which it promised. The singular purpose of the Declaration was to establish the agreement of the two sides to recognize each other as the two economic blocs of Europe. It is likely that the USSR hoped the Declaration might restore some of the authority of COMECON by regarding it and the EC as two independent blocs dealing with each other as equals. But COMECON had long ceased to be a bloc either in political or economic terms. The governments of east-central Europe (led by Hungary, whose economic system in 1988 was very different from the Soviet model) wanted nothing more than an accommodation with the Community: their goal was to revive their own national economies rather than the prestige of COMECON.[16] For its part, the Community could only regard the Joint Declaration as a victory over COMECON, whose members now rushed to conclude separate agreements with Brussels. The Declaration did not therefore inaugurate the new era which the Soviets hoped for; it marked instead the formal end of Moscow's opposition to the integration of Europe.

The post-communist leaders of east-central Europe had good reason to contemplate the meaning of European integration. No longer the battlefield of more powerful and longer established neighbours, and no longer constrained by the ideological competition of the two postwar superpowers, their countries were at last free to participate in the experiment of European union. The new leaders embraced the concept of a 'European home' because it recognized the strength of their cultural ties to Paris, Vienna and Berlin but above all because it offered the prospect of political security and economic well-being. Moreover, as the 1994 speech by Vaclav Havel illustrates, the people of east-central Europe were anxious to do something which their geography and political fate had denied them: to support Europe as a single democratic entity (DOCUMENT 39).

Havel was conscious of representing the hopes of one of Europe's smaller countries when he addressed the Parliament in Strasbourg on 8 March 1994. One of the 'successor states' after 1919, Czechoslovakia was the only viable democracy in the region. It was independent for only twenty years before it was shamefully sacrificed to Hitler's Germany in September 1938. Restored in 1945, Czechoslovakia succumbed to a communist coup in 1948; the country then became one of the industrial centres of COMECON. A brief period of liberal reform under Alexander Dubcek in 1968 encouraged notions of a more humane Eurocommunism until it was extinguished by forces of the Warsaw Pact. For the next twenty years Czechoslovakia was among the most dutiful and doleful of Moscow's client states, disturbed but never unsettled by Helsinki-inspired defenders of civil liberties. Following the end of the communist regime in 1989, Havel became president of his country; with the division of the country into two independent nations in 1992, Havel remained President of the Czech Republic.

We might interpret Havel's speech as a variety of Euroscepticism. Compared to the ideas normally expressed by Eurosceptics, however, Havel's doubts are rather different. He was not unduly worried about the loss of Czech sovereignty and he did not particularly fear that the political and cultural traditions of his small country would be lost in an amalgam of nationalities. Unlike Thatcher and de Gaulle, Havel considered European unity a 'magnanimous attempt' to give Europe 'a lasting security'. He saw no alternative to the European Union – except perhaps Aristide Briand's nightmare of a European gangland directed by fools, fanatics and demagogues. His doubts centred on the mechanistic order of the Union, the accumulation of 'dry official texts' which had gradually created a working combine of states.

He was certain that something was missing. The Union was systemic and administrative but it was not spiritual and emotional. The Union could never survive as a 'conglomerate of states' (he consciously used Margaret Thatcher's words); nor could it last very long without a clear sense of its value as a 'human community'. It may well be that Havel's words reflected his own experience: he had lived and worked (as a playwright) in a state which sanctified the external (technical and administrative talents, productivity and modernization) while it ignored or denounced the internal (the role of conscience, metaphysical explanations of human identity). Havel did not want a gentle and efficient version of communism to drive the European Union; he wanted a community which was strong and permanent because it transcended 'technical and administrative details'.

The thoughtful speculations of the Czech President would have seemed a wonderful luxury to the leaders of another small country – had they ever noticed them. Bosnia's fate since the breakup of Yugoslavia was a tragic contrast to the political and economic stability of the Czech Republic since its separation (the 'velvet divorce') from Slovakia. A mountainous landlocked state, Bosnia is not a 'nation' as such; its ethnic divisions (Orthodox Serbs, Catholic Croatians and Bosnian Muslims) have deprived it of any significant experience of democratic government; the ethnic communities have little or no desire to live together in a single multinational state. The ambitions of the larger republics (Serbia and Croatia) have not favoured the existence of a truly independent Bosnia and international attempts to identify Bosnia's 'ethnic realities' by mapping the state's internal linguistic boundaries proved futile in the face of the more ruthless strategy of 'ethnic cleansing'.

Three years of war in Bosnia and Croatia were extremely embarrassing to the rest of Europe. The European Union contented itself with offers of humanitarian aid and denunciations of genocide; for a long time there was a naive faith in the revision of linguistic maps as the basis of a peace treaty. To the rest of the world, the Union's efforts in solving a major European crisis seemed half-hearted, dependent on American intervention and Russian indifference. In the event, the Croatian and Bosnian government victories in mid-1995 brought the war to a close, and the American-sponsored agreement (signed in Dayton in November 1995) achieved what the Europeans had manifestly failed to achieve on their own.

With peace in sight, the EU was finally able to announce a clear and comprehensive policy on Bosnia. The *Policy Paper* published in Brussels by the EU Foreign Affairs Council (30 October 1995) was a highly detailed statement (DOCUMENT 40). The *Paper* was uncompromising in demanding the full restoration of human rights, respect for borders, the return of refugees and free elections in Bosnia; it claimed for the EU the right to send a 'High Representative' to oversee the implementation of the settlement. The tone of the *Policy Paper* is not unlike that of a teacher correcting troublesome children: further trouble will only mean the end of the Union's reconstruction aid. A certain measure of naivety remains, too, in the EU's expectations of 'open, free and normal economic relations' among states so long at war with civilian populations, the willingness of Serbia to grant autonomy to the Albanian Muslim district of Kosovo and the readiness of all three states to accept 'the lowest possible level of armaments' after the war.

The *Policy Paper* claims, rightly, that the European Union always sought peace in Bosnia. The *Paper* refrains, properly, from claiming that it was the European Union which imposed peace in Bosnia. That was done by the defeat of the Bosnian Serbs and by the quick replacement of a small and ineffective UN taskforce by a large NATO army which included American troops. The implications of Europe's apparent inability to do very much about a serious threat to peace on the edge of the Union itself will no doubt be discussed for years to come. There will be reasons aplenty for the Union's indecisiveness. The dangerous complexity of Balkan politics, the long memories of what this corner of Europe has meant to European interstate relations and the reluctance of Europeans to participate in a large-scale military venture without the Americans – these are all plausible explanations of Europe's record in Bosnia. But what effect have these explanations on Europe's credibility as a world power? Must Europe's foreign policy take on the same variegations of other aspects of its integration? When a problem involves Europe's security, will there be sufficient cohesion to the foreign policy of the Union? Will the fifteen (or more) member states coordinate policies in a rapid and convincing manner? Or will there be multiple policies, reflecting the interests of two or more 'tiers' or levels of member states? If the settlement imposed on the three Balkan states unravels, or if a similar emergency develops elsewhere on Europe's fringe (Cyprus? the Caucasus region?), Europe's ability to coordinate policy will again be put to the test. If such tests are not met and resolved quickly and fairly, Europe's confidence in itself may suffer more than its reputation as an external force in the world.

ENDNOTES

1 D. Dinan: *Ever Closer Union? An Introduction to the European Community* (London: Macmillan, 1994), p. 159.

2 *Ibid.*, pp. 145–7.

3 J. Lodge: 'EC policymaking: institutional considerations', in J. Lodge (ed.) *The European Community and the Challenge of the Future* (London: Pinter, 1989), p. 29.

4 Loukas Tsoukalis: *The New European Economy. The Politics and Economics of Integration* (Oxford: Oxford University Press, 1993), pp. 64–5; Dinan: *Ever Closer Union?*, p. 149.

5 D. Puchala: 'The economic and political meaning of 1992', in *The Technological Challenges and Opportunities of a United Europe* (Savage, Maryland: Barnes and Noble, 1990), p. 22; *Economist*, 9 July 1988, p. 30.

6 T. Hitiris: *European Community Economics* (Hemel Hempstead: Harvester-Wheatsheaf, 1991), chapter 10.

7 Stephen George: *Politics and Policy in the European Community* (Oxford: Oxford University Press, 2nd edn., 1991), p. 211.

8 Dinan: *Ever Closer Union?*, p. 397.

9 European Commission: Bulletin S/4–90, *The European Community and German Unification*, pp. 9–16; European Parliament: Sessional Document A3–183/90 (9 July 1990)

10 A. S. Milward, F. Lynch, et al.: *The Frontier of National Sovereignty. History and Theory, 1945–1992* (London: Routledge, 1993), p. 19.

11 Clive Church and David Phinnemore: *European Union and European Community* (Hemel Hempstead: Harvester-Wheatsheaf, 1994), p. 7.

12 L. J. Brinkhorst: [Chapter 1], in F. A. M. Alting van Geusau (ed.) *The Lomé Convention and a New International Economic Order* (Leyden: A. W. Sijthoff, 1977), pp. 12–13.

13 W. Laqueur: *Europe in Our Time* (London: Viking Penguin, 1992), p. 432.

14 Alex Pravda: 'The politics of foreign policy', in S. White and A. Pravda (eds) *Developments in Russian and Post Soviet Politics* (London: Macmillan, 1993, 3rd edn.), p. 209.

15 M. Gorbachev: *Perestroika. New Thinking For Our Country and The World* (New York: Harper and Row, 1988), chapter 1.

16 Simon Nuttall: *European Political Cooperation* (Oxford: Clarendon, 1993), pp. 275–6.

ADDITIONAL READINGS

C. Archer and E. Butler: *The European Community, Structures and Process* (London: Pinter, 1992).

M. Baldassari and R. Mundell: *Building the New Europe* (London: Macmillan, 1993).

R. Barrell: *Macroeconomic Policy Coordination in Europe: The ERM and Monetary Union* (London: Sage, 1992).

M. Burgess and A. Gagnon (eds): *Comparative Federalism and Federation. Competing Traditions and Future Challenges* (Hemel Hempstead: Harvester-Wheatsheaf, 1993).

A. W. Cafruny and G. G. Rosenthal: *The State of the European Community: Maastricht and Beyond* (London: Longman, 1993).

A. Clapham: *Human Rights and the European Community: A Critical Overview*, 2 vols (Baden-Baden: Nomus-Velagsgesellschaft, 1991).

D. Coombes: *Understanding European Union* (London: Longman, 1994).

R. Dahrendorf et al.: *Whose Europe? Competing Visions for 1992* (London: Institute for Economic Affairs, 1989).

J. Delors: *Our Europe. The Community and National Development* (London: Verso, 1992).

J. Dudley: *1993 and Beyond* (London: Kogan Page, 1993).

G. Edwards and E. Regelsberger (eds): *Europe's Global Links: The European Community and Inter-regional Cooperation* (London: Pinter, 1990).

E. Engels and W. Wessels: *The European Union in the 1990s* (Bonn: Europa Union Verlag, 1993).

S. Garcia: *European Identity and the Search for Legitimacy* (London: Pinter, 1993).

M. J. Hogan: *The End of the Cold War: Its Meanings and Implications* (Cambridge: Cambridge University Press, 1992).

A. Hyde-Price: *European Security Beyond the Cold War* (London: Sage, 1991).

M. Lister: *The European Community and the Developing World* (Aldershot: Avebury, 1988).

P. M. Lützeler (ed.): *Europe after Maastricht. American and European Perspectives* (Providence, RI and Oxford: Berghahn Books, 1994).

G. Merrit: *Eastern Europe and the USSR* (London: Kogan Page, 1991).

A. Moravcik: 'Negotiating the Single European Act', in *The New European Community: Decision-making and Institutional Change* (Boulder, Colorado: Westview Press, 1991).

P. Nell: 'EFTA in the 1990s: the search for a new identity', *Journal of Common Market Studies* (June 1990), 28(4), pp. 327–358.

S. Nello: *The New Europe: Changing Economic Relations between East and West* (Hemel Hempstead: Harvester-Wheatsheaf, 1991).

T. Pedersen: *European Union and the EFTA Countries* (London: Pinter, 1994).

J. Pinder: *The European Community and Eastern Europe* (London: Pinter, 1991).

——— and R. Pryce: *Maastricht and Beyond: Building the European Union* (London: Routledge, 1994).

'THE EUROPEAN CONGLOMERATE'

In a speech at the College of Europe in Bruges, the British Prime Minister Margaret Thatcher attacked what she saw as the dangers of central control by the 'European superstate'. The following extracts of her speech appeared in *The Times* on 21 September 1988.

The European Community is the practical means by which Europe can ensure the future prosperity and security of its people in a world in which there are many other powerful nations and groups of nations.

We Europeans cannot afford to waste our energies on internal disputes or arcane institutional debates. Europe has to be ready, both to contribute in full measure to its own security and to compete commercially and industrially, in a world in which success goes to the countries which encourage individual initiative and enterprise, rather than to those which attempt to diminish them.

My first guiding principle is this: willing and active cooperation between independent sovereign states is the best way to build a successful European Community. To try to suppress nationhood and concentrate power at the centre of a European conglomerate would be highly damaging and would jeopardize the objectives we seek to achieve. Europe will be stronger precisely because it has France as France, Spain as Spain, Britain as Britain, each with its own customs, traditions and identity. It would be folly to try to fit them into some sort of Identikit European personality.

Some of the founding fathers of the Community thought that the United States of America might be its model. But the whole history of America is quite different from Europe. People went there to get away from the intolerance and constraints of life in Europe.

They sought liberty and opportunity; and their strong sense of purpose has, over two centuries, helped create a new unity and pride in being American – just as our pride lies in being British or Belgian or Dutch or German.

I want to see us work more closely, on the things we can do better together than alone. Europe is stronger when we do so, whether it be in trade, in defence, or in our relations with the rest of the world.

But working more closely together does not require power to be centralized in Brussels or decisions to be taken by an appointed bureaucracy. Indeed, it is ironic that just when those countries such as the Soviet Union, which have tried to run everything from the centre, are learning that success depends on dispersing power and decisions away from the centre, some in the Community seem to want to move in the opposite direction. *comp. Community to Soviet Union*

We have not successfully rolled back the frontiers of the state in Britain only to see them reimposed at a European level with a European superstate exercising a new dominance from Brussels. Certainly we want to see Europe more united and with a greater sense of common purpose. But it must be in a way which preserves the different traditions, parliamentary powers and sense of national pride in one's own country, for these have been the source of Europe's vitality through the centuries.

My second guiding principle is this. <u>Community policies must tackle present problems in a practical way, however difficult that may be.</u> If we cannot reform those Community policies which are patently wrong or ineffective, which are rightly causing public disquiet, then we shall not get the public's support for the Community's future development.

You cannot build on unsound foundations, financial or otherwise, and it was the fundamental reforms agreed last winter which paved the way for the remarkable progress which we have since made on the single market. But we cannot rest on what we have achieved to date.

For example, the task of reforming the common agricultural policy is far from complete.

against CAP

Of course, we must protect the villages and rural areas which are such an important part of our national life – but not by the instrument of agricultural prices. Tackling these problems requires political courage.

My third guiding principle is <u>the need for Community policies which encourage enterprise.</u> If Europe is to flourish and create the jobs of the future, enterprise is the key.

The lesson of the economic history of Europe in the 1970s and 1980s is that central planning and detailed control don't work and that personal endeavour and initiative do; that a state-controlled economy is a recipe for low growth, and that free enterprise within a framework of law brings better results.

The aim of a Europe open to enterprise is the moving force behind the creation of the single European market by 1992. By getting rid of barriers, by making it possible for companies to operate on a Europe-wide scale, we can best compete with the United States, Japan and the other new economic powers emerging in Asia and elsewhere.

And that means action to free markets, action to widen choice, action to reduce government intervention. Our aim should not be more and more detailed regulation from the centre: it should be to deregulate and to remove the constraints on trade.

Britain has been in the lead in opening its markets to others. The City of London has long welcomed financial institutions from all over the world, which is why it is the biggest and most successful financial centre in Europe.

We have opened our market for telecommunications equipment, introduced competition into the market, for services and even into the network – steps others in Europe are only now beginning to face.

In air transport, we have taken the lead in liberalization and seen the benefits in cheaper fares and wider choice. Our coastal shipping trade is open to the merchant navies of Europe. I wish I could say the same of many other Community members.

Regarding monetary matters, let me say this. The key issue is not whether there should be a European central bank. The immediate and practical requirements are to implement the Community's commitment to free movement of capital – in Britain we have it; and to the abolition throughout the Community of the exchange controls – in Britain we abolished them in 1979; to establish a genuinely free market in financial services, in banking, insurance, investment, to make greater use of the ECU.

Britain is this autumn issuing ECU-denominated Treasury bills, and hopes to see other Community governments increasingly do the same.

It is to such basic practical steps that the Community's attention should be devoted. When those have been achieved, and sustained over a period, we shall be in a better position to judge the next moves.

It is the same with the frontiers between our countries. Of course we must make it easier for goods to pass through frontiers. Of course we must make it easier for our people to travel throughout the Community. But it is a matter of plain common sense that we cannot totally abolish frontier controls if we are also to protect our citizens from crime and stop the movement of drugs, of terrorists, and of illegal immigrants. [...]

And before I leave the subject of the single market, may I say that we certainly do not need new regulations which raise the cost of employment and make Europe's labour market less flexible and less competitive with overseas supplies. If we are to have a European company statute, it should contain the minimum regulations.

And certainly we in Britain would fight attempts to introduce collectivism and corporatism at the European level – although what people wish to do in their own countries is a matter for them.

My fourth guiding principle is that Europe should not be protectionist. The expansion of the world economy requires us to continue the process of removing barriers to trade, and to do so in the multilateral negotiations in the GATT. It would be a betrayal if, while breaking down constraints on trade within Europe, the Community were to erect greater external protection.

My last guiding principle concerns the most fundamental issue – the European countries' role in defence. Europe must continue to maintain a sure defence through NATO. There can be no question of relaxing our efforts even though it means taking difficult decisions and meeting heavy costs.

It is to NATO that we owe the peace that has been maintained over 40 years. Things are going our way: the democratic model of a free enterprise society has proved itself superior; freedom is on the offensive, a peaceful offensive the world over, for the first time in my lifetime.

We must strive to maintain the United States' commitment to Europe's defence. That means recognizing the burden on their resources of the world role they undertake, and their point that their Allies should play a full part in the defence of freedom, particularly as Europe grows wealthier.

NATO and the WEU have long recognized where the problems with Europe's defences lie, and have pointed out the solutions. The time has come when we must give substance to our declarations about a strong defence effort with better value for money.

It's not an institutional problem. It's not a problem of drafting. It's something at once simpler and more profound: it is a question of political will and political courage, of convincing people in all our countries that we cannot rely forever on others for our defence. [...]

---------------------------------- 33 ----------------------------------

THE SINGLE EUROPEAN ACT

In order to achieve still greater cohesion in economic, political and foreign policies, certain aspects of earlier treaties had to be amended.
This was the purpose of the Single European Act of 1986. The following passages from the Act are taken from the *Bulletin of the European Communities* (Supplement 2/86), published by the Commission of the European Communities.

TITLE I

COMMON PROVISIONS

Article 1

The European Communities and European Political Cooperation shall have as their objective to contribute together to making concrete progress towards European unity.

The European Communities shall be founded on the Treaties establishing the European Coal and Steel Community, the European Economic Community, the European Atomic Energy Community and on the subsequent Treaties and Acts modifying or supplementing them.

Political Cooperation shall be governed by Title III. The provisions of the Title shall confirm and supplement the procedures agreed in the reports of Luxembourg (1970), Copenhagen (1973), London (1981), the Solemn Declaration on European Union (1983) and the practices gradually established among the Member States.

Article 2

The European Council shall bring together the Heads of State or of Government of the Member States and the President of the Commission of the European Communities. They shall be assisted by the Ministers for Foreign Affairs and by a Member of the Commission.

The European Council shall meet at least twice a year. [...]

CHAPTER II

PROVISIONS AMENDING THE TREATY ESTABLISHING THE EUROPEAN ECONOMIC COMMUNITY

SECTION I

INSTITUTIONAL PROVISIONS

Article 6 [...]

2. *In Article 7, second paragraph of the EEC Treaty the terms 'after consulting the Assembly' shall be replaced by 'in cooperation with the European Parliament'.*
   [...]
4. *In Article 54(2) of the EEC Treaty the terms 'the Council shall, on a proposal from the Commission and after consulting the Economic and Social Committee and the Assembly,' shall be replaced by 'the Council shall, acting on a proposal from the Commission, in cooperation with the European Parliament and after consulting the Economic and Social Committee [...]'*
7. In Article 57(2) of the EEC Treaty, the third sentence shall be replaced by the following:
   'In other cases the Council shall act by a qualified majority, in cooperation with the European Parliament.'

Article 7

Article 149 of the EEC Treaty shall be replaced by the following provisions:

Article 149

1. *Where, in pursuance of this Treaty, the Council acts on a proposal from the Commission, unanimity shall be required for an act constituting an amendment to that proposal.*
2. *Where, in pursuance of this Treaty, the Council acts in cooperation with the European Parliament, the following procedure shall apply:*
   (a) *The Council, acting by a qualified majority under the conditions of paragraph 1, on a proposal from the Commission and after obtaining the Opinion of the European Parliament, shall adopt a common position.*
   (b) *The Council's common position shall be communicated to the European Parliament. The Council and the Commission shall inform the European Parliament fully of the reasons which led the Council to adopt its common position and also of the Commission's position.*
   If, within three months of such communication, the European Parliament approves this common position or has not taken a decision within that period, the Council shall definitively adopt the act in question in accordance with the common position.
   (c) *The European Parliament may within the period of three months referred to in point (b), by an absolute majority of its component members, propose*

amendments to the Council's common position. The European Parliament may also, by the same majority, reject the Council's common position. The result of the proceedings shall be transmitted to the Council and the Commission.

If the European Parliament has rejected the Council's common position, unanimity shall be required for the Council to act on a second reading [. . .]

Article 8

The first paragraph of Article 237 of the EEC Treaty shall be replaced by the following provision:

'Any European State may apply to become a member of the Community. It shall address its application to the Council, which shall act unanimously after consulting the Commission and after receiving the assent of the European Parliament, which shall act by an absolute majority of its component members.'

Article 9

The second paragraph of Article 238 of the EEC Treaty shall be replaced by the following provision:

'These agreements shall be concluded by the Council, acting unanimously and after receiving the assent of the European Parliament, which shall act by an absolute majority of its component members.' [. . .]

SECTION II

PROVISIONS RELATING TO THE FOUNDATIONS AND THE POLICY OF THE COMMUNITY

SUBSECTION I

INTERNAL MARKET

Article 13

The EEC Treaty shall be supplemented by the following provisions:

Article 8 A

The Community shall adopt measures with the aim of progressively establishing the internal market over a period expiring on 31 December 1992. [. . .]

The internal market shall comprise an area without internal frontiers in which the free movement of goods, persons, services and capital is ensured in accordance with the provisions of this Treaty. [. . .]

Article 15

The EEC Treaty shall be supplemented by the following provisions:

Article 8 C

When drawing up its proposals with a view to achieving the objectives set out in Article 8 A, the Commission shall take into account the extent of the effort that certain economies showing differences in development will have to sustain during the period of establishment of the internal market and it may propose appropriate provisions.

If these provisions take the form of derogations, they must be of a temporary nature and must cause the least possible disturbance to the functioning of the common market.

Article 16

1. Article 28 of the EEC Treaty shall be replaced by the following provisions:

Article 28

Any autonomous alteration or suspension of duties in the common customs tariff shall be decided by the Council acting by a qualified majority on a proposal from the Commission.

2. In Article 57(2) of the EEC Treaty, the second sentence shall be replaced by the following:

'Unanimity shall be required for directives the implementation of which involves in at least one Member State amendment of the existing principles laid down by law governing the professions with respect to training and conditions of access for natural persons.'

3. In the second paragraph of Article 59 of the EEC Treaty, the term 'unanimously' shall be replaced by *'by a qualified majority'*.

4. In Article 70(1) of the EEC Treaty, the last two sentences shall be replaced by the following:

'For this purpose the Council shall issue directives, acting by a qualified majority. It shall endeavour to attain the highest possible degree of liberalization. Unanimity shall be required for measures which constitute a step back as regards the liberalization of capital movements.' [...]

Article 17

Article 99 of the EEC Treaty shall be replaced by the following provisions:

Article 99

The Council shall, acting unanimously on a proposal from the Commission and after consulting the European Parliament, adopt provisions for the harmonization of legislation concerning turnover taxes, excise duties and other forms of indirect taxation to the extent that such harmonization is necessary to ensure the establishment and the functioning of the internal market within the time limit laid down in Article 8 A. [...]

Article 19

The EEC Treaty shall be supplemented by the following provisions:

Article 100 B

1. *During 1992, the Commission shall, together with each Member State, draw up an inventory of national laws, regulations and administrative provisions which fall under Article 100 A and which have not been harmonized pursuant to that Article.*
   The Council, acting in accordance with the provisions of Article 100 A, may decide that the provisions in force in a Member State must be recognized as being equivalent to those applied by another Member State....

SUBSECTION II

MONETARY CAPACITY

Article 20

1. A new Chapter 1 shall be inserted in Part Three, Title II of the EEC Treaty, reading as follows:

CHAPTER I

COOPERATION IN ECONOMIC AND MONETARY POLICY

(ECONOMIC AND MONETARY UNION)

Article 102 A

1. *In order to ensure the convergence of economic and monetary policies which is necessary for the further development of the Community, Member States shall cooperate in accordance with the objectives of Article 104. In so doing, they shall take account of the experience acquired in cooperation within the framework of the European Monetary System (EMS) and in developing the ECU, and shall respect existing powers in this field.*
2. *In so far as further development in the field of economic and monetary policy necessitates institutional changes, the provisions of Article 236 shall be applic-*

able. The Monetary Committee and the Committee of Governors of the Central Banks shall also be consulted regarding institutional changes in the monetary area.' [...]

SOCIAL POLICY
Article 21

The EEC Treaty shall be supplemented by the following provisions:

Article 118 A

1. *Member States shall pay particular attention to encouraging improvements, especially in the working environment, as regards the health and safety of workers, and shall set as their objective the harmonization of conditions in this area, while maintaining the improvements made.*
2. *In order to help achieve the objective laid down in the first paragraph, the Council, acting by a qualified majority on a proposal from the Commission, in cooperation with the European Parliament and after consulting the Economic and Social Committee, shall adopt, by means of directives, minimum requirements for gradual implementation, having regard to the conditions and technical rules obtaining in each of the Member States.*
   Such directives shall avoid imposing administrative, financial and legal constraints in a way which would hold back the creation and development of small and medium-sized undertakings.
3. *The provisions adopted pursuant to this Article shall not prevent any Member State from maintaining or introducing more stringent measures for the protection of working conditions compatible with this Treaty.*

Article 22

The EEC Treaty shall be supplemented by the following provisions:

Article 118 B

The Commission shall endeavour to develop the dialogue between management and labour at European level which could, if the two sides consider it desirable, lead to relations based on agreement.

ECONOMIC AND SOCIAL COHESION
Article 23

A Title V shall be added to Part Three of the EEC Treaty, reading as follows:

TITLE V

ECONOMIC AND SOCIAL COHESION

Article l30 A

In order to promote its overall harmonious development, the Community shall develop and pursue its actions leading to the strengthening of its economic and social cohesion.
In particular the Community shall aim at reducing disparities between the various regions and the backwardness of the least-favoured regions.

Article 130 B

Member States shall conduct their economic policies, and shall coordinate them, in such a way as, in addition, to attain the objectives set out in Article 130 A. The implementation of the common policies and of the internal market shall take into account the objectives set out in Article 130 A and in Article 130 C and shall contribute to their achievement. The Community shall support the achievement of these objectives by the action it takes through the structural Funds (European Agricultural Guidance and Guarantee Fund, Guidance Section, European Social Fund, European Regional Development Fund), the European Investment Bank and the other existing financial instruments.

Article 130 C

The European Regional Development fund is intended to help redress the principal regional imbalances in the Community through participating in the development and structural adjustment of regions whose development is lagging behind and in the conversion of declining industrial regions. [. . .]

SUBSECTION V

RESEARCH AND TECHNOLOGICAL DEVELOPMENT

Article 24

A Title VI shall be added to Part Three of the EEC Treaty, reading as follows:

TITLE VI

RESEARCH AND TECHNOLOGICAL DEVELOPMENT

Article 130 F

1. *The Community's aim shall be to strengthen the scientific and technological basis of European industry and to encourage it to become more competitive at international level.*
2. *In order to achieve this, it shall encourage undertakings, including small and*

medium-sized undertakings, research centres and universities in their research and technological development activities; it shall support their efforts to cooperate with one another, aiming, in particular, at enabling undertakings to exploit the Community's internal market.

SUBSECTION VI

ENVIRONMENT

Article 25

A Title VII shall be added to Part Three of the EEC Treaty, reading as follows:

TITLE VII

ENVIRONMENT

Article 130 R

1. *Action by the Community relating to the environment shall have the following objectives:*
   (i) *to preserve, protect and improve the quality of the environment:*
   (ii) *to contribute towards protecting human health;*
   (iii) *to ensure a prudent and rational utilization of natural resources.*
2. *Action by the Community relating to the environment shall be based on the principles that preventive action should be taken, that environmental damage should as a priority be rectified at source, and that the polluter should pay. Environmental protection requirements shall be a component of the Community's other policies.*
3. *In preparing its action relating to the environment, the Community shall take account of:*
   (i) *available scientific and technical data;*
   (ii) *environmental conditions in the various regions of the Community;*
   (iii) *the potential benefits and costs of action or of lack of action;*
   (iv) *the economic and social development of the Community as a whole and the balanced development of its regions.*
4. *The Community shall take action relating to the environment to the extent to which the objectives referred to in paragraph I can be attained better at Community level than at the level of the individual Member States. Without prejudice to certain measures of a Community nature, the Member States shall finance and implement the other measures.*
5. *Within their respective spheres of competence, the Community and the Member States shall cooperate with third countries and with the relevant international organizations. The arrangements for Community cooperation may be the subject of agreements between the Community and the third parties concerned, which shall be negotiated and concluded in accordance with Article 228.*

The previous paragraph shall be without prejudice to Member States' compe-

tence to negotiate in international bodies and to conclude international agreements. [...]

[CHAPTER III, Articles 26–29, provides for amending the Treaty Establishing the European Atomic Energy Community]

TITLE III

PROVISIONS ON EUROPEAN COOPERATION IN THE SPHERE OF FOREIGN POLICY

Article 30

European Cooperation in the sphere of foreign policy shall be governed by the following provisions:

1. The High Contracting Parties, being members of the European Communities, shall endeavour jointly to formulate and implement a European foreign policy.
2. (a) The High Contracting Parties undertake to inform and consult each other on any foreign policy matters of general interest so as to ensure that their combined influence is exercised as effectively as possible through coordination, the convergence of their positions and the implementation of joint action.

   (b) Consultations shall take place before the High Contracting Parties decide on their final position.

   (c) In adopting its positions and in its national measures each High Contracting Party shall take full account of the positions of the other partners and shall give due consideration to the desirability of adopting and implementing common European positions. [...]

   (d) The High Contracting Parties shall endeavour to avoid any action or position which impairs their effectiveness as a cohesive force in international relations or within international organizations.
3. (a) The Ministers for Foreign Affairs and a member of the Commission shall meet at least four times a year within the framework of European Political Cooperation. They may also discuss foreign policy matters within the framework of Political Cooperation on the occasion of meetings of the Council of the European Communities.

   (b) The Commission shall be fully associated with the proceedings of Political Cooperation.

   (c) In order to ensure the swift adoption of common positions and the implementation of joint action, the High Contracting Parties shall, as far as possible, refrain from impeding the formation of a consensus and the joint action which this could produce.
4. The High Contracting Parties shall ensure that the European Parliament is closely associated with European Political Cooperation. To that end the Presidency shall regularly inform the European Parliament of the foreign policy issues which are being examined within the framework of Political Cooperation

and shall ensure that the views of the European Parliament are duly taken into consideration. [...]

6. (a) The High Contracting Parties consider that closer cooperation on questions of European security would contribute in an essential way to the development of a European identity in external policy matters. They are ready to coordinate their positions more closely on the political and economic aspects of security.

(b) The High Contracting Parties are determined to maintain the technological and industrial conditions necessary for their security. They shall work to that end both at national level and, where appropriate, within the framework of the competent institutions and bodies.

(c) Nothing in this Title shall impede closer cooperation in the field of security between certain of the High Contracting Parties within the framework of the Western European Union or the Atlantic Alliance.

7. (a) In international institutions and at international conferences which they attend, the High Contracting Parties shall endeavour to adopt common positions on the subjects covered by this Title. [...]

(b) The Presidency shall be responsible for initiating action and coordinating and representing the positions of the Member States in relations with third countries in respect of European Political Cooperation activities. It shall also be responsible for the management of Political Cooperation and in particular for drawing up the timetable of meetings and for convening and organizing meetings. [...]

34

EUROPEAN SOCIAL RIGHTS

The Community Charter of the Fundamental Social Rights of Workers was adopted by the Member States on 9 December 1989, and was published by the Commission of the European Communities in 1990.

THE HEADS OF STATE OR GOVERNMENT OF THE MEMBER STATES OF THE EUROPEAN COMMUNITY MEETING AT STRASBOURG ON 9 DECEMBER 1989[1]

Whereas, under the terms of Article 117 of the EEC Treaty, the Member States have agreed on the need to promote improved living and working conditions for workers so as to make possible their harmonization while the improvement is being maintained; [...]

Whereas the completion of the internal market is the most effective means of creating employment and ensuring maximum well-being in the Community; whereas employment development and creation must be given first priority in the completion of the internal market; whereas it is for the Community to take up the

[1] Text adopted by the Heads of State or Government of 11 Member States.

challenges of the future with regard to economic competitiveness, taking into account, in particular, regional imbalances;

Whereas the social consensus contributes to the strengthening of the competitiveness of undertakings, of the economy as a whole and to the creation of employment; whereas in this respect it is an essential condition for ensuring sustained economic development;

Whereas the completion of the internal market must favour the approximation of improvements in living and working conditions, as well as economic and social cohesion within the European Community while avoiding distortions of competition;

Whereas the completion of the internal market must offer improvements in the social field for workers of the European Community, especially in terms of freedom of movement, living and working conditions, health and safety at work, social protection, education and training;

Whereas, in order to ensure equal treatment, it is important to combat every form of discrimination, including discrimination on grounds of sex, colour, race, opinions and beliefs, and whereas, in a spirit of solidarity, it is important to combat social exclusion;

Whereas it is for Member States to guarantee that workers from non-member countries and members of their families who are legally resident in a Member State of the European Community are able to enjoy, as regards their living and working conditions, treatment comparable to that enjoyed by workers who are nationals of the Member State concerned;

Whereas inspiration should be drawn from the Conventions of the International Labour Organization and from the European Social Charter of the Council of Europe; [...]

Whereas, by virtue of the principle of subsidiarity, responsibility for the initiatives to be taken with regard to the implementation of these social rights lies with the Member States or their constituent parts and, within the limits of its powers, with the European Community; whereas such implementation may take the form of laws, collective agreements or existing practices at the various appropriate levels and whereas it requires in many spheres the active involvement of the two sides of industry;

Whereas the solemn proclamation of fundamental social rights at European Community level may not, when implemented, provide grounds for any retrogression compared with the situation currently existing in each Member State;

HAVE ADOPTED THE FOLLOWING DECLARATION CONSTITUTING THE 'COMMUNITY CHARTER OF THE FUNDAMENTAL SOCIAL RIGHTS OF WORKERS':

TITLE I

FUNDAMENTAL SOCIAL RIGHTS OF WORKERS

Freedom of movement

1. Every worker of the European Community shall have the right to freedom of

movement throughout the territory of the Community, subject to restrictions justified on grounds of public order, public safety or public health.

2. The right to freedom of movement shall enable any worker to engage in any occupation or profession in the Community in accordance with the principles of equal treatment as regards access to employment, working conditions and social protection in the host country.

3. The right of freedom of movement shall also imply:
   (i)   harmonization of conditions of residence in all Member States, particularly those concerning family reunification;
   (ii) elimination of obstacles arising from the non-recognition of diplomas or equivalent occupational qualifications;
   (iii) improvement of the living and working conditions of frontier workers.

Employment and remuneration

4. Every individual shall be free to choose and engage in an occupation according to the regulations governing each occupation.

5. All employment shall be fairly remunerated.
   To this end, in accordance with arrangements applying in each country:
   (i)   workers shall be assured of an equitable wage, i.e. a wage sufficient to enable them to have a decent standard of living;
   (ii) workers subject to terms of employment other than an open-ended full-time contract shall benefit from an equitable reference wage;
   (iii) wages may be withheld, seized or transferred only in accordance with national law; such provisions should entail measures enabling the worker concerned to continue to enjoy the necessary means of subsistence for him or herself and his or her family.

6. Every individual must be able to have access to public placement services free of charge.

Improvement of living and working conditions

7. The completion of the internal market must lead to an improvement in the living and working conditions of workers in the European Community. This process must result from an approximation of these conditions while the improvement is being maintained, as regards in particular the duration and organization of working time and forms of employment other than open-ended contracts, such as fixed-term contracts, part-time working, temporary work and seasonal work.
   The improvement must cover, where necessary, the development of certain aspects of employment regulations such as procedures for collective redundancies and those regarding bankruptcies.

8. Every worker of the European Community shall have a right to a weekly rest period and to annual paid leave, the duration of which must be progressively harmonized in accordance with national practices.

9. The conditions of employment of every worker of the European Community shall be stipulated in laws, a collective agreement or a contract of employment, according to arrangements applying in each country.

Social protection

According to the arrangements applying in each country:

10. Every worker of the European Community shall have a right to adequate social protection and shall, whatever his status and whatever the size of the undertaking in which he is employed, enjoy an adequate level of social security benefits.

    Persons who have been unable either to enter or re-enter the labour market and have no means of subsistence must be able to receive sufficient resources and social assistance in keeping with their particular situation.

Freedom of association and collective bargaining

11. Employers and workers of the European Community shall have the right of association in order to constitute professional organizations or trade unions of their choice for the defence of their economic and social interests.

    Every employer and every worker shall have the freedom to join or not to join such organizations without any personal or occupational damage being thereby suffered by him.

12. Employers or employers' organizations, on the one hand, and workers' organizations, on the other, shall have the right to negotiate and conclude collective agreements under the conditions laid down by national legislation and practice.

    The dialogue between the two sides of industry at European level which must be developed, may, if the parties deem it desirable, result in contractual relations in particular at inter-occupational and sectoral level.

13. The right to resort to collective action in the event of a conflict of interests shall include the right to strike, subject to the obligations arising under national regulations and collective agreements.

    In order to facilitate the settlement of industrial disputes the establishment and utilization at the appropriate levels of conciliation, mediation and arbitration procedures should be encouraged in accordance with national practice.

14. The internal legal order of the Member States shall determine under which conditions and to what extent the rights provided for in Articles 11 to 13 apply to the armed forces, the police and the civil service.

Vocational training

15. Every worker of the European Community must be able to have access to vocational training and to benefit therefrom throughout his working life. In

the conditions governing access to such training there may be no discrimination on grounds of nationality.

The competent public authorities, undertakings or the two sides of industry, each within their own sphere of competence, should set up continuing and permanent training systems enabling every person to undergo retraining more especially through leave for training purposes, to improve his skills or to acquire new skills, particularly in the light of technical developments.

Equal treatment for men and women

16. Equal treatment for men and women must be assured. Equal opportunities for men and women must be developed.

    To this end, action should be intensified to ensure the implementation of the principle of equality between men and women as regards in particular access to employment, remuneration, working conditions, social protection, education, vocational training and career development.

    Measures should also be developed enabling men and women to reconcile their occupational and family obligations.

Information, consultation and participation for workers

17. Information, consultation and participation for workers must be developed along appropriate lines, taking account of the practices in force in the various Member States.

    This shall apply especially in companies or groups of companies having establishments or companies in two or more Member States of the European Community.

18. Such information, consultation and participation must be implemented in due time, particularly in the following cases:
    (i)   when technological changes which, from the point of view of working conditions and work organization, have major implications for the work-force, are introduced into undertakings;
    (ii)   in connection with restructuring operations in undertakings or in cases of mergers having an impact on the employment of workers;
    (iii) in cases of collective redundancy procedures;
    (iv)   when transfrontier workers in particular are affected by employment policies pursued by the undertaking where they are employed.

Health protection and safety at the workplace

19. Every worker must enjoy satisfactory health and safety conditions in his working environment. Appropriate measures must be taken in order to achieve further harmonization of conditions in this area while maintaining the improvements made.

    These measures shall take account, in particular, of the need for the training, information, consultation and balanced participation of workers as regards the risks incurred and the steps taken to eliminate or reduce them.

The provisions regarding implementation of the internal market shall help to ensure such protection.

Protection of children and adolescents

20. Without prejudice to such rules as may be more favourable to young people, in particular those ensuring their preparation for work through vocational training, and subject to derogations limited to certain light work, the minimum employment age must not be lower than the minimum school-leaving age and, in any case, not lower than 15 years.

21. Young people who are in gainful employment must receive equitable remuneration in accordance with national practice.

22. Appropriate measures must be taken to adjust labour regulations applicable to young workers so that their specific development and vocational training and access to employment needs are met.

    The duration of work must, in particular, be limited – without it being possible to circumvent this limitation through recourse to overtime – and night work prohibited in the case of workers of under 18 years of age, save in the case of certain jobs laid down in national legislation or regulations.

23. Following the end of compulsory education, young people must be entitled to receive initial vocational training of a sufficient duration to enable them to adapt to the requirements of their future working life; for young workers, such training should take place during working hours.

Elderly persons

According to the arrangements applying in each country:

24. Every worker of the European Community must, at the time of retirement, be able to enjoy resources affording him or her a decent standard of living.

25. Any person who has reached retirement age but who is not entitled to a pension or who does not have other means of subsistence, must be entitled to sufficient resources and to medical and social assistance specifically suited to his needs.

Disabled persons

26. All disabled persons, whatever the origin and nature of their disablement, must be entitled to additional concrete measures aimed at improving their social and professional integration.

    These measures must concern, in particular, according to the capacities of the beneficiaries, vocational training, ergonomics, accessibility, mobility, means of transport and housing.

TITLE II

IMPLEMENTATION OF THE CHARTER

27. It is more particularly the responsibility of the Member States, in accordance with national practices, notably through legislative measures or collective agreements, to guarantee the fundamental social rights in this Charter and to implement the social measures indispensable to the smooth operation of the internal market as part of a strategy of economic and social cohesion.
28. The European Council invites the Commission to submit as soon as possible initiatives which fall within its powers, as provided for in the Treaties, with a view to the adoption of legal instruments for the effective implementation, as and when the internal market is completed, of those rights which come within the Community's area of competence.
29. The Commission shall establish each year, during the last three months, a report on the application of the Charter by the Member States and by the European Community.
30. The report of the Commission shall be forwarded to the European Council, the European Parliament and the Economic and Social Committee.

35

MAASTRICHT TREATY

Agreement on European union was reached at Maastricht in December 1991 and the Treaty was signed there the following February. It incorporated or updated provisions of several earlier treaties, including the Single European Act and EURATOM. These articles are taken from the full text of the Treaty as it appeared in the *Official Journal of the European Communities*, vol. 35, no. C 191 (29 July 1992).

TITLE I

COMMON PROVISIONS

Article A

By this Treaty, the High Contracting Parties establish among themselves a European Union, hereinafter called 'the Union'.

This Treaty marks a new stage in the process of creating an ever closer union among the peoples of Europe, in which decisions are taken as closely as possible to the citizen.

The Union shall be founded on the European Communities, supplemented by the policies and forms of cooperation established by this Treaty. Its task shall be to organize, in a manner demonstrating consistency and solidarity, relations between the Member States and between their peoples.

Article B

The Union shall set itself the following objectives:

- to promote economic and social progress which is balanced and sustainable, in particular through the creation of an area without internal frontiers, through the strengthening of economic and social cohesion and through the establishment of economic and monetary union, ultimately including a single currency in accordance with the provisions of this Treaty;
- to assert its identity on the international scene, in particular through the implementation of a common foreign and security policy including the eventual framing of a common defence policy, which might in time lead to a common defence;
- to strengthen the protection of the rights and interests of the nationals of its Member States through the introduction of a citizenship of the Union;
- to develop close cooperation on justice and home affairs;
- to maintain in full the 'acquis communautaire' and build on it with a view to considering, through the procedure referred to in Article N(2), to what extent the policies and forms of cooperation introduced by this Treaty may need to be revised with the aim of ensuring the effectiveness of the mechanisms and the institutions of the Community.

The objectives of the Union shall be achieved as provided in this Treaty and in accordance with the conditions and the timetable set out therein while respecting the principle of subsidiarity as defined in Article 3b of the Treaty [of Rome] establishing the European Community.

Article C

The Union shall be served by a single institutional framework which shall ensure the consistency and the continuity of the activities carried out in order to attain its objectives while respecting and building upon the 'acquis communautaire'.

The Union shall in particular ensure the consistency of its external activities as a whole in the context of its external relations, security, economic and development policies. The Council and the Commission shall be responsible for ensuring such consistency. They shall ensure the implementation of these policies, each in accordance with its respective powers.

Article D

The European Council shall provide the Union with the necessary impetus for its development and shall define the general political guidelines thereof.

The European Council shall bring together the Heads of State or of Government of the Member States and the President of the Commission. They shall be assisted by the Ministers for Foreign Affairs of the Member States and by a Member of the Commission. The European Council shall meet at least twice a year, under the chairmanship of the Head of State or of Government of the Member State which holds the Presidency of the Council.

The European Council shall submit to the European Parliament a report after each of its meetings and a yearly written report on the progress achieved by the Union.

Article E

The European Parliament, the Council, the Commission and the Court of Justice shall exercise their powers under the conditions and for the purposes provided for, on the one hand, by the provisions of the Treaties establishing the European Communities and of the subsequent Treaties and Acts modifying and supplementing them and, on the other hand, by the other provisions of this Treaty.

Article F

1. The Union shall respect the national identities of its Member States, whose systems of government are founded on the principles of democracy.
2. The Union shall respect fundamental rights, as guaranteed by the European Convention for the Protection of Human Rights and Fundamental Freedoms signed in Rome on 4 November 1950 and as they result from the constitutional traditions common to the Member States, as general principles of Community law. [...]

PART TWO

CITIZENSHIP OF THE UNION

Article 8

1. Citizenship of the Union is hereby established.
   Every person holding the nationality of a Member State shall be a citizen of the Union.
2. Citizens of the Union shall enjoy the rights conferred by this Treaty and shall be subject to the duties imposed thereby.

Article 8a

1. Every citizen of the Union shall have the right to move and reside freely within the territory of the Member States, subject to the limitations and conditions laid down in this Treaty and by the measures adopted to give it effect.
2. The Council may adopt provisions with a view to facilitating the exercise of the rights referred to in paragraph 1; save as otherwise provided in this Treaty, the

Council shall act unanimously on a proposal from the Commission and after obtaining the assent of the European Parliament.

Article 8b

1. Every citizen of the Union residing in a Member State of which he is not a national shall have the right to vote and to stand as a candidate at municipal elections in the Member State in which he resides, under the same conditions as nationals of that State. This right shall be exercised subject to detailed arrangements to be adopted before 31 December 1994 by the Council, acting unanimously on a proposal from the Commission and after consulting the European Parliament; these arrangements may provide for derogations where warranted by problems specific to a Member State.
2. ... every citizen of the Union residing in a Member State of which he is not a national shall have the right to vote and to stand as a candidate in elections to the European Parliament in the Member State in which he resides, under the same conditions as nationals of that State. This right shall be exercised subject to detailed arrangements to be adopted before 31 December 1993 by the Council, acting unanimously on a proposal from the Commission and after consulting the European Parliament; these arrangements may provide for derogations where warranted by problems specific to a Member State.

Article 8c

Every citizen of the Union shall, in the territory of a third country in which a Member State of which he is a national is not represented, be entitled to protection by the diplomatic or consular authorities of any Member State, on the same conditions as the nationals of that State. Before 31 December 1993, Member States shall establish the necessary rules among themselves and start the international negotiations required to secure this protection.

Article 8d

[Every citizen of the Union shall be entitled to petition the European Parliament and to apply to the European Union Ombudsman.]

Article 8e

The Commission shall report to the European Parliament, to the Council and to the Economic and Social Committee before 31 December 1993 and then every three years on the application of the provisions of this Part. This report shall take account of the development of the Union.

On this basis, and without prejudice to the other provisions of this Treaty, the

Council, acting unanimously on a proposal from the Commission and after consulting the European Parliament, may adopt provisions to strengthen or to add to the rights laid down in this Part, which it shall recommend to the Member States for adoption in accordance with their respective constitutional requirements.

TITLE XVI

ENVIRONMENT

Article 130r

1. Community policy on the environment shall contribute to pursuit of the following objectives:
   - preserving, protecting and improving the quality of the environment;
   - protecting human health;
   - prudent and rational utilization of natural resources;
   - promoting measures at international level to deal with regional or worldwide environmental problems.
2. Community policy on the environment shall aim at a high level of protection taking into account the diversity of situations in the various regions of the Community. It shall be based on the precautionary principle and on the principles that preventive action should be taken, that environmental damage should as a priority be rectified at source and that the polluter should pay. Environmental protection requirements must be integrated into the definition and implementation of other Community policies.

   In this context, harmonization measures answering these requirements shall include, where appropriate, a safeguard clause allowing Member States to take provisional measures, for non-economic environmental reasons, subject to a Community inspection procedure.
3. In preparing its policy on the environment, the Community shall take account of:
   - available scientific and technical data;
   - environmental conditions in the various regions of the Community;
   - the potential benefits and costs of action or lack of action;
   - the economic and social development of the Community as a whole and the balanced development of its regions.
4. Within their respective spheres of competence, the Community and the Member States shall cooperate with third countries and with the competent international organizations. The arrangements for Community cooperation may be the subject of agreements between the Community and the third parties concerned, which shall be negotiated and concluded. . . .

   The previous subparagraph shall be without prejudice to Member States' competence to negotiate in international bodies and to conclude international agreements.

Article 130s

1. The Council ... after consulting the Economic and Social Committee, shall decide what action is to be taken by the Community ...
2. ... the Council, acting unanimously on a proposal from the Commission and after consulting the European Parliament and the Economic and Social Committee, shall adopt:
   - provisions primarily of a fiscal nature;
   - measures concerning town and country planning, land use with the exception of waste management and measures of a general nature, and management of water resources;
   - measures significantly affecting a Member State's choice between different energy sources and the general structure of its energy supply.

   The Council may, under the conditions laid down in the preceding subparagraph, define those matters referred to in this paragraph on which decisions are to be taken by a qualified majority.
3. In other areas, general action programmes setting out priority objectives to be attained shall be adopted by the Council ... after consulting the Economic and Social Committee.

   The Council, acting under the terms of paragraph 1 or paragraph 2 according to the case, shall adopt the measures necessary for the implementation of these programmes.
4. Without prejudice to certain measures of a Community nature, the Member States shall finance and implement the environment policy.
5. Without prejudice to the principle that the polluter should pay, if a measure based on the provisions of paragraph 1 involves costs deemed disproportionate for the public authorities of a Member State, the Council shall, in the act adopting that measure, lay down appropriate provisions in the form of:
   - temporary derogations and/or
   - financial support from the Cohesion Fund to be set up no later than 31 December 1993 ...

Article 130t

The protective measures adopted pursuant to Article 130s shall not prevent any Member State from maintaining or introducing more stringent protective measures. Such measures must be compatible with this Treaty. They shall be notified to the Commission. ...

TITLE V

PROVISIONS ON A COMMON FOREIGN AND SECURITY POLICY

Article J

A common foreign and security policy is hereby established which shall be governed by the following provisions.

Article J.1

1. The Union and its Member States shall define and implement a common foreign and security policy, governed by the provisions of this Title and covering all areas of foreign and security policy.
2. The objectives of the common foreign and security policy shall be:
   - to safeguard the common values, fundamental interests and independence of the Union;
   - to strengthen the security of the Union and its Member States in all ways;
   - to preserve peace and strengthen international security, in accordance with the principles of the United Nations Charter as well as the principles of the Helsinki Final Act and the objectives of the Paris Charter;
   - to promote international cooperation;
   - to develop and consolidate democracy and the rule of law, and respect for human rights and fundamental freedoms.
3. The Union shall pursue these objectives:
   - by establishing systematic cooperation between Member States in the conduct of policy, in accordance with Article J.2;
   - by gradually implementing, in accordance with Article J.3, joint action in the areas in which the Member States have important interests in common.
4. The Member States shall support the Union's external and security policy actively and unreservedly in a spirit of loyalty and mutual solidarity. They shall refrain from any action which is contrary to the interests of the Union or likely to impair its effectiveness as a cohesive force in international relations. The Council shall ensure that these principles are complied with.

Article J.2

1. Member States shall inform and consult one another within the Council on any matter of foreign and security policy of general interest in order to ensure that their combined influence is exerted as effectively as possible by means of concerted and convergent action.
2. Whenever it deems it necessary, the Council shall define a common position. Member States shall ensure that their national policies conform to the common positions.
3. Member States shall coordinate their action in international organizations and at international conferences. They shall uphold the common positions in such fora.
   In international organizations and at international conferences where not all the Member States participate, those which do take part shall uphold the common positions.

Article J.3

The procedure for adopting joint action in matters covered by the foreign and security policy shall be the following:

1. The Council shall decide, on the basis of general guidelines from the European Council, that a matter should be the subject of joint action.

   Whenever the Council decides on the principle of joint action, it shall lay down the specific scope, the Union's general and specific objectives in carrying out such action, if necessary its duration, and the means, procedures and conditions for its implementation.

2. The Council shall, when adopting the joint action and at any stage during its development, define those matters on which decisions are to be taken by a qualified majority.

   Where the Council is required to act by qualified majority pursuant to the preceding subparagraph, the votes of its members shall be weighted in accordance with [provisions of the Treaty of Rome] and for their adoption, acts of the Council shall require at least fifty-four votes in favour, cast by at least eight members. [...]

6. In cases of imperative need arising from changes in the situation and failing a Council decision, Member States may take the necessary measures as a matter of urgency having regard to the general objectives of the joint action. The Member State concerned shall inform the Council immediately of any such measures.

7. Should there be any major difficulties in implementing a joint action, a Member State shall refer them to the Council which shall discuss them and seek appropriate solutions. Such solutions shall not run counter to the objectives of the joint action or impair its effectiveness.

Article J.4

1. The common foreign and security policy shall include all questions related to the security of the Union, including the eventual framing of a common defence policy, which might in time lead to a common defence.

2. The Union requests the Western European Union (WEU), which is an integral part of the development of the Union, to elaborate and implement decisions and actions of the Union which have defence implications. The Council shall, in agreement with the institutions of the WEU, adopt the necessary practical arrangements.

3. Issues having defence implications dealt with under this Article shall not be subject to the procedures set out in Article J.3.

4. The policy of the Union in accordance with this Article shall not prejudice the specific character of the security and defence policy of certain Member States and shall respect the obligations of certain Member States under the North Atlantic Treaty and be compatible with the common security and defence policy established within that framework.

5. The provisions of this Article shall not prevent the development of closer cooperation between two or more Member States on a bilateral level, in the framework of the WEU and the Atlantic Alliance, provided such cooperation does not run counter to or impede that provided for in this Title. [...]

Article J.5

1. The Presidency shall represent the Union in matters coming within the common foreign and security policy.
2. The Presidency shall be responsible for the implementation of common measures; in that capacity it shall in principle express the position of the Union in international organizations and international conferences. [...]
4. ... Member States represented in international organizations or international conferences where not all the Member States participate shall keep the latter informed of any matter of common interest.

   Member States which are also members of the United Nations Security Council will concert and keep the other Member States fully informed. Member States which are permanent members of the Security Council will, in the execution of their functions, ensure the defence of the positions and the interests of the Union, without prejudice to their responsibilities under the provisions of the United Nations Charter.

Article J.6

The diplomatic and consular missions of the Member States and the Commission Delegations in third countries and international conferences, and their representatives to international organizations, shall cooperate in ensuring that the common positions and common measures adopted by the Council are complied with and implemented.

They shall set up cooperation by exchanging information, carrying out joint assessments and contributing to the implementation of the [provisions in the Treaty of Rome].

Article J.7

The Presidency shall consult the European Parliament on the main aspects and the basic choices of the common foreign and security policy and shall ensure that the views of the European Parliament are duly taken into consideration. The European Parliament shall be kept regularly informed by the Presidency and the Commission of the development of the Union's foreign and security policy.

The European Parliament may ask questions of the Council or make recommendations to it. It shall hold an annual debate on progress in implementing the common foreign and security policy.

Article J.8

1. The European Council shall define the principles of and general guidelines for the common foreign and security policy.
2. The Council shall take the decisions necessary for defining and implementing the common ... policy on the basis of the general guidelines adopted by the European Council. [...]

The Council shall act unanimously, except for procedural questions. [...]

3. Any Member State or the Commission may refer to the Council any question relating to the foreign and security policy and may submit proposals to the Council.

4. In cases requiring a rapid decision, the Presidency, of its own motion, or at the request of the Commission or a Member State, shall convene an extraordinary Council meeting within forty-eight hours or, in an emergency, within a shorter period. [...]

36

LOMÉ CONVENTION IV

The Lomé Conventions have guided the European Community's relations with many countries in the Third World. The following excerpt is from the General Provisions (Part One) of the fourth Lomé Convention, signed on 15 December 1989. The full text was published by the *Africa, Caribbean-Pacific Courier*, no. 120 (Brussels, March-April 1990), pp. 12–16.

CHAPTER 1

OBJECTIVES AND PRINCIPLES OF COOPERATION

Article 1

The Community and its Member States, of the one part, and the ACP States, of the other part (hereinafter referred to as the Contracting Parties), hereby conclude this cooperation Convention in order to promote and expedite the economic, cultural and social development of the ACP States and to consolidate and diversify their relations in a spirit of solidarity and mutual interest.

The Contracting Parties thereby affirm their undertaking to continue, strengthen and render more effective the system of cooperation established under the first, second and third ACP–EEC Conventions and confirm the special character of their relations, based on their reciprocal interest, and the specific nature of their cooperation.

The Contracting Parties hereby express their resolve to intensify their effort to create, with a view to a more just and balanced international economic order, a model for relations between developed and developing states and to work together to affirm in the international context the principles underlying their cooperation.

Article 2

ACP–EEC cooperation, underpinned by a legally binding system and the existence of joint institutions, shall be exercised on the basis of the following fundamental principles:

- equality between partners, respect for their sovereignty, mutual interest and interdependence;
- the right of each State to determine its own political, social, cultural and economic policy options; – security of their relations based on the acquis of their system of cooperation.

Article 3

The ACP States shall determine the development principles, strategies and models for their economies and societies in all sovereignty.

Article 4

Support shall be provided in ACP–EEC cooperation for the ACP States' efforts to achieve comprehensive self-reliant and self-sustained development based on their cultural and social values, their human capacities, their natural resources and their economic potential in order to promote the ACP States' social, cultural and economic progress and the well-being of their populations through the satisfaction of their basic needs, the recognition of the role of women and the enhancement of people's capacities, with respect for their dignity.

Such development shall be based on a sustainable balance between its economic objectives, the rational management of the environment and the enhancement of natural and human resources.

Article 5

1. [...] Cooperation operations shall thus be conceived in accordance with the positive approach, where respect for human rights is recognized as a basic factor of real development and where cooperation is conceived as a contribution to the promotion of these rights.
   In this context development policy and cooperation are closely linked with the respect for and enjoyment of fundamental human rights. [...]
2. [...] ACP–EEC cooperation shall help abolish the obstacles preventing individuals and peoples from actually enjoying to the full their economic, social and cultural rights and this must be achieved through the development which is essential to their dignity, their well-being and their self-fulfilment. To this end, the Parties shall strive, jointly or each in its own sphere of responsibility, to help eliminate the causes of situations of misery unworthy of the human condition and of deep-rooted economic and social inequalities.
   The Contracting Parties hereby reaffirm their existing obligations and commitment in international law to strive to eliminate all forms of discrimination based on ethnic group, origin, race, nationality, colour, sex, language, religion or any other situation. This commitment applies more particularly to any situation in the ACP States or in the Community that may adversely affect the pursuit of the objectives of the Convention, and to the system of apartheid, having regard also

to its destabilizing effects on the outside. The Member States (and/or, where appropriate, the Community itself) and the ACP States will continue to ensure, through the legal or administrative measures which they have or will have adopted, that migrant workers, students and other foreign nationals legally within their territory are not subjected to discrimination on the basis of racial, religious, cultural or social differences, notably in respect of housing, education, health care, other social services and employment.

3. At the request of the ACP States, financial resources may be allocated, in accordance with the rules governing development finance cooperation, to the promotion of human rights in the ACP States through specific schemes, public or private, that would be decided, particularly in the legal sphere, in consultation with bodies of internationally recognized competence in the field. Resources may also be given to support the establishment of structures to promote human rights. Priority shall be given to schemes of regional scope.

Article 6

1. With a view to attaining more balanced and self-reliant economic development in the ACP States, special efforts shall be made under this Convention to promote rural development, food security for the people, rational management of natural resources, and the preservation, revival and strengthening of agricultural production potential in the ACP States.

2. The Contracting Parties recognize that priority must be given to environmental protection and the conservation of natural resources, which are essential conditions for sustainable and balanced development from both the economic and human viewpoints.

Article 7

The Community and the ACP States shall give special importance and high priority to regional cooperation and integration. In this context, the Convention shall offer effective support for the ACP States' efforts to organize themselves into regional groupings and to step up their cooperation at regional and inter-regional level with a view to promoting a new, more just and more balanced economic order.

Article 8

The Contracting Parties acknowledge the need to accord special treatment to the least-developed ACP States and to take account of the specific difficulties confronting the landlocked and island ACP States. They shall pay special attention to improving the living conditions of the poorest sections of the population.

Cooperation shall comprise, inter alia, special treatment when determining the volume of financial resources and the conditions attached thereto in order to enable the least-developed ACP States to overcome structural and other obstacles to their development. [...]

Article 11

Within the scope of their respective responsibilities, the institutions of this Convention shall examine periodically the results of the application thereof, provide any necessary impetus and take any relevant decision or measure for the attainment of its objectives. Any question that might directly hamper the effective attainment of the objectives of this Convention may be raised in the context of the institutions.

Consultations shall take place within the Council of Ministers at the request of either Contracting Party in cases provided for in this Convention or where difficulties arise with the application or interpretation thereof. [...]

CHAPTER 2

OBJECTIVES AND GUIDELINES OF THE CONVENTION IN THE MAIN AREAS OF COOPERATION

Article 13

Cooperation shall be aimed at supporting development in the ACP States, a process centred on man himself and rooted in each people's culture. It shall back up the policies and measures adopted by those States to enhance their human resources, increase their own creative capacities and promote their cultural identities. Cooperation shall also encourage participation by the population in the design and execution of development operations.

Account shall be taken, in the various fields of cooperation, and at all the different stages of the operations executed, of the cultural dimension and social implications of such operations and of the need for both men and women to participate and benefit on equal terms.

Article 14

Cooperation shall entail mutual responsibility for preservation of the natural heritage. In particular, it shall attach special importance to environmental protection and the preservation and restoration of natural equilibria in the ACP States. Cooperation schemes in all areas shall therefore be designed to make the objectives of economic growth compatible with development that respects natural equilibria and brings about lasting results in the service of man. [...]

Article 16

Cooperation in the field of mining and energy shall be directed at promoting and expediting, in the mutual interest, diversified economic development, deriving full benefit from the ACP States' human potential and natural resources, and at fostering better integration of these and other sectors and their complementarity with the rest of the economy. [...]

Support shall be provided for the ACP States' efforts to devise and implement energy policies suited to their situation, notably the gradual reduction of the dependence of the majority of them on imported petroleum products and the development of new and renewable sources of energy. [...]

Article 17

The Community and the ACP States acknowledge that industrialization is a driving force – complementary to agricultural and rural development – in promoting the economic transformation of the ACP States in order to achieve self-sustained growth and balanced and diversified development. Industrial development is needed to enhance the productivity of the ACP economies so that they can meet basic human needs and step up the competitive participation of the ACP States in world trade by way of selling more value-added products.

Article 18

Given the extreme dependence of the economies of the vast majority of ACP States on their export of commodities, the Contracting Parties agree to pay particular attention to their cooperation in this sector with a view to supporting ACP States' policies or strategies designed:

– on the one hand, to foster diversification, both horizontal and vertical, of the ACP economies, in particular through the development of processing, marketing, distribution and transport (PMDT) and,
– on the other hand, to improve the competitiveness of the ACP States' commodities on world markets through the reorganization and rationalization of their production, marketing and distribution activities. [...]

CHAPTER 3

WIDENING PARTICIPATION IN COOPERATION ACTIVITIES

Article 20

In accordance with Articles 2, 3 and 13 and in order to encourage all parties from the ACP States and the Community which are in a position to contribute to the autonomous development of the ACP States to put forward and implement initiatives, cooperation shall also support, within limits laid down by the ACP States concerned, development operations put forward by economic, social and cultural organizations in the framework of decentralized cooperation, in particular where they combine the efforts and resources of organizations from the ACP States and their counterparts from the Community. This form of cooperation shall be aimed in particular at making the capabilities, original operating methods and resources of such parties available to the development of the ACP States.

The parties referred to in this Article are decentralized public authorities, rural and village groupings, cooperatives, firms, trade unions, teaching and research centres, non-governmental development organizations, various associations and all groups and parties which are able and wish to make their own spontaneous and original contribution to the development of ACP States. [...]

CHAPTER 4

PRINCIPLES GOVERNING THE INSTRUMENTS OF COOPERATION

Article 23

In order to contribute towards achieving the aims of this Convention, the Contracting Parties shall deploy cooperation instruments that correspond to the principles of solidarity and mutual interest, adapted to the economic, cultural and social situation in the ACP States and in the Community and to developments in their international environment.

These instruments shall be directed mainly, by strengthening the established mechanisms and systems, at:

- increasing trade between the Parties;
- supporting the ACP States' efforts to achieve self-reliant development by stepping up their capacity to innovate and to adapt and transform technology;
- supporting the ACP States' structural adjustment efforts and thus contributing to the attenuation of the debt burden;
- helping the ACP States to gain access to the capital markets and encouraging direct private European investment to contribute towards the development of the ACP States;
- remedying the instability of export earnings from the ACP States' agricultural commodities and helping those countries to cope with serious disruptions affecting their mining industries.

Article 24

In order to promote and diversify trade between the Contracting Parties, the Community and the ACP States are agreed on:

- general trade provisions;
- special arrangements for Community import of certain ACP products;
- arrangements to promote the development of the ACP States' trade and services, including tourism;
- a system of reciprocal information and consultation designed to help apply the trade cooperation provisions of this Convention effectively.

Article 25

The aim of the general trade arrangements, which are based on the Contracting Parties' international obligations, shall be to provide a firm and solid foundation for trade cooperation between the ACP States and the Community.

They shall be based on the principle of free access to the Community market for products originating in the ACP States, with special provisions for agricultural products and a safeguard clause.

In view of the ACP States' present development needs, the arrangements shall not comprise any element of reciprocity for those States as regards free access. [...]

Article 26

The Community shall contribute towards the ACP States' own development efforts by providing adequate financial resources and appropriate technical assistance aimed at stepping up those States' capacities for self-reliant and integrated economic, social and cultural development and also at helping to raise their populations' standard of living and well-being, and promote and mobilize resources in support of sustainable, effective and growth-oriented structural adjustment programmes.

Such contributions shall be made on a more predictable and continuous basis. They shall be provided at very highly concessional terms. Particular account shall be taken of the situation of the least-developed ACP States. [...]

--------- 37 ---------

THE WHOLENESS OF EUROPE

Two years after becoming the Soviet leader, Mikhail Gorbachev published his views on 'a common European home'. The following passages are taken from his book, *Perestroika, New Thinking for Our Country and the World* (New York: Harper and Row, 1988), pp. 180–3, 190–1.

This metaphor came to my mind in one of my discussions. Although seemingly I voiced it in passing, in my mind I had been looking for such a formula for a long time. It did not come to me all of a sudden but after much thought and, notably, after meetings with many European leaders.

Having conditioned myself for a new political outlook, I could no longer accept in the old way the multi-coloured, patchwork-quilt-like political map of Europe. The continent has known more than its share of wars and tears. It has had enough. Scanning the panorama of this long-suffering land and pondering on the common roots of such a multi-form but essentially common European civilization, I felt with growing acuteness the artificiality and temporariness of the bloc-to-bloc confrontation and the archaic nature of the 'iron curtain'. That was probably how the idea of a common European home came to my mind, and at the right moment this expression sprang from my tongue by itself. [...]

Europe is indeed a common home where geography and history have closely interwoven the destinies of dozens of countries and nations. Of course, each of them has its own problems, and each wants to live its own life, to follow its own traditions. Therefore, developing the metaphor, one may say: the home is common, that is true, but each family has its own apartment, and there are different entrances too. But it is only together, collectively, and by following the sensible norms of coexistence that the Europeans can save their home, protect it against a conflagration and other calamities, make it better and safer, and maintain it in proper order.

Some people may think this a beautiful fantasy. However, this isn't fantasy, but the outcome of a careful analysis of the situation on the continent. If the world needs new relations, Europe needs them above all. One may say that the nations of Europe have conceived them in suffering, and deserve them.

The concept of a 'common European home' suggests above all a degree of integrity, even if its states belong to different social systems and opposing military–political alliances [...]

One can mention a number of objective circumstances which create the need for a pan-European policy:

1. Densely populated and highly urbanized, Europe bristles with weapons, both nuclear and conventional. It would not be enough to call it a 'powder keg' today [...] *Control weapons*

2. Even a conventional war, to say nothing of a nuclear one, would be disastrous for Europe today. This is not only because conventional weapons are many times more destructive than they were during the Second World War, but also because there are nuclear power plants consisting of a total of some 200 reactor units and a large number of major chemical works. The destruction of those facilities in the course of conventional hostilities would make the continent uninhabitable. *avoid war*

3. Europe is one of the most industrialized regions of the world. Its industry and transport have developed to the point where their danger to the environment is close to being critical. This problem has crossed far beyond national borders, and is now being shared by all of Europe. *environmental effects*

4. Integrative processes are developing intensively in both parts of Europe [...] The requirements of economic development in both parts of Europe, as well as scientific and technological progress, prompt the search for some kind of mutually advantageous cooperation. What I mean is not some kind of 'European autarky', but better use of the aggregate potential for Europe for the benefit of its peoples, and in relations with the rest of the world. *integration aids development*

5. The two parts of Europe have a lot of their own problems of an East–West dimension, but they also have a common interest in solving the extremely acute North–South problem. [...] West European states, like the Soviet Union and other socialist countries, have broad ties with the Third World, and could pool their efforts to facilitate its development. *development of 3rd world*

Such are, by and large, the imperatives of a pan-European policy determined by the interests and requirements of Europe as an integrated whole.

EUROPE'S OPPORTUNITIES

Now, about the opportunities the Europeans have and the prerequisites they need to be able to live as dwellers in a 'common home'.

1. The nations of Europe have the most painful and bitter experience of the two world wars. The awareness of the inadmissibility of a new war has left the deepest of imprints on their historical memory. It is no coincidence that Europe has the largest and the most authoritative antiwar movement, one which has engulfed all social strata.
2. European political tradition as regards the level of conduct in international affairs is the richest in the world. European states' notions of each other are more realistic than in any other region. Their political 'acquaintance' is broader, longer, and hence closer.
3. No other continent taken as a whole has such a ramified system of bilateral and multilateral negotiations, consultations, treaties and contacts at virtually every level. It has to its credit such a unique accomplishment in the history of international relations as the Helsinki process. Hopeful results were produced by the Stockholm Conference. Then the torch was taken up by Vienna where, we hope, a new step in the development of the Helsinki process will be made. So, the blueprints for the construction of a common European home are all but ready.
4. The economic, scientific, and technical potential of Europe is tremendous. It is dispersed, and the force of repulsion between the East and the West of the continent is greater than that of attraction. However, the current state of affairs economically, both in the West and in the East, and their tangible prospects, are such as to enable some modus to be found for a combination of economic processes in both parts of Europe to the benefit of all.

Such is the only reasonable way for a further advance of European material civilization.

Europe 'from the Atlantic to the Urals' is a cultural–historical entity united by the common heritage of the Renaissance and the Enlightenment, of the great philosophical and social teachings of the nineteenth and twentieth centuries. These are powerful magnets which help policy-makers in their search for ways to mutual understanding and cooperation at the level of interstate relations. A tremendous potential for a policy of peace and neighbourliness is inherent in the European cultural heritage. Generally, in Europe the new, salutary outlook knows much more fertile soil than in any other region where the two social systems come into contact. [...]

EUROPEAN COOPERATION

The building of the 'European home' requires a material foundation – constructive cooperation in many different areas. We, in the Soviet Union, are prepared for this, including the need to search for new forms of cooperation, such as the launching of joint ventures, the implementation of joint projects in third countries, etc. We are raising the question of broad scientific and technological cooperation not as beggars who have nothing to offer in return. Unfortunately, this is the area where most of the artificial barriers are being erected. Allegations have been made that this involves 'sensitive technology' of strategic importance. [...]

Many opportunities and areas exist for peaceful scientific and technological cooperation. There is the experience of the joint project to study Halley's comet through the space probe Vega. This project found new construction materials and other discoveries were made in radio electronics, control systems, mathematics, optics, etc. [...]

As to cooperation in utilizing thermonuclear energy, a scientific base has been created by scientists from a number of countries working on ideas suggested by their Soviet colleagues. [...] There are also such possibilities as joint exploration and use of outer space and of planets of the solar system, and research in the fields of superconductivity and biotechnology.

True, all this would increase the European states' mutual interdependence, but this would be to the advantage of everyone and would make for greater responsibility and self-restraint.

Acting in the spirit of cooperation, a great deal could be done in that vast area which is called 'humanitarian'. A major landmark on this road would be an international conference on cooperation in the humanitarian field which the Soviet Union proposes for Moscow. At such a conference the sides could discuss all aspects of problems which are of concern to both East and West, including the intricate issue of human rights. That would give a strong new impetus to the Helsinki process. [...]

_____ 38 _____

'OFFICIAL RELATIONS' (THE JOINT DECLARATION)

The postwar division of Europe was virtually concluded in June 1988 with the Joint Declaration on the Establishment of Official Relations between the European Economic Community and the Council for Mutual Economic Assistance. This brief but important statement was published in the *Official Journal of the European Communities*, No. L 157/35 (24 June 1988).

JOINT DECLARATION

on the establishment of official relations between the European Economic Community and the Council for Mutual Economic Assistance

THE EUROPEAN ECONOMIC COMMUNITY,
of the one part, and

THE COUNCIL FOR MUTUAL ECONOMIC ASSISTANCE,
of the other part,
HAVING REGARD to the acts establishing the European Economic Community
and the Council for Mutual Economic Assistance, and in particular the Treaty of
Rome,
ON THE BASIS OF the Final Act of the Conference on Security and Cooperation
in Europe, and taking account of the results of the subsequent stages of the CSCE
process,
DESIROUS of contributing, by the activities they pursue within their fields of
competence, to the further development of international economic cooperation, an
important factor in economic growth and social progress,
DECLARE AS FOLLOWS:

1. The European Economic Community and the Council for Mutual Economic
   Assistance establish official relations with each other by adopting this Declaration.
2. The Parties will develop cooperation in areas which fall within their respective
   spheres of competence and where there is a common interest.
3. The areas, forms and methods of cooperation will be determined by the Parties
   by means of contacts and discussions between their representatives designated
   for this purpose.
4. On the basis of the experience gained in developing cooperation between them,
   the parties will, if necessary, examine the possibility of determining new areas,
   forms and methods of cooperation.
5. As regards the application of this Declaration to the Community, it shall apply
   to the territories in which the Treaty establishing the European Economic
   Community is applied and under the conditions laid down in that Treaty.
6. This Declaration is drawn up in duplicate in the Bulgarian, Czech, Danish,
   Dutch, English, French, German, Greek, Hungarian, Italian, Mongolian, Polish,
   Portuguese, Romanian, Russian, Spanish and Vietnamese languages, each text
   being equally authentic.

Done at Luxembourg, on the twenty-fifth day of June one thousand nine hundred
and eighty-eight.

_____ 39 _____

THE MEANING OF EUROPEAN INTEGRATION

Vaclav Havel, the playwright and dissident who became President of the Czech Republic, addressed the European Parliament on 8 March 1994. The following text of his speech was published by the European Parliament in Strasbourg in March 1994.

Mr Chairman,
Members of Parliament.

I am most grateful to you for the honour of addressing the European Parliament and I can scarcely think of a better way of using this opportunity than to try to answer three questions. First, why is the Czech Republic, which I represent here, requesting membership in the European Union? Secondly, why is it in the interest of all of Europe to expand the European Union? And thirdly, what, in my opinion, are the more general tasks confronting the European Union today?

Europe is a continent of extraordinary variety and diversity – geographically, ethnically, nationally, culturally, economically and politically. Yet at the same time all its parts are and always have been so deeply linked by their destiny that this continent can accurately be described as a single – albeit complex – political entity. Anything crucial in any area of human endeavour occurring anywhere in Europe always has had both direct and indirect consequences for our continent as a whole. The history of Europe is, in fact, the history of a constant searching and reshaping of its internal structures and the relationship of its parts. Today, if we talk about a single European civilization or about common European values, history, traditions, and destiny, what we are referring to is more the fruit of this tendency toward integration than its cause.

From time immemorial, Europe has had something that can be called an inner order, consisting of a specific system of political relations that circumscribed it and tried in one way or another to institutionalize its natural interconnectedness. This European order, however, usually was established by violence. The more powerful simply imposed it upon those less powerful. In this sense, the endless series of wars in Europe can be understood as an expression of the constant effort to alter the status quo and replace one order with another. From the ancient Roman Empire, through the Holy Roman Empire, and down to the power systems created by the Congress of Vienna, the Treaty of Versailles and finally by Yalta – all these were merely historical attempts to give European coexistence a certain set of game rules. A thousand times in its history Europe has been unified or divided in various ways; a thousand times one group has subjected another, forced its version of civilization on another and established self-serving political relations; a thousand times Europe's internal balance has been dramatically sought, found, transformed, and torn down. And a thousand times the French, the Swedes, the Germans or the Czechs have dealt with apparently internal matters, only to have their actions affect the rest of Europe.

I do not believe, therefore, that the idea of a European Union simply fell out of the sky, or was born in the laboratory of political theoreticians or on the drawing boards of political engineers. It grew quite naturally out of an understanding that European integrity was a fact of life, and from the efforts of many generations of Europeans to project the idea of unity into a specific 'supranational' European structure.

We may all be different, but we are all in the same boat. We can fight for our places and means of coexistence on this boat, but we also can agree on them peacefully. I understand European unity as a magnanimous attempt to choose the second of these possibilities, and to give Europe – for the first time in its history – the kind of order that would grow out of the free will of everyone, and be based on mutual agreement and a common longing for peace and cooperation. It would be a stable and solid order, one based not merely on military and political treaties, which anyone can break or ignore at will, but on such a close cooperation between European nations and citizens that it would limit, if not exclude, the possibility of new conflicts. [...]

This alone is enough to demonstrate that this newest type of European order is not, or need not be, a mere utopia, but that it can work in real terms.

I do not perceive the European Union as a monstrous superstate in which the autonomy of all the various nations, states, ethnic groups, cultures, and regions of Europe would gradually be dissolved. On the contrary, I see it as the systematic creation of a space that allows the autonomous components of Europe to develop freely and in their own way in an environment of lasting security and mutually beneficial cooperation based on principles of democracy, respect for human rights, civil society, and an open market economy.

The Czech Lands lie at the very centre of Europe and sometimes even think of themselves as its very heart. For this reason, they have always been a particularly exposed place, unavoidably involved in any European conflict. In fact, many European conflicts began or ended there. Like a number of other Central European countries, we have always been a dramatic crossroads of all kinds of European intellectual and spiritual currents and geopolitical interests. This makes us particularly sensitive to the fact that everything that happens in Europe intrinsically concerns us, and that everything that happens to us intrinsically concerns all of Europe. We are among the expert witnesses to the political reality of Europe's interconnectedness. That is why our sense of co-responsibility for what happens in Europe is especially strong, and also why we are intensely aware that the prospect of European integration presents an enormous historic opportunity to Europe as a whole, and to us.

I think I have essentially answered my first question – that is, why the Czech Republic wants to become a member of the European Union. Yes, we are able and happy to surrender a portion of our sovereignty in favour of the commonly administered sovereignty of the European Union, because we know it will repay us many times over, as it will all Europeans. The part of the world we live in can hope for a gradual transformation from an arena of eternally warring rulers, powers, nations, social classes and religious doctrines, competing for territories of influence or hegemony, into a forum of down-to-earth dialogue and effective cooperation between all its inhabitants in a commonly shared, commonly administered and commonly cultivated space dedicated to coexistence and solidarity.

I believe my thoughts about the interconnectedness of Europe have, to a considerable degree, answered the second question as well: why the European Union should gradually expand. Europe was divided artificially, by force, and for that very reason its division had to collapse sooner or later. History has thrown down a gauntlet we can, if we wish, pick up. If we do not do so, a great opportunity to create a continent of free and peaceful cooperation may be lost. Only a fool who has learned nothing from the millennia of European history can believe that tranquility, peace and prosperity can flourish forever in one part of Europe without regard for what is happening in the other. The era of the Cold War, when the enforced cohesion of the Soviet Bloc contributed to the cohesion of the West, is definitively over.

We must all accept that the world is radically different today than it was five years ago. The vision of Europe as a stabilizing factor in the contemporary international environment, one that does not export war to the rest of the world but rather radiates the idea of peaceful coexistence, cannot become reality if Europe as a whole is not transformed. The gauntlet simply must be taken up. What is going on in the former Yugoslavia should be a grave reminder to any of us who think that in Europe we can ignore with impunity what is going on next door. Unrest, chaos and violence are infectious and expansionary. We Central Europeans have directly felt the truth of this countless times, and I think it is our responsibility repeatedly to draw others' attention to this experience, especially those fortunate enough not to have undergone it as often as we have.

Western Europe has been moving toward its present degree of integration for nearly fifty years. It is clear that new members, particularly those attempting to shed the consequences of Communist rule, cannot be accepted overnight into the European Union without seriously threatening to tear the delicate threads from which it is woven. Nevertheless, the prospect of its expansion, and of the expansion of its influence and spirit, is in its intrinsic interest and in the intrinsic interest of Europe as a whole. There is simply no meaningful alternative to this trend. Anything else would be a return to the times when European order was not a work of consensus but of violence. And the evil demons are lying in wait. A vacuum, the decay of value, the fear of freedom, suffering and poverty, chaos – these are the environments in which they flourish. They must not be given that opportunity.

For if the future European order does not emerge from a broadening European Union, based on the best European values and willing to defend and transmit them, it could well happen that the organization of this future will fall into the hands of a cast of fools, fanatics, populists and demagogues waiting for their chance and determined to promote the worst European traditions. And there are, unfortunately, more than enough of those.

Members of Parliament, allow me now to turn to the third question I have posed. That is, the question of the tasks with which, in my opinion, the European Union is now confronted. There are certainly many of them, and all of them are difficult. One, however, appears to me especially important, and it is this I would like to talk about.

I confess that when I studied the Maastricht Treaty and the other documents on which the European Union is based, I had a somewhat ambiguous response. On the one hand, it is undoubtedly a respectable piece of work. It is scarcely possible to believe that a common framework could be given to such a complex and diverse legal and economic order, involving so many different European countries. It is amazing that common rules of the game have been created, that all the legislative, administrative and institutional mechanisms that enable the smooth running of this great body have been invented and that, in so colourful a political environment, agreement on an enormous number of concrete matters was reached and many different interests harmonized in a way that will benefit everyone. It is, I repeat, a remarkable labour of the human spirit and its rational capacities.

However, into my admiration, which initially verged on enthusiasm, there began to intrude a disturbing, less exuberant feeling. I felt I was looking into the inner workings of an absolutely perfect and immensely ingenious modern machine. To study such a machine must be a great joy to an admirer of technical inventions, but for me, whose interest in the world is not satisfied by admiration for well-oiled machines, something was seriously missing, something that could be called, in a rather simplified way, a spiritual or moral or emotional dimension. The treaty addressed my reason, but not my heart.

Naturally, I am not claiming that an affirmation of the European Union can be found in a reading of its documents and norms alone. They are only a formal framework to define the living realities that are its primary concern. And the positive aspects of those realities far outweigh whatever dry official texts can offer. Still, I cannot help feeling that my sensation of being confronted with nothing more than a perfect machine is somehow significant: that this feeling indicates something or challenges us in some way.

The large empires, complex supranational entities or confederations of states that we know from history, those which, in their time, contributed something of value to humanity, were remarkable not only because of how they were administered or organized, but also because they were always buoyed by a spirit, an idea, an ethos – I would even say by a charismatic quality – out of which their structure ultimately grew. For such entities to work and be vital, they always had to offer, and indeed did offer, some key to emotional identification, an ideal that would speak to people or inspire them, a set of generally understandable values that everyone could share. These values made it worthwhile for people to make sacrifices for the entity that embodies them, even, in extreme circumstances, the sacrifice of their very lives.

The European Union is based on a large set of values, with roots in antiquity and in Christianity, which over 2,000 years evolved into what we recognize today as the foundations of modern democracy, the rule of law and civil society. This set of values has its own clear moral foundation and its obvious metaphysical roots, whether modern man admits it or not. Thus it cannot be said that the European Union lacks a spirit from which all the concrete principles on which it is founded grow. It appears, though, that this spirit is rather difficult to see. It seems too hidden behind the mountains of systemic, technical, administrative, economic, monetary and other measures that contain it. And thus, in the end, many people might be left with the understandable impression that the European Union – to put it a bit crudely – is no more than endless arguments over how many carrots can be exported from somewhere, who sets the amount, who checks it and who will eventually punish delinquents who contravene the regulations.

That is why it seems to me that perhaps the most important task facing the European Union today is coming up with a new and genuinely clear reflection on what might be called European identity, a new and genuinely clear articulation of European responsibility, an intensified interest in the very meaning of European integration in all its wider implications for the contemporary world, and the re-creation of its ethos or, if you like, its charisma. [...]

It should be perfectly clear to everyone that this is not just a conglomerate of states created for purely utilitarian reasons, but an entity that in an original way fulfils the longings of many generations of enlightened Europeans who knew that European universalism can – when projected into political reality – become the framework for a more responsible human existence on our continent. More than that, it is the way to achieve the genuine inclusion of our continent as a partner in the multicultural environment of contemporary global civilization.

Naturally, my intention is not to advise the European Union on what it should do. I can only say what I, as a European, would welcome.

I would welcome it, for instance, if the European Union were to establish a charter of its own that would clearly define the ideas on which it is founded, its meaning and the values it intends to embody. Clearly, the basis of such a charter could be nothing other than a definitive moral code for European citizens. All those hundreds of pages of agreements on which the European Union is founded would thus be brought under the umbrella of a single, crystal-clear and universally understandable political document that would make it obvious at once what the European Union really is. At the same time, it also would be to its advantage if it were made even more obvious who represents it and embodies and guarantees its values. If the citizens of Europe understand that this is not just an anonymous bureaucratic monster to limit or even deny their autonomy, but simply a new type of human community that actually broadens their freedom significantly, then the European Union need not fear for its future.

You will certainly understand that at this moment my concern is not so much any particular suggestion but something deeper: how to make the spirit of the European Union more vivid and compelling, more accessible to all. For it seems to me that this is a project of such historical importance that it would be an unforgivable sin were it to languish and ultimately disappoint the hopes invested in it only because its very meaning were drowned in disputes over technical details.

Ladies and gentlemen, I have come from a land that did not enjoy freedom and democracy for almost sixty years. You will perhaps believe me when I say that it is this historical experience that has allowed me to respond at the deepest level to the revolutionary meaning of European integration today. And perhaps you will believe me when I say that the very depth of that experience compels me to express concern for the proper outcome of this process and to consider ways to strengthen it and make it irreversible.

Allow me, in conclusion, to thank you for approving the Europe Agreement on the association of the Czech Republic with the European Union two weeks after it was signed. In doing so, you have shown that you are not indifferent to the fate of my country.

40

BOSNIA

Late in 1995, peace came to Bosnia and other republics which once constituted Yugoslavia. The Foreign Affairs Council of the European Union commented on the implementation of the peace accords and the course of economic reconstruction in a *Policy Paper* which was published in Brussels on 30 October 1995.

In view of the forthcoming peace talks, the Council has adopted the following conclusions:

1. INTRODUCTION

Since the beginning of the conflict in former Yugoslavia, the European Union has spared no effort to promote peaceful and lasting solutions. The Union has also been the principal contributor in the work to relieve the terrible suffering of the civilian population.

The European Union reaffirms its determination to do everything possible to help achieve a successful outcome in the forthcoming negotiations.

The European Union, represented by the European mediator Mr Carl Bildt, will devote special attention both to questions relating to the constitutional framework of Bosnia–Herzegovina and to the solving of territorial issues. The clear definition and implementation of structures of the State of Bosnia–Herzegovina will be essential to the development of the relations with the European Union. The Union also calls on the parties to make every effort to agree on all remaining questions relating to the map. It reaffirms its full readiness to help on these important issues.

The European Union will work, on the basis of agreements reached in Geneva and New York, to achieve the following goals:

1. The continuing existence of Bosnia–Herzegovina as a single State in its internationally recognized borders, consisting of two entities: the Federation of Bosnia–Herzegovina and the Republika Srpska.

2. Bosnia–Herzegovina must be a multiethnic state, a democracy founded on respect for the human person and the rule of law.
3. Basic human rights and the rights of minorities as enshrined in international law have to be fully recognized and respected.
4. Full respect for the rights of refugees and displaced persons, in particular the right of voluntary return.
5. A framework for early, free and fair elections in Bosnia–Herzegovina.
6. Economies based on market principles and regional cooperation.
7. Mutual recognition among all states of the former Yugoslavia, within their internationally recognized borders.
8. The establishment of a process to define arms control, disarmament and confidence-building measures.

The European Union will give its full support to the implementation of the peace process, in coordination with other members of the international community. In this context, the representative of the European Union acts in close cooperation with the Presidency and the Commission with their respective competences.

The European Union wishes to confirm its willingness to contribute to the international effort aimed at the reconstruction of the regions devastated by the war, once peace is established. To that end, the European Union will coordinate its action with other members of the international community in order to provide long-term assistance with the objectives of supporting economic development, reinforcement of civil society, reconciliation and regional economic cooperation.

In the perspective of peace, the European Union is developing its long-term policy towards the region, to help build stability and prosperity. [...]

The EU reminds the parties of their responsibility for reaching a peaceful solution on the basis of respect for the internationally recognized borders of the Republic of Croatia and respect for the rights of the local Serb population. The EU will ... take part in the future transitional arrangements. Failure to reach a negotiated solution will have serious consequences in future relations with the EU.

The European Union believes it is necessary to create the conditions for the early return of the displaced Serb population from the United Nations protected areas in the Republic of Croatia. The government of Croatia must fully restore them in their civil and political rights as well as their properties. [...]

2. HUMANITARIAN ASSISTANCE

The EU reaffirms its determination to provide humanitarian assistance as long as the need exists. This assistance will seek to overcome humanitarian dependence as soon as possible and to assure a 'continuum' with the reconstruction effort. From the beginning of the conflict, the European Union has made a great effort, contributing with 1.6 billion ECU, and will continue to do so.

Humanitarian aid must reach all those who need it throughout the entire territory of former Yugoslavia, impartially and without conditionality. All interested parties should cooperate fully in its delivery. [...]

3. REFUGEES AND DISPLACED PERSONS

The right of refugees and displaced persons to return freely to their homes throughout the whole territory of former Yugoslavia in conditions of security or to receive just compensation is a fundamental principle. The right must be enshrined in the peace agreement. The practical application of these rights should be ensured in cooperation with the UNHCR as the lead agency and other institutions. The European Union will in any case encourage the return of refugees by the means at its disposal, including the channelling of the international aid.

The European Union will seek the commitment of the countries of origin to accept the return of their citizens and those others who have left their territory and have been accorded temporary protection by third countries.

The readiness of the countries of origin to allow the return of all refugees is one of the criteria for participation in the reconstruction and development programmes.

4. HIGH REPRESENTATIVE

In order to ensure the overall political coordination and coherence of the implementation of the peace settlement, the European Union considers necessary the designation of a High Representative who should be entrusted by the UN Security Council with the tasks referred to in the peace settlement.

In view of the contribution of the European Union in these aspects, the High Representative should come from the EU. The High Representative would report regularly as required, to the Council of the European Union and to the international organizations involved in the implementation process. [...]

5. CONSTITUTIONAL ISSUES AND FREE ELECTIONS IN BOSNIA

On the basis of Geneva and New York documents, the EU calls on all parties to continue the negotiations aimed to agree on a basic constitutional framework for Bosnia–Herzegovina.

The future constitution of Bosnia–Herzegovina must contain provisions for:

- a democratic political system based on free and fair elections;
- institutional arrangements at central government level, adequate to ensure effective functioning of the State, inter alia with structures responsible for foreign relations and foreign trade; it must have the possibility of concluding and implementing international treaties;
- a functioning market economy.

Free and democratic elections should take place as soon as conditions permit. The signatories of the peace agreement should undertake firm commitments in this regard. In this context, the European Union calls on the OSCE to adopt an early decision to send missions to Bosnia–Herzegovina in order both to evaluate when conditions allow for elections to take place and to monitor the electoral process itself.

When the elections take place the return of refugees should already be under way, allowing them to participate in elections in their places of origin. [...]

6. RECONSTRUCTION AND REGIONAL DEVELOPMENT

A) Reconstruction is a major task for the international community. The European Union is willing to contribute to this task in the context of the widest possible burden-sharing with other donors and in the light of detailed identified needs.

Reconstruction should be concentrated in those areas most affected by war: the whole territory of Bosnia–Herzegovina and certain areas of Croatia.

Reconstruction assistance for Bosnia–Herzegovina depends on the implementation of the provisions of the peace plan.

The granting of reconstruction assistance to Croatia should be linked to the creation of real return options by the Croat government for the Serbs in the UN protected areas and to strict respect for human and minority rights, as well as to a constructive attitude to the implementation of the peace plan.

Since the International Financial Institutions, and in particular the IMF and the World Bank can play a major role in reconstruction, it is important that Bosnia–Herzegovina does become a member of both institutions as soon as possible. To that end, a maximum effort should be made to help Bosnia–Herzegovina to clear its arrears with these institutions.

B) The European Union is convinced of the need to support economic development and the establishment of normal relations among all the states and the peoples of the former Yugoslavia. Only the granting of longer term measures in the region at a later stage will enable it to enjoy a sustained economic recovery.

The objective of the EU should include:

- the establishment and reinforcement of democratic political institutions which guarantee the rule of law, human rights and fundamental freedoms;
- the reinforcement of civil society and the strengthening of non-governmental bodies and cultural and educational institutions;
- support for economic stabilization and transition to market economies;
- the rebuilding and modernization of energy, water, transport and telecommunications networks;
- the development of the private sector, specially smaller firms and the promotion of investments;
- the establishment of open, free and normal economic relations between the states of former Yugoslavia;
- the participation of the countries concerned in the open international economic system;

- the development of trade and cooperation with the European Union and other international partners.

The granting of longer term measures will be subject to criteria of conditionality which should include the following elements:

- implementation of the terms of the peace agreement;
- respect for human rights, minority rights and the right to return of all the refugees and displaced persons;
- with respect to the FRY (Serbia and Montenegro), the granting of a large degree of autonomy within it for Kosovo;
- respect for the principles of market economy;
- cooperation with the international war crimes tribunal. [...]

7. FUTURE AGREEMENTS

As a follow-up to the European Union efforts to bring peace and stability to the region, the EU seeks to establish, as soon as conditions permit, a long-term relationship with the countries of the region. These relationships should take the form of agreements in the framework of a regional approach.

The agreements should be based on experience gained from previous agreements with the EU and should have an element of clear political and economic conditionality, including in particular respect for human rights, minority rights, the right to return of displaced persons and refugees, democratic institutions, political and economic reform, readiness to establish open and cooperative relations between these countries, full compliance with the terms of peace agreement and, with regard to the FRY (Serbia and Montenegro), the granting of a large degree of autonomy within it to Kosovo.

The willingness of the concerned states to engage in regional cooperation and to speed the process of economic and political reform will be determining factors in the future relations with the European Union.

8. ARMS CONTROL AND CSBM IN THE REGION

Following the signing of the peace agreement, the establishment of a stable military balance based on the lowest possible level of armaments will be a necessary element in preventing the recurrence of conflict in the former Yugoslavia.

The European Union considers urgent that a process be started in the context of OSCE to define arms control, disarmament and confidence and security-building measures. The EU will seek the commitment of the governments concerned, on signing the peace agreement, to begin constructive and bona-fide negotiations on confidence and security measures, arms control and reduction as well as regional security.

INDEX

295